Economic Performance and Financial Sector Reform in Central and Eastern Europe

Capital Flows, Bank and Enterprise Restructuring

Edited by

Andrew W. Mullineux

Professor of Money and Banking, University of Birmingham, UK

Christopher J. Green

Professor of Banking and Finance, University of Loughborough, UK

Edward Elgar
Cheltenham, UK • Northampton, MA, USA

Chapters 2 and 4 to 12 are reproduced in revised form from papers presented at the September 1996 Tallinn Conference on 'Economic Performance and Financial Sector Reform in Central and Eastern Europe' which was organized in the context of the European Commission's Phare ACE Programme 1994. Their content does not, however, express the Commission's official views. Responsibility for the information and views set out in the papers lies entirely with the editors and authors.

Published by
Edward Elgar Publishing Limited
Glensanda House
Montpellier Parade
Cheltenham
Glos GL50 1UA
UK

Edward Elgar Publishing, Inc.
6 Market Street
Northampton
Massachusetts 01060
USA

A catalogue record for this book
is available from the British Library

Library of Congress Cataloguing in Publication Data
Economic performance and financial sector reform in Central [and]
Eastern Europe : capital flows, bank and enterprise restructuring /
edited by Andrew W. Mullineux, Christopher J. Green.
Papers of a conference, held in Tallinn, Estonia, 20–21 September
1996.
1. Finance—Europe, Eastern—Congresses. 2. Banks and banking—
Europe, Eastern—Congresses. 3. Europe, Eastern—Economic
policy—1989- —Congresses. I. Mullineux, A. W. II. Green,
Christopher J.
HG186.A3E8524 1998
332.1'0947—dc21 98–17099
CIP

ISBN 1 85898 806 3

Typeset by Manton Typesetters, 5–7 Eastfield Road, Louth, Lincs, LN11 7AJ, UK

Printed and bound in Great Britain by Bookcraft (Bath) Ltd.

Contents

Figures

Tables

Contributors

Mr Parminder Bahra Department of Economics, University of Loughborough

Professor Marek Belka Institute of Economics, Polish Academy of Sciences

Dr David G. Dickinson Department of Economics, University of Birmingham

Professor J. Kimball Dietrich School of Business Administration, University of Southern California

Professor Eric Girardin LARE, University of Montesquieu, Bordeaux

Ms Céline Gondat Larralde LARE, University of Montesquieu, Bordeaux

Professor Christopher J. Green Department of Economics, University of Loughborough

Dr Niels Hermes Department of Economics, University of Groningen

Professor Miroslav Hrnčíř Czech National Bank

Professor Dwight Jaffee Haas School of Business, University of California, Berkeley

Professor Alfred Janc University of Economics, Poznań

Dr Jan Klacek Czech National Bank

Dr Tadeusz Kowalski University of Economics, Poznań

Mr Vahur Kraft President, Bank of Estonia

Professor Anna Krajewska Department of Economics, University of Lodz, Poland

Professor Robert Lensink Department of Economics, University of Groningen

Professor Andy Mullineux Department of Economics, University of Birmingham

Dr Victor Murinde Department of Accounting and Finance, Business School, University of Birmingham

Ms Agata E. Pawlowska Department of Economics, University of Birmingham

Dr Aita Tammeraid Department of Accounting, Tallinn Technical University

Professor Amine Tarazi Department of Economics, University of Limoges

Dr Asta Teearu Department of Accounting, Tallinn Technical University

Professor Alfred Vanags Department of Economics, Queen Mary and Westfield College

Professor Vello Vensel Department of Economics, Tallinn Technical University

Professor Clas Wihlborg Department of Economics, Gothenburg School of Economics and Commercial Law

Foreword*

Vahur Kraft

Ladies and gentlemen,

I am extremely pleased to be here to address the Conference on Economic Performance and Financial Sector Reform in Central and Eastern Europe on behalf of the Bank of Estonia.

I am glad that these problems attract a notably wide interest and that so many well-known specialists engaged in economic research have gathered here in Tallinn to discuss the issues.

At the present time the countries of Central and Eastern Europe are undergoing an economic transition period; they are developing market economy structures and concentrating on lining up with the EU. The long-term goals set by different countries are quite similar. But we have chosen different ways to reach these goals. All of us have our own experiences, our own successes and our own small failures to report. We all learn from our own experiences, of course. But it is also useful to know and learn from the experiences of other countries having similar problems.

The processes presently going on in Central and Eastern Europe needn't necessarily be so unique that they would not have analogues elsewhere in the world. Much useful experience can be gained from the countries of the Pacific Rim and Latin America, for example. In our everyday work we all probably tend to pay too little attention to the analysis of the experience of others, and thus avoid reaching some conclusions that it could be extremely profitable for us to reach.

It is a welcome sign that the Action for Cooperation in the Field of Economics (ACE) projects of the EU PHARE programme pay quite a lot of attention to research in the field of financial sector developments. Different countries of Central and Eastern Europe have adopted quite different monetary policy principles. There are different exchange rate mechanisms, there are considerable variations in the roles of the central banks as well as in the

* Keynote speech by the President of the Bank of Estonia at the Conference on Economic Performance and Financial Sector Reform in Central and Eastern Europe, Tallinn, Estonia, 20–21 September 1996.

objectives of their monetary policy and instruments used to attain these objectives. We have been successful to a varying degree in attracting foreign capital inflows. The countries that have experienced larger inflows have taken differing attitudes towards sterilizing them. We are all well aware of the difficulties of modelling and forecasting developments in a rapidly changing financial sector.

Almost all of us have faced difficulties in the banking sector at one time or another. In Estonia a serious banking crisis occurred in late 1992. The experience brought about changes in the regulatory framework and caused shifts in the attitudes of both the banks and the customers. Latvia and Lithuania faced problems in their banking sector last year.

We have much to learn from each other. But it is not always easy for us to see our experience in the wider context of the developments and the theoretical work of the rest of the world. That is why we are especially satisfied to note the involvement of scientists from the EU countries, besides those from Central and Eastern Europe, in the ACE programmes dealing with problems that are extremely important from our point of view. We are also glad to note that the interest in the problems of the financial sectors of our countries is not limited to Europe and there are well-known American specialists working in this field.

I hope this conference offers new knowledge and that the coming discussions and the publications prepared as a result of it should be instrumental in the ongoing reforms of the financial sector as well as the economic development of the Central and East European countries.

I would like to wish the participants of the conference a productive and satisfying two days.

Preface and acknowledgements

This book contains papers presented at a conference organized by Vello Vensel and his colleagues at the Tallinn Technical University and Teet Rajasalu, Bank of Estonia. The conference was held in Tallinn, Estonia, on 20–21 September 1996. It brought together two teams of researchers supported by the European Commission's PHARE/ACE Programme. The team led by Professor Chris Green (Department of Economics, University of Loughborough) with the support of Dr Victor Murinde (Department of Accounting and Finance, University of Birmingham) held contract number 94–0685–R. The team led by Professor Maxwell Fry (Business School, University of Birmingham), assisted by Professor Andy Mullineux and Dr David Dickinson (Department of Economics, University of Birmingham), held contract number 94–0772–R. The papers have since been updated in the light of comments received at the conference and subsequent group workshops.

This book is thus a joint venture undertaken by the two groups and has been edited by representatives of the two groups ably assisted by Victor Murinde. The research programmes of the two groups produced too many papers to be included in just one volume. It therefore became necessary to focus on two main themes, and to leave out papers that did not 'fit in'. Most of the chapters are grouped into the two sections: 'Bank and Enterprise Restructuring' (Part I); and 'Exchange Rate Regimes and Capital Flows' (Part II). The papers left out have been published in working paper series and elsewhere. However, the papers finally included in this book benefited greatly from discussion with and comments from all the participants of both groups and the guest participants in the conference. The editors would, therefore, like to thank them all for their contributions. We would also like to thank Mr Vahur Kraft (President, Bank of Estonia) for giving us permission to publish the keynote speech he gave at the conference. Finally, we would like to thank Vensel and his colleagues and Teet Rajasalu for making the conference that gave birth to this book a success, and the EC's PHARE/ACE Programme for the funding that made it all possible.

The members of the 'Green Team' were: Niels Hermes (University of Groningen); Alfred Janc (University of Economics, Poznań); Tadeusz Kowalski (University of Economics, Poznań); Robert Lensink (University of Groningen); Victor Murinde (University of Birmingham); Aita Tammeraid (Tallinn

Technical University, Estonia); Asta Teearu (Tallinn Technical University, Estonia); Vello Vensel (Tallinn Technical University, Estonia).

The members of the 'Fry Team' were: Maxwell Fry, Andy Mullineux, David G. Dickinson (University of Birmingham); Eric Girardin and Céline Gondat-Larralde (Department of Economics, University of Montesquieu IV, Bordeaux); Amine Tarazi (University of Limoges); Marek Belka (Polish Academy of Sciences), Andrzej Raczko, Jarek Bauc, Bogusław Grabowski (University of Lodz); Jan Klacek, Miroslav Hrnčíř, and Roman Matousek (Czech National Bank); Inna Shteinbuka (Ministry of Finance, Latvia); Salomeja Jasinkaite and Dalia Vidickiene (New Economy Institute, Lithuania); Tatiana Houbenova-Delissivkova and Victor Yotsov (Bulgarian Academy of Science); and Jose F. Könings (Katholiek University, Leuven).

1. Introductory overview: issues surrounding bank and enterprise restructuring in Central and Eastern Europe

Victor Murinde and Andy Mullineux

1 BACKGROUND

The financial sector reform[1] of the transition economies in Eastern Europe, the Baltics, Russia, and the other countries of the Commonwealth of Independent States (CIS) began with the separation of the banking sector into two tiers: central and commercial banks. The aim was to emulate the banking structure in established capitalist economies, but the important difference was that the banks remained largely state owned. Subsequently, individual transition economies have chosen quite distinct approaches in progressing with the reforms of the financial sector (EBRD 1995, p. 153).

In developed market economies, the banking sector dominates the intermediation of savings and loans. It is expected that banks in transition economies will play an integral part in the financial reforms; for example, by facilitating the restructuring of state-owned enterprises (SOEs), mobilizing funds for privatization or takeover of SOEs, providing mechanisms to monitor and control management in order to enhance corporate governance, supporting securities and equities markets, increasing liquidity and encouraging expertise in risk evaluation (Blommestein and Spencer 1994).

In most transition economies, banking sector restructuring involved initially reforming the single bank (monobank) which, in the central planning era, played the traditional roles of a central bank and commercial banks. Typically, a two-tier system, in which the central and commercial banking functions were separated, was created. The 'monobank' took deposits from households, but decisions on the distribution of credit rested with the central planning agencies. Bank officials did not have the experience of assessing project viability or risk; their role was a passive one of accounting and responding to orders from the planning agency. For example, the officials were required to ensure that credit lines to selected enterprises were maintained in order to meet output targets. Credit was underwritten by the state, and bank officials had no incentive to stop credit. Because credit was freely available, managers of enterprises had little incentive to improve the productivity of their enterprises. The monobank effectively created as much credit as was seemingly required without being constrained by the opportunity cost of funds or the need to evaluate lending risk. Consequently, the flow of funds involving households, the monobank, planning agencies and industrial firms led to the buildup of bad and unserviceable loans. Transition economies thus face a number of immediate fundamental problems when attempting to restructure the banking system: the bad loans problem; low savings and investment levels; and the securities markets which are illiquid and provide little new capital (see Doukas et al. 1998). Further, in many cases privatization of state-owned banks (SOBs) and enterprises cannot proceed until outstanding bad debt problems have been addressed.

One noticeable consequence of bank restructuring is the rapid proliferation of small private banks. This has been due largely to the liberal entry requirements and licensing of new private banks. For example, between 1990 and 1992, 60 new private banks were established in Poland and 43 in Czechoslovakia. However, many of these banks soon ran into difficulties because the banks were poorly capitalized and the regulatory and supervisory structure was weak.

Lax entry requirements were, for example, evident in the Baltic countries. In Estonia between 1989 and 1992, liberal entry rules resulted in the creation of 42 new private banks. The high rate of inflation had caused the minimum capital requirement to fall and many of these poorly capitalized banks ran into difficulties. By the end of 1993, the total number of banks was halved, with the three largest banks closed (one closed, the other two merged to form a new entity) by the authorities, because of liquidity problems (EBRD 1995). The central bank and government did not come to the rescue of the troubled banks. Instead the insolvent banks were closed down without compensating the depositors. The number of banks in operation in 1996 was 14, although this may be reduced in the future.[2] The closure of insolvent banks has been supplemented with tighter regulations such as increased minimum reserve requirements. Latvia faced similar consequences after its banking crisis in 1995, although the governor of the central bank suggested that this was initially the result of fraudulent activity in the banking sector. Lithuania was also faced with a banking crisis in 1995; it was resolved with approaches similar to those implemented in the other Baltic countries.

Approaches to helping troubled new banks are confined by two extremes: easy exit (usually through failure), which may destabilize the banking sector; and supporting poorly functioning enterprises, which encourages bad behaviour (the moral hazard problem). Policies such as minimum capital (and reserve) requirements may be used to weed out the smaller banks and encourage the banking sector to behave in a more responsible way (CEPR 1995).

Along with the introduction of a two-tier banking system, many countries cut or reduced subsidies to enterprises, making them more reliant on non-state financial sources. The evidence from Romania and the Czech Republic (but not Russia, where state funding had remained relatively unchanged) suggests that, at the outset of transition, firms were heavily dependent upon internal financing as state subsidies were cut, but that outside financing becomes more important once the reform of the financial sector has begun.[3] Interestingly, enterprises in transitional countries are more dependent upon external and equity financing than enterprises in developing countries (EBRD 1995, p. 95).

The privatization of banks was envisaged as a means of instilling discipline in the banking sector. However, because the bad debt problems remained unresolved it proved difficult to privatize the existing banks in the early stages of the transition (see Goldstein and Gultekin 1998). Although new private banks were established, these suffered from the problems outlined above, and furthermore were small relative to the existing state banks.

The slow progress in financial reform in the stabilization phase (broadly pre-1995) impacted directly on economic performance. For example, rigidities in the banking sector constrained the scope for financial intermediation, and consequently the savings rate steadily declined. In addition, there was a decline in business and government savings (see Table 1.1).

The impact of security markets has been small. The Czech and Slovak Republics have achieved the highest market capitalization to GNP ratios,

Table 1.1 Domestic savings in the transition period, 1990–1995

	Gross savings rate		Government savings rate		Household savings rate	
	Hungary	Poland	Hungary	Poland	Hungary	Poland
1990	—	0.39	5.1	5.1	9.1	—
1991	—	—	3.1	3.7	15.1	—
1992	0.18	0.23	0.6	4.5	12.5	—
1993	0.11	0.13	1.3	3.2	8.0	10.4
1994	0.15	0.17	–1.5	3.1	9.7	10.5
1995	—	—	—	3.0	—	13.9

Source: Bahra et al. (1997).

which are comparable with Western European economies. However, as in almost all the transition economies, market liquidity is low. It may also be argued that the size of the securities market in the Czech and Slovak Republics reflects the mass (voucher-based) privatization schemes, rather than the generation of new capital. In the other transitional countries, market capitalization is still very low (EBRD 1995, p. 165).

In spite of the restructuring efforts, by the end of 1995 the banking and financial sectors still played a relatively small role in transitional economies when compared to developing and developed countries. In many of the countries, the banking sector was still characterized by bad loans, failures and state domination. There was, therefore, a long way to go until the objectives of financial sector reform were to be met, and before the banking sectors become more efficient (better) and stable.

2 THE ISSUES

The key issues relating to bank and enterprise restructuring in Central and Eastern Europe are best discussed within the context of the overall process of economic transition. These issues include: resolution of the banks' bad loans problem; the appropriate structure of the financial system ('universal banking' versus 'Anglo-Saxon'); and institutional and regulatory issues surrounding the building of bank and non-bank financial institutions.

The Banks' Bad Loans Problem

Following the creation of the two-tier banking system, credit was no longer given on demand. Debtor firms' collateral was introduced as a basis against which loans could be issued and the general monetary tightening in the stabilization phase gave rise to acute credit rationing (a 'credit crunch'). In order to ease the effects of the credit crunch, some SOEs were given greater autonomy. In Poland, for example, firms were allowed to keep and use profits, hold bank deposits, lend to other firms and pay bonuses to workers (Fries and Lane 1994). It also became apparent that the initial stage of the reform process was problematic because the constraints imposed by central planning had been removed, but an effective financial control (or corporate governance) system had not been established. SOEs increased their indebtedness by defaulting on loans and increasing inter-enterprise arrears.

High default rates on loans inhibit improvements in the banking sector, distort credit allocation, waste valuable human resources and complicate the valuation of banks. This, in turn, delays the privatization process. In terms of the macroeconomy, bad loans have serious implications for stability and the fiscal position of transitional governments. The government amasses the contingent liabilities in the form of large foreign exchange debts, the bad debts of commercial banks (which were primarily loans by SOBs to SOEs), unfunded pension liabilities, and government guarantees for loans to large SOEs. As a result, the government is likely to face growing revenue requirements, especially with an underdeveloped taxation system, which previously relied on SOEs' profits, and an underdeveloped government bond market. SOEs that failed to secure bank credit usually continued production, relying on voluntary or involuntary credits from other enterprises. As noted by Ickes and Ryterman (1994), the managers of SOEs engaged in such activities because they believed that the state, as owner of enterprises and banks, would underwrite their activities. In addition, SOBs continued to lend because they would otherwise have had to declare their bad loans. Because they had insufficient capital provisions, this would have been tantamount to declaring themselves bankrupt.

Hence, the immediate problem facing the financial reform effort in transition economies is the accumulation of bad loans in the banking sector. In Hungary, Poland and the Czech Republic, for example, the volume of bad loans *increased* until 1994. As a percentage of bank loans in Hungary, bad loans increased from 9.4 in 1991 to 20.7 in 1992 and 42.6 in 1993, but fell to 30.2 in 1994. Bad loans increased steadily in Poland from 16.5 (in 1991) to 26.8 (in 1992) and 27.4 (in 1993) and further to 29.0 in 1994. In the Czech Republic, despite the early establishment of a 'consolidation bank' to take over bad loans, the increase was dramatic; from 2.7 (in 1991) to 19.3, 22.1 (in 1992/93) and 38.8 in 1994.

Many solutions to the bad loans problem have been proposed (see Saunders and Sommariva 1993; Borish et al. 1996). Enterprise managers or bank officials tend to perpetuate past behaviour unless there is a credible signal from the government that it will not bail them out if debts accumulate once again (see the panel discussion in Part III, Chapter 13). A simple write-off requires that not only the debts (assets), but also the liabilities of the bank should be written off; making it likely that savers will lose their deposits and creating an expectation of future forgiveness (moral hazard problem). If the government cannot afford to recapitalize the banks, inflation is an option since it reduces the value of (non-index linked) outstanding debts.

In general, the proposals for resolving the bad debt problem can be grouped under two general categories. The first is the 'decentralization approach' under which banks retain enterprise borrowing and lending decisions. This helps the bank staff to develop their skills in project assessment and address some of the sectoral and geographical biases prevalent in the banking sectors of many transitional economies. Poland, for example, created nine regionally based state-owned commercial banks and Bulgaria created commercial banks defined by industrial portfolio. This approach may not remove the moral hazard problem, however, since bank officials may continue to lend money to inefficient enterprises in the hope of recovering earlier loans. The moral hazard problem could be alleviated by the creation of 'workout departments'. These exist within banks (although in time they could be privatized separately) and operate with market-orientated supervisory boards. Underpinning workout departments are legal reforms, which impose certain limits and duties. Such an approach has been undertaken in Poland, where the Law on Financial Restructuring of Enterprises and Banks set a deadline by which all bad loans had to be restructured or sold off (no new loans were allowed to be offered unless in conjunction with some restructuring agreement). Enterprises failing to do so were declared bankrupt (Kwalec et al. 1994, p. 55). The Polish scheme allowed banks to swap (with enterprises) debt for equities. It is sometimes argued that allowing banks to own equity in an enterprise to which they are giving loans may lead to conflicts of interest and a concentration in power (Fries and Lane 1994, p. 31). Alternatively, this may be viewed as an incentive compatible solution as frequently argued in the case of German universal banking (see the next subsection for further discussion).

A similar approach is the 'bad bank solution', under which individual banks set up subsidiary banks whose sole responsibility is to manage bad loans. This leaves a more stable and liquid 'good bank' which is better placed to offer new loans. Equity in the bad bank may be sold off to risk-loving investors, thus leaving bank credit to more reliable projects. Furthermore, any worsening of the bad loan portfolio will be borne by equity and debt holders of the bad bank. However, such a scheme may be inhibited by the absence of secondary markets (Saunders and Sommariva 1993, p. 946).

More commonly, a centralized approach is adopted under which banks transfer or sell bad loans to a government-sponsored institution. This allows the banks to be free of their inherited debt and increases the speed and likelihood of privatization, which according to Blommestein and Spencer (1994) is generally considered to be the most effective way of instilling market discipline in the operations of the banking sector. However, critics argue the reverse, namely that it creates a moral hazard problem in the sense that banks will expect to be bailed out again if they make further bad loans – which they are likely to, given their inexperience and the fact that they are operating in the highly uncertain, at least prior to stabilization, transition environment.

The Polish approach seems to have induced more restructuring than in the Czech Republic, where a consolidated bank was established early on and the centralized approach adopted. Fries and Lane (1994) suggest that the centralized approach should only be taken when there are a large number of debts and where the long-term objective is privatization. Critics add that the centralized approach does not give bank staff experience in handling bad debts and therefore future judgements will be poor (although the debt resolution agency does provide a training ground for improved credit assessment).

In addition, centralized schemes could run into problems because of an initial shortage of experienced staff and, moreover, centralized agencies could drain limited resources in transitional countries, although joint ventures with foreign banks may ease this problem. The centralized approach can take many forms, leading to a variety of financial structures with the development of different instruments.

1. Banks may be recapitalized, and then privatized at a later stage (ibid., p. 32). This instils confidence into the banking system; if depositors' funds have little security, then banks may continuously face the prospect of investors and depositors seeking more secure assets, such as foreign currency and gold, and possibly starting a run on the bank. In the face of inadequate private capital the potential sources of non-private funds for recapitalization of banks are additional funds from the government/state Treasury department and external agencies, such as the European Bank for Reconstruction and Development (EBRD). This allows banks to make new loans and alleviate credit constraints while reducing the pressure on bank officials in charge of low net worth banks to take on risky projects. In addition, if the recapitalizing institution is an outsider (that is, not the state) there is increased monitoring.[4]
2. The centralized approach also involves bankruptcy procedures and enterprise restructuring. In order for existing loans to be serviced, the indebted enterprises must be restructured. In some instances it may be prudent for enterprises to be liquidated in order to recover as much as possible from asset sales (this has the advantage of freezing the firm's debt position). Hastening the liquidation of inefficient enterprises would also improve the quality of lending. These decisions may, however, be hampered by the absence of formal bankruptcy procedures. Bulgaria, for example, finally managed to pass bankruptcy laws in 1996. In the early phase of the transition it may be advantageous for banks to enter into informal or private restructuring, rather than resort to the law courts and bankruptcy procedures.[5] The establishment of effective bankruptcy laws and court procedures are an important supporting institutional change.
3. The centralized approach may also take the form of debt-for-equity swaps where the enterprise swaps equity for debt with the bank. By doing so, the bank reduces its seniority of claims in the event of the enterprise declaring itself bankrupt and may encourage other investors. In addition, with closer ties, bank staff have greater control over the enterprise, thus increasing monitoring and supervision.[6]

4. Banks can also swap bad loans at a discount. This does not remove the bad loans altogether; however, such a scheme would encourage the development of a secondary market in debt, especially once institutions such as insurance and pension firms begin to operate.[7] This scheme would also reduce the sectoral and geographic concentrations that exist in bank portfolios.
5. Bad loans may also be swapped for government bonds, that is, 'asset carve out' or 'debt socialization'. By offering government bonds, non-performing assets are replaced with earning assets. However, unless there is a functioning secondary market for government bonds, banks would have to hold on to the bonds until maturity. This would effectively reduce liquidity in the banking sector (Saunders and Sommariva 1993, p. 949).[8]

Transition economies have, with mixed results, adopted their own mix of these approaches (Borish et al. 1996, p. 40). Using enterprise and financial sector performance, government credibility and fiscal stability as criteria to evaluate alternative policies, Levine and Scott (1993) favour government assumption of debt obligations because it allows early privatization and it also minimizes subsequent government intervention. The 'true' moral hazard problem is that governments may behave in an *ad hoc* way, thereby reducing credibility. However, the government has to be in a position to pay the bonds upon maturity. This requires a sound tax base (but at least it buys time to set up a sound tax base), otherwise macroeconomic stability will be jeopardized (see Fries and Lane 1994; Borish et al. 1996).

The greatest problem has been to establish firm dividing lines between old and new loans. Additionally, recapitalization inhibits efforts to harden budget constraints. In order to address this problem, most transitional countries have introduced capital adequacy regulations that reflect Basle Committee or European Union (EU) standards. There have also been attempts to classify asset values, although there are some 'departures from Basle Committee and EU standards in the definition of regulatory capital, as well as the scope for discretion in application of loan classification and provisioning rules' (EBRD 1995, p. 154).

Universal Banking Versus the Anglo-Saxon Banking System

What sort of (post-reform) structure will the financial sector assume? Should it be allowed to hold equity, as continental European (and Japanese) banks do; or not (as in the so-called 'Anglo-Saxon' (UK/US) systems)? The answer is, of course, academic in the case of countries joining the EU, which has adopted the 'continental model'.

Many authors have expounded on the merits of universal banking (see Mayer 1990; Corbett and Mayer 1991), citing successful examples such as Germany (Niggle 1995).[9] Stiglitz (1992, p. 180), for instance, suggests that: 'the desirability of maintaining strong walls between the financial and production sectors of the economy runs counter to what many observers see as very successful models of financial structure of Japan and Germany'. Universal banking enables bank representation on the supervisory boards of enterprises, with the effect that banks have greater control and therefore have greater confidence to make long-term investments. They can monitor enterprises more closely and can influence day-to-day running decisions of enterprises to the extent that poor management can be disciplined (Blommestein and Spencer 1994, p. 163; Caprio and Levine 1994). Furthermore, universal banking overcomes the problems associated with excessive fragmentation of ownership. When ownership is too diverse, monitoring becomes a public good and individual costs become excessively high. Universal banks, however, have an incentive to monitor closely because they are both lenders to and owners of enterprises, so that an incentive-compatible solution is achieved (Stiglitz 1992, p. 182).

However, others argue that universal banking is not appropriate in the Eastern European context. There are already serious doubts in the Czech Republic, where investment funds are often owned by banks, corporate governance has been poor, and there has been little enterprise restructuring. Valuing equity is difficult and, if it forms a significant part of a bank's asset portfolio, then some of the economic problems of the transition countries become institutionalized within the banking sector (as they have done in Japan in the mid-1990s). Second, the use of bank staff in the management of enterprises removes already scarce human capital from banking activities. Furthermore, there is no reason to suggest that bank staff are any better at managing enterprises than existing enterprise managers. Further, bank managers may continue to lend to insolvent enterprises in the hope of recovering earlier losses, or to protect the value of shares. Given the unstable nature of the transitional economies, universal banks may become 'captive' to their corporate clients, thus hindering corporate governance (Blommestein and Spencer 1994, p. 193). Universal banking may also lead to cartelization in the financial sector, inhibiting the development of securities markets. Additionally, Lee (1996) suggests that because of the tied nature of projects, a universal banking structure reduces the distribution of accumulated knowledge in project evaluation. When firms are not tied to banks through equity, there is greater competition for good projects, leading to better intermediation. There is also evidence which suggests that banks are becoming less interested in holding equity because the costs of doing so outweigh the benefits (Dittus 1996). Recently, equities have had relatively low yields in banking portfolios and, in the mid-1990s, German and Japanese banks announced plans to shed their holdings of company equity.

Building Non-bank Financial Institutions and Markets

The banking sector is the most important source of enterprise credit in transitional countries.[10] However, the non-banking sector (generally taken to mean stock markets, bond markets and all money markets, including the foreign exchange market) can also help facilitate the objectives of transformation. For instance, privatization and mechanisms for corporate control will benefit from developed equity and capital markets. A greater variety of instruments, such as equities, bills and bonds can increase the demand for financial services, thereby encouraging savings and the mobilization of funds. They can help instil financial discipline, increase liquidity and efficiency, agglomerate capital, pool and diversify risk, and, like the banks, intermediate between savers and borrowers, offering risk capital and long-term debt financing for restructuring or expansion. Furthermore, the financial sector has the potential capacity to unleash the incentives that ensure efficient use of funds through monitoring, project selection and enforcement of contract (Stiglitz 1992, p. 161). Moreover, privatization of enterprises creates new shareholders or large shareholding institutions, such as pension funds, mutual investment funds and insurance companies, which require equity and money markets if they are to function efficiently and will, in turn, add liquidity to those markets.

There is evidence from recent research, especially from the countries of East Asia and Latin America, which shows a positive correlation between financial deepening[11] and economic growth (King and Levine 1993). The evidence also suggests that causality runs predominantly from financial deepening to economic growth, but that it may be bi-directional. It is found that financial deepening improves overall productivity by mobilizing resources, screening projects, diversifying risk and revealing the potential rewards from engaging in innovation. Indeed, financial deepening may be at least as important as human capital accumulation. Thus the scale and scope of the financial system should be increased. Further, empirical analysis also suggests that as equity financing increases, enterprises increase their debt to equity ratios and increase their leverage (Demigiric-Kunt and Maksimovic 1996; King and Levine 1993).

The development of transition economies will be greatly facilitated by the establishment of equity (stock) markets, bond (government and corporate) markets and money markets (foreign exchange, inter-bank[12]). Indeed, many of the schemes that address the bad loans problems (such as privatization and debt for government bond or equity swaps) entail the creation of equity and government bonds. However, there are many obstacles to overcome before the non-banking financial sector becomes a sizeable part of the financial sector. First, an efficient banking sector is a necessary condition for equities, capital and other non-banking financial markets to function (Calvo and Kumar 1994). Second, in transitional countries, non-banking finance markets show similar characteristics to those in other emerging markets in that they are: thinly spread; highly illiquid, with only a small number of players; highly volatile; prone to speculative bubbles and collapse; and vulnerable to fraudulent activities. The corollary of this argument is that pricing mechanisms are inefficient.

Equity markets help widen and transfer ownership, especially after privatization. However, effective control and ownership requires a sound legislative foundation (for example, private property rights) plus regulations to protect investors from agency problems. Furthermore, development is hampered if the degree of liquidity in the market does not allow for easy transactions, and is further undermined if there is an inefficient payments settlements system – a characteristic of all transitional economies. In addition, information regarding assets is not widely available, leading to incorrect valuation and instability. Credibility and confidence in such markets can be enhanced if 'avenues for the dissemination of information about the market and listed companies' are developed (Blommestein and Spencer 1994). This is the key. Indirect finance is intermediated through banks because there is information asymmetry. Capital market (direct) finance can only develop as this asymmetry is reduced, that is, as more information is made publicly available. This, too, takes time, since firms need to build a track record, and an auditing process has to be established to verify the quality of the published information.

In some respects, stock market development and wide share ownership may be inappropriate for transitional countries. When ownership is wide and thin, investors have little interest in the control and restructuring. They are more concerned with the liquidity of the secondary markets that facilitate portfolio diversification and speculation than with strategic investment. There are conflicts between shareholders and enterprise managers that prevent effective control and lead to instability in the face of hostile takeover and merger threats, which may in turn contribute to a culture of 'short-termism'. Instead, it is suggested that effective corporate control can arise if investors are offered debt contracts instead of equity contracts. More generally, the appropriate ownership structure will place heavy emphasis on control by those who are best placed to exercise it, namely, the banks that are closely associated with the funding of the real economy (Corbett and Mayer 1991, p. 70). Furthermore, the institutional participants that dominate developed equity markets, such as insurance and pension funds, are not yet fully developed in the transition economies. Without these institutions, equity markets will not provide much in the way of new capital to the financial sector (Blommestein and Spencer 1994).

As the central banks in transition economies become independent, governments will find it increasingly difficult to finance budget deficits through printing money, and it will therefore be important to develop government bond markets (Steinherr and Gilibert 1994). By providing relatively safe homogeneous assets with a range of maturities, governments will help to develop commercial corporate bond markets. In turn, these markets will stimulate the development of derivative markets, which can provide important hedges against risks and shocks in the transitional economies (Blommestein and Spencer 1994). It is to be noted that the issuance of bonds (unless they are index linked) is only likely to be possible after stabilization has been achieved, since prior to that, governments' anti-inflation reputation is weak. In the mid-1990s, Poland still did not have an active government bond market. Buyers are needed to enable sales of bonds, and this is why the establishment of pension funds, following the planned privatization of pensions in Poland, is of crucial importance.

To support transition to a market economy with greater private ownership, institutional reforms are necessary, yet most transitional countries are currently still struggling to establish effective bankruptcy procedures. The previous discussion has shown that the lack of a bankruptcy law meant that there was no threat to inefficient firms. Property rights must also be established at an early stage to enable collateral to be provided (Dewatripont and Roland 1996).

A payments or settlements system is central to a market-based economy. It directly affects the ability of central banks to operate monetary management, since it has a bearing upon the reserve requirements set down by the central bank. When the payments system is not operating efficiently, banks may have to hold either large (or volatile) reserves (or floats) or ask the central bank to accommodate with overdrafts. In the case of the former, credit available for investment is reduced, and in the latter, central bank monetary management is hampered. This affects the development and functioning of money markets, and also increases the difficulty of implementing macroeconomic stabilization policies. Moreover, under high rates of inflation, delays could sharply reduce the value of receipts and thus increase credit demand by government and enterprises (Balino et al. 1994). Additionally, an inefficient payments system may result in increased informal market activities (Ickes and Ryterman 1994). As the rate of economic growth increases, the demands on the payments system increase, hence the development of an efficient function payments mechanism is essential.

3 THE RELATIONSHIP BETWEEN PRIVATIZATION AND BANKING SECTOR RESTRUCTURING

The relationship between privatization and the reform of the banking sector in transition economies should be emphasized (Takla 1994). Lipton and Sachs (1990) observed that privatization redefines property rights and brings about the functioning of basic institutions of a market financial system, including corporate governance, equity ownership, stock exchanges, and bank and non-bank financial intermediaries. For example, voucher privatization of large firms was based on distribution of shares (for a nominal fee) to the population in the former Czech and Slovak Federal Republics with unexpected consequences for banks, firms and the government. Perhaps the integral element of the relationship between the two derives from the unique nature of privatization and the banking system in transition economies. While privatization in developed market economies refers to the transfer of ownership of public corporations (a fairly small ratio of total enterprises) from state to private hands, mainly by public offering, privatization in transition economies has been complicated by the fact that the SOE sector overwhelmingly dominated the private sector. While privatization was motivated by the objective of increasing corporate and national efficiency and to raise money for government in both transition and 'developed' economies, the shortage of domestic savings, and the rudimentary nature of financial institutions, markets and instruments, made it difficult for transition economies to achieve these objectives.

The manner in which privatization proceeds is an important issue since immediate privatization may simply convert a state monopoly into a private monopoly, and thus create a need to establish appropriate 'anti-trust' regulations and procedures. It should be noted that banks may have to be restructured before privatization. This involves resolving the bad debt problem discussed earlier. This in turn will free SOEs from debts, making them more 'privatizable'. Early privatization will send positive signals, confirming government commitment to a market economy and to new emerging private and existing state banks (Caprio and Levine 1994), as well as maximizing their present discounted value (Thorne 1993, p. 987). However, valuation is difficult and may affect government credibility. Undervaluation will lead to charges of a give-away, while overvaluation leads to undercapitalization to which managers may respond by entertaining riskier projects (Stiglitz 1992, p. 170).

4 THE CONTENTS OF THIS BOOK

This book brings together research results on issues relating to financial sector reform in Central and Eastern Europe. It has a particular focus on bank and enterprise restructuring, macroeconomic policy and capital flows and aims to contribute to policy debates highlighted above. The foreword contains the keynote speech by the President of the Bank of Estonia, and the book consists of three parts following on from this introductory overview. Part I (Chapters 2 to 7) contains studies of bank and enterprise restructuring. Part 2 (Chapters 8 to 11) concentrates on related macroeconomic issues pertaining to exchange rate regimes and capital flows. The final part consists of an examination of macroeconomic effects of financial reform (Chapter 12) and a summary of the panel discussion which concluded the conference (Chapter 13).

In Chapter 2, Belka and Krajewska undertake an evaluation of the Polish 'case-by-case' approach to enterprise restructuring and bank consolidation. Each case involves negotiations between bank creditors and state-owned enterprises, leading to financial and wider enterprise restructuring as well as to privatization and resolution of bad debt problems. The evaluation is based on a survey of 110 (out of 630) enterprises in which Bank Consolidation Agreements (BCAs) had been concluded by 18 March 1996. Numerous shortcomings and faults in the programme are identified. A need to streamline bankruptcy procedures is highlighted, and suggestions for increasing the effectiveness of the restructuring programme are provided.

In Chapter 3, Tammeraid, Teearu and Vensel draw on the results of a special interview study of Estonian business firms undertaken in 1997, and utilizes the previous annual surveys in 1994–96, in order to undertake a quantitative measurement of enterprise restructuring and the state and changes in the Estonian business environment, with respect to the regulation mechanism, disputes resolution mechanism, financial contractual relations, and availability of business support services. The 49 firms which responded to questionnaires during interviews were mostly privately owned small- and medium-sized joint-stock companies from different industries and various regions of Estonia. The evidence leads to at least five main conclusions. First, own savings were the main source of finance for firms' start-up, but formal or informal loans were used in some rare cases. Second, informal finance was important for funding working capital and enterprise growth. Third, government regulations did not constrain the decisions taken by Estonian manufacturing firms in normal operation, expansion or closing down. Fourth, there existed a number of disputes and conflicts between economic agents, but Estonian legislation was not sufficient for resolving these disputes, rather direct negotiation with the other party seemed to work. Finally, Estonian governmental institutions or business associations did not support business; main support services were rendered by commercial banks, Estonian universities and training schools, the Estonian Chamber of Commerce and the Estonian Tax Office.

The results of the Tammeraid–Teearu–Vensel study on Estonia offer a good basis for comparison with those obtained in the study by Kowalski and Janc in Chapter 4. Kowalski and Janc analyse financial contractual relationships within the small and medium-sized enterprise (SME) sector in Poland in order to disentangle the main factors and mechanisms that influence the way the sector functions. The analysis focuses on the results of an interview study carried out on a representative sample of 74 SMEs located mainly in the Wielkopolska region of Poland. Among the factors explored were formal entrance rules, formal exit rules, bankruptcy procedures within the private sector, and the institutional and financial environment. It is found that the role played by the government in creating entrance and exit rules is not perceived by economic agents as being a constraint to the growth of the SMEs. Rather, the findings suggest that the growth of the SMEs is influenced by the potential of the SMEs to attract external finance.

In Chapter 5, Pawlowska and Mullineux provide a further analysis of SME financing based on a survey of both banks and SMEs in Poland (1989–94). Their findings generally confirm that there was significant rationing in the supply of credit by banks to SMEs in the early phase of the Polish transition. In addition, 'counselling and information' gaps were identified. Given the widespread market failure, government intervention is recommended through the provision of loan guarantees and financial support for institutions providing advisory services to the SME sector, *inter alia*.

In Chapter 6, Gondat Larralde and Tarazi present an analysis of entry conditions, structure and performance of the banking structure in 11 transition economies. The aim is to check whether (or not) results normally obtained in North American and Western European economies hold for those in Central and Eastern Europe. It is found that the expected positive relationship between concentration of market share and profitability is not evident in the transition economies. Further investigation shows that there is some evidence of a positive relationship in banking markets which are weakly concentrated, that is, when the three-bank asset concentration ratio is less than 60 per cent, namely in Latvia, Hungary and Poland. In the remaining countries (Bulgaria, Croatia, the Czech Republic, Estonia, Lithuania, Romania, Slovenia and the Slovak Republic), where the three-bank asset concentration ratio was greater than 60 per cent, there was no positive relationship between concentration and profitability. The authors fear that these results could in part be due to poor data availability and quality, but also note that, in the earlier phase of the transition, banks remained 'captured', by state-owned and recently privatized large firms, in old and often unprofitable relationships.

Finally in Chapter 7, Lensink uses a general equilibrium model to analyse the impact of interest rate deregulation and changes in reserve requirements, which are the most important financial reform measures adopted by the

Polish government in accordance with International Monetary Fund (IMF) and World Bank recommendations. Simulations are used to study the effects of interest rate deregulation and changes in the reserve reqiuirements of banks.

Part II consists of four chapters focusing on macroeconomic policy, exchange rates and capital flows. In Chapter 8, Hrnčíř explains the role that the fixed exchange rate regime has played in the various stages of the transition in the Czech Republic. Four stages of transition are identified: the financially closed economy prior to convertibility; rudimentary financial openness, following the establishment of current account convertibility; advanced financial openness, following the establishment of capital account convertibility; and compatibility with the monetary integration projects of the EU. The first stage is regarded as a pre-transition phase and the last as a post-transition stage. It is argued that the role of the exchange rate and the appropriate exchange rate policy changes as progress is made with the transition through the middle two stages from pre-stabilization, when a fixed nominal anchor might be helpful, post-stabilization with capital account liberalization, when there is greater exposure to excessive capital inflows (and sudden capital outflows), and their associated problems. In the pre-1997 transition period covered by the chapter, it is argued that there had been a change in the equilibrium real exchange rate necessitating the introduction of more flexibility in the 'fixed' exchange rate system through the widening of the fluctuating band in February 1996, from the narrow ± 0.5 per cent adopted in 1990, to the much wider ± 7.5 per cent.

In Chapter 9, Dickinson and Mullineux consider a number of factors influencing capital flows in the transition economies of Poland, Hungary, the Baltic states and the Czech Republic, and the impact of these flows on macroeconomic policy options. Capital flows are found to be influenced by general macroeconomic uncertainty and it is argued that, along with political stability, macroeconomic policy credibility is a particularly important determinant of these flows. Links between currency convertibility, the exchange rate regime and policy credibility are explored. The chapter concludes with a discussion of factors influencing the speed at which transition economies should move to full capital account convertibility.

In Chapter 10, Hermes, Lensink and Murinde investigate the issue of capital flight in a sample of Eastern European countries, using a different approach. It is argued that there is a high level of uncertainty over the future outcomes of the process of political and economic transition in Eastern Europe, which may trigger capital flight. Yet, the success of policy reforms is conditional on foreign exchange availability and the reduction (or even the reversal) of capital flight. On the basis of data availability alone, Hungary, Poland and Romania are selected as sample countries for the study of the determinants and magnitude of capital flight in transition economies. Capital flight is measured by the residual method, which measures capital flight as the sum of the change in gross external debt, net foreign direct and portfolio investment inflows minus the current account deficit and the net change in foreign reserves.[13] A model is developed in which the determinants of capital flight relate to aspects of uncertainty over future policy reforms and their outcomes. The variables used to proxy uncertainty include an increase in external government and government guaranteed debt, an increase in aid inflows, overvaluation of the exchange rate, an increase in the government budget deficit, and bleak prospects for export growth. The empirical findings are that capital flight is a country-specific phenomenon for the sample countries. However, the results also indicate that the financial reforms of 1990–95 in these countries were successful in reducing capital flight.

In Chapter 11, Girardin and Klacek undertake an econometric investigation of the sterilization of capital inflows in the Czech and Polish cases. Monetary policy reaction functions for the 1992 to 1995 period are estimated using monthly data. It is found that the change in the net foreign assets of the banking system has a pronounced negative influence on domestic credit in Poland, but a positive influence in the Czech Republic.

Part III focuses on broader policy issues and consists of Chapters 12 and 13. In Chapter 12, Bahra, Green and Murinde report the results of a policy-modelling exercise for transitional economies. In the light of the experience with financial sector reforms in Estonia and Poland, the chapter proposes and implements a methodology that involves simulations and policy experiments to study the effects of financial sector reforms in transition economies within a small disaggregated macroeconomic model. It is found that the response of most economic indicators to an interest rate shock tends to be different in the two transition economies, notwithstanding the broadly common heritage of the economies. Poland exhibits stronger curb-market interest rate effects which permeate the macroeconomy, while the effects tend to be rather concealed in Estonia.

The concluding chapter is the aforementioned summary of the wide-ranging panel discussion.

NOTES

1. Financial sector reform is interpreted here to encompass reforms in financial institutions (especially banks, but also including non-banks) and financial markets (especially stock markets).
2. See various issues of *The Banker* in 1997.
3. However, SOEs generated little profit (if any); their profits went to the state as revenue.
4. Recapitalization may also reassure depositors and add to the stability of the system.

5. This is because the court system is slow and inefficient, thus allowing transfer pricing activities, such as incumbent managers setting up their own firms and then selling the state-owned enterprise assets to it at below book value. In addition, the assets of the mainly manufacturing state sector are user specific and old and will not realize much in the way of sales. Moreover, secondary markets are thin and prices low, especially during a recession when asset prices are generally driven downwards. Potential buyers may also be faced by credit constraints.
6. There is, though, no reason to suggest that bank staff will perform these jobs better. Also as both lender and equity owner there could be a conflict in interests with perhaps an increase in ownership concentration and monopolization.
7. Critics argue that this may be too late; the problem needs urgent attention to get privatization moving.
8. There is also no reason to believe that states will be better at recovering the bad loans, in fact they could be worse. Also, given the nature of the loans, bonds may yield zero (or very low) interest. Moreover, given that there are costs involved with managing such schemes, banks may find that they are operating with negative interest margins on such investments.
9. Although doubts about the benefits of the system have long been held in Germany and reached a peak in the mid-1990s, following a series of corporate governance failures and a period of poor economic performance.
10. Indeed, banks remain the most important source of external credit in all economies.
11. Financial deepening is interpreted as the effect of the substitution between financial and real assets, indicated by the ratio M2/GNP, where M2 is narrow money plus bank liabilities (see Murinde 1996).
12. For example, the banking system cannot function efficiently if surplus funds lie idle.
13. See Murinde et al. (1996) for the competing measures of capital flight, including the hot money method and the asset method.

REFERENCES

Bahra, P., C.J. Green and V. Murinde (1997), 'Coping with financial sector reform in transition economies', Discussion Papers in Corporate Finance, University of Birmingham.

Balino, T., J. Dhawan and V. Sundararajan (1994), 'Payment systems reforms and monetary policy in emerging market economies in Central and Eastern Europe', *International Monetary Fund Staff Papers*, **41** (3), 383–410.

Blommestein, J. (1993), 'Financial sector reform and monetary policy in central and eastern Europe', in D. Fair and R. Raymond (eds), *The New Europe, Evolving Economic and Financial Systems in East and West. Financial and Monetary Policy Studies 26*, Boston: Kluwer Academic.

Blommestein, J. and S. Spencer (1994), 'The role of financial institutions in the transition to a market economy', in G. Caprio, D. Folkerts-Landau and T. Lane (eds), *Building Sound Finance in Emerging Market Economies*, Washington, DC: IMF.

Borish, M., M. Long and M. Noel (1996), 'Lessons from bank and enterprise restructuring in the transition economies of Europe and Central Asia', *World Economy*, **19** (1), 39–62.

Calvo, G. and F. Coricelli (1993), 'Output collapse in Eastern Europe – the role of credit', *International Monetary Fund Staff Papers*, **40** (1), 32–52.

Calvo, G. and M. Kumar (1994), 'Money demand, bank credit, and economic performance in former socialist economics', *International Monetary Fund Staff Papers*, **41** (2), 314–49.

Caprio, D. and R. Levine (1994), 'Reforming finance in transitional socialist economies', *World Bank Research Observer*, **9** (1), 1–24.
Centre for Economic Policy Research (CEPR) (1995), 'Banking sector development in Central and Eastern Europe', *Economic Policy Initiative*, No. 1, London: CEPR.
Corbett, J. and C. Mayer (1991), 'Financial reform in Eastern Europe, progress with the wrong model', *Oxford Review of Economic Policy*, **7** (4), 57–75.
Coricelli, F. (1996). 'Finance and growth in economies in transition', *European Economic Review*, **40** (3–5), 645–53.
Demigiric-Kunt, A. and V. Maksimovic (1996), 'Stock market development and financing choices for firms', *World Bank Economic Review*, **10** (2), 341–69.
Dewatripont, M. and G. Roland (1996), 'Transition as a process of large scale institutional change', *The Economics of Transition*, **4** (1), 1–30.
Dittus, P. (1996), 'Why east European banks don't want equity', *European Economic Review*, **40** (3–5), 655–62.
Doukas, J., V. Murinde and C. Wihlborg (1998), 'The main issues in financial sector reform and privatisation in transition economies', in J. Doukas, V. Murinde and C. Wihlborg (eds), *Financial Sector Reform and Privatisation in Transition Economies*, Amsterdam: Elsevier Science (North-Holland), pp. 1–17.
European Bank for Reconstruction and Development (EBRD) (1995), *Transition Report*, London: EBRD.
European Bank for Reconstruction and Development (EBRD) (1996), *Transition Report*, London: EBRD.
Fries, S. and T. Lane (1994), 'Financial and enterprise restructuring in emerging market economies', in G. Caprio, D. Folkerts-Landau and T. Lane (eds), *Building Sound Finance in Emerging Market Economies*, Washington, DC: IMF.
Goldstein, M.A. and N. Bulent Gultekin (1998), 'Privatisation in post-Communist economies', in J. Doukas, V. Murinde and C. Wihlborg (eds), *Financial Sector Reform and Privatisation in Transition Economies*, Amsterdam: Elsevier Science (North-Holland), pp. 281–325.
Ickes, B. and R. Ryterman (1994), 'Financial underdevelopment and macroeconomic stabilisation in Russia', in G. Caprio, D. Folkerts-Landau and T. Lane (eds), *Building Sound Finance in Emerging Market Economies*, Washington, DC: IMF.
King, R. and R. Levine (1993), 'Financial intermediation and economic development', in X. Vives (ed.), *Capital Markets and Financial Intermediation*, Cambridge: Cambridge University Press.
Kwalec, S., S. Sikora and P. Rymaszewski (1994), 'Dealing with bad debts – the case of Poland', in G. Caprio, D. Folkerts-Landau and T. Lane (eds), *Building Sound Finance in Emerging Market Economies*, Washington, DC: IMF.
Lee, J. (1996), 'financial development by learning', *Journal of Development Economics*, **50** (1), 147–64.
Levine, R. and D. Scott (1993), 'Old debts and new beginnings – a policy choice in transitional socialist economies', *World Development*, **21** (3), 319–30.
Lipton, D. and J. Sachs (1990), 'Creating a market economy in Eastern Europe: the case of Poland', *Brookings Papers on Economic Activity*, **2**, 293–341.
Mayer, C. (1990), 'Financial systems, corporate finance and economic development', in G. Hubbard (ed.), *Information, Capital Markets and Investment*, Chicago: National Bureau of Economic Research.
Murinde, V. (1996), *Development Banking and Finance*, Aldershot: Avebury.
Murinde, V., N. Hermes and R. Lensink (1996), 'Comparative aspects of the magni-

tude and determinants of capital flight in six Sub-Saharan African economies', *Savings and Developmental Quarterly Review*, **xx** (1), 61–78.
Niggle, C. (1995), 'The role of the financial sector in the socialist economies in transition – the 2nd primitive accumulation of capital', *Review of Social Economy*, **53** (3), 311–31.
Saunders, A. and A. Sommariva (1993), 'Banking sector and restructuring in Eastern Europe', *Journal of Banking and Finance*, **17**, 931–57.
Steinherr, A. and P. Gilibert (1994), 'Six proposals in search of financial sector reform in Eastern Europe', *MOCT–MOST, Economic Policy in Transitional Economies*, **4** (1), 101–14.
Stiglitz, J. (1992), 'The design of financial systems for the newly emerging democracies of Eastern Europe', in C. Clague and G. Rausser (eds), *The Emergence of Market Economies in Eastern Europe*, Cambridge, MA, and Oxford: Blackwell.
Stiglitz, J. (1993), 'The role of the state in financial markets', *Proceedings of the World Bank Annual Conference on Development Economics*, Washington, DC: World Bank, pp. 19–52.
Takla, L. (1994), 'The relationship between privatisation and the reform of the banking sector: the case of the Czech Republic and Slovakia', in S. Estrin (ed.), *Privatisation in Central and Eastern Europe*, London and New York: Longman.
Thorne, A. (1993), 'Eastern Europe experience with banking reform – is there a role for banks in the transition?', *Journal of Banking and finance*, **17** (5), 959–1000.

PART I

Bank and Enterprise Restructuring

2. The Polish bank and enterprise restructuring programme: expectations and reality

Marek Belka and Anna Krajewska

1 THE GENESIS OF BAD DEBTS AND LAWS PERTAINING TO BANK AND ENTERPRISE FINANCIAL RESTRUCTURING

The shock therapy introduced by Leszek Balcerowicz in January 1990 radically changed the situation of state-owned enterprises. The packet of stabilization measures adopted at that time brought about a drastic drop in demand and increased the costs of credit. Meanwhile, the liberalization of prices and foreign trade weakened the competitiveness of Polish products. The year 1991 witnessed the collapse of exports to the former COMECON, which further intensified the demand barrier. The difficult financial situation of state-owned enterprises was aggravated by the discriminating tax system (the dividend and the tax of wage increases above prescribed limits). Enterprises were unable to fulfil their obligations on time, and payment arrears increased uncontrollably.

In that difficult situation, state-owned enterprises began the adjustment process to the novel conditions. The main symptoms of these adjustments were cuts in production, the shedding of unnecessary assets, the curbing of employment, the establishment of new ties with the market, changes in management, an enhanced role for economic–financial and marketing departments, and greater caution in taking credit.[1]

Although state-owned enterprises in fact started the difficult process of restructuring, many of them carried a huge burden of growing debts. Some of these debts were inherited from the command-type economy, but in most firms the debt problems dated back to the beginning of the transformation period.

At the beginning of 1990 there was a quite common conviction in many enterprises that the recession would end soon and, hence, it was not necessary to reduce production too much even if it involved taking high-priced credit. Not all enterprises suspended the investments they had made before 1990, either. Many investors came to the conclusion that from the viewpoint of the firm's investments it would be more advisable to take high-priced credit and complete an investment project, because it would be needed when the economy managed to overcome the recession. Therefore, enterprises (and especially those that did not believe in the success of reforms and were convinced that the recession would be overcome soon) continued to take credit, although the possibilities of paying it back were shrinking. At the same time, banks could not object to the growing demand for credit.

During the early stage of the transformations, the worsening portfolio of credits in the banking sector was not fully identified by banks themselves. Difficulties of estimating the value of overdue credits were a result, among others, of differentiated methodologies of identifying them among all the credits extended by banks.

The diagnostic studies of the financial situation of the nine biggest banks to be established from the structure of the National Bank of Poland at the beginning of 1992, carried out by independent auditors on the orders of the Ministry of Finance, confirmed the growing share of bad debts in the overall portfolio of credits. The share of credit which was classified as doubtful or lost ranged from 9 to 20 per cent in June 1990, and from 24 to 68 per cent in June 1992.[2] There was a real danger that the liquidity of certain banks would be shaken.

The deteriorating financial situation of enterprises was accompanied by their growing arrears in contributions towards the budget (overdue taxes and obligations to the social insurance system) and overdue obligations towards suppliers. The scale of credit granted by enterprises to one another increased considerably, to a large extent this forced out and undermined the liquidity of the enterprises.

In conditions of a normal stabilized economy, unsettled obligations and loss of liquidity lead to the enterprise's liquidation and bankruptcy. However, the scale of overdue liabilities and the causes behind the intensifying financial difficulties of enterprises made it necessary to find a compromise solution. Such an opportunity was created by the Enterprise and Bank Restructuring Act, adopted on 3 February 1993.[3]

In accordance with the assumptions accepted by the legislators, the Act was expected to accomplish three main goals.

1. It should lead to reducing the debt burden of state-owned enterprises and joint-stock companies belonging to the State Treasury which had some hopes for survival, create prospects for their growth and help them in implementing the adopted restructuring and privatization programme. To

this goal were subordinated the bank conciliation agreements allowing, for example, debts to be written off, repayments to be made in instalments and debt/equity swaps.

2. It should eliminate from the market those enterprises which did not have any hope of further independent operation on the market, through the public sale of bank debts, liquidation or announcement of the firm's bankruptcy.
3. It should pave the way for restructuring the banking sector through solving the problem of bad debts, that is, doubtful and lost credits, which appeared in banks at the beginning of the transformation period (as of 31 December 1991) by adopting one of the restructuring 'paths' proposed for them (bank conciliation agreement, debt repayment, sale of debts, liquidation or bankruptcy).

Because the implementation of the enterprise restructuring programme poses a threat for the liquidity of the banking system, it was envisaged that state-owned banks would receive additional capital sufficient to ensure that losses incurred by them should not lead to the collapse of the financial system of the economy. At the beginning of 1992, in accordance with a recommendation from the Minister of Finance, the nine biggest commercial banks identified their bad debts and they received additional capital to the amount of 40 trillion old zloty (11 trillion zloty went to seven commercial banks established from the structure of the National Bank of Poland and 29 trillion zloty was allocated to the Bank Gospodarki Zywnosciowej (Food Economy Bank), the PKO BP (Polish Savings Bank) and the PeKaO SA (Polish Care Bank)).[4]

2 MAIN CHARACTERISTICS OF A BANK CONCILIATION AGREEMENT (BCA)

A bank conciliation agreement (BCA) is applicable only in relation to state-owned enterprises and joint-stock companies which have a majority of their shares held by the State Treasury.

Only a debtor enterprise unable to fulfil the accepted obligations for exceptional reasons beyond its control and having a chance of survival and growth in a future may apply for BCA. In turn, a BCA may be initiated only by a bank whose claims represent at least 10 per cent of the debtor's obligations (the bank's claims should reach at least one billion old zloty) or 20 per cent of the debtor's total obligations. A BCA cannot cover claims guaranteed by a pledge or mortgage, or claims resulting from social insurance obligations or from employment.

A BCA covers:

1. The debtor's obligation to take definite measures aimed at improving the enterprise's situation, stipulated by the restructuring programme;
2. the creditors' obligation to take measures supporting the implementation of the restructuring programme through debt restructuring or facilitated access to new funds, and particularly through:
   - postponing the deadline for repayment of obligations,
   - lowering the interest rate on claims,
   - abstaining from charging the interest on all or a part of the claims during a specified period,
   - capitalizing the due interest temporarily,
   - rescheduling the repayment of the interest and the principal,
   - swapping a part of the claims for equity,
   - writing off a part of the claims including the interest,
   - giving new loans, credits or credit guarantees to the debtor; and
3. provisions aimed at safeguarding the fulfilment of a BCA and control over its implementation; these include, among others, appointing the council of creditors, and determining its rights and means of exercising control over the debtor.

A BCA is concluded when the conciliation proposal defining the means of settling all claims covered by the BCA is accepted by the debtor and by creditors holding jointly more than 50 per cent of the total amount of the claims being dealt with in the agreement, including the claims of the bank conducting the conciliation programme.

A BCA cannot be started more than three years from the day the Act came into force. The deadline for starting a BCA lapsed on 18 March 1996. This prescription determines the nature of a BCA as a procedure of an incidental character. Such and no other definition of a BCA was prompted by the legislators' conviction that the economic situation in the country would be normalized within the next three years.

About 650 BCAs were concluded by 18 March 1996. New BCAs can no longer be set up, but those already started can be continued.

3 DEPT/EQUITY SWAPS AND 'REGULAR' BCAs: SURVEY RESULTS

Choice of the Sample

The sample in the survey comprises 110 enterprises in which BCAs were concluded. Half of the sample (55 cases) are BCAs which were concluded to convert debts into equity. These are enterprises in which the agreements have become valid and the Minister of Privatization has already transferred powers to carry out a debt/equity swap. By 18 March 1996, the Minister of Privatization transferred such powers to 74 joint-stock companies. Thus, the sample in the survey (55 joint-stock companies) makes up 75 per cent of such cases. The information about these companies was gathered by the Ministry of Privatization and the companies were chosen primarily on the basis of a criterion such as the progress made in the equity transfer.

The other half of the sample (also 55 cases) includes firms implementing BCAs in which debt/equity swaps are not planned ('regular' BCAs). This part of the sample was chosen randomly. The information was gathered by conducting questionnaire surveys directly in firms and analysing the provisions of agreements signed by them.

The analysed BCAs were conducted by 15 banks and the Industrial Development Agency SA. Eighty-three agreements (75.5 per cent of the sample) were concluded by nine commercial banks (founded from the structure of the National Bank of Poland), of which 79 conciliation procedures were led by banks belonging to the group of seven commercial banks that had received additional capital allowing for the restructuring of bad debts.

Characteristics of the Sample

Mainly large enterprises were covered by BCAs. The fixed assets of 70 per cent of the firms in the survey exceeded 50 billion old zloty (Table 2.1). Bigger assets belonged to firms in which debt/equity swaps took place. More than 50 per cent of the firms had fixed assets exceeding 100 billion old zloty, and about 34 per cent of the firms that entered into regular BCAs had fixed assets whose value surpassed 100 billion old zloty.

A majority of the firms (63 per cent) employed more than 500 people in the period directly preceding the signing of the BCAs, while 16 per cent of the firms had more than 2000 employees each (Table 2.2). Much bigger, taking into account the number of employees, were the joint-stock companies from debt/equity swaps: 73 per cent had more than 500 employees, of which 21 per cent employed more than 2000 people. The biggest joint-stock companies employed 7008 and 5890 people. In the case of regular BCAs, more than half

Table 2.1 Fixed assets of surveyed firms

Value of fixed assets (zloty million)	Total sample		Debt/equity BCAs		Regular BCAs	
	Number of firms	%	Number of firms	%	Number of firms	%
0–10	3	2.7	1	1.8	2	3.6
10.1–50	31	28.2	11	20.0	20	36.4
50.1–100	25	26.4	15	27.3	14	25.5
100.1–500	35	31.8	22	40.0	13	23.6
Above 500	12	10.9	6	10.9	6	10.9
Total	110	100.0	55	100.0	55	100.0

Table 2.2 Size of employment in surveyed firms

	Total sample		Debt/equity BCAs		Regular BCAs	
Number of employees	Number of firms	%	Number of firms	%	Number of firms	%
0–500	39	35.5	15	27.3	24	43.6
501–1000	30	27.2	16	29.1	14	25.5
1001–2000	23	20.9	12	28.1	11	20.0
Above 2000	18	16.4	12	21.8	6	10.9
Total	110	100.0	55	100.0	55	100.0

(56.4 per cent) were firms with less than 500 employees, while large firms with more than 2000 employees represented 10.9 per cent of the sample.

In half of the firms in the survey, the value of their obligations was in the range of 100–500 billion old zloty. They were quite evenly spread between the two groups: 52.7 per cent in BCAs with debt/equity swaps and 47.3 per cent in regular BCAs (Table 2.3). On the other hand, major disproportions could be observed with regard to the firms at the opposite ends of the debt scale. The group with the lowest obligations – less than 100 billion old zloty – included 29.1 per cent of firms in which debt/equity swaps took place, and a high 43.6 per cent of firms with regular BCAs. The situation looked different in the group of firms with the biggest obligations exceeding 500 billion zloty: 18.2 per cent and 9.1 per cent (regular BCAs), respectively. In most

Table 2.3 Obligations of surveyed firms

Value of obligations assets (zloty million)	Total sample		Debt/equity BCAs		Regular BCAs	
	Number of firms	%	Number of firms	%	Number of firms	%
0–100	40	36.4	16	29.1	24	43.6
100.1–200	28	25.5	15	27.3	13	23.7
200.1–300	16	14.5	9	16.3	7	12.7
300.1–500	11	10.0	5	9.1	6	10.9
above 500	15	13.6	10	18.2	5	9.1
Total	110	100.0	55	100.0	55	100.0

cases (about 60 per cent), the value of obligations surpassed the value of fixed assets – in extreme cases several times over.

The creditors of the firms under analysis are banks, investment institutions (mainly the Industrial Development Agency), the State Treasury, the Social Insurance Office, and suppliers. In about a half of all cases, because of the overdue interest, the obligations towards banks and other creditors exceeded the value of the main claim.

The firms point to the following reasons for suspending their debt servicing or failing to make repayments: fall in domestic demand, collapse of the eastern market, difficulties connected with collecting receivables, growing competition on the part of imports, growing tax burden, higher prices and other elements of costs, and particularly a sudden growth of credit costs. The information shows that the firms in which BCAs involved debt/equity swaps were more strongly linked with the eastern market than were the other firms. This is true especially for large electro-engineering and light industry firms.

The analysed information about the causes of growing debt of enterprises does not contain any indications connecting the increase of bad debts with the lack of financial discipline of joint-stock companies or weaknesses of the banking supervision. The information seems to reveal a tendency, common among both debtors and bank creditors, to interpret the growth of bad debts in objective categories, that is, the effects of 'shock therapy' in the economy being independent of enterprises and banks. The interpretation of insolvency causes by most creditors and debtors clearly minimizes the impact of debtors' passiveness and peace of mind and banks' patience with the scale and structure of bad debts, and especially the share of obligations resulting from an unpunctual servicing of credits in the total value of debts.

Financial Restructuring of the Analysed Firms

The measures envisaged by BCAs aim at debt restructuring and facilitating access to new capital for debtors.

The legislators accepted an assumption that the BCA should take into account the interests of creditors without injuring them. In practice it allows a few categories of creditors (in most cases two or even three) to be distinguished, usually taking into account the amount of the claim and proposing the scale and type of concessions on the part of particular creditors, which would be comparable but not necessarily identical. Special privileges such as accelerated repayment deadlines and smaller write-offs of the total amount of the claim, are given to creditors with small claims. The point of departure for such a solution was a conviction justified by the observation that small claims are, as a rule, owed to creditors whose survival may depend upon their repayment. In particular, this applies to small and medium-sized private firms and cooperatives. An additional argument was also the fact that these units take part in the enterprise and bank restructuring process only as passive partners of the BCA, while large state-owned enterprises have a dual role of being both active and passive partners in the restructuring process.

The classification of creditors in the category of large or small creditors was strongly individualized. Depending on the scale and structure of debts, small creditors have claims of less than 3 billion old zloty in BCAs whose objectives are debts amounting to many billions; less than 10–20 billion old zloty with a relatively small value of the total debt was covered by the BCA.

As regards BCAs involving debt/equity swaps, only in four cases were creditors treated in a similar manner (with only large creditors participating in debt/equity swaps). In ten regular BCAs, all creditors were treated equally.

A very important element in a BCA is an obligation assumed by creditors to write off a part of their claim, with either the remaining part being repaid in instalments, or the conversion into equity of a part or all of the remaining claim.

In most cases the write-off of claims was defined in percentage points, taking into account the total amount of debt, that is, the main claim plus interest (Table 2.4). Such a procedure was applied in 68 BCAs (62 per cent of all surveyed firms). This procedure was less common in the case of BCAs with debt/equity swaps (29 BCAs, that is, 53 per cent of all BCAs in this group) than with regular BCAs (39 BCAs, that is, 71 per cent). The remaining agreements provided for a differentiated (in percentage points) degree of the write-off of the principal part of the debt and the interest, or only the overdue interest, was written off. In 18 cases the overdue interest was written off fully (of which in 11 cases it concerned only BCAs involving debt/equity swaps). In these cases when the write-off of the principal and the overdue

Table 2.4 Debt write-off in the BCAs (in percentages)

The reduction of debt (%)	Number of firms																	
	Total sample						Debt/equity BCAs						Regular BCAs					
	Large creditors			Small creditors			Large creditors			Small creditors			Large creditors			Small creditors		
	1	2	3	1	2	3	1	2	3	1	2	3	1	2	3	1	2	3
0						30				1		17						13
1–30	1		9	1		5			9	1		5	1					
31–40	2		2	1		7	1		1			7	1		1	1		
41–50	3	2	11	1	3	11		1	6	1		3	3	1	5		3	8
51–60	1		9			6			2			2	1		7			4
61–70		3	21		5	6		2	9		4			1	12		1	6
71–80	1	4	13		1	4		3	3		1	1	1	1	10			3
81–90	1	1	5			3	1	1	1						4			3
100		18			9	2		11			6	2		7	—		3	
Does not concern						14						4						10

Notes:
1 = principal capital.
2 = interest.
3 = total debts.

interest was differentiated, the write-off of the interest was usually about twice as high as that of the principal.

In most cases the BCAs differentiated the written-off claims for different categories of creditors. In all cases when the extent of written-off debt was differentiated, small creditors were treated much better than large ones. In 47 cases small creditors were fully repaid (27 with debt/equity swaps and 20 with regular BCAs). The median level of written-off debt of large creditors in BCAs stipulating different types of written off debt can be seen in Table 2.5.

Table 2.5 Median level of written-off debt

Type of written-off debt	Type of BCA	
	Debt/equity swaps (%)	Regular (%)
Principal	65.0	50.0
Interest	86.4	94.4
Total claims	47.6	67.4

In the agreements which did not provide for debt/equity swaps, the following settlements of claims were negotiated:

1. Small creditors were paid on a one-off basis in the period from one to six months when the agreement became valid or their claims were rescheduled into instalments to be paid, as a rule, within a year after the agreement became valid. In 82 per cent of BCAs, small creditors had to be paid a year after the agreement became valid, and in the remaining 18 per cent during the second year of the agreement's execution.
2. The repayment of debt to large creditors was rescheduled into longer instalments, with a one-year or longer grace period sometimes being given. The deadlines for repayment are as follows: 1995, one BCA; 1996, six BCAs; 1997, 33 BCAs; 1998, 13 BCAs; 1999, one BCA; and 2000, one BCA. It can be seen that for 60 per cent of BCAs the debt repayment was rescheduled over a period of three years (until 1997), for 27 per cent – a period of four to six years, and only for 13 per cent a period shorter than three years.

In the analysed BCAs, under which a part of the claims remaining after write-offs was converted into equity, the following solutions were accepted:

1. Debt/equity swaps included, in principle, creditors classified in the category of large creditors. Only in three cases did small creditors take part in debt/equity swaps.
2. In 27 joint-stock companies under survey (that is, 50 per cent) the whole debt to large creditors after write-off was converted into equity and debtors had to settle all their debts to small creditors.
3. The division of claims into the part repaid by the debtor and the part swapped for equity is shown in Table 2.6. The data concern 25 joint-stock companies. No information was received for three joint-stock companies. On average, 34.4 per cent of the amount of claims remaining after the write-off will be repaid within two to three years from the moment the BCA becomes valid, while 65.6 per cent will be converted into equity.

Table 2.6 Division of debt remaining after write-off

Repayment (%)	Debt/equity swaps (%)	Number of firms
3	97	1
6	94	1
15	85	1
20	80	2
25	75	5
30	70	2
35	65	2
40	60	3
48	52	1
50	50	1
52	48	1
60	40	2

Note: Repayment + debt/equity = 100%.

The write-off of a part of the claim and the conversion of most of the remaining claim into equity changes radically the scale and structure of debts of these companies. They have to repay only a small part of debts to large creditors and small claims are written off to a much smaller extent. A compensation for firms involved in regular BCAs is a higher degree of the debt write-off.

A major relief to be found in almost all BCAs is the creditor's agreement to stop collecting the interest from the moment the conciliation procedure is started until the time it becomes valid, and also, in most BCAs, during the period of repaying the interest according to the accepted schedule. The principle of not collecting the interest, which checks the growth of debt, will lead to a more harmonious repayment of the remaining part of the debt.

The analysed BCAs were concluded in 15 banks. A comparison of the terms of financial restructuring accepted in different BCAs clearly shows that the greatest interest in debt/equity swaps was displayed by banks classified as 'weak' banks at the time of entering the programme, in which a big share of all credit was considered to be doubtful or lost. Strong banks and those with an intermediate position were less interested in the takeover of enterprises under the restructuring programme.We can suppose that for these banks, taking over the equity of a large number of firms, despite a risk connected with this operation, was synonymous with the strengthening of their position resulting from the control over a group of large firms which are of major importance in a given region. It was also a sign of their expansiveness and ability to take a risk, as well as their elasticity in operation and their attempts to enter the sphere of investment activity.

Enterprise Restructuring Programmes

A condition for concluding a BCA is that the debtor must submit a restructuring programme which must be approved by the bank and the creditors. These programmes for concluding the analysed BCAs appear to be differentiated considerably both with regard to the substantive standard and the amount of detailed information to be found in them. There are well-prepared and well-argued restructuring programmes and there are those which appear to be wishful thinking, not supported either by a reliable analysis of the economic situation or by the capabilities of the analysed firms.

The information concerning restructuring programmes frequently makes reference to the programmes already launched in firms or are an updated version of programmes worked out earlier but not implemented because of the deficit of funds or resistance of employees (in most cases both these factors were at work). The programmes were developed by external units or formulated by specialized consultancy firms.

The submitted restructuring programmes usually involve reducing the labour force, a wage freeze, reduction of socio-welfare functions, shedding of unnecessary production and socio-welfare assets, or elimination of unprofitable production. Hence, they are connected with a number of measures likely to arouse the resistance of employees. The practice confirms that in most cases, restructuring programmes call for forcing-out compliance, that is for firm pressure to be exerted by the owners. Neither the so-called 'founding organs' in relation to state-owned enterprises nor organs representing the State Treasury in joint-stock companies can force out the necessary but unpopular restructuring moves. Privatization is, thus, a necessary condition of the restructuring of many enterprises.

The surveys indicate, however, that creditors – owners of joint-stock companies – do not intend to get deeply involved in the enterprise restructuring process. Their aim is to ensure that shares reach their highest possible value, at the lowest possible cost, and to sell them at a profit after the execution of the agreement. New, compulsory owners of joint-stock companies, as a rule, have no clear idea about what to do with the firm, which was not an object of their interest and investment initiatives until an application for the BCA was submitted. Consequently, a hypothesis could be formulated here that a substantial restructuring of most of the joint-stock companies under survey has been postponed until some later time.

The chances for restructuring in the new ownership situation also depend on the determination and capabilities of the management of firms and the employees' approval for the necessary strategy of savings and cutbacks. Ideas about how to make the firm successful are usually conceived by its managers. The lack of creative and efficient managers, the resistance to change in management structures and methods, management habits and methods, and the resistance of employees to accept redundancies and changes in working practices may also be a major barrier to restructuring.

Some of the measures to be found in restructuring programmes call for financial outlays. Some BCAs contain a promise that credit will be given provided the requirements formulated in the restructuring programme are fulfilled. On the other hand, some BCAs contain a provision imposing an obligation on joint-stock companies to accept credit for restructuring purposes from the bank conducting the bank conciliation procedure, which testifies to the development of investment orientation in banks and in large part to the bank's confidence in the suitability of the restructuring programme and in its own ability to supervise its implementation effectively. This situation gives rise to one effect of the new law not intended by the legislators, that is, the origination of a new debt.

Prospects of Privatization

The analysis of ownership structures of the creditor-owned joint-stock companies, which have appeared (or will appear) through debt/equity swaps, shows that the conversion process results in the emergence of both ownership forms, with a decisive domination of the owner and joint-stock companies over a large number of dispersed owners.

Table 2.7 shows the structure of shares in the analysed 55 joint-stock companies owned by creditors. The data to be found in it indicate that the biggest blocks of shares have been distributed as shown in Table 2.8. Seven-

Table 2.7 *Structure of shares in surveyed firms*

	Number of firms holding the following percentage of the shares										
Type of owner	0	1–10	11–20	21–30	31–40	41–50	51–60	61–70	71–80	81–90	Above 90
Leading bank	0	22	12	8	6	1	3	3	0	0	0
Other banks	41	7	5	1	1	0	0	0	0	0	0
Strategic creditor	22	12	9	3	4	4	1	0	0	0	0
Creditors	0	6	15	11	7	7	1	1	6	0	1
Treasury	2	1	2	26	12	3	3	0	4	2	0

Table 2.8 Owners of biggest blocks of shares

	Total	Of which over 50%
Bank conducting BCA	12	6
Main creditor	8	1
Creditors	17	9
State Treasury	18	9
Total	55	25

teen joint-stock companies appear not to have a dominant owner-creditor (31 per cent) and in 18 companies (32.7 per cent) a dominant position is held by the State Treasury.

The debt/equity swaps led to the emergence of four ownership forms in joint-stock companies owned by their creditors:

1. joint-stock companies with the bank as a dominant owner;
2. joint-stock companies with the strategic owner;
3. joint-stock companies of the State Treasury with a group of creditors; and
4. creditor-owned joint-stock companies with a big number of dispersed creditors ('cooperatives' of creditors).

Because of the goals attributed to debt/equity swaps by the legislators, that is, the restructuring and privatization of debtors and the development of investment banking, the most desirable ownership structure for these joint-stock companies is one in which the owner–strategic investor is a bank or the main creditor (provided the latter is a firm), which can take over the function of a strategic investor. About 36 per cent of joint-stock companies under survey have this form of ownership.

Joint-stock companies with a dominant ownership position held by the State Treasury usually have as their co-owners a group of creditors or the bank conducting the BCA (with a small share). On the other hand, about 31 per cent of joint-stock companies, in which a dominant position is held by groups of creditors, have the most dispersed structure of ownership. An extreme example of such a structure is a company in which creditors hold 92 per cent of the equity and the State Treasury holds 8 per cent. The absence of a dominant owner is also characteristic for joint-stock companies, in which the degree of involvement of the bank, the main creditor, creditors and the State Treasury is at a similar level. This means that the process of creating the strategic investor is postponed in the majority of joint-stock companies, and it can take place only as a result of trade in shares.

In the analysed group of BCAs, the real privatization, that is the takeover of a dominant block of shares by a private firm, took place in only five cases. The privatized foreign trade organizations which have taken over a majority interest in joint-stock companies are well prepared to undertake an efficient and direct supervision of the implementation of restructuring programmes in these firms.

Some banks – owners of large blocks of shares – seek solutions to the problem of equity management by specialized managers. They also recruit external experts or pass over the equity management to specialized managerial firms. The information gathered in banks[5] shows that they are becoming involved in the financial restructuring of the firms covered by BCAs, seeking to raise the value of shares held by them. It is the intention of banks to sell the shares after two to three years. Hence, according to our assessment, banks' activities do not resemble the involvement of owners but rather functions performed by a privatization agency. As the strategic investor, banks intend to provide assistance in financing indispensable restructuring measures, which are to ensure that financial liquidity is restored and maintained by the joint-stock company during the agreement's validity. Because of the assistance provided by banks, the joint-stock companies covered by BCAs will be made ready to be sold to investors, who will launch a full range of adaptation and modernization activities in the future.

The group of creditor-owned companies, in which the State Treasury holds the position of the strategic investor, has marginally altered the earlier set-up. Various problems connected with funding the necessary restructuring of the debtor and finding the strategic investor may become a major barrier to the effectiveness of creditor-owned companies which have this ownership structure.

Difficulties connected with the emergence of a strategic investor from among shareholders of joint-stock companies with a dispersed structure of ownership, especially in the situation when compulsory (and also major) investors in some of the joint-stock companies are suppliers of energy, for example, or problems connected with finding a strategic investor may also influence, to a large extent, the chances of restructuring and survival of these firms.

Supervision of Enterprises Covered by Restructuring Programmes

A weaker than assumed effect of the Restructuring Act is apparent both in the fact that many of the BCAs do not envisage debt/equity swaps and in the slow emergence of strategic investors, which means that the success of this programme is largely dependent upon the effective supervision of firms included in it. BCAs are connected with changes in the forms and content of enterprise supervision. A condition of joining a BCA is the enterprise's transformation into a joint-stock company belonging to the State Treasury. This results in a new structure of management within the firm and in external supervision.

It is not permitted for employee self-government to exist in joint-stock companies. In this way, one of the elements of the 'Bermuda triangle' is eliminated. Also, the second element, that is trade unions, is weakened considerably, because they are deprived of their previous formal co-determination rights which often used employee self-management as a convenient platform for exerting an influence on the firm's activity. In this situation, the role of management boards in joint-stock companies increases. As a rule they are more inclined than the employee self-government and trade unions, to launch major restructuring measures, even if such measures call for more intensive efforts and cutbacks. The management boards can exert a greater influence on the content and course of restructuring programmes, as they do not have to seek the approval of the employee self-government for their activities, while employees no longer play the main role in appointing directors.

The establishment of a joint-stock company belonging to the State Treasury also implies institutional changes in the system of external supervision. The earlier founding body of a state-owned enterprise (the minister or head of an administrative province) is replaced by the Minister of Privatization, who appoints the first supervisory board in the newly established joint-stock company, which (at least formally) is a representative of interests of the new founding body.

The Enterprise and Bank Restructuring Act requires that a new body be appointed, charged with the task of supervision of the restructuring programmes. This is the council of creditors, and it is generally composed of a few (usually three) representatives of the main creditors including the leading bank. Independently of the council of creditors, the bank exercises a day-to-day control over the implementation of the BCA.

The survey findings show that changes in the management of joint-stock companies and in external supervision connected with BCAs have exerted a positive influence on the adaptation of enterprises to new conditions. It refers especially to those BCAs in which debt/equity swaps take place, which is synonymous with a change of owner. Such a situation calls for the appointment of new supervisory boards. Representatives of the Ministry of Privatization are replaced on these boards by representatives of the bank and creditors. Investigations show that these new supervisory boards are generally more active and they are more successful in convincing joint-stock companies to embark upon restructuring programmes.

Meanwhile, representatives of the Ministry of Privatization representatives are rarely Ministry of Privatization employees, but are instead people drawn predominantly from the various profession who have completed short courses and passed exams giving them the right to sit on the supervisory board. They generally have neither a strong motivation nor clear criteria to guide the restructuring they are overseeing, and in most cases their familiarity with problems faced by companies, to which they have been assigned, is minimal. It must also be remembered that the Ministry of Privatization has not as yet developed an effective system of cooperation with its representatives on supervisory boards of joint-stock companies. There are no mechanisms allowing for either the transfer of suggestions and opinions between the Ministry and members of supervisory boards, or a system for evaluating its representatives on supervisory boards by the Ministry.

Debt/equity swaps result in supervisory boards being dominated by representatives of banks and large creditors. They are usually well acquainted with joint-stock companies executing BCAs, while banks and enterprises delegating them to supervisory boards formulate their tasks clearly and control their accomplishment.

In banks holding the shares of joint-stock companies and executing BCAs, there prevails an approach today, according to which the most advantageous solution is to bring about a rapid improvement of the situation in the joint-stock companies and then to find a strategic investor for them, who will buy them at a high price. On the other hand, the restructuring of a joint-stock company is seldom perceived as an attractive source of income in the longer term, and therefore it is not worth maintaining a stable ownership control over it. Such an approach is undoubtedly due to the generally unfavourable situation of joint-stock companies executing BCAs (financial, market, technical) in recent years. It can be expected that the improved condition of the market, which has been observed for some time now, and the strengthening of some of the joint-stock companies, will change this approach into a more long-term orientation of owners.

4 ASSESSMENT OF THE EFFECTS OF THE ENTERPRISE AND THE BANK RESTRUCTURING PROGRAMME

As has been said above, the main goals of the enterprise and the bank restructuring programme were:

1. to create opportunities for enterprises that could repay their debts and bring about their restructuring so that they could be privatized;
2. to eliminate ineffective or unprofitable enterprises from the market; and
3. to restructure the credit portfolios of Polish banks.

The regulations permitting the reduction of the debt burden of state-owned enterprises through BCAs expired on 18 March 1996. The agreements already signed will be executed during the next few years. The experience gained so far allows only an initial assessment of positive effects and weaknesses of the restructuring programme to be carried out.

Of the three goals named above, the one accomplished most satisfactorily was the third objective. Banks were mobilized to restructure their bad debt portfolios. State-owned banks received restructuring bonds from the State Treasury allowing them to raise additional capital and improve their financial position. Hence, they were able to carry out the debt reduction programme without fearing that they would lose their liquidity. Also, private banks frequently found that a BCA concluded with difficult debtors was a better solution than announcing their bankruptcy.

It is worth stressing that the supervision and control of banks and creditors over enterprises have been intensified. The banks conducting BCAs and the council of creditors exert pressures for changes, pass opinions and control more important moves of the management board, and initiate, wherever it is necessary, changes in the board composition.

Debt/equity swaps provided an impetus for the internal modernization of bank structure and the emergence of investment banking dealing not only with equity investments but also with attracting capital for investments and co-participating in the management of privatized firms. Not all banks availed themselves of this opportunity. The biggest headway in building such a model was made by the Lodz bank, PBG, where an investment fund was established, to which the shares taken over through BCAs were transferred. The fund will be managing these assets in order to raise their value.

The degree to which the first goal will be achieved will be known in two to three years. The conciliation agreements were concluded for four to five years. In that time, the enterprises undertook to repay their debts and carry out their remedial programmes (restructuring programmes). Initially it can be stated that BCAs protected many enterprises from bankruptcy. Debt reduction and restructuring allowed many enterprises to improve their situation economically. In 1993, only 19.2 per cent of the BCAs analysed by us, under which debt/equity swaps took place, recorded a positive net financial effect, and in 1994 debt reduction and restructuring increased the share of enterprises recording a net profit to 59.6 per cent. In 1993, 12.7 per cent of enterprises covered by regular BCAs achieved a net profit, while in 1994 their share rose to 63.6 per cent.

These results should be approached with caution because they are tainted with many distortions. The firms covered by bank-led conciliation agreements included their written-off debts in the extraordinary profits, which led to a seeming improvement in their financial results. But it is the operating profit that reflects the real restructuring effort. The research conducted by the World Bank on the effects brought about by conciliation agreements shows that the first years of implementation of the restructuring programmes did not contribute greatly to improvements in the operating profit. In the examined 62 enterprises, the number of firms with operating profits above 5 per cent fell in the years 1994–95, in spite of the revival recorded in the economy and a more than 6 per cent economic growth.[6] It also follows from the report prepared by the Supreme Chamber of Control that conciliation agreements have not yet produced a marked improvement in the economic situation of the firms. In most cases, the agreements boiled down only to considerable debt write-offs (on average by 54 per cent). This may considerably worsen the financial situation of some creditors.

Among the reasons for the low efficacy of the bank-led conciliation agreements, the report[7] mentions the following factors:

- a lack of legal instruments which would induce creditors to take an active part in restructuring the state-owned firms by buying shares/stocks for debts;
- the privileged position of the banks, whereby additional funds were obtained from the budget irrespective of the effects brought about by the restructuring programme implemented by firms with which they started conciliation agreements;
- the 'moderation' of the banks which were not eager to give credits to enterprises undergoing restructuring programmes, which – given the fact that these enterprises had to repay debts – limited their financial liquidity and hampered their current production activity; and
- dilatoriness on the part of the central administration bodies in carrying out ownership transformations.

Debt restructuring procedures also have other weaknesses. Namely, bank conciliation agreements did not protect creditors and they sometimes supported bad firms at the expense of good ones. Two groups of enterprises had the greatest chance of signing BCAs: (i) relatively good firms which had prospects for overcoming their financial difficulties (here the restructuring programme fulfilled its legislative goals); (ii) firms which had a strong political leverage but their financial standing was very bad, and which had poor prospects for the future. These firms were often restructured in a dual manner – first, by means of the court conciliation agreement, which proved to be of little effect, and second, through the BCA. This led to the softening of financial constraints in the public sector. The findings of the Supreme Chamber of Control indicate that about 20 per cent of BCA participants do not repay their debts, generate losses and are threatened by bankruptcy. It can be expected that these are primarily enterprises belonging to the second group.

Despite these reservations, the preliminary Polish estimates received from the Supreme Chamber of Control show that 60–65 per cent of BCAs are successful.[8] Firms recover their creditworthiness, repay instalments, restructure their product range and regain the market.

Summing up the effects to date of the bank-led conciliation agreements it should be said that although they did not solve all the problems, they fulfilled their goals. It is true that there was no universal ridding of their debts by the firms. However, the Act permitted the bank portfolios to be cleared of bad debts, without which their privatization would probably be impossible.

The experience acquired during the implementation of the restructuring programme will be most helpful for the amendment of the Bankruptcy Law and the Court Conciliation Agreement by introducing certain elements of the BCA. Because of the inefficiencies of the judicial system, the restructuring solutions for enterprises facing problems should be made the responsibility of arbitration courts.

The combination of the bank restructuring mechanism and the process of solving firms' indebtedness was a unique solution in the countries of Central and Eastern Europe. The Hungarians gave banks only an additional capital of US$2.5 billion and sold them to foreign investors. The Czechs did not draw up a special programme for firm restructuring; they changed their firms' outstanding debts into Treasury Bonds and transferred them to the Consolidation Bank.

Among the measures taken by banks within the bank and enterprise restructuring programme, an important element was procedures aimed at eliminating those organizations which, in the bank's opinion, were not and would not be able to operate effectively without recourse to policies which had nothing to do with the rules of market competition. This group of measures encompassed: the sale of debts, the announcement of the debtor's bankruptcy and the launching of liquidation proceedings.

The market of debts is one of Poland's youngest financial markets. It did not start operating until 1993, when banks were allowed to sell their claims publicly under the Bank and Enterprise Financial Restructuring Act. The Act envisages the following modes of selling debt:

- through auction;
- through a publicly announced offer; and
- through negotiations started on the basis of public invitation.

The surveys conducted by the Market Economy Research Institute indicate that banks did not sell their claims through a publicly announced offer, because of difficulties connected with fixing the minimal price and hopes that a higher price could be obtained using a different procedure.

The invitation to negotiations was used in the vast majority of cases, because banks consider it to be the simplest method of allowing the price and terms of the agreement to be agreed in detail. An additional aspect in favour of this form of selling claims was also the possibility of the bank's participation in the restructuring process undertaken by the buyer.[9] However, whenever the invitation to negotiations proved to be unsuccessful, banks would try to sell the claims through an auction (some banks used this form of bargaining exclusively). This form of restructuring appeared to be very ineffective. In terms of quantity, only 30.3 per cent of claims put on sale were sold and in terms of value only 12.7 per cent. It also appears that banks managed to recover only 22 per cent of the total value of debts put on sale including about 49 per cent of the principal and only 2 per cent of the interest.[10]

The small interest displayed in bank claims was undoubtedly unattractiveness of the claims put on sale. After all, they were in most cases the debts classified by banks in the fourth group of bank risk – lost credit of enterprises coping with serious financial difficulties, for which the bank found it economically unjustifiable to use positive restructuring paths.

The situation is also highly complicated on the supply side. In the course of the restructuring programme it appeared that banks did not use this technically simplest and recommended path (the immediate return of financial resources, with practically no additional outlays), because the tax regulations in this field, and particularly those concerning income tax, contain incentives that encourage banks to seek, first of all, the execution against credit provided by them, and only then to sell their claims. When selling claims it was necessary to add to the debt minimal price 40 per cent tax in relation to the target reserve created for this claim, because in this case the Income Tax from Legal Entities Act did not permit the inclusion of the reserve among the costs of obtaining the revenue (revenue – costs of obtaining revenue = taxable income) unless the claims were likely to be made irrevocable.[11] It was the reason why banks were reluctant to embark upon this form of restructuring, and even if they did, the results were poor. It can be also presumed that the causes of failure of these few attempts to sell claims (particularly during the period immediately following the passing of the Act, that is, before the obligatory deadline for selling the claims of banks benefiting from additional funds received from the budget) should be sought merely in their infrequent character. After all, it can hardly be expected that there will be a demand in the market for a product offered in such an insignificant quantity, with the total offer being very uncertain. All the causes mentioned above show that this instrument of restructuring proved to be a failure.[12]

An alternative procedure to eliminate ineffective economic units is the announcement of enterprise bankruptcy. The experience derived from the restructuring programme revealed numerous shortcomings and faults in this procedure. The chief criticisms made by the banks which decided to clean their credit portfolio in this way included:

- that bankruptcy proceedings were long drawn-out;
- that there was little chance of recovering claims because, on the one hand, of the low seniority of the bank in the sequence of satisfying particular claims and, on the other hand, there were problems connected with selling the debtor's fixed assets (in the division of a bankrupt's estate, the bank would recover on average only 10.1 per cent of the bankrupt's debt);[13] and
- that political pressure was exerted on the bank whenever the debtor was one of a few employers in a region threatened by unemployment and, simultaneously, employed a large workforce.

Past experience shows that bankruptcy proceedings should be streamlined and their effectiveness should be increased through:

1. the liquidation or change of priorities in satisfying creditors so that most of them are interested in the execution of bankruptcy proceedings and in submitting bankruptcy applications;
2. the introduction of sanctions forcing debtors to disclose financial information and to cooperate with trustees in bankruptcy;
3. a change in the system of compensation for trustees in bankruptcy by making their compensation dependent on the completion of the bankruptcy procedure, for example, delaying payment of a significant part of the compensation until the bankruptcy proceedings are completed;[14] and
4. specifying the time during which the court is obliged to dismiss or accept the application for the announcement of the bankruptcy and the commencement of bankruptcy proceedings.

NOTES

1. See, for example, Pinto et al (1994).
2. The original text, in Polish, is Grzegorzewski (1995).
3. Enterprise and Bank Restructuring Act of 3 February 1993 and Amendments to some Acts, Dziennik Ustaw, 4 March 1993, No. 18, item 82 (in Polish).
4. See the report by Pawlowicz (1995, p. 42).
5. See also the earlier report by Pawlowicz (1994, p. 38).
6. See the study by Gray and Holle (1996, p. 28).
7. See the report by Sadurski (1997) in Polish.
8. See Domagala (1966) in Polish.
9. See Cholewa (1995) in Polish.
10. See Pawlowicz, (1995), pp. 21, 23.
11. See Cholewa (1995) in Polish.

12. An opinion expressed by P. Cyburt (director of Workout Department and Board member of the Powszechny Bank Kredytowy SA) in a newspaper discussion, 'Harvesting test', *Zycie Gospodarcze*, No. 15, 1994; and A. Parafiniewicz and J. Zebrowski, 'Role of the banks in the implementation of bank and enterprise restructuring programme', *Bank*, No. 15, 1993.
13. See Pawlowicz, (1995), p. 29.
14. See Jabłoński (1995).

REFERENCES

Cholewa, M. (1995), 'Trade in debts', *Zycie Gospodarcze*, No. 29 (in Polish).

Cholewa, M. (1995), 'Ultimate Solution', *Bank*, No. 5, (in Polish).

Domagala, J. (1966), 'Putting them on their Feet', *Zycie Gospodarcze*, No. 11 (in Polish).

Gray, Ch. W. and A. Holle (1996), *Bank-led Restructuring in Poland. An Empirical Look at the Bank Conciliation Process*, Policy Research Working Paper 1650, World Bank Policy Research Department, September.

Grzegorzewski, Z. (1995), 'Enterprises for sale', *Bank*, No. 26 (in Polish).

Jabłoński, H. (1995), 'Bankruptcy law – necessary and desirable amendments', *Bank*, No. 2.

Pawlowicz, L. (1995), *Enterprise and Bank Restructuring. Second Report on Surveys*, Gdansk: Gdansk Academy of Banking (in Polish).

Pawlowicz, L. (1994), *Enterprise and Bank Restructuring. First Report on Surveys*, Gdansk: Gdansk Academy of Banking (in Polish).

Pinto, B., Belka, M. and S. Krajewski (1994), *Transforming State Enterprises in Poland: Evidence on Adjustment by Manufacturing Firms*, Brookings Papers on Economic Activity, No 1.

Sadurski, K. (1997), 'Report by the SCLC. To postpone restructuring', *Gazeta Wyborcza*, 14–15 June (in Polish).

3. Enterprise restructuring and changes in the business environment in Estonia*

Aita Tammeraid, Asta Teearu and Vello Vensel

1 INTRODUCTION

Singular among the factors that underpin the transformation of former centrally-planned economies in Central and Eastern Europe (CEE) into well-functioning market economies is the change in the business environment that engenders enterprise restructuring.[1] Given that firms interact with one another, households, governmental as well as non-governmental organizations, it is not surprising that the market and non-market business environments are important in the developed Western countries (see, for example, Baron 1993). However, business environmental issues are difficult to pin down analytically in transition economies because the main market structures are still not well developed (for example, development of financial markets), and market forces are functioning weakly. Moreover, lessons from the stabilization and liberalization programmes adopted in CEE have sometimes contradicted the predictions that derive from traditional economic theory and some 'mainstream' economic models.[2]

Existing studies offer a tall order of the main objectives that economies should ideally pursue during the transition process (see, for example, Hillman 1994; Yavlinsky and Braginski 1994; Citrin and Lahiri 1995; and Banerjee et al. 1995). On top of the agenda is the privatization and restructuring of the former state-owned enterprises in all industries. This involves the development of the private sector in order to establish a competitive business environment to replace the planned allocation of resources and concentrated production of the pre-transition era. The process also involves the restructuring of the financial sector, especially the development of a private commercial banking system as well as financial markets. The liberalization of prices, capital movements, and

* This research has been supported under the European Commission's PHARE/ACE Programme under two successive contracts, numbered 94–0685–R and P96–6152–R. Support from the Royal Swedish Academy of Sciences and the University of Gothenburg for the first years of the field research, and from the Estonian Science Foundation for some of the subsequent years, is also gratefully acknowledged.

the international trade regime are also undertaken, alongside monetary reform and the introduction of a stable convertible domestic currency. Some more general reforms include defining the new role of government, development of budgetary discipline, and introducing market-orientated fiscal instruments and social security programmes. These transition activities, in particular appropriate institution-building, political democratization, and changes in the values and behaviour of economic agents, cause rapid changes in the business environment and thus influence firm survival and the potential for firm and national competitiveness. It should also be emphasized that all these changes must be flexible, ready to meet unexpected developments in the basic structures of an emerging market economy. Institutional and environmental changes require substantial changes in individual attitudes: all agents in the economy (producers–consumers, owners–workers, firms–households and so on) have to change their economic behaviour radically.

In Estonia, major steps have been taken to create a business environment which favours the growth of new business activities: for example, full liberalization of prices, interest rates and trade regime; successful monetary reform, tight monetary policy and high fiscal discipline; moderate governmental regulations; restructuring and rapid development of the commercial banking sector, and the privatization and restructuring of the Estonian manufacturing sector (see, for example, Kilvits 1995; Lugus and Hachey 1995; Vensel 1996; Grennes 1997). However, there are still some problems which constrain economic recovery and growth; these problems, though, seem to be shared by other transition economies (see Mullineux 1994, 1995; Aghion et al. 1994; Calvo and Coricelli 1993; Zecchini 1997). For Estonia, in particular, it is crucial to study the key problems of the development of the business environment and the restructuring of the economy, in the context of Estonia's desire to join the European Union (EU) as per her declaration in November 1995 (see Ziacik 1995; Purju 1996) and the positive response of the EU member states at their meeting in December 1997.[3] Estonia has successfully undertaken the first step towards joining the EU by signing the Europe Agreement or Associate Agreement.

A key issue in the development of the business environment in Estonia is whether (or not) there exists a mechanism for conflict resolution. In general, conflict resolution mechanisms and regulatory mechanisms are both important components of the legal infrastructure. Existing literature in this area emphasizes the survival prospects of business firms in the transition economies, especially in Russia (see, for example, Alm and Sjoquist 1995; Commander et al. 1996; Linz 1997). The literature suggests that firms' survival and competitiveness potential are determined by the characteristics of the market structure, the characteristics of the firm, and the characteristics of the firms' top-level managers. These issues are also studied in the developed economies, for example on the basis of Darwinian view of organizations (see Kole and Lehn 1997). Deregulation in transition economies provides a good opportunity to observe and to study the Darwinian process at work! This view is consistent with recent findings in survey studies which suggest that private ownership dramatically improves firms' performance, survival and competitiveness potential (Frydman et al. 1997; Pohl et al. 1997).[4]

In addition, the development of the business environment in Estonia rests on the operation of the enforcement mechanism. Where this mechanism is non-operational, self-enforcement mechanisms become the option. As Klein and Murphy (1997, p. 417) observe, 'unfortunately, however, transactions cannot rely entirely on self-enforcement, because the magnitude of the private sanction that can be imposed for nonperformance is limited'. The role of the state in this context, during the transition process, is characterized by means of three basic models (Frye and Schleifer 1997, p. 355). The first is the 'invisible hand' model. The legal environment in this model is such that the government is not above the law; the regulatory environment requires that the government follows rules; there is little corruption. The second is the 'helping hand' model. The government is above the law but uses aggressively regulatory power to help business. State officials enforce contracts. The third is the 'grabbing-hand' model. The legal environment is such that government is above the law and uses power to extract rents. The legal system does not work; the Mafia replaces state as enforcer. The regulatory environment is characterized by predatory regulations, disorganized corruption, bribes and bureaucracy.[5]

This chapter is motivated to address the above issues in the context of the current reforms in Estonia. It presents some results of the special interview study of Estonian business firms undertaken in 1997. Specifically, the 1997 interview study was a logical continuation of the studies undertaken in 1994, 1995 and 1996 (see Liikane et al. 1994; Vensel and Wihlborg 1998; Tammeraid et al. 1996). In this context, the major contribution of this chapter to the existing literature is that it undertakes a quantitative measurement of the state and changes in the Estonian business environment, with respect to the regulation mechanism, dispute resolution mechanism, financial contractual relations, and availability of business supporting services. The evidence offers key information on the most important factors influencing the competitiveness of Estonian business firms. Forty-nine firms responded to questionnaires during interviews. Respondent firms were mostly privately owned small and medium-sized joint-stock companies from different industries and various industrial regions.

The rest of this chapter is structured as follows. Section 2 deals with the general sample characteristics. Section 3 focuses on investment and infrastructure, and Section 4 discusses microstructure, corporate governance and

Table 3.1 General characteristics of sample firms

Characteristics	1994	1995	1996	1997
1. Distribution by industries				
Light industry	7 (17.9%)	5 (10.9%)	5 (11.4%)	4 (8.3%)
Food industry	7 (17.9%)	4 (8.7%)	7 (15.9%)	6 (12.5%)
Construction industry	4 (10.3%)	4 (8.7%)	5 (11.4%)	4 (8.3%)
Transportation	3 (7.7%)	7 (15.2%)	2 (4.5%)	2 (4.2%)
Wood-processing industry	3 (7.7%)	3 (6.5%)	3 (6.8%)	3 (6.3%)
Metal-processing industry	4 (10.3%)	1 (2.2%)	4 (9.1%)	4 (8.3%)
Trade industry	4 (10.3%)	9 (19.5%)	10 (22.7%)	15 (31.3%)
Other industries	7 (17.9%)	13 (28.3%)	8 (18.2%)	10 (20.8%)
2. Distribution by production location				
Tallinn (the capital)	15 (38.5%)	24 (57.1%)	24 (51.0%)	24 (49.0%)
North Estonia	16 (41%)	11 (26.2%)	10 (21.3%)	14 (28.6%)
South Estonia	6 (15.4%)	5 (11.9%)	10 (21.3%)	7 (14.3%)
Other regions	2 (5.1%)	2 (4.8%)	3 (6.4%)	3 (8.1%)
3. Distribution by legal status				
Corporate	25 (65.8%)	36 (80%)	40 (83.3%)	38 (77.6%)
State-owned enterprise	7 (18.4%)	3 (6.7%)	1 (2.1%)	1 (2.0%)
Limited liability enterprise	3 (7.9%)	3 (6.7%)	3 (6.3%)	7 (14.3%)
Partnership	1 (2.6%)	2 (4.4%)	1 (2.1%)	1 (2.0%)
Sole proprietorship	1 (2.6%)	1 (2.2%)	1 (2.1%)	0
Subsidiary of a corporation	2 (5.3%)	0	2 (4.1%)	2 (4.1%)
4. Distribution by ownership structure				
Domestic private owners	23 (59%)	32 (72%)	42 (88%)	37 (75%)
Domestic and foreign private	6 (15%)	8 (18%)	2 (4%)	10 (21%)
State ownership	7 (18%)	2 (5%)	0	1 (2%)
State, domestic and foreign private	1 (3%)	2 (5%)	1 (2%)	0

Foreign private owners	0	0	2 (4%)	0
State and domestic private	2 (5%)	0	1 (2%)	1 (2%)
5. Distribution by start-up year				
Started before 1980	7 (18%)	5 (10.6%)	7 (15.2%)	4 (8.7%)
Started 1981–1990	3 (7.7%)	3 (6.4%)	3 (6.5%)	9 (19.5%)
Started 1991	13 (33.3%)	10 (21.3%)	11 (23.9%)	11 (23.9%)
Started 1992	8 (20.5%)	12 (25.5%)	8 (17.4)	11 (23.9%)
Started 1993	8 (20.5%)	11 (23.4%)	9 (19.6%)	5 (10.9%)
Started 1994	0	6 (12.8%)	7 (15.2%)	5 (10.9%)
Started 1995	0	0	1 (2.2%)	1 (2.2%)
6. Size distribution of sample Firms				
Small, 1–20 workers	7 (20.6%)	16 (38.1%)	15 (32.6%)	17 (36.2%)
1–5	3	7	5	4
6–10	2	5	6	8
11–20	2	4	4	5
Medium, 21–200 workers	19 (55.9%)	17 (40.5%)	23 (50%)	26 (55.3%)
21–50	8	7	9	16
51–100	6	6	6	4
101–200	5	4	8	6
Large, 201–	8 (23.5%)	9 (21.4)	8 (17.4%)	4 (8.5%)
201–500	6	7	6	3
501–	2	2	2	1
7. Distribution by sources of start-up financing (%)				
Own savings	57.9	63.6	51.6	57.5
Loan from domestic bank	10.5	11.4	10.9	1.0
Loan from relatives, friends	8.0	9.2	6.2	3.3
Loan from foreign bank or donor agency	2.6	6.8	1.6	0.8
Loan from money-lender	10.5	4.5	4.7	3.7
Other sources (parent firm, loan from supplier, foreign partner, etc.)	10.5	4.5	25.0	33.7

adjustment procedures. Section 5 examines the financial contractual relations, while Section 6 discusses the regulation mechanism. Dispute resolution mechanisms are explored in Section 7, and business support services in Section 8. Section 9 concludes.

2 GENERAL SAMPLE CHARACTERISTICS

The most important general characteristics of the sample firms are presented in Table 3.1, showing the distribution of sample firms by industries, production location, legal status, ownership structure, start-up year, size of firm, and sources of the firm's start-up financing. The sample covers the key industries of the Estonian economy. Quite typical for a small country, more than one-half of manufacturing output is produced in the capital city (Tallinn) and its suburbs.

The evidence presented in Table 3.1 highlights some of the main changes in the business environment. Based on the distribution of firms by legal status in different years, it is shown that there is a decreasing share of state-owned enterprises and some corresponding increase in the share of limited liability enterprises; this evidence suggests that the privatization process has the prospect of becoming a success story. In both domestic firms (by ownership) and the firms in which ownership is mixed (domestic and foreign), there is a diminishing share of state ownership while the share of private ownership is increasing. The average share of foreign ownership in private (rather than state) firms was 43 per cent. Most of the sample firms started after year 1990 and obtained their start-up financing from own savings, mainly because the firms had only limited access to the credit market (especially commercial banks). Most of the sample firms were medium sized, with 21–200 permanent workers.

In general, the main findings on the sample characteristics are fourfold. First, the sample consists mainly of companies which are small sized (36 per cent) and medium sized (55 per cent). Second, 75 per cent of total firms are domestically-owned private firms, while 78 per cent of the total are joint-stock companies. Third, most firms started on the basis of own savings (58 per cent) after the year 1990 (72 per cent). Fourth, most firms are operating in Tallinn (49 per cent) and in Northern Estonia (28 per cent).

3 INVESTMENT AND INFRASTRUCTURE

An important component of the interview survey was to capture the developments in the investment behaviour of enterprises with respect to their acquisition of buildings and equipment. The idea was to determine changes in the behaviour of enterprises in terms of the initial as well as the additional investment for acquisition of buildings and equipment; an attempt was also made to assess the business infrastructure as an aspect of the environment for enterprises.[6]

The data on the initial investment by the sample firms for the acquisition of buildings and equipment are reported in Table 3.2. The equipment acquired by firms was mostly imported; what is more interesting, however, is that most of this equipment was used rather than new.

Table 3.2 Firms' initial investment for acquisition of buildings and equipment

Characteristics	1994	1995	1996	1997
1. Acquisition year				
Before 1990	2 (8%)	5 (12%)	1 (3%)	3 (6%)
1991	0	5 (12%)	7 (17%)	5 (11%)
1992	6 (24%)	13 (30%)	8 (20%)	0
1993	17 (68%)	11 (25%)	12 (30%)	20 (43%)
1994	0	9 (21%)	10 (25%)	11 (23%)
1995	0	0	2 (5%)	5 (11%)
1996	0	0	0	2 (4%)
1997	0	0	0	1 (2%)
N/A	14	4	8	2
2. Distribution by equipment age				
New equipment	7 (26%)	13 (30%)	15 (37%)	15 (33%)
Used equipment	9 (33%)	20 (47%)	12 (29%)	16 (36%)
Both, new and used	11 (41%)	10 (23%)	14 (34%)	14 (31%)
N/A	12	4	7	4
3. Distribution by acquisition source				
Imported equipment (100%)	11 (41%)	14 (34%)	12 (30%)	19 (44%)
Mostly imported	6 (22%)	11 (27%)	12 (30%)	10 (23%)
Domestic equipment (100%)	2 (7%)	5 (12%)	3 (7%)	2 (5%)
Mostly domestic	4 (15%)	7 (17%)	9 (23%)	7 (16%)
Imported purchased in Estonia	4 (15%)	4 (10%)	4 (10%)	5 (12%)
N/A	12	6	8	6

The data on the additional investment by the sample firms for the subsequent acquisition of buildings and equipment are reported in Table 3.3. Together with the evidence in Table 3.2, the data in Table 3.3 suggest that almost all the respondent firms (95.8 per cent) have made additional investment for the acquisition of buildings and equipment after the initial investment in 1994. In general, the average size of the latest additional investment was about 1.3 million kroons.

Table 3.3 Characteristics of firms' latest additional investment

Characteristics	1994	1995	1996	1997
1. Year of latest investment				
1992	3 (13%)	2 (6%)	—	
1993	9 (39%)	3 (8%)	—	
1994	11 (48%)	19 (53%)	8 (20%)	
1995	0	12 (33%)	23 (58%)	5 (11%)
1996	0	0	9 (22%)	20 (42%)
1997	0	0	0	22 (47%)
N/A	16	11	8	2
2. Distribution by equipment age				
New equipment	10 (44%)	24 (69%)	24 (57%)	29 (66%)
Used equipment	6 (26%)	6 (17%)	7 (17%)	11 (25%)
Both, new and used equipment	7 (30%)	5 (14%)	11 (26%)	4 (9%)
N/A	16	12	6	5
3. Distribution by acquisition source				
Imported equipment (100%)	14 (61%)	19 (53%)	25 (64%)	26 (59%)
Mostly imported equipment	4 (17%)	8 (22%)	3 (8%)	5 (11%)
Domestic equipment (100%)	3 (13%)	2 (6%)	2 (5%)	1 (2%)
Mostly domestic equipment	0	4 (11%)	2 (5%)	2 (5%)
Imported, but purchased in Estonia	2 (9%)	3 (8%)	7 (18%)	10 (23%)
N/A	16	11	9	5

The sources of financing for the latest additional investment in 1997 are presented in Table 3.4. It is shown that the most important source of funding was retained earnings. However, for the acquisition of buildings, the main source of funding is shown to be bank loans (35.9 per cent). The evidence also shows that only two firms were able to purchase land; this evidence is consistent with the existing land reform problems in Estonia in the sense that

Table 3.4 Financing sources of the latest investment, 1997 (percentages)

Source	Land	Building	Equipment
Retained earnings	75	45.2	43.9
Own savings	0	0	7.1
Loan from relatives, friends	0	0	0.4
Bank loan	0	35.9	16.8
Supplier credit	25	0	7.8
Loan from a money-lender	0	0	3.8
Other sources (leasing, accumulated depreciation etc.)	0	18.9	20.2

economic agents are not allowed to acquire land directly without going through the state machinery.

In general, however, enterprises face some infrastructure problems. In the interview exercises, we used a Likert-type 5–point scale, with 1 indicating no problems and 5 indicating great problems. The results of the interview with the sample firms are reported in Table 3.5, showing the relevance of problems with various infrastructure elements in the sample period. The results suggest that the greatest problem faced by enterprises was associated with the 'communications services' element of infrastructure, which includes telephones, fax and related communication facilities. Most firms felt that the quality of communications services was poor; the service was criticized as unreliable and costly.

Table 3.5 Average estimates of problems with elements of infrastructure

Infrastructure elements	1994	1995	1996	1997
Communication services	2.0	2.5	2.3	2.12
Roads	1.4	2.0	2.0	1.79
Security	2.0	1.9	1.7	1.73
Electricity	1.8	1.8	1.8	1.73
Freight transport	1.3	1.6	1.4	1.48
Removal of wastes	1.3	1.6	1.6	1.45
Water	1.4	1.5	1.8	1.33
Harbours, airports	1.2	1.4	1.5	1.24
Workers' transportation	1.3	1.3	1.5	1.34

To overcome the above infrastructure problems, a number of Estonian manufacturing firms have their own infrastructure elements. The most common private infrastructure facilities owned by firms include security systems, communications system, water systems, removal of waste systems, electricity generation, and roads. Table 3.6 reports the number and share of firms which have their own (private) business infrastructure elements.

4 MICROSTRUCTURE,[7] CORPORATE CONTROL AND ADJUSTMENT PROCEDURES

We investigated the main markets for output, encompassing both the foreign and domestic markets. We found that 28 firms (57 per cent of sample firms) were exporters. The average share of exports in the output of exporters was

Table 3.6 Number and share of firms which have their own infrastructure elements

Infrastructure elements	1994	1995	1996	1997
Freight transport	13 (33.3%)	26 (76.5%)	18 (62.1%)	27 (58.7%)
Security systems	10 (25.6%)	24 (70.6%)	20 (62.5%)	24 (52.2%)
Communication systems	4 (10.3%)	15 (44.2%)	12 (40%)	17 (37.0%)
Workers' transportation	7 (17.9%)	11 (32.3%)	7 (22.6%)	8 (17.4%)
Water systems	9 (23%)	9 (26.5%)	11 (36.7%)	9 (20%)
Removal of waste systems	11 (28.2%)	9 (26.5%)	8 (27.6%)	9 (20%)
Electric generators	2 (5.1%)	7 (19.4%)	3 (10%)	3 (6.7%)
Roads	0	7 (20.6%)	6 (19.3%)	5 (10.9%)

39 per cent, and the share of exports in 12 firms was more than 50 per cent. The exporters used the following different export market channels to distribute their products: direct foreign buyers – 83.9 per cent; private trading firms – 12.5 per cent; and state-owned trading firms – 3.6 per cent.

The domestic distribution channels by the sample firms was as follows:

1. private firm, final consumer: 36.3 per cent
2. state-owned firm, final consumer: 11.0 per cent
3. private wholesale or retail trade firm: 32.2 per cent
4. state-owned wholesale or retail trade firm: 4.3 per cent
5. others (for example, private person): 16.2 per cent

In addition, the interviewed firms determined their main competitors in the output market. It was found that the main competitors were domestic firms – 85.7 per cent; foreign competitor in exports market – 8.2 per cent; and importers – 6.1 per cent.

In terms of the pricing policy, the sample firms mentioned two main output pricing methods (first-order choice followed by second-order choice):

1. following market prices: 12 (25 per cent), 0;
2. mark-up pricing: 14 (29 per cent), 2 (5 per cent);
3. following imports prices: 5 (11 per cent), 1 (3 per cent);
4. different prices in different markets: 10 (21 per cent), 2 (5 per cent);
5. high pricing signalling high quality of output: 0, 2 (5 per cent);
6. following price leaders: 3 (6 per cent), 19 (50 per cent);
7. government guidelines: 0, 1 (3 per cent);
8. pricing based on bilateral agreements: 3 (6 per cent), 10 (26 per cent);
9. association determines: 1 (2 per cent), 1 (3 per cent).

We also examined location factors as cardinal aspects of the business environment. We found that two main factors were important in determining the firm location, as follows (first-order factor followed by second-order factor):

1. availability of land: 2 (4 per cent), 0;
2. existence of infrastructure: 17 (36 per cent), 0;
3. existence of qualified labour: 1 (2 per cent), 2 (8 per cent);
4. availability of raw materials: 2 (4 per cent), 0;
5. closeness to clients: 9 (20 per cent), 11 (46 per cent);
6. closeness to family and home: 1 (2 per cent), 2 (8 per cent);
7. government regulations: 1 (2 per cent), 1 (4 per cent);
8. others: 14 (30 per cent), 8 (34 per cent).

We also found that 40 per cent of the respondent firms have more than one production location, and 37 per cent of the firms have administration, sale or other buildings separately from the production location.

Given the efforts being made to establish a well-functioning legal system, we investigated the legal rights firms have to their locations. We found that legal rights to the business location were determined as follows:

1. real estate register: 11 (23 per cent);
2. rental contracts: 29 (59 per cent);
3. other rights (for example, land usage contracts): 9 (18 per cent);

On the crucial question of research and development (R&D), we attempted to ascertain during the interview whether firms are establishing R&D facilities. As the sample firms consisted mainly of small and medium-sized firms, there were hardly any hired researchers, engineers or technicians who were concerned with R&D issues. However, 26 firms (53 per cent of respondents) had hired engineers (average number 4.9), and only eight firms (16 per cent) had hired engineers who were included in R&D (average number 4.7) activities; 19 firms (39 per cent) had hired technicians (average number 2.4), and eight (16 per cent) firms had hired technicians who were included in R&D (average number 1.4); ten firms (20 per cent of interviewed firms) had made expenditures on R&D averaging about EEK (kroons) 100 thousand; while 14 firms (29 per cent) reported having workers (engineers and technicians) who were concerned with the improvement of productivity.

The nature of the labour market is also another important aspect of the business environment that was investigated during the interviews. Respondents reported usage of different modes of hiring new workers, namely:

1. relatives or friends of the owner or the employer: 17 per cent;
2. recommendations of business partners: 5 per cent;
3. verbal conversation: 35 per cent;
4. job announcements: 35 per cent;
5. intermediation of the Labour Office: 0;
6. others (on-the-job training, public contest): 8 per cent.

Overall, labour mobility was reported quite high. Respective average labour mobility coefficients during the last year were as follows:

1. hiring coefficient: 18 per cent;
2. firing coefficient: 16 per cent;
3. own leaving coefficient: 11 per cent;
4. retiring coefficient: 4 per cent.

As regards corporate governance, almost all firms had some kind of board of directors; the average number of board members for the sample firms was 3.2. Five firms were managed solely by the managing director. The average distribution of shares and voting rights in joint-stock companies was as follows:

1. managing director: 15.1 per cent;
2. board members: 30.9 per cent;
3. employees of the firm: 19.5 per cent;
4. foreign owners: 4.5 per cent;
5. other firms: 9.9 per cent;
6. government or banks: 0;
7. others (for example, parent firm, previous employees): 20.1 per cent.

In general, the above represents important milestones in the development of corporate governance in Estonia.

Finally, in the climate of economic transition, we would expect enterprises to evolve some kind of adjustment procedures. In general, however, firms had problems in coping with two major factors, namely high interest rates and uncertainty in revenues. On a Likert-type 5-point scale with 1 for no problems and 5 for very great problems, the sample firms scored 3.7, 3.6, 3.5 and 3.1 during 1994–97, respectively, with regard to coping with high interest rates. On the same Likert-type 5-point scale, the sample firms scored 3.2, 3.0, 2.9 and 2.9 during 1994–97, respectively, with regard to coping with uncertainty in revenues.

We found that due to high interest rates and uncertainty in revenues, some firms had suffered serious losses on the balance sheet. In order to cope with these losses, the firms pursued the following options:

1. arrangement of more suitable sale policies: 35 per cent;
2. reducing the cost of production: 25 per cent;
3. rehabilitation of the operating capacity: 19 per cent;
4. reducing production: 6 per cent;
5. raising output prices: 4 per cent;
6. other measures (for example, change of ownership form, change of managers, establishment of branches): 11 per cent.

We also found that 46 per cent of respondent firms used adjustment measures to deal with high inflation. In addition to relative primitive price adjustments, the firms also used other adjustment measures, namely, more active activities in the stock market, deeper financial analysis of the balance sheet, and managing stocks.

5 FINANCIAL CONTRACTUAL RELATIONS

Financial contractual relations are an important component of the business environment in the transition process in Estonia (see Vensel and Wihlborg 1998). In what follows, we explain our findings on financial contractual relationships in Estonia in the context informal lending, informal borrowing and the activities of the official financial system.

In terms of informal lending, about one-third of respondent firms reported the usage of informal lending during 1995, 1996 and 1997. Table 3.7 reports the distribution of firms by informal loan recipients. We found that the average amount of granted loans was EEK 140 thousand (from EEK 10 to 1000 thousand). These were mainly short-term and medium-term (1–24 months) loans, with average maturity a little more than one year, and with an average loan rate of 11.3 per cent (with a lower rate for other firms, 7.3 per cent, and employees, 11.6 per cent). Collateral was required in only 21.7 per cent of the cases; output was mentioned as a collateral from other firms and salary as

Table 3.7 Distribution of firms by informal loan recipients (percentages)

Loan recipient	1993	1994	1995	1996	1997
Relatives and friends	6.7	14.8	27.8	5.3	3.2
Suppliers	6.7	0	0	0	17.4
Clients	13.3	14.8	0	0	0
Employees	33.3	48.2	55.6	73.7	76.7
Other firms	40.0	22.2	16.6	21.0	2.7

a guarantee required from employees. If the loan recipient was not able to pay the loan at maturity, the maturity would be prolonged (45 per cent); interest penalties (20 per cent) or initiating legal procedures (20 per cent) would be used. Informal finance was mostly the first loan for corporate loan recipients (88.2 per cent). The average interest rate for informal lending was 11.3 per cent; in previous years this was 15.4 per cent (from 8 to 36 per cent).

In terms of the informal borrowing, 12 firms (24.5 per cent of the total number) reported the use of informal borrowing during the last three years, while 37 firms did not use the sector. The main reasons for informal borrowing are presented in Table 3.8. Relatives and friends and equity-holders of the firm were reported as the main suppliers of the loan, in some cases money-lenders and informal groups were mentioned. The amounts of informal loans were quite different, on average about EEK 500 thousand. In some firms, current balance owing was very large, up to EEK 2 million. Maturities varied from one month to some years; the average was about 300 days. The average annual interest rate was very high, 27.3 per cent, because of the extremely high interest rate of loans from informal sector money-lenders (65 per cent!). Other loan rates were much lower: from relatives and friends at 16 per cent; from informal groups as low as 8 per cent. Collateral was required only in three cases; the reported average value was EEK 417 thousand. Loan rescheduling was mentioned only in the case of non-payment at maturity.

Table 3.8 Primary reasons for informal borrowing

Reasons	1994	1995	1996	1997
More favourable interest rate	2 (33%)	5 (46%)	1 (12.5%)	1 (8.3%)
More flexible repayment schedule	1 (17%)	3 (28%)	2 (25%)	7 (58.4%)
Fewer formalities	2 (33%)	0	0	0
Collateral is not needed	0	2 (18%)	2 (25%)	1 (8.3%)
Did not got a loan from a bank	1 (17%)	2 (18%)	1 (12.5%)	3 (25%)

However, the formal financial sector plays an important role. In terms of borrowing from formal institutions, 56.3 per cent of interviewed firms reported the usage of overdraft facilities; 84 per cent of these firms received overdrafts from one bank and others from two or three different banks. Only 27 firms (55.1 per cent of the total number) had previously had access to loans, whereas 22 firms had no access at all. Table 3.9 presents data on the main explanations why the firms did not apply for formal sector credit.

The average reported current balance owing from bank loans was about EEK 3 million, while from other institutions (for example, the Estonian Privatization Agency) firms had received loans of about one million kroons.

Table 3.9 Reasons why the firm did not apply for a formal loan

Reasons	1994	1995	1996	1997
High interest rates	9	1	3	2
Do not wish to get into debt	5	5	3	5
Do not need a loan	4	11	4	11
Complicated loan application procedure	2	3	1	1
Insufficient collateral/guarantee	1	3	0	6
Probably will not be approved for a loan	1	3	0	2
Other reasons	2	0	0	0

The average loan application acceptance time was about four months. The average amount of institutional loans was EEK 2.1 million, and the average maturity was about two years, on an average annual interest rate of 16.7 per cent (from 10 to 25 per cent). Collateral was required in 86.2 per cent of the cases; the average value of the collateral was EEK 5.3 million. Buildings, equipment and output were mentioned among the type of collateral. In the event of non-payment at maturity, the following measures were mainly used: initiating legal procedure (34.5 per cent), interest penalties (27.6 per cent), and rescheduling the loan (17.2 per cent).

Generally, the primary reasons why firms did not apply for a loan were uniform across the sample; either they thought they did not need a loan (33.3 per cent), or they did not wish to get into debt (25 per cent). Leasing contracts for acquisition of buildings and equipment were reasons given by 29 firms (60 per cent of those who responded).

We also investigated the behaviour of firms with respect to their deposits with financial institutions. All respondent firms held cheque accounts at financial institutions. Table 3.10 reports the distribution of firms by the number of cheque accounts. Most of the cheque accounts have been open for only a short time, on average 3.7 years. Seven firms reported having savings accounts. Fourteen firms hold shares of other firms, two firms held deposit accounts in foreign banks, two firms reported holding Treasury Bills, and two firms had other securities (privatization securities and Russian government bonds). Twenty-one firms (43.8 per cent of respondents) reported having foreign currency deposits in Estonian commercial banks.

One firm reported making deposits or contributions in an informal sector group. The number of members in the group was 13, and the monthly amount of contribution amounted to EEK 3000; the group was operating continuously on the basis of the special agreement. No firm reported the use of safekeeping/deposit services of individual intermediaries.

Table 3.10 Distribution of firms by number of cheque accounts

No. of cheque accounts	1994	1995	1996	1997
One	17	19	14	12
Two	11	16	15	21
Three	4	4	5	7
Four	1	5	5	6
Five and more	6	0	3	3

In terms of contractual relations with suppliers, the distribution of shares of primary suppliers of the three main raw materials and intermediate inputs by type of supplier was as follows:

1. state-owned enterprise: 4.6 per cent;
2. private domestic firm: 51.4 per cent;
3. private foreign firm: 37.6 per cent;
4. others: 6.4 per cent.

Almost all suppliers (92.7 per cent) were business partners, with an average business relationship of about three years. The main form of transaction was purchase on credit (88.9 per cent of reported cases); advance payments were required rarely (8.3 per cent) and cash payments were also rare (2.8 per cent). The frequency of purchases was different depending on the production process, but these were mainly weekly (51.5 per cent of reported cases) and monthly purchases (43.7 per cent). In 43.2 per cent of the cases, collateral was not required for credit purchases; signed invoices were mostly mentioned as collateral (76 per cent). In the case of non-payment at maturity, the following measures were used:

1. rescheduling the maturity: 40.9 per cent;
2. interest penalties: 36.4 per cent;
3. interruption of credits: 11.3 per cent;
4. initiating legal procedure: 6.8 per cent;
5. interruption of delivery and other measures: 4.6 per cent.

In terms of the contractual relations with clients, the distribution of principal clients and the share of written contracts were as follows:

1. private firm, final consumer: 41.6 per cent, share of written contracts 73.7 per cent;

2. state-owned firm, final consumer: 17.5 per cent, share of written contracts 81.0 per cent;
3. private wholesale or retail trade firm: 24.1 per cent, share of written contracts 84.0 per cent;
4. state wholesale or retail trade firm: 6.6 per cent, share of written contracts 100.0 per cent;
5. others (for example, private persons): 10.2 per cent, share of written contracts 36.4 per cent.

The distribution of the main forms of sales were as follows: credit sales –53.0 per cent; cash payments –26.5 per cent; advance payments –15.1 per cent; and consignment –5.4 per cent. The average maturity of credit sales was about 20 days. In 32.6 per cent of the cases, collateral was not required; signed invoices were the main collateral (79.3 per cent). The main measures or penalties in the case of non-payment at maturity were:

1. prolonging the maturity: 31.0 per cent;
2. interest penalties: 26.2 per cent;
3. interruption of credit: 26.2 per cent;
4. interruption of delivery: 11.9 per cent;
5. initiating legal procedure: 4.7 per cent.

6 REGULATION MECHANISM

A key component of the business environment relates to government regulation of the activities of enterprises during economic reform. During the interviews, we investigated the issue of ownership regulation; nine firms (18.3 per cent of those who responded) reported that government regulations affect their ownership structure. Some firms were of the opinion that regulatory acts require reduction of the state ownership, and the removal of bottlenecks in raising equity and in changing ownership procedures. The average estimates of the relevance of various regulations to the operating of the firm were measured using a Likert-type 5-point scale with 1 for no relevance and 5 for very relevant; the results are reported in Table 3.11.

In terms of expansion regulations, the average estimates of the relevance of regulations/restrictions affecting firms' expansion decisions are also reported in Table 3.11. Three most important first-order restrictions were mentioned, namely, obtaining investment facilities, taxes and lack of demand for output. The second-order restrictions were taxes, obtaining investment facilities, and lack of demand and competition with imports. In general, the most important restrictions were mentioned: taxes (22 answers), obtaning investment facili-

Table 3.11 Average estimates of the relevance of various regulations/restrictions to firms' various decisions

Regulations/restrictions	1994	1995	1996	1997
1. Relevance of restrictions to firms' operating decisions				
Domestic finance restrictions	2.2	1.7	1.6	1.98
Earnings repatriation restrictions	2.0	1.5	1.2	1.40
Restrictions on activities	1.7	1.5	1.5	1.32
Capital requirements	1.7	1.5	1.9	1.66
Exchange restrictions on business travel	1.7	1.3	1.2	1.21
Foreign loan restrictions	1.7	1.9	1.5	1.27
Restrictions on technology licences and royalties	1.6	1.2	1.3	1.12
Joint venture restrictions	1.3	1.0	1.0	1.34
Restrictions on payment of salaries to non-residents	1.2	1.6	1.4	1.29
2. Relevance of hindrances in the case of reducing production				
Large financial cost of firing workers	3.1	3.5	3.5	2.35
Government restrictions against firing workers	1.9	1.6	2.0	1.40
Trade union restrictions against firing workers	1.4	1.2	1.5	1.29
3. Relevance of hindrances in the case of closing down the business				
Large financial cost of firing workers	3.0	3.3	3.1	2.58
Legal procedure of bankruptcy or liquidation	1.9	2.4	2.1	2.00
Government restrictions against firing workers	1.8	2.5	2.7	1.87
Government restrictions on selling the enterprise	1.4	2.4	1.6	1.65
Trade union restrictions against firing workers	1.3	1.4	1.6	1.38
4. Relevance of restrictions affecting firms' expansion decisions				
Obtainability of credits	3.5	4.2	3.1	2.34
Taxes	3.0	4.1	3.5	2.98
Obtaining investment facilities	3.7	3.4	3.7	3.41
Prices of public services	2.2	2.5	2.3	2.32
Lack of demand for output	3.1	2.4	2.9	2.63
Infrastructure and location problems	1.4	2.2	2.1	2.00
Ownership regulations	2.2	2.1	1.8	1.53
Competition with imports	2.9	2.0	2.4	2.69
Lack of business supporting services	2.6	1.9	1.8	1.80
Labour regulations	1.7	1.5	1.6	1.39
Price controls	1.6	1.5	1.14	1.37
Getting licences	1.5	1.5	1.5	1.64
Activity restrictions	1.3	1.3	1.3	1.15
Exchange controls	1.3	1.1	1.05	1.05

ties (20 answers), competition with imports (16 answers), lack of demand (15 answers), and obtainability of credits (12 answers).

In terms of labour relations, most of the interviewed firms were of the opinion that labour regulations did not affect their hiring and firing decisions. It was also felt by 46 firms (93.9 per cent) that reducing minimum wages would not affect the hiring decisions; and 42 firms (85.7 per cent) argued that the removal of firing restrictions and compensation payments would not reduce the number of permanent workers; while 46 firms (94.0 per cent) answered that the removal of hiring restrictions would not reduce the number of workers in general; and 44 firms (90.0 per cent) argued that liberalization in the hiring laws of foreign labour would not increase the number of workers hired.

In terms of price and exchange controls, the opinions of firms on price controls affecting the enterprises are presented in Table 3.12. In terms of capacity utilization and compensation, firms were of the opinion that low production capacity utilization exists in the Estonian manufacturing sector: the production amount could be on average 17.3 per cent higher (37 per cent in the 1996 year study), if restrictions on labour supply and output demand are taken into account – 6.7 per cent (12 per cent in the 1996 year study). Ten firms applied for export compensation (20 per cent), and seven of them received it. Five firms applied for other compensation or subsidies, and two of the applications were successful (from the Export Council and from the Environment Ministry).

Table 3.12 Estimates of price control and relevance of problems with foreign currency exchange

	1994	1995	1996	1997
1. Price control estimates (%)				
Input prices	34.2	46.7	51.2	43.8
Output prices	24.0	13.2	8.8	11.1
2. Relevance of problems with foreign currency exchange				
Delays in obtaining foreign currency	1.4	1.1	1.08	1.04
Required documentation	1.15	1.14	1.08	1.02
Obtainability of foreign currency	1.15	1.05	1.03	1.00

In the context of licensing and registration, only two of all the interviewed firms were not registered. It is neither very complicated nor expensive to get a licence. The problem is that the number of licensed activities has grown during the last couple of years.

7 DISPUTE RESOLUTION MECHANISM

The first dispute resolution mechanism relates to late payments and non-payments by clients: 39 firms (81.3 per cent; in the 1996 study, 87 per cent) of those that responded have had late payment or non-payment problems during the previous year, and most of the firms have had between one and five disputes during the year. The main reasons for late payment or non-payment were clients' payment difficulties, bankruptcies and lack of consideration towards business partners. The distribution of late payment or non-payment disputes by the other party is presented in Table 3.13. In 12 cases (25 per cent) the dispute occurred during the firm's first transaction with the other party; in general, the duration of business relations with the other party was very short, for example, one to three years. In 80 per cent of reported dispute cases, direct bargaining with the other party was used; only one arbitration case was reported. A lawyer was hired to resolve the conflict in eight cases only, and in 11 cases the firm went to the court. The dispute was settled in 20 cases (50 per cent), but only 17 firms (43.6 per cent) were satisfied with the outcome and 22 firms were not satisfied. Fourteen firms (41 per cent) are still doing business with the other party.

Table 3.13 Distribution of disputes by the other party

Other party	1994	1995	1996	1997
1. Disputes with suppliers				
Other domestic firm	22 (67%)	29 (78%)	35 (88%)	35 (88%)
Governmental institution	6 (18%)	2 (6%)	1 (2%)	1 (2%)
Foreign firm	5 (15%)	3 (8%)	3 (8%)	3 (8%)
Individual	0	3 (8%)	1 (2%)	1 (2%)
2. Disputes with clients				
Other domestic firm	8 (61%)	16 (80%)	19 (73%)	10 (45%)
Foreign firm	4 (31%)	2 (10%)	7 (27%)	12 (55%)
Individual	1 (8%)	0	0	0
Governmental institution	0	2 (10%)	0	0

With respect to delivery timing, 18 firms (37.5 per cent; in the 1996 study, 46.7 per cent) have had problems with late delivery or non-delivery of inputs/services as well as with the deficient quality of inputs/services. The number of times firms have had these problems with suppliers during the last year fluctuated mainly between two and five, but some firms have had such disputes with suppliers on ten or more occasions. Table 3.13 contains evidence on the distribution of disputes regarding delivery and quality of inputs. It is shown that there is rapid growth in the share of disputes with foreign firms.

Only three firms reported that it was the first transaction with the other party; duration of business relations with the other party was mainly between one and three years. Direct bargaining with the other party was used in 91 per cent of cases: private arbitration was not used. In two cases, a lawyer was hired and the firm went to the court. Disputes were mostly settled (82.6 per cent of cases), and 73.9 per cent of firms were satisfied with the outcome. In 18 cases firms are still doing business with the other party.

As regards labour disputes, disputes with competitors, governmental institutions and commercial banks, six firms (12.2 per cent; in the 1996 year study, 19.1 per cent) reported having labour disputes during the last year. Labour disputes were connected with problems concerning the amount of salary and with the legal problems of firing employees. In four cases direct bargaining with the other party was used, and in two cases the firm hired a lawyer, but only one firm went to court. In five cases (83.3 per cent) disputes were settled, four firms were satisfied with the outcome, and two firms are still doing business with the other party.

Only ten firms (20.4 per cent; in the 1996 year study, 14.9 per cent) reported having disputes with their competitors during the last year. The main reasons for these disputes were the use of dumping by competitors, unethical competition and breaking agreements. These disputes were mostly not settled. Thirteen firms (26.5 per cent; in the 1996 year study, 18 per cent) have had disputes with the governmental institutions, in four cases the other party was the tax authority, and in five cases it was the customs office. The main reason for disputes was a different interpretation of laws and other legal acts. In seven cases, direct bargaining was used; the disputes were settled in half of the cases, but a few firms were satisfied with the outcome (15.4 per cent).

Six firms (12.2 per cent) reported having disputes with commercial banks during the last year; the main reason for these disputes was late transfer of payments by the bank. Disputes were settled in three cases; in these cases the firms were satisfied with the outcome, and five firms are still doing business with the bank.

As regards legislation and the enforcement mechanism, 22 firms (45.8 per cent, in the 1996 year study, 32.5 per cent) were of the opinion that Estonian legislation is sufficient for the resolution of disputes and conflicts between economic agents, while the remaining 26 firms found legislation insufficient because of contradictions in the acts; also, overregulation and wilfulness of civil servants were mentioned. The Business Law and the Bankruptcy Law were mainly mentioned as weak and controversial acts. At the moment, there is no debt legislation in Estonia.

Only 24 firms (49 per cent; in the 1996 year study, 31.6 per cent) were satisfied with the enforcement mechanism. Firms were of the opinion that legislation must relate to real life rather than to an ideal theoretical framework that cannot be realized; not all essential relationships between economic agents are regulated, and the court system is weak. Twenty-six firms (65 per cent of those that responded) supported the use of self-enforcement mechanisms (for example, negotiations, direct bargaining).

Recently there has been a slight decrease in the number of different disputes between economic agents. Although the legal framework seems to have improved (a few more firms are satisfied with the Estonian legislation and enforcement mechanism), the overall situation in the development of the legal framework is not yet satisfactory.

8 BUSINESS SUPPORT SERVICES

The first category of business support services in Estonia includes governmental, educational, and other institutions.[8] The hierarchical order of Estonian governmental, educational and other institutions supporting business is estimated by interviewing firms; the results are reported in Table 3.14. Services obtained by firms include getting information, consulting and legal advice services, and business contacts.

The second category of business support services in Estonia comprises commercial banks. The results of the interview exercise show that when choosing a bank that will service the firm, the three most important criteria were:

Table 3.14 Hierarchical order of institutions supporting the business

Institution	1994	1995	1996	1997
Training schools	21	21	19	21
Estonian universities	11	19	15	12
Commercial banks	10	16	21	16
Estonian Tax Office	16	15	14	14
Estonian Commercial Chamber	6	9	15	16
Estonian Privatization Agency	7	7	5	3
Estonian Small Business Association	3	4	6	3
Estonian Central League of Industry	2	4	6	3
Ministry of Economic Affairs	0	4	13	7
Ministry of Foreign Affairs	4	3	4	3
International financial institutions	1	3	3	2
Estonian Manufacturers' Association	3	2	3	2
Estonian Labour Office	2	2	7	5
Estonian Export Council	1	2	8	6

1. First-order criteria
   distance to the bank location: 14 answers (25 per cent);
   trustworthiness of the bank: 11 answers (39.5 per cent);
   obtainability of credits/loans: 9 answers.
2. Second-order criteria
   trustworthiness of the bank: 10 answers (12.5 per cent);
   obtainability of credits/loans: 8 answers (27.1 per cent);
   quality of banking services: 8 answers (22.9 per cent).
3. Third-order criteria
   quality of banking services: 10 answers (12.5 per cent);
   trustworthiness of the bank: 7 answers (12.5 per cent).

The average estimates of the quality of banking services on a Likert-type 5-point scale with 1 for poor quality and 5 for excellent quality are presented in Table 3.15. Among the weak or non-existent banking services mentioned were the quality of electronic communication systems, the availability of cheaper working capital and investment credits, financial advice and consulting services, faster foreign transfers, and the functioning of on-line systems. Most of the firms that responded were of the opinion that they were fully satisfied with the quality of banking services in Estonia. But some firms are anticipating the entry of foreign banks into the Estonian banking market, falling interest rates, stability and soundness in the banking system, and the introduction of the deposit insurance system. Some firms reported that their business confidence is undermined by lack of ownership of real estate and land, small equity and working capital, weak payment capability, and unfinished privatization procedures.

Table 3.15 Average estimates of the quality of banking services

Banking service	1994	1995	1996	1997
Arrangement of domestic payments	4.4	4.4	4.5	4.29
Arrangement of foreign exchange	3.8	4.4	4.0	4.14
Speed of banking operations	4.1	4.2	4.2	3.86
Arrangement of foreign payments	3.6	4.1	4.0	4.11
Financial consulting	3.8	3.7	3.7	3.28
Crediting of working capital	2.9	3.0	3.6	3.56
Crediting of investments	1.9	2.7	3.0	3.39
Budgeting assistance	2.0	2.6	2.4	2.32

9 CONCLUSIONS

The results of the special interview study of Estonian business firms undertaken in 1997 as well as the previous exercises undertaken in 1994, 1995 and 1996 have made it possible to undertake a quantitative measurement of enterprise restructuring and the state of and changes in the Estonian business environment, with respect to the regulation mechanism, dispute resolution mechanism, financial contractual relations, and availability of business supporting services. The evidence reported and discussed in this chapter can be structured into five conclusions.

First, own savings were the main source of firms' start-up financing, but formal or informal loans were used in some rare cases. In general, Estonian manufacturing firms have no serious problems with various infrastructure elements; more severe problems were connected with communication services and the quality of roads. A large number of firms have their own infrastructure, including freight transport, security systems and communication systems.

Second, informal finance is important for funding enterprise. About one-third of the firms that responded reported the use of informal lending and 24.5 per cent of firms reported the use of informal borrowing during the last year. All interviewed firms held cheque accounts in various financial institutions. The use of bank loans for financing their investments has grown during the last year. But some of the firms were of the opinion that they do not need a loan, nor do they wish to get into debt.

Third, government regulations do not seriously affect the decisions of Estonian manufacturing firms regarding operating, expanding or closing down the business. Some more relevant exceptions are the large financial cost of firing workers in the case of reducing production (2.35 points) or in the case of closing down the business (2.58 points), and competition with imports (2.69 points), taxes (2.98 points) and obtaining investment facilities (3.41 points) in the case of a firm wanting to expand.

Fourth, there exist a number of disputes and conflicts between economic agents, but Estonian legislation is inadequate to resolve these disputes (in the opinion of 54 per cent of firms interviewed), enforcement mechanism is not working well (51 per cent), and 65 per cent of firms support the use of self-enforcement mechanisms. Direct bargaining with the other party was the method mostly used, quite often disputes were not settled, and firms were not satisfied with the outcome.

Finally, Estonian governmental institutions or business associations do not provide support for businesses. The main business-supporting services (for example, providing information, advice and consulting services) are rendered by commercial banks, Estonian universities and training schools, the

Estonian Chamber of Commerce, and the Estonian Tax Office. The quality of banking services has improved and is in general high. Budgeting assistance (2.32 points), financial consultation (3.28 points), and long-term crediting of investments (3.39 points) are more problematic issues.

NOTES

1. The argument here is that competitiveness at the firm level depends on the development of the business environment.
2. The issue is also whether traditional economic theory can be applied uncritically to the transformation process in the transition economies.
3. There are several important reasons behind Estonia's bid to join the EU, including political and security issues.
4. We argue that conflict resolution is at the heart of the Darwin theory in the context of the development of the business sector in transition economies.
5. The three models offer collectively yet another angle in which the results of the survey reported in this chapter could be interpreted; however, we do not strictly pursue this line of enquiry.
6. It may also be argued that the acquisition of buildings and equipment by enterprises is a reflection of the state of (as well as changes in) the business environment.
7. We use the term microstructure here in terms of firm output and pricing factors, distribution and sales, as well as the labour market.
8. The other institutions supporting business are lawyers' offices, accounting and auditing firms, and the Ministry of Environment.

REFERENCES

Aghion, P., O.J. Blanchard and W. Carlin (1994), 'The economics of enterprise restructuring in Central and Eastern Europe', CEPR Discussion Paper No. 1058.

Alm, J. and R. Sjoquist (1995), 'Provision of social services by Russian firms', *Comparative Economic Studies*, **35** (3), Winter.

Banerjee, B., V. Koen, T. Krueger, M.S. Lutz, M. Marrese and T.O. Saavalainen (1995), 'Road maps of the transition: the Baltics, the Czech Republic, Hungary, and Russia', IMF Occasional Paper No. 127, Washington, DC: IMF.

Baron, D.P. (1993), *Business and Its Environment*, Englewood Cliffs, NJ: Prentice-Hall.

Calvo, G.A. and F. Coricelli (1993), 'Output collapse in Eastern Europe: the role of credit', *IMF Staff Paper*, **40** (1), 32–51.

Citrin, D.A. and A.K. Lahiri (1995), 'Policy experiences and issues in the Baltics, Russia, and other countries of the Former Soviet Union', IMF Occasional Paper No. 133, December, Washington, DC: IMF.

Commander, S., Q. Fan and M. Schaffer (eds) (1996), *Enterprise Restructuring and Economic Policy in Russia*, Washington, DC: World Bank.

Frydman, R., C.W. Gray, M. Hessel and A. Rapaczynski (1997), 'Private ownership and corporate performance: some lessons from transition economies', World Bank Working Paper No. 1830, September.

Frye, T. and A. Schleifer (1997), 'The invisible hand and the grabbing hand', *American Economic Review*, **87** (2), May, 354–8.

Grennes, T. (1997), 'The economic transition in the Baltics', *Journal of Baltic Studies*, **28**, Spring, 9–24.

Hillman, A.L. (1994), 'The transition from socialism: an overview from a political economy perspective', *European Journal of Political Economy*, **10**, 191–225.

Kilvits, K. (1995), *Industrial Restructuring in Estonia*, Tallinn: Institute of Economics, Estonian Academy of Sciences.

Klein, B. (1996), 'Why hold-ups occur: the self-enforcing range of contractual relationships', *Economic Inquiry*, **34** (3), July, 444–63.

Klein, B. and K.M. Murphy (1997), 'Vertical integration as a self-enforcing contractual arrangement', *The American Economic Review*, **87** (2), May, 415–20.

Kole, S. and K. Lehn (1997), 'Deregulation, the evolution of corporate governance structure, and survival', *American Economic Review*, **87** (2), May, 421–5.

Liikane, K., A. Tammeraid, A. Teearu and V. Vensel (1994), 'Preliminary results of the interview study of firms' financial contractual relations in EMEs (Estonia): an overview', Gothenburg Studies in Financial Economics, Study No. 1993:1, Gothenburg University.

Linz, S.J. (1997), 'Russian firms in transition: champions, challengers and chaff', *Comparative Economic Studies*, **39** (2), Summer, 1–36.

Lugus, O. and G. Hachey (eds) (1995), *Transforming the Estonian Economy*, Tallinn: Institute of Economics, Estonian Academy of Sciences.

Mullineux, A. (1994), 'Banking sector restructuring, debt consolidation, and small and medium sized enterprise financing in formerly centrally planned economies', University of Birmingham, International Finance Group Working Paper IFGWP–94–02.

Mullineux, A. (1995), 'Progress with financial sector reform in six transforming economies', University of Birmingham, International Finance Group Working Paper IFGWP–95–04, March.

Pohl, G., R.E. Anderson, S. Claessen and S. Djankov (1997), 'Privatization and restructuring in Central and Eastern Europe', World Bank Technical Paper No. 368, May.

Purju, A. (1996), 'Foreign trade of Estonia: factors supporting integration', Stockholm Institute of East European Economies, Working Paper No. 113, July.

Schleifer, A. (1996), 'Origins of bad policies: control, corruption, and confusion', *Rivista di Politica Economica*, **86** (6), June, 103–24.

Tammeraid, A., A. Teearu and V. Vensel (1996), 'Development of financial contractual relationships in Estonia: empirical results of firms' interview study', in A. Janc and T. Kowalski (eds), Reformy finansowe w krajach tworzących gospodarkę rynkową. Modele i badania empiryczne, Poznań, Wydawnictwo Akademii Ekonomicznej.

Vensel, V. and C. Wihlborg (1996), 'Financial conditions and constraints on entrepreneurship in the Estonian manufacturing sector', in A. Janc and T. Kowalski (eds.), Reformy finansowe w krajach tworzących gospodarkę rynkową. Modele i badania empiryczne, Poznań, Wydawnictwo Akademii Ekonomicznej.

Vensel, V. and C. Wihlborg (1998), 'Financial constraints on entrepreneurship in Estonia', in J. Doukas, V. Murinde and C. Wihlborg (eds), *Financial Sector Reform and Privatisation in Transition Economies*, Amsterdam: Elsevier Science Publishers, Ch. 3, pp. 35–67.

Yavlinsky, G. and S. Braginski (1994). 'The inefficiency of laissez-faire in Russia:

hysteresis effects and the need for policy-led transformation', *Journal of Comparative Economics*, **19** (1) August, 88–116.
Zecchini, S. (ed.) (1997), *Lessons from the Economic Transition: Central and Eastern Europe in the 1990s*, London: Kluwer Academic Publishers.
Ziacik, T.L. (1995), 'Estonia's progress on the road to European monetary integration: an assessment and comparison', *Bank of Estonia Bulletin*, Tallinn, No. 7, 45–56.

4. Financial contracts and relations in the small and medium-sized enterprise sector in Poland

Tadeusz Kowalski and Alfred Janc

1 INTRODUCTION

The small and medium-sized enterprise (SME) sector is the major driving force of market transformation in Poland. However, its contribution to employment and GDP formation is still much lower than in stabilized market economies. In the transformation period of 1990–95, SMEs created more than 1.5 million new jobs. The majority of SMEs employed less than five employees. The sector's dynamics, its development of contractual relationships and its financial interdependence will have a strong impact on the functioning and growth potential of the whole economy.

This chapter analyses financial contractual relationships within the SME sector and its links with the financial, legal and institutional environment. It aims to present the main factors and mechanisms that influence the way the SME sector functions. Market transformation has been characterized by a very high uncertainty, especially in the first stage. The scope of qualitative and quantitative adjustments and changes that were taking place rendered the traditional theory of entry and competition less applicable.[1] There is a need to collect and study empirical evidence and to use it as a starting point for drawing more general hypotheses and conclusions. In order to attain this goal we have analysed the empirical results of an interview study carried out on a representative sample of 74 enterprises located mainly in the Wielkopolska region. Special emphasis has been laid on examination of the nature of financial relations within this group of SMEs.[2] Entrepreneurs' perceptions and assessment of economic and institutional environment operation was also examined.

The assumed hypothesis was that liberalization of formal entrance rules has created an open arena for the development of entrepreneurship.[3] We also ascertained that another group of factors, that is, actual formal exit rules, could hinder the small business development, mainly due to their poor execution. Insufficient support from the financial and institutional environment might also be seen as a hindrance to the proper functioning and growth of the SME sector. Therefore we acknowledged that formal entrance and exit rules, their execution and also the conditions in the institutional and financial environment, shaped the formation of both contractual relationships and demand and supply of capital within the SME sector. Furthermore, we assumed that with liberalization of formal entrance rules the majority of small firms went on operating within market niches relatively free from competition.[4] It enabled such firms to function and develop despite high relative transaction costs.[5] These factors probably explain the lack of financial transparency in the SME sector and reluctance to reveal financial data.

Our analysis is focused on institutional arrangements and contractual relations which affect both the actions of various stakeholders and finally the very development of the SME sector in Poland. Thus the analysis covers:

- contractual governance (relations of firms' management with their suppliers, customers and competitors);
- work governance (relations of management and employees); and
- corporate governance (relations of management with the firms' creditors and shareholders.

The last dimension of the analysis is of a lesser importance since the SME sector is typically based on family firms with credit relations in the first stage of development.

The relevant Polish literature usually points out the following most important obstacles to SME development: difficult terms of credit, an unfavourable tax system, and insufficient harmonization of regulations.[6] Another group of barriers comprises low level of technology, worn and obsolete productive assets, demand constraints, and insufficient managerial knowledge especially within financial management and marketing.

2 FORMAL ENTRANCE RULES

Formal start-up requirements introduced in Poland at the beginning of the transformation period were modelled along those in stabilized market economies. Regulations in force to a large extent limit the scope of discretionary bureaucratic decisions. Moreover, the regulations do not require prolonged procedures. Because of liberalization of formal requirements, the private sector in Poland developed at a fast rate (Table 4.1). The table shows that liberalization of formal entrance rules brought about a rapid increase in the number of newly established private enterprises, especially in 1990–92. Small

Table 4.1 Number of private sector start-ups in Poland, 1990–1995

Legal status	1990	1991	1992	1993	1994	1995
Commercial Law Companies (CLC)	21 117	14 451	10 528	16 229	9 138	5 015
CLC with foreign capital participation	1 216	3 151	5 335	5 035	4 570	4 349
Sole proprietorships	322 007	284 510	210 627	153 211	96 606	133 797

Sources: Own calculation based on the Ministry of Finance (MF), Central Statistical Office (GUS) and Central Office of Planning (CUP) data.

firms established by individuals constituted the great majority. By December 1995, there were 2.1 million sole proprietorships and 112 thousand commercial law companies.

The structure of the Polish private sector is dominated by firms owned by single owners (Table 4.2). Data shows also that Commercial Law Companies (CLC) amounted to only 5 per cent of all private enterprises in 1995. This ownership pattern is characteristic of a typical premature market economy system. The dominance of very small firms owned by individual agents is also connected with the cultural and historical conditions in Poland, where there is no long tradition, in the private sector, of separation between management and ownership (corporatization).

Table 4.2 Structure of private sector in Poland according to the legal status of firms, 1990–1995

Legal status	1990	1991	1992	1993	1994	1995
CLC	1.47	2.84	3.43	3.97	4.21	4.17
CLC with foreign capital participation	0.05	0.14	0.60	0.81	0.99	1.13
Sole proprietorships	98.48	97.02	95.97	95.22	94.80	94.70
Total	100.00	100.00	100.00	100.00	100.00	100.00

Sources: Own calculation based on the Ministry of Finance (MF), Central Statistical Office (GUS) and Central Office of Planning (CUP) data.

The branch structure of the private sector is dominated by trade and services. About 16 per cent of private enterprises operate within industry, 10.16 per cent in the construction sector, 4.55 per cent in transportation, while 41.07 per cent are involved in trade and 28.04 per cent in services. Such a structure stems mainly from the insufficient level of savings available for the private sector and also from relatively high start-up costs in both the production and construction sectors. The current sectoral structure results also from the underdevelopment of services and trade inherited from the rigid mechanism of centrally planned allocation of resources.

3 FORMAL EXIT RULES

Economic entity formal exit rules (completion of activity) are regulated by the commercial code, bankruptcy law, settlement law and other acts.[7] The existing legal solutions and the efficiency of procedures in particular have determined turnover safety as well as effectiveness of resource reallocation from the state-owned sector to the private sector. This relationship matters, especially in the period of the economy's ownership restructuring and re-creation of market economy institutions, procedures and standards. Generally, one may assume that the completion of economic activity may result from an owner's sovereign decision and from bankruptcy.[8] Because of the nature of the contemporary economic processes in Poland, the improvement in efficiency of bankruptcy legal procedures has been a *sine qua non* condition, supporting the allocation function of market mechanism.

Liquidation of State-owned Enterprises

Enterprise liquidation under the terms of Article 19 of the State-owned Enterprise Law means liquidation of assets of a failed enterprise in order to satisfy the creditors and delete this enterprise from the state enterprise register. This regulation has great potential for the elimination of ineffective entities and could be a useful means of takeovers of state-owned enterprises (SOEs) by small private firms. However, the actual effectiveness of resource reallocation on the basis of Article 19 has not been high.[9] This has resulted mainly from social obstacles as well as prolonged bureaucratic and legal procedures and from the slow pace of asset appraisal. Substantial economic depreciation and obsolescence have also played a negative role.

Privatization in accordance with the State-owned Enterprise Law, Article 37 (*capital path*) which was aimed at transferring all a bankrupt's assets to new management, has influenced the small business development even less.[10] The failure of this way of supporting the transfer of assets to the private sector was connected with insufficient capital available to managers. Data on state sector restructuring through both liquidation privatization and the capital path is shown in Table 4.3.

Comparison of the number of newly established private entities with the number of SOEs undergoing liquidation and privatization proves that the

Table 4.3 Number of state-owned enterprises under ownership restructuring, 1990–1995

Year	Capital path		Completed privatization	
	STC*	Privatizing	Liquid. (Art. 37)	Liquid. (Art. 19)
1990	58	6	15	3
1991	202	21	167	16
1992	220	24	293	67
1993	47	48	232	100
1994	196	35	238	117
1995	235	26	109	93
Total	958	160	1054	396

Note: * State Treasury's companies (STCs) only, created by Ministry of Ownership Restructuring (MPW).

Source: Own calculation, based on Dynamika przekształceń własnościowych (1996).

restructuring of the Polish economy has been performed mainly through establishing a private sector from scratch. Privatization of the state sector has appeared to be a difficult and sensitive issue because of a lack of home capital on the one hand and social considerations on the other. The remaining state-owned sector book value is still very high. Continuation of this sector privatization has a potential positive impact on the supply (accessibility) of productive assets for the emerging private sector. Delays in privatization have caused depreciation of assets to be restructured and this has thus led to losses. A byproduct of the delay was also the process of *spontaneous privatization,* undermining to some extent public perception and acceptance of economic transformation.

The data in Table 4.3 show that by December 1995 160 enterprises had been privatized along the capital path method. However, most SOEs have been restructured by means of liquidation. By December 1995, state sector ownership restructuring had covered almost 3500 enterprises, cutting the number of SOEs by nearly half.

Bankruptcy Procedures within the Private Sector

The inefficiency of the bankruptcy legal procedures has concerned not only the state sector. With an increasing number of bankruptcy cases under investigation, the existing legal regulations and underdevelopment of the economic judiciary infrastructure have proved critical. The system's ability to identify cases of criminal bankruptcy declarations (as a result of purposeful action) is very limited. As shown in Table 4.4, the greatest number of bankruptcy cases were brought to court in 1993. At the same time, case settlements took more time. This stems both from the weaknesses of the judiciary infrastructure and from the increasingly complicated nature of cases under investigation.

Table 4.4 Bankruptcy cases brought to district courts in Poland, 1991–1995

Bankruptcy cases	1991	1992	1993	1994	1995
Number of cases brought to court	1250	3661	5249	4193	2992
Number of settled cases	656	2155	4324	4056	3246

Source: Hadasik (forthcoming).

4 INSTITUTIONAL AND FINANCIAL ENVIRONMENT

Policy on the Small Business Sector

Policy on the small business sector has been criticized by entrepreneurs for its passive approach and neutrality. This policy has been pursued mainly by the Ministry of Labour and Social Policy (MPiPS) and the Ministry of Industry and Commerce (MPiH). There is a programme of SME development, which is run by MPiPS and co-financed by the World Bank. Its goal is to create and maintain institutional and financial infrastructure supporting the SME sector. The main elements of the programme are the establishment of entrepreneurship incubators and support centres, and entrepreneurship growth funds. MPiH policy has aimed at sector developing in order to reduce unemployment and increase the private sector's share in the economy.[11] This programme envisaged the use of budgetary means in order to increase credit guarantee funds and aid assistance from PHARE. The scale of the programme is limited and it has a minor impact on the SMEs. A well-designed policy towards SMEs should aim at stabilizing both the institutional and legal environment and at supporting technology transfer and the growth of credit guarantee funds.

Small Business Financing

The financing of the small business sector is perceived to be a major hindrance to its functioning and development. This situation stems from both external (financial environment) and internal (specificity of SMEs, culture features and the current development of SMEs) factors. Within the first group of factors, the objectively low level of the economy's monetization and the still poor qualitative and quantitative development of financial intermediation play a major role. This might be expressed by the low ratio of bank assets and domestic credit to GDP (Table 4.5).

Table 4.5 Development of financial intermediation, 1992–1994 (percentages)

Specification	Poland	Hungary	Czech Republic
Bank assets/GDP* 100%	45	62	114
Domestic credit/GDP*100%	40	62	92

Source: *Business Central Europe*/IMF, *International Financial Statistics*.

According to a survey conducted by the Centre of National Opinion Research (CBOS), more than 60 per cent of adults have never been serviced by any bank.[12] The same research shows that about 80 per cent of bank clients have pointed to the excessively high credit cost as a reason for profitless credit for firms.

The SME sector's credit guarantee institutions have had at their disposal about PLN 80 million (about US$30 million). In 1995 however, only 50 per cent of state funds were used.[13] The major institution is the PLN 45 million Credit Guarantee Fund of the state-owned Bank of Domestic Economy (BGK). Venture capital funds play a minor, auxiliary role and have barely improved access to capital for a great number of SMEs.[14]

The SME sector is highly diversified. The majority of ultra-small and small firms have a rather passive policy aimed at preserving existing positions and jobs created by the founders for themselves and their families. Even under lower real interest rate conditions these firms will be reluctant to develop credit relations with the formal credit market. However, there is also a group of SMEs exhibiting strong growth dynamics and a clear mission and strategy. As their retained profits have been insufficient to finance growth, they have had to use external sources of finance.

The various categories of SMEs have different potential for growth as well as different financial standing and credit demands (external finance). From the banking sector's point of view, SMEs have been on the one hand a group of clients showing great growth potential (in the sense of bank product demand and especially credit) but also represent a credit risk which is difficult to measure. Hence, the low extent of SME external financing stems from the features mentioned above as well as the conservative policy of the banking sector. The latter is a function of both an experience of bad loans accumulated at the beginning of the 1990s and a high level of the public sector borrowing requirement (PSBR) which helps the banks to develop a secure asset portfolio. That is why there could be two equivalent hypotheses concerning the banking sector's attitude towards the SME sector:

- banks are reluctant to grant credit to SMEs because they (properly) estimate the credit risk as being too high; the result is that the most dynamic SMEs function within limited credit access (rationing) and/or they enjoy credit access with above-average interest rates;
- banks are reluctant to grant credit to SMEs because they are not competent to estimate credit risk correctly, primarily because banks' methods and procedures of identifying profitable enterprises and projects are poor.[15]

5 DATA ON ANALYSED SMEs

General Characteristics of the Sample

The interview study was carried out on a representative sample of 74 enterprises located mainly in the Wielkopolska region. Distribution of the sample firms by industry is shown in Table 4.6. Within the interviewed group of enterprises, service and trade firms were dominant – 60.8 per cent (including 'others').

The distribution of the group by legal status is shown in Table 4.7. Civil corporations and sole proprietorships prevail and constitute more than 60 per

Table 4.6 Distribution of the sample firms by industry

Industry	Number of firms	Percentage
Light industry	7	9.4
Food industry	5	6.8
Construction	6	8.1
Transportation	1	1.4
Wood-processing industry	3	4.1
Metal-processing industry	7	9.4
Services	28	37.8
Others	17	23.0

cent of the sample. Limited liability companies are also important for the SME sector since this form offers flexibility to the founders and the obligatory costs to establish such entities are low.

Table 4.7 Distribution of representing group by legal status

Legal status	Number of firms	Percentage
Corporation	5	6.8
Limited liability enterprise	24	32.4
Civil corporation	15	20.3
Sole proprietorship	30	40.5

Table 4.8 shows distribution of firms by ownership structure. In the sample of interviewed firms domestic owners dominate (90.5 per cent of firms). There were only three firms with foreign private owners acting without local shareholders.

Table 4.8 Distribution of sample group by ownership structure

Ownership forms	Number of firms	Percentage
Domestic private owners	61	82.4
Domestic and foreign private owners	2	2.7
Foreign private owners	3	4.1
Domestic and foreign joint state and private owners	2	2.7
Domestic state and private owners	6	8.1

Most of the enterprises from the representing group started up after 1989. More than 58 per cent of the start-ups were launched in 1989–92. Distribution of enterprises by start-up year is shown in Table 4.9.

Information about the number of employees at the start-up stage is shown in Table 4.10.

Because of limited credit accessibility, and a reluctance to use high real interest credits, own savings were the main start-up financing source. Start-up financing sources are shown in Table 4.11. Compound financing forms, that is, own savings together with credit financing, dominated within the category 'others'.

Table 4.9 Distribution of representing group by start-up year

Start-up year	Number of firms	Percentage
Before 1980	4	5.4
1981–1988	5	6.8
1989–1990	23	31.1
1991	8	10.8
1992	12	16.2
1993	6	8.1
1994	7	9.4
1995–1996	9	12.2

Table 4.10 Number of employees at the start-up stage

Number of employees	Number of firms	Percentage
1–3	41	55.4
4–8	18	24.3
More than 8	15	20.3

Table 4.11 Start-up financing sources

Sources	Number of firms	Percentage
Own savings	53	71.6
Loan from domestic commercial banks	5	6.7
Loans from friends and relatives	2	2.7
Loan from foreign banks or donor agencies	0	
Loan from money-lenders	1	1.4
Others	13	17.6

In 13 cases (17.6 per cent) firms purchased buildings, in one case buildings were obtained through affranchisement. In 11 cases (14.9 per cent) firms purchased land, whereas in one case land was donated. Eight enterprises (10.8 per cent) had no fixed assets, 24.3 per cent of firms rented their equipment or leased it. Only about one-fifth of the interviewed firms declared that they had bought machinery, equipment or land from SOEs (either still functioning or liquidated). The low rate of flow of fixed assets from the SOEs to the emerging private SMEs is caused, according to the survey, by the following reasons: low quality of equipment offered, lack of finance, and also lack of sufficient information on the sales.

Financial Contractual Relations

Contracts with suppliers and receivers

The answers to the question about types of suppliers were determined by the share of service firms within the representing group. Table 4.12 shows the answers given by firms interviewed.

Table 4.12 Number of suppliers

Number of suppliers	Number of firms	Percentage
Just 1	14	18.9
2–3	19	25.7
4 and more	19	25.7
No answer	22	29.7

The frequency of purchases declared by firms ranged from one to 40 a month. In a few cases firm suppliers were the only available supply source. The duration of business relationships with suppliers ranged from one to 72 months. No suppliers were relatives of firm owners. Forms of supplier settlements are shown in Table 4.13. The dominance of cash, and cash and belated payment (48.6 per cent) settlements reflect the inflationary environment and the need to maintain liquidity.

Table 4.13 Form of supplier settlement

Settlement form	Number of firms	Percentage
Cash only	18	24.3
Invoice with belated payment	18	24.3
Cash and invoice with belated payment	18	24.3
No answer	20	27.1

Clients of interviewed firms, that is, goods receivers and service purchasers, varied greatly. Table 4.14 shows the type of clients. Table 4.15 shows the kinds of goods sold and services offered. Almost all enterprises have more

Table 4.14 Type of client/receiver

Type of client	Number of firms	Percentage
Public enterprise only	14	18.9
Domestic private firm only	19	25.7
Foreign enterprise only	6	8.1
Other receivers	30	40.5
No answer	5	6.8

Table 4.15 Kinds of goods and services

Goods and services	Number of firms	Percentage
Local good (sold to clients within 50 km)	6	8.1
Domestic good (sold to clients at a distance over 50 km)	22	29.7
Local service	15	20.3
Domestic service	10	13.5
Export service	2	2.7
Other goods and services	14	18.9
No answer	5	6.8

than one purchaser. In none of the cases were relatives clients. It was impossible to generalize business relationship duration with suppliers. Despite the fact that interviewed firms belonged to ultra-small or small enterprises, only 28.4 per cent operated on local markets; the rest declared that they offered both services and goods on domestic and export markets.

Forms of purchase settlements are shown in Table 4.16. In 77 per cent of enterprises belated payments, with the aid of which they settled their dues,

Table 4.16 Form of purchase settlement

Form of settlement	Number of firms	Percentage
Cash only	17	23.0
Invoice with belated payment	31	41.9
Cash and invoice with belated payment	14	18.9
Other forms (no answer included)	12	16.2

refer to the total due amount. In two-thirds of cases the time elapsing between delivery and full payment was less than 14 days. Only one firm among those interviewed was paid its dues after the purchaser had sold its goods.

Formal and informal lending/borrowing

Among the firms interviewed, one-third of them financed their activities using bank credit. The average number of credit applications approved within the sample group in recent years amounted to five, whereas in the last 12 months it was three; about 40 per cent of the credit applications approved within the 5-year period were granted in the last 12 months. Eight firms (10.8 per cent) had access to credit lines.

Table 4.17 Criteria used by firms in selecting banks

First-rank criteria	Second-rank criteria	Third-rank criteria
Bank credibility	Bank employees' qualifications	Distance to the bank
Timing of operations	Quality of products and services	Quality of products and services
Quality of products and services	Timing of operations	Access to credit
Distance to the bank	Distance to the bank	Bank employees' qualifications

In most cases, commercial banks were the cash credit sources. In only one case was the business relationship with the credit bank of less than three months' duration. The credit bank was general located near to the firm interviewed (at a distance of 0.3 to 10 kilometres). It is worth emphasizing that the expectation period of credit approval was short and there was no need to have many meetings with bankers to obtain credit (from one to five). Credit interest rates ranged from 60 per cent (credits obtained in 1992) to 25 per cent (credits obtained in 1996). Maturity ranged from 120 days to three years. Types of collateral varied greatly. Ranking of criteria used by the interviewed firms in selecting banks is shown in Table 4.17. The most important factors were bank credibility, timing of operations, quality of service and products and distance to the bank facilities. Other criteria included employees' qualifications, and access to credit.

The firms were also asked about their assessment of the quality of bank products and services (Table 4.18). A comparison between the results for 1994 and 1995 shows that there was an improvement in the quality of all bank services and products. The improvement was especially noticeable in investment credit, foreign settlements and forex transactions. Forex trans-

Table 4.18 Assessment of quality of bank products

Bank products and services	1994	1995
Timing of bank operations	2.82	3.58
Home settlements	3.27	3.64
Foreign settlements	2.71	3.54
Forex transactions	2.87	3.96
Short-term loans	2.62	3.37
Investment credit	2.26	3.20
Financial advice	2.00	2.67
Assistance in financial planning	1.68	1.90
Access to information	3.05	3.71

Note: 5-point scale: 1 = very low quality, 5 = very high quality.

actions are assessed by the managers as good. Other products, despite improvement, are still on a lower level. The firms assessed assistance in financial planning and financial advice offered to them by banks as rather poor.

Only in eight cases (10.8 per cent) was informal borrowing declared. Relatives were the borrowing sources in three cases, friends in three cases, and suppliers and owners in one case each.

Financial institution deposits

A great majority of the firms interviewed held accounts at financial institutions, mainly current accounts. In most of the cases, the year of the account opening corresponded with the year of the firm's start-up. The amount of interest paid on the account ranged from 3 to 16 per cent. Firms declared neither possession of Treasury Bonds nor other financial instruments. No firm reported deposits held with informal financial intermediaries.

Regulation Mechanism

Ownership and firm functioning regulations

All interviewed firms had their activities registered (including economic activity entry). Registration cost was described as low. The registration period for 25 firms (33.8 per cent) lasted less than seven days. Twenty-seven firms (36.4 per cent) registered their activities within two weeks of the application being filed, 17 firms (20.3 per cent) within three or four weeks, and five firms (6.8 per cent) within two months.

A great majority of the firms reported no obstacles to registration. Difficulties in the form of document supplements or meeting sanitary and custom requirements were reported in single cases. Only 11 firms (14.9 per cent) registered their activity with the aid of intermediaries.

Table 4.19 shows the influence of price regulation on the firms interviewed. Thirty-five firms (47.3 per cent) reported that the price regulation influences their activities. Thirteen firms (17.6 per cent) charged external firms with price inspection and calculation. It has to be noted, however, that except for energy prices, fuels, minimum wage rate and some other minor items there were no state regulations of prices in the analysed period.

Table 4.19 Influence of price regulation

Range of influence	Number of firms	Percentage
With the majority of goods/services	11	14.9
With the majority of outlays	14	18.9
With the majority of goods and outlays	10	13.5
Small or none	39	52.7

Retrospectively, the firms remarked that no particular aspects of their activities were burdensome. The influence of government regulations was mentioned in some cases. The average of estimates of system regulations affecting a firm's activities are shown in Table 4.20. Change in the ownership

Table 4.20 System regulations affecting firm operating activities, 1995–1996

Kind of regulations	Average of estimates in 1995	Average of estimates in 1996
Number of required registrations/licences	1.83	1.9
Productive registration/licences obtaining	1.78	1.65
Import registration/licences obtaining	2.51	1.95
Registration/licences costs	2.24	2.48
Outlay price regulation	1.93	2.11
Firm's good price regulation	2.41	1.84
Government regulation relevant employment	1.68	2.16
Trade union activity	1.73	1.42
Others	1.78	2.33

Note: 5-point scale: 1 = no obstacles, 5 = very severe obstacles.

structure is planned by a few firms interviewed. System regulations, according to the survey are perceived as stable. In five cases the respondents declared some deterioration of the regulations (employment, registration/licences costs, and outlay price). Average score of the regulations in both years was very similar (1.99 in 1995 and 1.98 in 1996).

Work condition regulations

According to the majority of firms, government regulations regarding mergers and acquisitions did not affect their activities. The question 'Does the firm plan to cut down production or reduce employment due to a drop in demand?' was answered negatively by more than 70 per cent of firms interviewed; at the same time more than 90 per cent of respondents found no legal obstacles to dismissal. Table 4.21 shows the particular obstacles to employment reduction as seen by firms. A comparison of the firms' perception of employment regulations reveals that there is stability in this respect with some improvement in 1996 (average estimates for 1995 and 1996 were 1.74 and 1.53, respectively). According to entrepreneurs, the position 'Others' includes: employee training outlays covered by firms, and moral factors.

Table 4.21 Employment reduction obstacles

Kind of obstacle	Average of estimates in 1995	Average of estimates in 1996
Union trade regulation or restrictions	1.24	1.38
Government regulation or restrictions	1.87	2.0
Others	2.12	1.2

Note: 5-point: 1 = no obstacles, 5 = very servere obstacles.

Employment regulation types which the firms are subject to are shown in Table 4.22. Labour force supply and accessibility on the local market are perceived to be good. Only about 20 per cent of firms declared that labour accessibility was insufficient. A similar percentage of firms noted that labour quality was not sufficient for their needs. About 35 per cent of firms assessed the quality as being high or very high and 42 per cent as sufficient. Those dissatisfied with the labour force declared that its most acute drawbacks include insufficient qualifications and overexpectations concerning wage rates.

Table 4.22 Employment regulations

Regulation types	Number of firms	Percentage
Minimum pay	41	55.4
Dismissal restrictions	6	8.1
Engagement restrictions/regulation	8	10.8
Restrictions relevant to specified period of employment	12	16.4
Others	7	9.5

Regulations affecting the expansion of firms

Only about 55 per cent of the firms interviewed intended to develop the scope of their activities. More enterprises (about 30 per cent) declared an intention to finance their expansion only with the aid of their own savings instead of with bank credit. Most of the firms declared a combination of savings, bank credit and relative borrowing in different proportions. Firms abstained from financing development with credit because of high interest rates. Interest rates on credit available to firms ranged from 25 to 32 per cent.

Managers were also asked to rank those factors necessary to improve competitive position on the market with regard to both imported goods and foreign competitors producing and operating in Poland. The ranking (decreasing importance) of factors affecting firms' abilities to compete with imports is shown in Table 4.23. In the case of factors perceived to be important for competing with imports, the most crucial were marketing support, preferential loans, reduced tax rates and technological support. In the case of competition with foreign firms producing in Poland the same factors were pointed out, with preferential loans and tax incentives being the most important. A rather striking conclusion is that import of new

Table 4.23 Ranking of factors affecting firms' ability to compete with imports

Marketing support
Preferential loans
Reduced tax rates
Technological support
Technical personnel
Equipment and production facilities
Import of technology

technologies and new production facilities (buildings/equipment) were ranked as second-range factors.

Conflict Resolution Mechanisms

Firms reported many disputes and conflicts with their clients and suppliers. The proportion of disputes and conflicts with public authorities/institutions is negligible. Eighty per cent of conflicts were caused by delays in payments from customers. The second most important source of conflicts was low quality of raw materials and semiproducts. Lack of payment, conflict employees and delays in the supply of products played a minor role.

The disputes and conflicts were settled mainly through direct negotiations, and only when there were no deals did the disputing parties go to court or to a lawyer to seek arbitration. In about 30 per cent of the cases, business relationships with dispute parties continued despite conflicts. According to the survey, family members were generally not involved in disputes and conflicts.

6 CONCLUSIONS

1. The analysis shows that the liberalization of formal entrance rules created development possibilities for all economic agents, SMEs included. The main group which benefited the most from the liberalization of the formal entrance rules was the SME sector. Its internal dynamics and growth potential needed to be assisted by the state policy. The main declared objective of this policy has been the promotion of the sector's growth. That should lead to: extension of the share of the private sector in the economy's structure, decrease in unemployment, exports increase, activation of local initiatives,and creation of a modern cooperation and service environment.
2. The number of tasks and functions attributed to SMEs in developed market economies is different from that in emerging market economies. The experience shows, however, that the sector development has always been supported by governmental actions and activities. The SME sector, with its job creation potential, should be able particularly to absorb those workers laid off in large state-owned firms being privatized and restructured. Our study shows that the role played by the government in such areas as creating entrance and exit rules has not been perceived as a major hindrance to the sector's growth in Poland. On the contrary, most firms reported no severe obstacles to registration rules and employment policies, and only some obstacles connected with employment regulations and price regulations were perceived.

3. The SME sector is highly diversified. Its effective functioning and development depends on its external and internal financing potential. The study shows limited access to finance in the first half of the 1990s. In the literature, loans from friends and relatives as well as from money-lenders are quoted as typical sources of finance. Our study has not confirmed such an observation. The dominant source in the form of own savings can be seen as a major limitation to the sector's growth. The tendency, however, has already started to change, with SMEs' growing interest for loans from commercial banks. The banks with large bad debts are reluctant to grant credit to firms which have a very short credit history. On the other hand, high real lending rates discourage SMEs from borrowing from banks. To make the fast growth of the SME sector sustainable there is a need to improve the credit and loan accessibility for the SMEs.
4. Our study also shows that contrary to what is generally assumed, the access and quality of infrastructure, equipment and technical staff were not perceived as obstacles. The entrepreneurs would rather demand tax reductions, preferential credit and marketing support as factors helping to compete with local suppliers and with imports.
5. The survey supported earlier assumptions and expectations that machinery and equipment of bankrupt state-owned firms were not utilized on a large scale by the emerging private SME sector. The fixed assets offered by existing or liquidated SOEs were perceived as being of low quality or of little use to the SMEs.
6. The analysed firms are characterized by a lack of financial transparency. This stems both from the fact that the SMEs operate in niches they want to protect and also from cultural considerations.
7. The new SMEs are in the first stage of development. They are very small and credit relations and financial management are in their infancy. The group is dominated by family-run, very small service and trade firms whose consolidation and investment plans are vague.

NOTES

1. Classical literature on entrance and exit and their relationship to competition includes: Bain (1956); Baumol et al. (1982); and Baumol and Willig (1986).
2. The questionnaire, similar to the one used by the Vello Vensel team, acted as a tool in our collecting of source information, see A. Tammeraid and T. Tammeraid, 'Possibilities of flow-of-funds accounting arrangement in Estonia: data description and accounting issues'; A. Tammeraid, A. Teearu and V. Vensel, 'Development of financial contractual relationships in Estonia: empirical results of firms' interview study'; V. Vensel and C. Wihlborg, 'Financial conditions and constraints on entrepreneurship in the Estonian manufacturing sector'. These papers are published in *Reformy finansowe w krajach tworzących gospodarkę rynkową. Modele i badania empiryczne* (1996).

3. See Wilczyński (1996).
4. This can be considered one of the factors influencing current and expected inflation rate.
5. See, for example, Pańkowska (1995).
6. See, for example, Zachowania przedsiębiorcze w przemyśle. Raport z badań empirycznych (1995); Bednarski (1996); Kondratowicz (1993).
7. Within this group, the State Enterprise Privatization Act (implemented on 13 July 1990) and the State Enterprises Act (implemented on 25 September 1981) play an especially important role.
8. See Letza and Kowalski (1993); Hadasik (forthcoming); and Hadasik and Kowalski (1997).
9. See Dynamika przekształceń własnościowych (1996).
10. A state-owned enterprise can be judged to be bankrupt by virtue of the Bankruptcy Act. See Dynamika ... (1996).
11. See Małe i średnie przedsiębiorstwa (1995).
12. See Raport CBOS o bankach (1995).
13. On guarantee funds see Chojnacki (1996) and *Rzeczpospolita*, no 139, 1996.
14. See Tamowicz (1995).
15. Most SMEs do not have any, or have at most a very short, 'credit history'. Furthermore, SMEs have a very low level of capital. This increases bank credit risk. Many of firms from this sector are reluctant to share information about their cost structure, volume of turnover or profit rate. This stems from the considerable share of non-registered turnover and penetration of household expenditures into enterprise costs, especially in family firms.

REFERENCES

Bain, J.S. (1956), *Barriers to New Competition*, Cambridge, MA: Harvard University Press.

Baumol, W.J., J.C. Panzar and R.D. Willig (1982), *Contestable Markets and the Theory of Industry Structure*, New York: Harcourt, Brace, Jovanovich.

Baumol, W.J. and R.D. Willig (1986), 'Contestability: developments since the book', Oxford. *Economic Papers*, Supplement 38, 9–36.

Bednarski, M. (1996), 'Skuteczność prywatyzacji przedsiębiorstw państwowych', in M. Okólski and U. Sztanderska (eds), *Studia nad reformowaną gospodarką*, Warszawa : Wydawnictwo Naukowe PWN.

Chojnacki, J. (1996), 'Poręczeniowe kolce', *Gazeta Bankowa*, No. 4.

Dynamika przekształceń własnościowych (1996), Ministerstwo Przekształceń Własnościowych, No. 27.

Hadasik, D. (forthcoming), Żastosowanie wielowymiarowej analizy porównawczej do oceny zagrożenia przedsiębiorstwa bankructwem, Zeszyty Naukowe Akademii Ekonomicznej w Poznaniu.

Hadaski, D. and T. Kowalski (1997), 'Bankruptcy in Poland in 1990–1995. Macroeconomic aspects and legal procedures', in T. Kowalski (ed.), *Financial Reform in Emerging Market Economies. Quantitative and Institutional Issues*, Poznań: Wydawnictwo Akademii Ekonomicznej.

Kondratowicz, A. (1993), 'Transformacja w sferze małych i średnich przedsiębiorstw', in M. Okólski and U. Sztanderska (eds), *Studia nad reformowana gospodarka*, Warszawa: Wydawnictwo Naukowe PWN.

Letza, S. and T. Kowalski (1993), 'Metody oceny zagrożenia bankructwem – podejście pragmatyczne, Ruch Prawniczy', *Ekonomiczny i Socjologiczny*, **LV** (4).

Małe i średnie przedsiębiorstwa w gospodarce narodowej. Polityka wobec małych i średnich przedsiębiorstw (1995), Ministerstwo Przemysłu i Handlu, Gospodarka Narodowa, No. 7.

Pańkowska, M. (1995), 'Teoria kosztów transakcyjnych według Oliviera Williamsona, Ruch Prawniczy', *Ekonomiczny i Socjologiczny*, **LVII** (3).
Raport CBOS o bankach. (1995, 1996), CBOS, Warszawa.
Reformy finansowe w krajach tworzących gospodarkę rynkową. Modele i badania empiryczne (1996), A. Janc and T. Kowalski (eds), Wydawnictwo Akademii Ekonomicznej w Poznaniu.
Tamowicz, P. (1995), Fundusze inwestycyjne typu venture capital, Instytut Badań nad Gospodarką Rynkową, Transformacja Gospodarki 60.
Wilczyński, W. (1996), 'Wzrost gospodarczy a transformacja ustrojowa. Polska pod koniec lat 90-tych XX wieku, Ruch Prawniczy', *Ekonomiczny i Socjologiczny*, **LVIII** (1).
Zachowania przedsiębiorcze w przemyśle. Raport z badań empirycznych (1995), Gospodarka Narodowa, No. 8–9.

5. Financing small and medium-sized enterprises in Poland, 1989–1994: an empirical investigation of credit rationing*

Agata E. Pawlowska and Andy Mullineux

1 INTRODUCTION

A key feature of successful 'market' (mixed) economy is a thriving sector of small and medium-sized enterprises (SMEs).[1] From the beginning of reformatory efforts in 1990 in Poland, SMEs have been developing vigorously and are playing an increasingly important role in the economy: in the period 1989–95, the private sector increased is share in GDP from 28.4 to 59 per cent. Its contribution in total employment soared from just above 33 to more than 62 per cent, which was mainly due to fast increasing employment in businesses employing less than five people. The number of private firms during the period 1990–95 has almost doubled, with the most substantial growth exhibited by private sector firms trading goods and services.

Thus, a vibrant SME sector is perceived by many as the engine of the impressive 7 per cent growth of GDP achieved in 1995. However, in order to sustain this development and enable further growth, SMEs need access to external finance to supplement internally generated (from retained profits) and privately sourced finance. In the environment of an underdeveloped financial system, the role of commercial banks as a major source of external finance becomes crucial. The subject of this chapter is the relationship between SMEs and bank sectors in Poland in the period 1989–95.

It has long been recognized that the SMEs, by comparison with large companies, have limited access to external finance, experience greater difficulty in raising capital (especially medium and long term), even when the security offered is perfectly sound (strong credit rationing), and that the terms

* This chapter draws heavily on a PhD dissertation by Agata E. Pawlowska, completed in 1997 at the Department of Economics, University of Birmingham, UK, under the supervision of Professor Andy Mullineux.

on which they can obtain such finance are relatively unfavourable (weak credit rationing).[2] This mismatch between the supply and terms (availability) of finance for SMEs was dubbed the *finance gap*, and was first identified by the Macmillan Committee in 1931, and subsequently confirmed by the 1969 Radcliffe Committee, the 1971 Bolton Committee and the 1979 Wilson Committee.[3] While there is no doubt about the existence of the gap, there is still a great deal of controversy as to the causal factors and its exact size, simply because it is difficult to measure it and assess whether the finance gap is due to imperfections in the supply of finance or to the weaknesses on the demand side.

Nevertheless, in the ongoing discussion, an agreement has been achieved as to the possible (negative) consequences of this market failure, especially in periods of economic recession, when the supply-side considerations exacerbate the difficulties and reduce the likelihood of entrepreneurship, which facilitates economic growth at the time it is required the most. It should be stressed that credit rationing (CR) is also believed to be present in the economies with more developed banking systems (because of asymmetric information and fixed costs), but the market failure is particularly acute in the early phases of transition for several reasons:

1. high level of *uncertainty* concerning economic prospects;
2. severe *asymmetric information adverse selection, adverse incentive and moral hazard problems*, resulting from lack of established standards, techniques and mechanisms to facilitate the exchange of credible and reliable information between interested parties and property rights execution;
3. *underdevelopment of the financial sector* in Poland, which in practice restricts the range of alternative sources of loanable funds for the real sector to the commercial banks; and
4. high *financing requirements of the government* facilitated through the sale of government papers, which, although relatively less profitable, are also less risky as compared to the loans extended to the real sector. Banks facing high standards of prudential regulations, a high level of non-performing assets, severe uncertainty and AI problems, will allocate their financial sources in less risky endeavours.

These factors may lead to a much more severe phenomenon of CR than otherwise, resulting in an underfinanced and underinvested SME factor. Adding other restrictions and regulatory deficiencies hampering the development of the (private) SME sector and slow pace of privatization of the economy, one can infer the most likely (negative) consequences for the entire economy, such as (i) higher unemployment as workers laid off by the restructuring state-owned enterprises (SOEs) fail to be absorbed by a vibrant SME sector; (ii) lack of foreign and domestic investment in R&D and modern technologies, perpetuating the uncompetitive structure of the economy and, in the long term, threatening the country's expert performance; (iii) decreasing wealth and living standards of the population; and finally (iv) slower growth of the economy.

Many developed countries have long ago acknowledged the significance of the consequences of the CR phenomenon on the private sector and the future of their national economies. Thus, government intervention in response to this market failure usually takes the form of providing loan guarantees to increase the availability and affordability of external finance for the SME sector (for example, the US, the UK, Germany, Japan and Canada). The arguments for government intervention in the countries of transition, justified from economic and social policy perspectives and policy recommendations, will accordingly be made in the final section.

This chapter focuses on the issue of financing SMEs in Poland in the six-year period 1989–94/95, and is based on data collected from responses to a questionnaire distributed to 60 SMEs and six banks (for details on survey design and the basic characteristics of both samples see Appendix 5A), and data describing the population of 70 banks published periodically in the Polish press and/or by the National Bank of Poland (NBP). Our investigation posed questions relating to the lending policies of and services provided by the banking sector in Poland. It is an attempt to illustrate the trends in SME financing in Poland in the discussed period and to evaluate the adequacy, and quality, of bank finance and services. We examine the possibility of the existence of a finance gap in the availability of capital for the SME sector and assess whether it was a consequence of credit rationing of SMEs by the banking industry or the weaknesses on the demand side.[4] A list of possible recommendations for the government is reserved for the final section.

This chapter is organized as follows: Section 2 provides a comprehensive analysis of bank financing raised by the surveyed firms and examines the price, non-interest price and non-price terms of the loan contract. Section 3 explores the reasons for rejections of loan applications from SMEs. Section 4 looks at the actual borrowing of sampled SMEs. In Section 5 we attempt to measure the efficiency and adequacy of the supplied bank services to their smaller customers. Section 6 raises the question of CR and the 'finance gap' and summarizes the evidence from the study, while a list of recommendations is offered in the final part.

2 BANK FINANCING OF SMES

In the population of sampled enterprises (Figure 5.1) *borrowing from commercial banking* was of secondary importance and accounted for 18.5 per cent of total financing in the period 1989–94. *Internally generated funds* (retained profits and amortization) on average have been the most important source of finance, accounting for almost 39 per cent of the total. *Trade credit* from domestic partners accounted for almost 16 per cent of the total; however, since it is particularly prone to reporting (or rather 'underreporting') errors, the numbers can actually be much higher. None the less, the relatively high values suggest that trade credit flows in the discussed period were far from insignificant.[5] *Tax and social security liabilities* accounted for 15 per cent of the total. As in the case of trade credit, the arrears to the budget are likely to be understated.

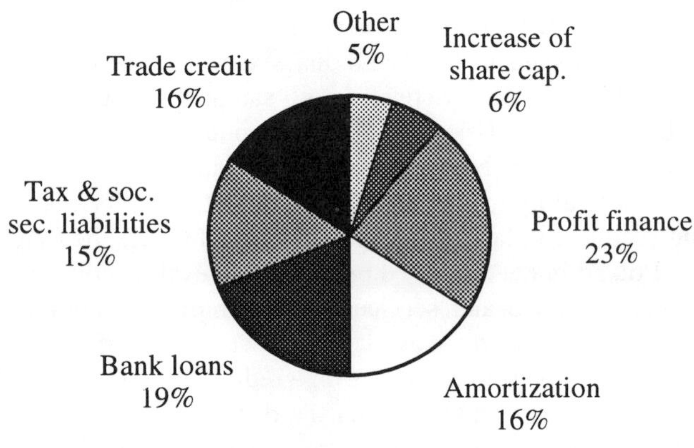

Figure 5.1 Patterns in SMEs' financing, 1989–1994

Most Frequently Requested Type of Financing

To rank the factors according to their importance and/or frequency of usage as assessed by the surveyed firms we have devised a simple measure, which is referred to in the text as the Index of Importance (IofI).[6] The investigation of importance of different types of bank financing to sampled SMEs facilitated by the IofI yielded the following results.[7] An overwhelming majority of firms (50 firms or 83.3 per cent of the total) selected short-term (ST) operating loans as the first most required type of financing, which resulted in a value of IofI more than four times higher than others. Medium- and long-term (M&LT) investment loans were indicated as the second most important source of finance by 35 SMEs. Ten firms chose debt factoring as the second most important source of finance (of which four were SOEs), 22 firms (12 SOEs) as the third and 15 (ten SOEs) as the fourth. The overall picture implies than debt factoring was third in importance, followed by bills discounting. The last position was assigned to leasing, which seemed to be of greater importance for private firms.

Consequently, 70 per cent of enterprises perceived that their demand for ST financing (including overdraft facilities, ST loans and debt factoring) was higher than that for M&LT maturity. However, this outcome did not imply that the provision of ST loans to finance working capital requirements of SMEs was more important than the M&LT financing of fixed assets. On the contrary, it is accepted that SMEs, as compared with large enterprises, are more frequently unable to raise their productivity without introducing at least minimal equipment, which in turn requires M&LT financing. But to obtain a bank loan of longer maturity, frequently an SME was required to provide evidence of already growing productivity. To overcome this vicious circle, as indicated by more than one-quarter of the managers of the sampled SMEs, they used ST loans to finance their LT projects, simply because it was much easier to convince the bank that granting ST rather than M&LT loan carries less risk.[8]

This conclusion was broadly confirmed by the results of the examination of loans by maturity based on data describing the entire banking sector published by the NBP: in the spectrum of five years (1991–95) the importance of ST credit has been decreasing systematically and its share in total bank lending to corporate sector declined by 15 percentage points reaching 41.6 per cent in 1995. This fact, together with the increasing importance of M&LT financing, can be interpreted as a good sign of a lower level of uncertainties in the economy because of the progress of the reforms and the increasing support of the banking sector for the LT growth of the economy, and can also indicate banks' more favourable assessment of LT credit risk. However, the most striking difference in lending practices between private and state-owned enterprises can be noted in the case of M&LT loans. While LT finance until 1993 accounted on average for more than 40 per cent in the case of SOEs, it remained at a disappointing level of 8 per cent in the case of private firms, which consequently may have forced them to finance their LT investments from short- and medium-term credits. This kind of behaviour, however, seems to have been reversed in 1994 and maintained in 1995, which may indicate that banks have been getting more confidence in the stable development of the private sector.[9]

Interest Rate

It is often said that SMEs are condemned to pay higher lending rates for the funds they borrow in comparison with larger enterprises. This can be justified partially by the lending costs of financial institutions, since several factors cause costs of lending to SMEs to be higher than the costs of lending to larger firms relative to the size of the loan, and also partly relative to riskiness. Consequently, higher margins (and/or higher fees) are set between the rate at which the banks obtain their funds and the lending rate they charge to SME borrowers than to larger/less-risky firms. It is difficult to provide a sound generalization as to the adequate margin (and the appropriate spread over the base margin for low-risk borrowers). A range between 4 and 6 percentage points above the prime lending rate has been suggested as a plausible spread for ST funds for the SMEs, as compared with a spread of 1.5 to 3 percentage points charged in lending to larger enterprises (Kochav et al. 1974, p. 24; Storey 1994, pp. 218–21).[10] Furthermore, it is also a common practice to vary interest rates conditional on other elements, such as size, purpose and maturity of the loan, financial standing of the borrower (for example, profitability, turnover), length of relationship between the bank and its customer, and so on.

In Poland (Table 5.1), as a consequence of a decreasing inflation, nominal interest rates on refinancing credit have declined (from 105 per cent in 1990 to 33 per cent in 1994), followed by rates on deposits and credits in the main commercial banks. Consequently, the interest rate charged on loans to surveyed SMEs has dropped in the 1990–95 period by 33 percentage points on average (that is, from 90 per cent in 1990 to 57 per cent in 1994). An onerous tendency in the spread between the borrowing and lending rates in the period 1991–94 can be noted:[11] while the nominal (real) spread in lending to an average enterprise in the economy (as a consequence of decreasing nominal interest rates) has been reduced by 2.5 (0.1) percentage points, in the case of lending to an average SME it has actually increased by 1.7 (4.3) percentage points. As a result, in 1994 the nominal (real) spread in aggregate equalled 14.5 (11.3) percentage points (which by international standards is already excessive), while that in lending to SMEs was almost twice as high![12] Moreover, throughout the entire period of 1991–94 the nominal spreads for small and smaller-medium (S&S) companies were higher than those for bigger-medium and large (B&L). On average the difference amounted to approximately 9.8 percentage points, which was statistically significant (at the significance level of 0.10). The difference between real spreads has been systematically closing since 1993, which is more explicit considering the real spread.

Why have interest spreads remained at such high levels throughout the discussed period? Which factors have played major roles in preventing the

Table 5.1 Nominal and real (N&R) interest rate spreads according to the surveyed sample and aggregated data (percentages)

	1991	1992	1993	1994	Ave 1991–94
1. Average rate charged on surveyed SMEs (%)	67.7	59.8	54.6	56.9	59.75
2. Six-month deposit rate in banks (%)	41.0	37.0	29.5	28.5	34.00
3. Quoted credit rate in commercial banks (%)	58.0	52.0	48.0	43.0	50.25
N&R spread between (3) and (2) in economy[1]	17.0 (11.4)	15.0 (11.3)	18.5 (13.4)	14.5 (11.3)	16.3 (11.8)
N&R spread between (1) and (2) for SMEs	26.7 (18.0)	22.8 (17.4)	25.1 (18.3)	28.4 (22.3)	25.75 (16.0)
for B&L firms[2]	25.5 (17.1)	20.8 (15.7)	25.0 (18.2)	28.2 (21.9)	24.88 (25 firms)
for S&S firms[2]	28.4 (19.1)	24.7 (18.6)	25.2 (18.1)	28.7 (22.2)	34.65 (21 firms)
difference between nominal spreads $_{t\text{-statistic incl.}}$[2]	$-2.9_{0.702}$	$-3.9_{0.612}$	$-0.2_{0.979}$	$-0.4_{0.957}$	$-9.77_{0.102}$

Notes:
1. Real spreads calculated according to the formula obtained from Buch (1996): $[(r^L - r^D)/(1 + \Delta P)] \times 100$ where ΔP denotes the change in the PPI, r^L is the lending rate and r^D is the deposit rate.
2. Averages in the last column for S&S and B&L firms were calculated on the basis of average employment in the period 1989–94.

spreads from falling? In order to answer these questions a crude attempt with the utilization of a simple simulation model is applied to assess the contribution of three factors to the spread, namely level of non-performing loans (NPL) obligatory reserve requirements (ORR) and inflation.[13] We run a simulation for prime (normal) credit based on the NBP. The obtained results, although they should not be taken stringently because of imperfections in the data, can, however, provide a useful approximation of orders of magnitude of the aforementioned parameters. Moreover, caution is needed due to the fact that the model does not contain the element of credit risk particularly associated with smaller lenders and uncertainty characteristic of the constantly changing environment of a transitional economy. Based on the simulation results (delineated in Table 5.2) the following conclusions can be drawn.

Table 5.2 Decomposition of the interest rate spreads (percentages)

	1991	1992	1993	1994	1995
Actual spread	17.0	15.0	18.5	14.5	10.8
Baseline simulation	17.4	16.1	17.1	16.1	9.2
Difference	–0.4	–1.1	1.4	–1.6	1.5
Difference compared with baseline simulation results					
without NPL	–7.1	–10.6	–12.0	–12.7	–6.6
without ORR	–8.5	–7.0	–6.2	–5.3	-3.6
with inflation = 0	–9.9	–6.0	–9.6	–8.0	–4.7

NPL explained the largest proportion of interest spread, on average 980 basis points. A very clear patterns emerged of close positive correlation between escalation of NPL phenomena and widening of the spread. In 1991, when the NPL have not yet become a problem, their contribution to the widening of the interest spread accounted for 710 basis points, whereas in the period 1993–94, when they reached a record-high share in banks' portfolio, it increased to 1235 basis points.[14] This may confirm the hypothesis (Thorne 1993) that banks suffering from NPL may have rationally maintained high spreads to help their recapitalization (increase loss loans reserves while adding to capital).

ORR, indicating the level of taxation of financial intermediation, on average accounted for 610 basis points of the spread. Their share has been decreasing gradually because of a reduction in ORR requirements set by the central bank and therefore, they cannot explain the steadiness and/or widening of the spread. Declining inflation was responsible for a systematically decreasing portion of the spread. It should be noted, however, that because of interactions between the different elements of the simulation model, they magnify the effects of each other, for example, higher inflation would magnify the distortionary effects of NPL (Dittus 1994a, b).

Despite all the imperfections of the simulation model, it appears that NPL, ORR and inflation explain interest spread in a satisfactory manner. Nevertheless, only NPL can explain widening of the spread until 1993, since the importance of the two remaining variables has been declining over time. Looking for other explanations one has to think of credit risk (not included in the calculations), 'bad experiences' of the banks, forcing them to more prudent and careful lending and probably stricter prudential rules and regulations introduced into the system. As a confirmation of this, one could consider the fact that the average difference between the actual and calculated spreads in case 1 is of a very small range (approximately 1 percentage point), whereas in case 2 it reached approximately 6.2 percentage points. This implies that the element of credit risk played a crucial role in setting lending rates. Additionally, low financial intermediation rates of the Polish banking sector may have driven up the cost of intermediation and thus contributed to the maintenance of high spreads.[15] The fact that the high spreads prevail in the banking industry despite its systematic development and decreasing NPL, ORR and inflation is most certainly due to the high concentration of the market, oligopolistic structure and regional segmentation, all of which jeopardize and hamper competition. High spreads and high credit price may adversely affect real sector development (especially SMEs, which are cut off from affordable credit) and consequently endanger the growth of the entire economy.

Additionally, we use a multiple regression analysis which permitted the identification of the most influential characteristics associated with the high credit price and a logistic regression analysis which allowed us to predict the probability of the firm being charged a high credit price. Average spread between charged lending and six-month deposit rates in the period 1989–94 was a dependent variable. The independent variables included: (i) three variables measuring bank–firm relationship obtained from a factor analysis using principal component extraction, (ii) a number of firm-specific characteristics such as size, age, profitability and so on, and (iii) two variables describing financing arrangements, such as level of collateral and owner's participation (for details, see Pawlowska 1997).

Six explanatory variables were significant at a different significance level (Table 5.3; we had to make some allowances concerning the significance level of *t*-statistics, but otherwise the analysis would not be possible). With the exception of participation level, all signs were expected: firms with a shorter and relatively less favourable relationship with the banking staff, unwilling to provide necessary information to the bank, able to secure the

Table 5.3 *Multiple regression results: dependent variable – interest rate spread*

Independent variable (variables in the equation)	Coefficient	*t*-ratio	Sig *t*-ratio	Other statistics
Overdue loans	–0.327	–1.440	0.158	*R* Square = 0.274
Level of collateral (C–L ratio)	–7.365	–1.422	0.163	
Owner's participation level	19.657	1.405	0.168	*F* = 2.38797
ADVICE – use of bank-provided advisory services	–3.326	–1.211	2.233	Significance *F* = 0.0468
APPROACH – relationship with the bank	–6.118	–2.164	0.037	
INFO – information flow	–3.115	–1.109	0.274	
(Constant)	32.911	3.829	0.001	

loan to a lesser extent and lacking expertise at preparing the credit application, business plan and/or feasibility study of the planned project, were to be charged a higher rate of interest on the loans. Surprisingly and contrary to common sense, the results suggested that firms with unpaid loans and participating to a higher degree in planned investment projects were to pay a higher rate of interest. We cannot find a reasonable explanation for this outcome and had to admit that this may be an error resulting from too small a sample.

Unfortunately, six statistically significant independent variables were able to explain only 28 per cent of the total variance of the dependent variable (all 12 variables explained 35 per cent), which may suggest that there were other subjective criteria used to determine the price of credit.[16] Surprisingly, firms' characteristics associated with their performance and financial stance were not influential. This fact may be due to a relatively small size of the sample and therefore should be recognized as a shortcoming of our analysis. However, it may also confirm a hypothesis we suggest in the next sections, that banks were not particularly concerned with the financial stance of a potential lender, but rather with the ability to post collateral in excess of the loan size. The confirmation of any of these suggestions would require further study, preferably on a more representative sample.

Using the same set of dependent variables we run a logistic regression in order to find the characteristics and the magnitude of their impact on the probability of the *event* defined as being charged a high rather than a low interest rate.[17] According to the findings, the value of collateral and owner's participation most significantly influenced the probability of being charged a high lending rate. Overall, the expected relationship was noted in the case of the firm's size, collateral level and type (that is, the bigger the firm, the higher the loan collateralization and the more business collateral pledged, the lower the probability of being charted a higher rate), and in the case of profitability, liquidity and loan collateralization (that is, the higher the profitability, liquidity and collateral-to-loan ratio (C–L ratio) the lower the probability of the event). Age did not seem to have a big impact. Unexpected outcomes were noted in the case of overdue loans, sales growth, owner's participation and restrictive covenants: the first two factors may suggest that in our sample, factors such as problematic loans and declining sales turnover were not the most important issues in the decision-making process whether to grant the loan or not. A surprising negative relationship between the owner's participation in the project and a high lending rate could be due to the fact that the S&S firms were usually required to participate to a higher degree in the planned project and at the same time they were charged a higher interest rate. This hypothesis, however, is highly speculative and thus not conclusive. The proof would require further studies. From the calculated probabilities of events it seems evident that in the surveyed sample, smaller firms were much more likely to be charged higher lending rates than their bigger counterparts.

Collateral Requirements

Availability of collateral plays a vital role in the willingness of banks to meet the demand of the firms. Because banks are restricted in their ability to differentiate interest rates to cover the default risk due to information and adverse selection problems, collateral offsets the losses in cases of default and provides incentives to repay the loan. Thus, collateral was required of almost all surveyed enterprises that received loans. By and large, surveyed SMEs did not have a partner to share the provision of security and thus supplied the required collateral themselves (89 per cent). One-third of enterprises met the security conditions with the participation of another firm, while only seven and nine firms (out of 55) received guarantees from banks or insurance companies, respectively.

The amount of collateral varied with the other factors. They were usually higher for younger firms and on start-up loans (57 per cent of respondents). Lower leverage ratio and higher profitability could result in a reduction of the requested amount of security (58 and 52 per cent, respectively). The payback period had little impact on the C–L ratio. An interesting association can be noted between the amount of collateral and the loan size: calculated correlation coefficients (although not very high, about half a percentage point on average in the period 1989–94) had a negative value, which implies that as the loan volume decreased, the level of collateralization increased. This outcome can be a consequence of the so-called 'divisibility problem' (Binks et al. 1988, p. 34), that is, because often pledged assets are not easily divided and in case of default they would have to be liquidated or sold in their entirety to repay the loan, therefore they have to be pledged as a whole. This in turn, artificially increases the C–L ratio, especially for smaller loans.

It is a rule of thumb (Binks et al. 1988) to set the C–L ratio at the level of 1.5 to 1.0. Analysis of the firm's population shows that bankers hit this target pretty well: on average, in the period 1989–94, the bulk of loans (67 per cent) contained requirements for a C–L ratio higher than 1.0, and the proportion of SMEs compelled to provide collateral in excess of that has escalated from 54 per cent in 1989 to 82 per cent in 1994. The same calculations made for C–L ratios above the 1.5 level appear even more striking: the share of firms required to provide collateral of more than 1.5 times the loan size has increased from 17 per cent in 1989 to 44 per cent in 1994. From 1992 onwards, all surveyed banks demanded the loan to be covered more than once, and half of the sample compelled their customers to provide collateral of more than 1.5 times the loan size.

The evidence also reinforces the common view that although in general all firms had to meet high collateral requirements, private and smaller firms were more likely to be required to provide higher security. With the exception of 1991, an average C–L ratio for S&S firms was slightly higher as compared to their B&L counterparts, although not statistically significant (Table 5.4).

What were the most likely explanation of the high C–L ratios experienced by the SMEs? Because the information available to the lender is imperfect, the banks would try to fully secure the loan guarding against asset price risks and increase their abilities to recover the money in case of default. Also difficulties in assessing the true value of pledged assets may have led to their undervaluation by the banks, which in time should try to overcome this problem by increasing the level of expertise of the bank staff at risk approval and value evaluation of pledged assets. Additionally, the divisibility problem resulted in the value of the assets being higher than the value of the loan. Further, a lack of institutions allowing banks to verify whether the assets have already been pledged against another loan (such as information bank) and the fact that in the case of default the banks have to compete with other creditors, certainly contributes to the policy of securing the value of the loan more than once. The ownership of assets used to secure loans may be the subject of restitution claims in the early phases of transition. Finally, banks may be seeking protection against asset price deflation and to cover the costs of holding and selling the collateralized assets (including 'fire-sale' losses).

Additionally, a high C–L ratio seemed to have been a consequence of deliberate bank policy aimed at bringing down the appraised value of pledged assets in anticipation of its lower present and future real commercial value ('gone concern' approach). Subsequently only a fraction of the estimated value of assets could have been pledged as collateral and the longer the loan maturity the lower the fraction (Table 5.5). Hence, more collateral was needed

Table 5.4 Average C–L ratio in sampled enterprises (number of firms in brackets)

	1989	1990	1991	1992	1993	1994	Average*
B&L firms	1.14 (29)	1.17 (27)	1.32 (26)	1.41 (22)	1.46 (21)	1.51 (18)	1.27 (31)
S&S firms	1.36 (6)	1.37 (9)	1.21 (14)	1.51 (20)	1.62 (26)	1.66 (25)	1.45 (24)
Difference $_{t\text{-statistic incl.}}$	−2.54 (35)	$-1.99_{0.365}$ (36)	$1.13_{0.619}$ (40)	$-0.97_{0.605}$ (42)	$-1.58_{0.367}$ (47)	$-1.50_{0.462}$ (43)	$-1.80_{0.275}$ (55)

Note: * Averages calculated on the basis of average employment in the period 1989–94.

Table 5.5 Rules of evaluation of assets pledged as collateral (percentages)

	Short and medium term	Long term
Real estate	50	30
Tangible assets	50–60	40
Liquid assets	60–70	50

Note: The percentages indicate the fraction of the value estimation accepted by the banks as collateral in the case of ST and M&LT loans.

Source: Data from internal documents of the surveyed banks.

to secure the loan in general and banks' requirements to secure the loan at least once resulted in excessive C–L ratios. While this type of behaviour is not unusual or exceptional among the policies of other banks worldwide, especially if there is a high probability of encountering difficulties in recovering overdue debts (Barro 1976), in the environment where the possibility of sharing the provision of collateral and/or obtaining a loan guarantee from other financial and non-financial institutions is close to zero, these excessive requirements could (and did) pose a great deal of difficulty for any enterprise, but could prove unattainable for SMEs. As a result, the SMEs would be rationed out of the credit market and if there were not other institutions in the financial market from which they could acquire external finance and internally generated funds were insufficient to allow for development or at least survival, the outcomes could be twofold depending on firms' economic–financial stance: the firms starved of capital either (i) abstain from investments or cease to exist, or (ii) switch to other sources of capital such as, for example, inter-enterprise or tax arrears. The results of empirical analysis on the firm level confirmed the latter hypothesis of replacing unavailable bank finance with payment arrears. In any case, the consequences for economic development might be of a high magnitude.

Other Non-interest and Non-price Terms of the Loan Contract

Requirements concerning the minimum level of firm's participation in a planned investment, restrictive covenants (RCs) and compensating balances (CBs) can be incorporated into the loan contract to reduce moral hazard problems by introducing positive incentives. The former one is very similar to one of the forms of collateral, that is, the higher involvement of the borrower in the planned project, the more incentives he/she has to engage in a less-risky venture, thus the lower probability of default. RCs and CBs on the other hand, besides alleviating the moral hazard problems, by specifying exactly the desirable and undesirable types of action, make the monitoring process of the firm's activities easier and less expensive for the bank (Apilado and Millington 1992).

Most of the respondents (75 per cent) were required to finance the planned project up to 50 per cent from their own sources, and one-third in more than 50 per cent. In the period 1989–94, banks increased their emphasis on requirements concerning a firm's participation, as the number of firms financing the new ventures up to the 50 per cent threshold has been systematically decreasing (in 1989, almost the entire sample, whereas in 1994 it was just above 60 per cent), so has the number of firms required to increase their financial involvement in the planned endeavour as a condition of the loan (36 per cent in 1994). On average in the discussed period, S&S firms were subject to slightly higher participation requirements by about 4 percentage points as compared to B&L firms (Table 5.6).

The vast majority of firms (89 per cent) admitted that a set of RCs was usually written into the loan contract and among the most frequently used were: a clause ensuring the banks' rights to monitor the loan, requirements concerned with maintaining pledged collateral in a good condition and in the possession of the borrower, and a clause specifying the exact purpose of the loan. Generally banks were not interested in participating the formulation and verification of strategic investment decisions, or in securing the minimum net worth of the firm. The latter could be especially surprising, however, taking into account the fact that to obtain the loan, firms very often pledge all or the majority of assets against the loan as collateral, and as these are covered by the separate RCs, there is no need to duplicate the restrictions.

During our interviews, a few firms mentioned that banks expressed their readiness to grant the loan conditionally to CBs kept at the firms' savings accounts amounting to two-thirds of the loan volume. The idea of keeping CBs as a guarantee had been recognized long before in the literature (Mishkin 1992; Hodgman 1961; Kane and Mankiel 1965), but these requirements seem to be excessive. Thus, not surprisingly, the managers did not accept such conditions, since it would be cheaper for them to increase their tax and inter-enterprise arrears and finance the planned project from a free credit, rather than pay a high lending rate.

Equity Finance

There are several instances of banks taking an active role in the restructuring, governance and provision of external funds facilitated through debt-for-equity swaps or outright purchasing of equity (Dittus 1996; Dittus and Prowse 1995; Mendelson and Peake 1993). These arguments notwithstanding, there

Table 5.6 Owners' participation requirements in the sampled firms (percentages; number of firms in brackets)

	1989	1990	1991	1992	1993	1994	Average*
B&L firms	27.76 (25)	30.64 (21)	30.62 (21)	40.58 (18)	51.12 (17)	49.57 (25)	37.52 (31)
S&S firms	29.50 (6)	29.50 (9)	35.88 (13)	34.88 (17)	44.66 (22)	38.98 (21)	41.77 (25)
Difference $_{t\text{-statistic incl.}}$	$-1.74_{0.825}$ (31)	$1.14_{0.875}$ (30)	$-5.26_{0.510}$ (34)	$5.70_{0.485}$ (35)	$6.46_{0.483}$ (39)	$10.59_{0.274}$ (36)	$-4.25_{0.464}$ (56)

Note: * Averages calculated on the basis of average employed in the period 1989–94.

are also a number of reasons justifying banks' reluctance to become owners of non-financial enterprises. As a result (confirmed by Dittus 1996 and our studies), it appears that banks deliberately refrained from gaining effective control in their customers' business and were content to adhere to basic corporate lending to the best and least-risky firms. Only if there was no other way to redeem their NPL, did they decide on the equity option.[18] Taking equity stakes in 'healthy' and prosperous firms (including SMEs) was not on the agenda of any of the interviewed banks. One can expect that because of the implementation of the Mass Privatization Programme and the development of the Privatization Investment Funds, the equity market will gradually expand and develop, closing the 'equity gap'. Whether, however, this will increase the availability of equity finance for the firms which are not covered by the Mass Privatization Programme, remains to be seen in the future.

SMEs on the other hand, either did not receive any interest from the banks, because their financial conditions were too poor, or were not interested because equity finance implied limitations of decision-making autonomy. A number of SMEs would be more receptive to an equity finance arrangement if it came from an institution that did not seek to control the every-day operations of the firm.

3 REJECTED LOAN APPLICATIONS FROM SMEs

Although most of the loan requests were approved, it is interesting to investigate the cases of rejection to uncover the reasons behind this decision. Out of the 60 firms, 17 (28.3 per cent) had their loan requests turned down, of which ten were state owned and seven were private. It is difficult to assess the differences in the rejection pattern according to the firms' size, given sample limitations. In order to check whether the grounds on which the banks rejected the surveyed SMEs were justified, we performed a discriminant analysis on two groups of enterprises: those that have had their loan applications rejected versus those that have been successful. From the obtained results (Table 5.7)[19] one can state that the bankers' decision not to grant the loan to the rejected firms was firmly justified on the basis of their financial characteristics. None the less, checking the firms' characteristics case by case, it turned out that five out of 13 firms were unjustifiably rejected, while four were granted loans regardless of their characteristics being no different from those firms that were rejected.[20] This translates into 21 per cent of 'grouped' cases classified incorrectly, and particularly into 39 per cent (five out of 13) of firms subject to strong CR (that is, they were complying with the requirements, willing to pay the credit price, but denied the credit altogether). Although, because of the small size of the sample, one cannot treat these

Table 5.7 Results of the discriminant analysis – rejection of the loan application (averages, 1989–94)

Actual group	Length (years)[1]	Advice usage (%)[2]	Profit-ability[3]	Liquidity ratio	Overdue loans (%)[4]	Growth ratio[5]	C–L ratio[6]	Owners' particip. (%)	Predicted group membership	
									Successful (%)	Rejected (%)
Successful	18	93.6	4.68	2.08	0.98	0.92	1.37	38.4	27 firms (87.1)	4 firms (12.9)
Rejected	17	76.9	–6.05	1.29	11.9	0.66	1.18	35.2	5 firms (38.5)	8 firms (61.5)

Notes:
1. Length of relationship with the bank.
2. Percentage of firms using external advice prior to applying.
3. Profitability = net profit/sales turnover.
4. Percentage of overdue in total loans.
5. Average growth rate of annual sales turnover.
6. Collateral-to-loan ratio.

results as conclusive, a high percentage of firms 'mistakenly' rationed may well indicate that a phenomenon of strong CR exists.

Another piece of evidence indicating the existence of CR is the assessment of the most important criteria that determine the banks' decision whether to grant the loan or not: the overwhelming majority of firms (86.7 per cent) and all sampled banks indicated full collateralization of the loan as being the most decisive criteria whether to grant the loan. A long-term and well-established relationship with the bank and a minimum of 30 per cent of shareholders'/owners' participation in the investment project were of second (fourth) and fourth (second) importance, respectively, for SME (banks). The third position was taken by 'the good financial projections of the planned investment project', which was also evaluated by a quarter of the SMEs as unimportant to the bank.[21]

Furthermore, 14 of the surveyed enterprises admitted that they found themselves in a situation where the bank had decided to grant the loan, but they had not taken it because of the excessive collateral requirements (nine firms), or interest rate (seven firms), or level of owner participation in the project (two firms), or excessive bank charges (two firms). Thus, they were subject to weak CR.

This extreme prudence and unwillingness of the banks to take any above-the-minimum credit risk confirms the hypothesis of security- rather than profit-orientation of their leading policies, resulting in a passive role as a financial intermediary.[22] This type of policy may have prevented many good (likely to succeed) projects from getting bank financing and many SMEs being subject to CR.

4 BORROWING OF SMEs

Has the extent of the SME's borrowing been affected by the relatively unfavourable terms of the loan contracts? Our analysis of the quality and volume of received loans over the period 1989–94 is arranged according to the loan type, so that the results are presented separately for ST and LT loans.[23] The main findings are as follows:

1. *Number of loans* On average, 61 loans were granted every year, of which approximately 65 per cent were given to SOEs. However, while the distribution of loans between private and public sectors have not changed significantly over the discussed period, the number of loans received by S&S firms has increased almost five times (that is, from 12 per cent of the total in 1989 to 54 per cent in 1994), resulting in a decreasing proportion of loans received by the B&L firms (from 90 to 46

per cent in respective years). These findings are contrary to the common opinion that there is bank discrimination against smaller-size customers.

2. *Frequency of loan receipt* On average, in the population of borrowers, a firm has received a ST loan 1.83 times, with the highest ratio of 2.36 in 1991.[24] A majority of enterprises (60 per cent) obtained a ST loan once, almost 25 per cent twice, 6 per cent three times and 16 per cent four times or more. The average number for SOEs equal 1.9 (1.8 excluding firms that obtained a loan more than five times), as compared with 1.7 for private firms, which implies that SOEs obtained ST loans slightly more often than their private counterparts. Comparing firms according to their employment, larger firms tend to borrow more frequently than the smaller ones. These differences, however, were not very significant, which again contradicts the opinion that there is bank discrimination against smaller firms.
3. *Loan size* More than half of the total number of loans granted were of medium value (that is, between PLZ 1001 and 5000 million), whereas small-value loans (that is, PLZ 1000 million or less) accounted for 40 per cent.[25] There is a distinctive pattern of loan allocations according to their size, among firms divided on the basis of ownership: almost 70 per cent of loans received by SOEs were of medium value and only 25 per cent were of low value, whereas for private firms this relation is exactly the opposite. The situation is less clear-cut when analysing firms divided on the basis of their size: comparing data from 1989 and 1994, it seems evident that S&S companies shifted their priorities from low- to medium-value loans.[26] The rationale for this outcome can be twofold: on the demand side, smaller firms were more often engaged in projects requiring high-value capital injection than were their bigger counterparts;[27] on the supply side, because of the banks' policy and the existence of fixed costs in loan contracts, obtaining a larger loan was relatively easier than securing a smaller one (Kulawczuk 1994, p. 84).
4. *Number of firms* On average, 56.5 per cent of all surveyed firms have received a ST operational loan, however, the proportion continued to decline from 71 per cent in 1989 to 65 per cent in 1994.[28] Only 15 per cent of firms on average have acquired an investment loan, of which loans of maturity exceeding three years were the most popular. Each year approximately 33 firms were granted ST loans, of which almost 60 per cent were B&L SOEs. None the less, the number of smaller and private borrowers has been systematically increasing, and in 1994 they accounted for 62 and 46 per cent of the total number of borrowers, respectively. In the period 1990–94, almost one-third of the total number of firms received low-value credits (PLZ 1000 million or less), but they accounted for only 9.4 per cent of the total volume of loans, while the 10 per cent of

firms that acquired high-value loans (more than PLZ 5000 million), accounted for almost one-third of the total. The vast majority of firms received medium-value loans (between 1000 and 5000 million zlotys), which accounted for almost 60 per cent of the total value.

5. *Borrowers' financial stance* Surprisingly, there were no strong relationships between loan size an the net financial results, and the profitability of the firms. This outturn corresponds to one of the findings that full collaterization of the loan, rather than the financial status of an enterprise, was a decisive factor in the decision-making process whether to grant the loan or not.

5 BANK SERVICES DEMANDED AND RECEIVED – MEASURING BANK PERFORMANCE

Measuring the importance of each of the bank services is facilitated by using the IofI formula. In order to collapse the two sets of data collected in question when the firms evaluated the importance and quality of services into one set of numbers, we have devised a simple measure which we refer to as the Index of Attainment (IofA).[29] In interpreting the value of the index, two things had to be taken into account:[30] (i) from the firms' standpoint there is relatively insignificant benefit if there has been an improvement in the provision of services which is perceived as unimportant, and (ii) from the bank's point of view, although a general improvement in the quality of the provision of all services may be positive, an improvement (deterioration) in the quality of undesired (required) services can be treated as a misallocation of scarce resources. Thus, the optimal situation would occur when the value of the index declines with the degree of importance attached to a specific service.

According to the importance of each of the bank services as perceived by SMEs and measured by the IofI, we divided them into four thematic groups: (i) bank services, (ii) terms of the loan contract, (iii) bank–firm relationships, and (iv) network development. A brief analysis of each group is presented in Table 5.8.

The most important bank attributes centred on the *quality, speed and range of bank services* that SMEs received as customers. More than three-quarters of respondents rated them as very important, and a quarter as important. However, the relatively low value of the IofA in the case of both quality of services and speed of decision-making process, suggests that their needs are far from being satisfied. The range of services offered, although it was ranked at fifth place according to the IofI, was considered important by three-quarters of the firms. The high value of the attainment index suggests that the development of new banking products and services has been successful.

Table 5.8 Banks' characteristics (IofI and IofA values)

Bank characteristics	IofI	IofA
Bank services		
1. Quality of bank services	27.95	0.30
2. Good reputation of the bank	26.00	0.40
3. Speed of decision making	24.18	0.28
Terms of loan contract		
4. Interest rate charged	24.18	0.28
5. Fees charged	19.84	–0.65
Bank–firm relationships		
6. Range of offered services	19.60	0.53
7. Collateral/administrative barriers	15.73	–0.26
8. Consulting/advice	12.36	0.30
9. Willingness to take risk	11.29	–0.19
10. Relations with bank staff	8.67	0.38
Network development		
11. Bank location	8.41	0.26
12. No. of branches in the country	4.20	0.28
13. No. of subsidiaries abroad	2.85	0.15

However, we obtained a slightly different view when asking whether they fit SMEs' needs. During our interviews a significant number of managers complained about banks' lack of understanding of the specific properties of small business. Banks are frequently very rigid in applying their requirements and are not prepared to make any allowances. Credit applications and the range of services offered are not well suited to meet smaller customers' needs.[31] The average time for receiving a bank decision on whether the loan had been granted was far too long and should have been shorter.[32] Moreover, in the light of a series of banking scandals involving massive frauds, critical errors with bank privatization and a few financial problems of smaller banks which took place in the past,[33] it is not surprising to find a high proportion of firms being concerned about banks' reputation and trustworthiness. However, judging by a relatively high value of the attainment index, banks have been trying to improve their image.

A second tier of significant bank attributes consisted of *price and non-interest-price terms of the loan contract.* Interest rate, fees and required collateral were considered as very important or important by approximately 67 and 32 per cent of the total number of respondents, respectively. Only in the case of interest rate charged on loans was the value of the IofA satisfactory, which was most likely due to the fact that half of the firms acknowledged its declining trend. In the case of collateral and fees, the values were negative, indicating that the situation has significantly worsened from firms' point of view over the six-year period. On the other hand, raising the level of fees/services charges was partly due to the fact that banks, as well as other financial institutions, increasingly employed them to augment their revenue, subjecting a growing number of services to charges.[34]

The group of bank characteristics ranked as the third most important pertained to the nature of the *bank–firm relationship*. Utilization of external advice and consultation concerning financial planning and budgeting was almost absent. However, 20 and 63 per cent, respectively, regarded its provision as very important or important in conducting their business. The value of the IofA equal to 0.3 may justify the low level of utilization of advisory services because of their poor provision. In spite of a 0.4 score in the case of the assessment of relations with the banks' staff, the concern of SMEs with banks' bureaucratic structure and with their lack of flexibility on rules and procedures draws attention to the issue of 'absolute impersonality' (that is, a 'strictly by numbers' approach). It seems that there was no such thing as close cooperation or a good relationship between the bank staff and the firm's management: only one bank and 11 firms (19 per cent) from the surveyed sample acknowledged the existence of a special department in their main bank dealing exclusively with SMEs, whereas 47 (81 per cent) of the remaining firms declared that if there was one, it would be much easier to cooperate with the bank. As a consequence, one can expect to find severe problems with asymmetric information and the associated reluctance (or at least prudence) in lending practices. It is impossible to measure the exact impact of asymmetric information on banks' readiness to take the risk of crediting SME, but it seems plausible to assume a positive association. Although more than 88 per cent of the sample considered a bank's willingness to take the risk and finance small businesses to be an important factor, more than half of the sample (55 per cent) noted its decreasing tendency over the six-year period 1989–94 (that is, 37 per cent found it unchanged and only 8 per cent found it increased). On the other hand, a very low score of the attainment index (–0.19) indicates that not a great deal of effort has been undertaken to improve the situation.[35]

The rest of the 13 characteristics, concerning *network development*, were of less concern. They included location of the bank, number of branches at home and abroad and so on. This result is largely to the fact that all the main banks of the surveyed firms have well-developed networks of branches and subsidiaries all around Poland, despite their original regional orientation.

6 ELABORATION OF CONSTRAINTS IN SMEs' FINANCE AND THEIR EFFECTS ON THE SME SECTOR: QUESTIONING THE EXISTENCE OF FINANCE GAPS, DISCRIMINATION AND CREDIT RATIONING

Many criticisms of the banking industry have been made by SMEs, and our goal in this section is to assess whether the survey's evidence supports them and whether these obstacles could have led to funding gaps, CR and discrimination against small firms in bank finance in Poland in the period 1989–94/95. Table 5.9 sets out five main areas in which the sampled SMEs have criticized the Polish banks, and the authors' own judgement of their validity based on the survey findings from the SMEs, banks and the overall score. Using the results yielded by the firm- and bank-level questionnaire, we attempted to verify the existence of finance gaps, discrimination against and CR of SMEs.[36]

Overall, evidence from the bank and firm questionnaires strongly supported the main criticisms of the banking sector. An old adage has it that banks only lend to those wealthy enough not to need to borrow. Unless an SME can post adequate collateral, banks wedded to the 'gone concern' approach (that is, most banks in economies at an early stage of transition, given the high level of uncertainty over future cash flows) will not lend to it. It is also not surprising that the banks ask for collateral of approximately 1.5 times the loan, given uncertainty over debt seniority, possible rival (restitution) claims on the assets pledged, and uncertainty about their market value. However, in an environment of an almost complete absence of any other institutions sharing/helping to provide an adequate loan collateralization, these requirements (although justified from the bank standpoint) may prove unattainable for many SMEs. Also, it is not unreasonable to assume that with the banks' increasing and improving expertise and experience at risk evaluation, the required amount of collateral will be more appropriate to the level of the firm's/project's riskiness (thus, lower for some SMEs), rather than uniformly high for all SMEs according to a 'better-safe-than-sorry' strategy.

Another problem faced by early-phase transition economies is of a more general nature. State-owned banks are generally undercapitalized – by international (Basle Accord) standards – and have sizeable bad loan problems. If the state is unwilling or unable to recapitalize the banks at an early stage (as in Poland) then the banks' only option is to try to increase revenue by setting lending rates much higher than rates paid to depositors (wide margins) and possibly also wide spreads by lending to SMEs at rates well in excess of prime lending rates (at the cost of aggravating the adverse selection problem and discouraging potential good borrowers, in particular). Also, excessive

Table 5.9 Drawing conclusions: are SMEs credit rationed by the Polish commercial banking sector?

Main criticisms	SME survey	Bank survey	Overall score	Possible implications	SME survey	Bank survey	Overall score
Too high collateral and other security measures	+	+	+	Unfair rejections (strong CR)	+/–	+/–	+/–
Excessive and unaffordable credit price	+	+	+	Discrimination against and weak CR of SMEs	+/–	+	+/–
Lack of business advice, counselling and consultancy	+	+	+	Limited availability of M&LT finance	≈ +	≈ +	≈ +
Lack of understanding and 'attitude problem' of banks	≈ +	≈ +	≈ +				
Alternative sources of finance unavailable	+	+/–	+/–				

Notes:
(+) justified criticism/supportive evidence.
(–) unjustified criticism/disapproving evidenced.
(+/–) mixed evidence.
(≈ +) broadly correct.

direct and indirect taxation of the banking sector contributes indirectly to the maintenance of low deposit and high lending rates (spreads).

In addition, given double-digit inflation, nominal interest rates have to be high in order to achieve the positive real interest rates necessary to exert downward pressure on inflation and encourage domestic saving and 'financial deepening'. It is thus potentially more difficult to generate a cash flow sufficient to service bank loans, and, as indicated in the survey responses, SMEs will be relieved as nominal rates fall (even if spreads and margins do not).

Finally, the rudimentary nature of the pre-transition monobanking or the succeeding 'two-tier' banking systems meant that, at the outset of the transition, banks offered only a limited range of services and operated with inexperienced loan officers, making them perhaps even more reluctant to lend commercially. The state-owned banks also remained tied to lending to the larger state-owned enterprises, limiting the supply of funds to SMEs (state or private) in general. Oligopolistic structure, financially weak private banks, limitations on entry and so on, further hamper price and non-price competition among the banks for depositors and the efficient uses of funds.

As expected, weak CR and discrimination was much more pronounced and the evidence for it was stronger. Strong CR, in general more difficult to prove, seemed to have existed especially during the period of 1992–93 (credit crunch), when the economy was in recession, the Polish government conducted contractionary monetary policy, financing requirements of the government were high because of the sizeable budget deficit and the banking sector witnessed severe problems with non-performing loans. With the economic improvement it is plausible to assume that the severity of strong CR started to diminish. 'Equity, information and counselling gaps' were very strongly pronounced, and these may have triggered the problems that the SME sector experienced with raising, especially M&LT, finance.

Summing up, although our survey yielded a mixture of evidence, whereby some place the blame for the existence of financial gaps on the supply side (for example, the banking sector), and some on the demand side (for example, the SMEs themselves), it has proved the existence of significant shortcomings and weaknesses present on both sides, which have most likely resulted in considerable differences in the banks' treatment of firms of different size, ownership and age. Usually, young, private and smaller firms were subject to less-favourable loan terms, which may be seen as some kind of discrimination against them. None the less, wherever the problems are found they will need to be resolved to ensure further development and expansion of the SME sector in Poland.

7 CONCLUSIONS AND POLICY RECOMMENDATIONS: TOWARDS IMPROVED AND EFFECTIVE SME FINANCING

The questionnaire responses are consistent with the findings of similar surveys of SMEs in more-developed (for example, G7) economies and are thus well documented elsewhere. Such problems are, however, exacerbated in transition economies by the higher level of uncertainty (greater information asymmetry) in the transition recession and problems with the supply and the quality of capital.

As stated above, the core problem, particularly overreliance on collateral and overdrafts and shortage of medium- to long-term fixed (and variable) rate loans, are well known in more-developed economies. Many countries address these market failures through loan guarantee schemes with fees charged to the borrower. The degree of subsidy in the fee and the extent of the guarantee (to the bank against loan loss) varies considerably (ranging from approximately 50 to 90 per cent). Not surprisingly, uptake is greater the lower the fee and the greater the guarantee. Some countries also use small business development banks/funds (for example, KfW in Germany, as described by Harm 1992) to disburse implicitly subsidized medium- to long-term, fixed or variable (according to the choice of the borrower), loans. The implicit subsidy derives from the non-profit (taxation) status of the KfW and government backing, which ensures that (largely bond) finance is raised cheaply. The level of importance accorded to the SME sector in developed countries has increased in recent years as it has come to be seen as the main source of new jobs. The EU has, for example, provided funds for disbursement (via the European Investment Bank) specifically targeting lending into the SME sector in order to create employment.

In transition economies it is even more important to generate new jobs quickly because the required pace of restructuring, which normally results in substantial workforce reduction, of the established (mainly state-owned) enterprises is much faster than in the developed economies, with which they are trying to compete from a starting point of much lower levels of labour productivity. Hence it is very important to ensure an adequate supply of external finance to SMEs with good growth prospects, whether they can post adequate collateral or not. Generous loan guarantees and the establishment of a fund to finance SME investment thus seem highly desirable at an early stage in the transition. Given lack of expertise in the banking system, it might be sensible to have the guarantees and SME investment loans disbursed by a specialist SME banks, staffed with experts from abroad (at least initially). A great deal of effort has been undertaken within the last few years, with substantial financial and technical help from the EU countries and the United

States. Yet, the scope of these programmes and the number of SMEs that have actually benefited from such assistance is rather insignificant. Thus, more incentives and more active involvement of both domestic and foreign institutions (including the government) is needed to make a significant difference.

Furthermore, over time the banks could been encouraged to enter into co-financing (with guarantees) agreements with the SME bank, which, as an SME lending culture and banking relationship are established, might progressively withdraw from lending itself. The SME bank (perhaps with regional branches) might also be a useful source of business advice, counselling and consultancy (in line with the UK's Business Link programme). Given that the SME bank is able to raise finance relatively cheaply, it would exert downward pressure on margins and spreads on SME investment loans, as in Germany.

As the transition progresses past the stablilization phase and into the post-transition recession recovery, attention could turn to equity financing. This will develop naturally following progress with privatization programmes, although, as in the UK, tax incentives may be needed to induce household capital into this more risky savings market. As the supply of venture funds increases, the financing options of the more ambitious SMEs will multiply. The guarantees will still be needed to induce an adequate supply of funds to smaller, bank-dependent, firms, however. The SME bank, through its lending and loan guaranteeing activities, will have an incentive to screen loans rigorously and, as in Germany, a double screening, by the proposing bank and the regional guaranteeing bank and/or the SME bank (KfW), would take place. This should increase the quality of lending. The SME bank could also pool information on credit risks in certain sectors of the economy, and on particular clients, for other banks to access.

The evidence from the questionnaires pointing to the existence of 'counselling and information gaps' was very strong. Advancement in these areas should be central and subject to increasing efforts, because it will benefit parties – the banks and their clients. Improvement of the availability, credibility and quality of supplied information should reduce the costs of screening and monitoring, and alleviate the problems of uncertainty and asymmetric information and this will result in cheaper, and safer lending. Further development of the banking sector and increased competition should also widen the menu of bank services and products. With their increasing variety it should be easier for SMEs to find services more suitable and adequate to their needs. Both initiatives should prompt the establishment of stronger links and broader cooperation between the firm, and its bank – a prerequisite for an established and long-lasting relationship.

Given the market failure, which is particularly serious in transition economies, the required government policy response is clear, namely: (i) the development and introduction of SME-friendly legal frameworks; (ii) the provision of subsidized loan guarantees and medium- to long-term fixed and variable rate loans to SMEs (especially growth-orientated ones with reasonably good prospects); and (iii) financial support for institutions providing advisory services to the SME sector, and collecting and disseminating credible information about potential customers (to the banks) and alternative sources of finance (to the firms). The cost of the subsidy will be offset by employment gains (saved costs of higher unemployment and beneficial social externalities) and the subsidy should be reduced as the gains through unemployment reduction decline. As the subsidy element in the loan guarantees declines, the government could begin to experiment with a risk-related guarantee premium charged to the banks (rather than to the customer).

Summarizing, our findings generally confirmed the hypothesis of credit rationing of SMEs exercised by the banking industry in the first years of transition in Poland. Our suggestions for closing the gap between demand and supply of finance to SMEs consisted of three parts.

First, what the financial system should do to improve the quality and quantity of services, and products provided (for example, promote a closer cooperation with their smaller customers by establishing SME departments, which should allow them to understand their needs better and offer suitable services; organize training courses for bank staff to increase their expertise at risk and creditworthiness evaluation, which should reduce the required level of loan collateralization; provide advice and counselling to their customers to improve the quality of information/reports received from them; resolve the NPL problem, which should help to break up the lines with the loss-making SOEs and direct more resources towards a dynamic and prosperous private sector; and so on).

Second, what actions the government should undertake to increase competition, reduce uncertainty, and increase availability of funds to the SME sector (for example, formulate an SME-friendly policy package aimed at strengthening the institutional and legal framework, and make a commitment that its consistency is not going to be disrupted when another stronger group starts lobbying for a change that suits its interests; improve the coordination and information flow between central and local governments, which should lead to a better, more efficient utilization of resources and avoid overlaps; remove the impediments to market entry for foreign banks and institutions, which should spur the competition and reduce the intermediation costs; get actively involved in the establishment, promotion and financial support of the institutions providing loan guarantees for the SME sector and those collecting and disseminating information about other sources of finance/quality of borrowers/and so on; reduce the level of direct and indirect taxation of the banking sector, and the level of NPL phenomenon; speed up the process of privatization of SOEs and state-owned banks; financially support the initiatives aimed at increasing the level of expertise of banks' staff and SMEs' management; introduce appropriate legal changes to encourage the development of alternative M&LT finance such as equity market, leasing and franchising; and so on).

Third, what SMEs can do to be perceived as more reliable and creditworthy (for example, increase the quality of information/reports provided to their bank especially during the screening process; if possible, try to employ an external adviser/expert to prepare the business plan/feasibility study; avoid 'double accounting'; enquire about other available sources of finance; try to develop a long-term relationship with their main bank; avoid delays in paying back their liabilities to the bank; and so on).

If the banks are to play a significant role in the economic recovery and growth, which, as the experiences of other countries have shown, is greatly facilitated by strong development and expansion of an efficient SME sector, increased and coordinated efforts to improve the relationships between those two sectors are essential and the involvement of all interested parties, including the government, is required. The long-term benefits of consistent policies promoting sound banking and efficient enterprise sector by far exceed any short-term costs.

NOTES

1. The following employment-based definition of an SME is used throughout this chapter: small enterprises employ 100 or fewer people; medium enterprises employ between 101 and 500 people; large enterprises employ more than 500 people. The comparisons are sometimes conducted by dividing sampled firms into two groups: small and smaller-medium firms (up to 250 employees; S&S), and bigger-medium and large firms (more than 250 employees; B&L).
2. Credit rationing is recognized as a direct consequence of asymmetric information, adverse selection, adverse incentive and moral hazard problems (Stiglitz and Weiss 1981). Two types of credit rationing are distinguished: 'strict' or 'non-price' credit rationing describes the situation in which there exists an excess demand for loans because the interest and non-interest price terms do not adjust to restore/maintain equilibrium in the credit market and some borrowers are rationed through the use of non-price conditions (Driscoll 1992). If the banks maintain the interest rate, but instead raise non-interest price conditions sufficiently, so that excess demand for loans is eliminated and market equilibrium is restored, and there are some borrowers unwilling to pay that price, then they are said to be subject to 'weak' or 'non-interest price' rationing, as indicated by Baltensperger (1978).
3. The finance gap can take three different forms, depending upon the type of finance concerned: the equity and debt gap (Macmillan gap) and the venture capital gap (Radcliffe gap). All gaps are recognized as a consequence of asymmetric information and uncertainty.
4. For the analysis of the most likely consequences of CR on SMEs' investment outlays and growth, see Pawlowska (1997).
5. For a more comprehensive discussion of inter-enterprise and tax arrears in economies of transition, see: Calvo and Coricelli (1994); Begg and Portes (1992); Schaffer (1995); Khan and Clifton (1992); Belka and Krajewska (Chapter 2 in this book); Rostowski (1994); Daianu (1994).

6. For details concerning the method of derivation of the IofI, see Appendix 3–6, Pawlowska (1997).
7. Loans division by maturity as appeared in the questionnaire is as follows: short term – up to one year; medium term – up to three years, and long term – over three years. This divisionis used throughout this chapter unless stated otherwise.
8. This tendency was also confirmed by the empirical analysis of enterprises (mostly medium and large in size) conducted in 1996 by Boguszewski et al. (1996). Another justification for higher demand for ST financing highlighted in our survey sample was high uncertainty in the long run (98 per cent of firms) jeopardizing any constructive assessment of the future profits and success of the investment project. Also, too low profitability of LT investment projects to pay back the principal plus the interest rate plus additional charges was mentioned by some 90 per cent of the sample. Only 14 per cent indicated banks' policy as the reason for their higher demand for ST financing.
9. In contrast to this result is the examination conducted by Maczynska and Zawadzski (1996) based on aggregated data describing firms operating in industry in the period 1993–95. According to their results, dynamics of ST bank finance of the manufacturing firms is still relatively higher than that of M&LT finance. They do not, however, distinguish between the enterprises on the basis of their ownership or size of employment. Moreover, the conclusiveness of this suggestion is undermined by the results of the analysis conducted by Boguszewski et al. (1996), who, based on aggregated data provided by GUS, proved that 62 per cent of the total value of LT bank credit extended in 1995 to the sampled enterprises went to 18 main branches of industry, of which coal mining, shipyards, energy and electricity, steel production and the car industry were among the main beneficiaries. Because these industries consist almost exclusively of large SOEs, it seems plausible to assume that the SME sector continued to be financed by ST credit.
10. For a very good discussion addressing the most important problems of credit–price discrimination against SMEs in general (part I) and in the Polish economy in particular (part II), plus a comprehensive list of relevant literature, see Luczka (1996a).
11. One can also look at the spread between the prime (refinancing) and lending rates. However, since the results are similar whichever method is used, we only present the conclusions drawn from using a six-month borrowing rate as an indication of banks' fund-raising cost.
12. Our results are broadly in line with the empirical analysis conducted in two commercial banks by Luczka (1996b). According to her results, in the period 1994–95 the average difference between lending rates charged on SMEs and that charged on large firms was approximately 12.72 percentage points in Bank A, and 9.5 percentage points in Bank B. The differences between the sampled banks related to the proportion of small and medium versus large customers receiving cheap, basic and expensive credit (for example, charged lending rates lower than, equal to or higher than the basic credit rate). In Bank A, the percentage share of small/medium/large size firms receiving cheap, basic and expensive credit was 4/24/72, 75/25/0 and 27/73/0, respectively. In Bank B, the ratios were higher and equalled: 38/51/10, 84/8/8 and 84/10/7, respectively. On average in both banks, SMEs were charged relatively higher lending rates, but loans in Bank A were more expensive.
13. The model, described in detail in Appendix 4–7, Pawlowska (1997), has been drawn from Dittus (1994a, 1994b). Our analysis, however, covers a longer period (five compared to two years), and the results obtained are different due to factual not assumed data.
14. Similar results were obtained by a group of economists from the World Bank (Pohl et al. 1996, p. 15): in their empirical analysis, assuming that NPL account for 25 per cent of the banks' portfolio and they will have to be written off over five years, in order to recover their loss banks would have to raise interest rate by about 7 percentage points. This increase would result in a lending spread of approximately 900 basic points.
15. On average, in the period 1990–95 monetary depth (calculated as M1/GDP) equalled 15.1 per cent and revealed a declining trend, whereas financial depth remained rather stable, oscillating around 35.0 per cent. For comparison, the financial depth ratio equals approximately 200 per cent in Germany, 100 per cent in Spain, 100 per cent in Hungary, 95 per

cent in the Czech Republic and 14 per cent in Russia. See Pawlowicz and Kulawczuk (1994), Pawlowska (1997).

16. On the other hand, however, one can think of the R^2 statistic as a squared correlation coefficient between the variables. Consequently, the correlation coefficient between the six statistically significant variables is approximately 0.529 (/0.28) and between all twelve variables 0.592 (/0.35). Thus, statistically there is a relatively strong relationship between the variables.
17. According to our adopted terminology, a firm charged a 'high credit price' when the spread between the lending and six-month deposit rate is equal to or higher than 15 percentage points. Thus, 'lower credit price' implies the spread less than 15 percentage points.
18. According to Dittus (1996) and Dittus and Prowse (1995), banks purposely avoid majority shareholding in excess of 20 per cent, forcing them to active corporate control. This type of behaviour would explain why after financial restructuring of SOEs there was no active shareholder to take responsibilities of further real restructuring of an enterprise as suggested by Belka and Krajewska (1996). For discussion about prerequisites for equity market and investment bank development, see Juchniewicz (1995), Lewszyk (1995).
19. The number of firms covered by the discriminant analysis was 13. Four firms were rejected because of missing data.
20. This worrying outcome, which if common may have significant negative consequences for the quality of the banks' portfolios, found confirmation in the empirical analysis (based on a firm-level questionnaire) of Boguszewski et al. (1996). According to their results, in 1995, 90 per cent (73 per cent) of firms experiencing severe (temporary) economic and financial problems were using bank finance, whereas 19 per cent (24 per cent) of firms in very good (good) conditions did not borrow at all. They estimated that in 1996 these relations will be subject to a positive change (that is, more good firms will apply and less troublesome enterprises will be granted a bank loan); however, the adverse impact on banks' portfolios is likely to be negative.
21. Very similar results were obtained in the research conducted by the group of economists from Gdansk Institute: the criteria influencing the banks' decision were ranked as follows: (i) full collateralization; (ii) good financial conditions of the company; (iii) LT relationships with the bank; (iv) sufficient participation of the firm in the planned project; (v) loan application prepared in a professional way; and (vi) a good idea. See Kulawczuk (1994, pp. 79–82).
22. For support of this postulate, see the results of the empirical research of the entire Polish commercial banking sector conducted in 1996 by the Research Institute of Business Outlook, PENTOR.
23. Because a small number of firms received investment loans, we decided to analyse investment loans by summing up the respective values in each year (although still recording the number of loans granted).
24. Excluding the firms that obtained a loan more than five times, the above indicators are slightly lower, that is, the average for the entire population equals 1.64, and the highest ratio of 1.80 was recorded in both 1990 and 1991. It is worthwhile noting that the highest ratio in 1991 coincides with the 'easy credit/money' policy conducted by the Polish government resulted in escalation of the non-performing loans in portfolios of the commercial banks.
25. Average size calculated excluding year 1989. High-value loans (that is, more than PLZ 5000 million) accounted for only 7 per cent, and were received by a small number of firms.
26. Additional evidence confirming this result is calculated by Pearson's correlation coefficient measuring the strength of relationship between firm and loan size. Its value has been steadily decreasing from 0.59 ($N = 29$) in 1989 to 0.26 ($N = 39$) in 1994, which implies that the discussed relationship has weakened over time. In the case of B&L firms, almost 55 per cent of the loans they received were of medium value.
27. This hypothesis finds confirmation in the results of an investment analysis conducted in Pawlowska (1997): according to the findings, S&S firms were not only responsible for

more than 60 per cent of total investment outlays, but more than 60 per cent of their projects were involved in new investment.

28. The respective figures for the population of borrowers (that is, excluding non-borrowers) were as follows: on average 86.4 per cent received an ST loan in the period 1989–94, with the following percentages in respective years: 80.6 per cent in 1989, 82.9 per cent in 1990, 94.6 per cent in 1991, 84.4 per cent in 1992, 87.5 per cent in 1993 and 88.6 per cent in 1994.
29. The derivation of this index is described in Appendix 3–7, Pawlowska (1997). The formula applied to calculate the index (as well as the name used) has been obtained from Binks et al. (1988, p. 93).
30. A value of the IoA of at least 0.40 means a good match; between 0.25 and 0.39, a reasonable match; between 0.10 and 0.24, a poor match; and below 0.09, a very poor match.
31. A few managers explicitly noted that banks favour bigger firms over small ones, and do not make any effort to encourage SMEs to develop closer relationships.
32. The above conclusions have also been emphasized in Gdansk Institute research: accordingly, 58 per cent of respondents perceived banks as uncompromising when dealing with SMEs, 36 per cent stressed banks' favouritism of bigger enterprises compared to smaller ones, 24 per cent regarded offered services and requirements as absolutely unsuitable for SMEs and 81 per cent considered that the turnaround time could be shorter if the organization was better. See Kulawczuk (1994, pp. 74–6; 83).
33. For example: the infamous 'Lech Grobelny case' in 1990, the 'Art-B scandal' in 1992, the privatization of Bank Slaski in 1993, and financial problems of the Lodzki Bank Rozwoju S.A., Interbank and Agrobank. For details, see Lipinski (1994, p. 3).
34. In order to estimate the real growth in fees one would have to calculate the proportion of banks' revenue derived from charges and the amount of charges per unit. Because of data shortage, we are unable to conduct this sort of examination.
35. For similar results, see Kreft (1994).
36. For details, see Pawlowska (1997).

REFERENCES

Alinska, A. and J. Kulawik (1994), 'Wybrane problemy z zakresu dostosowywania sie bankow spoldzielczych do warunkow gospodarki rynkowej' (Selected issues concerning adjustment of cooperation banking sector to market-orientated economy), *Bank i Kredyt*, No. 12, 31–8.

Apilado, V.P. and J.K. Millington (1992), 'Restrictive loan covenants and risk adjustment in small business lending', *Journal of Small Business Management*, January, 38–48.

Baltensperger, E. (1978), 'Credit rationing. Issues and questions', *Journal of Money, Credit, and Banking*, **10** (2), 170–183.

Barro, R.J. (1976), 'The loan market, collateral, and rates of interest', *Journal of Money, Credit, and Banking*, **8** (4), 439–56.

Begg, D. and R. Portes (1992), 'Enterprise debt and economic transformation: financial restructuring of the state sector in Central and Eastern Europe', *CEPR Discussion Paper*, No. 695, June.

Belka, M. and A. Krajewska (1996), 'The Polish Bank and enterprise restructuring program: debt/equity swaps. Survey results', Mimeo.

Binks, M. and C.T. Ennew (1996), 'Growing firms and credit constraint', *Small Business Economics*, **8**, 17–25.

Binks, M., C. Ennew and G. Reed (1988), 'The survey by the forum of private business on banks and small firms', in 'Small Business and Banks, A Two Nation Perspective', Report prepared for the Forum of Private Business and the National Federation of Independent Business, Mimeo.

Boguszewski, P., K. Puchalska and A. Bolek (1996), 'Wybrane elementy sytuacji ekonomicznej przedsiebiorstw w 1995r. w swietle badan ankietowych i danych GUS' (Some problems concerning the economic and financial situation in enterprises in 1995. Results of an empirical analysis based on micro-data and aggregated information provided by GUS), *Bank i Kredyt*, No. 10, 32–7.

Bolton, J.E. (1971), *The Bolton Committee, Small Firms. Report of the Committee of Inquiry on Small Firms*, Cmnd. 4811, London: HMSO.

Buch, C.M. (1996), *Creating Efficient Banking Systems. Theory and Evidence from Eastern Europe*, Kieler Studien 277, Institut für Weltwirtschaft an der Universität Kiel, Tübingen: Mohr.

Calvo, G.A. and F. Coricelli (1994), 'Inter-enterprise arrears in economies in transition', *Empirica*, **21** (1), 37–55.

Chojnacki, I. (1992), 'Za, a nawet przeciw ...' (For, and even against ...), *Gazeta Bankowa*, No. 23, 1, 19.

Cowling, M., J. Samuels and R. Sugden (1991), *Small Firms and Clearing Banks*, Association of British Chambers of Commerce Report.

Daianu, D. (1994), 'Inter-enterprise arrears in a post-command economy: thoughts from a Romanian perspective', *IMF Staff Paper*, No. WP/94/54.

Dittus, P. (1994a), 'Corporate governance in Central and Eastern Europe: the role of banks', *BIS Economic Papers*, No. 42.

Dittus, P. (1994b), 'Bank reform and behavior in Central Europe', *Journal of Comparative Economics*, **19**, 335–61.

Dittus, P. (1996), 'Why Eastern European banks don't want equity', *European Economic Review*, **40**, 655–62.

Dittus, P. and S. Prowse (1995), 'Corporate control in Central Europe and Russia. Should banks own shares?', *World Bank Policy Research Working Paper*, No. 1481.

Driscoll, M.J. (1992), 'Credit rationing in Europe', in A.W. Mullineux (ed.) (1992), *European Banking*, Oxford: Basil Blackwell, 65–91.

Harm, C. (1992), 'The financing of small firms in Germany', *World Bank Working Paper*, Country Economics Department, WPS 899, Washington, DC.

Harris, D.G. (1973), 'Some evidence on differential lending practices at commercial banks', *Journal of Finance*, **27** (5), 1303–11.

Hester, D.D. (1979), 'Customer relationships and terms of loans: evidence from a pilot survey', *Journal of Money, Credit, and Banking*, **11** (3), August, 349–57.

Hodgman, D.R. (1961), 'The deposit relationship and commercial bank investment behavior', *Review of Economic Statistics*, **XLII**, 257–68.

Juchniewicz, L. (1995), 'Uwarunkowania rozwoju bankowosci inwestycyjnej w Polsce' (Prerequisites for investment banking development in Poland), *Bank i Kredyt*, **11**, 4–10.

Kane, E.J. and B.G. Mankiel (1965), 'Bank portfolio allocation, deposit variability, and the availability doctrine', *Quarterly Journal of Economics*, **LXXIX**, 113–34.

Khan, M.S. and E.V. Clifton (1992), 'Inter-enterprise arrears in transforming economies: the case of Romania', *IMF Working Paper*, No. PPAA/92/1.

Kochav, D. et al. (1974), 'Financing the development of small scale industries', *World Bank Staff Working Paper*, No. 191, November.

Kondratowicz, A. and W. Maciejewski (1994), *Small and Medium Private Enter-*

prises in Poland: Their Dynamics and Institutional Environment, Warsaw: Adam Smith Research Center.

Kreft, J. (1994), *Biznesmeni oceniaja banki* (Banks' evaluation by Polish businessmen), *Gazeta Bankowa*, 27 August, No. 35, 1, 11.

Kulawczuk, P. (1994), 'Dzialalnosc kredytowa bankow w opinii firm prywatnych' (Banking sector evaluation by SMEs), in Pawlowicz and Kulawczuk (1994), pp. 63–91.

Lewszyk, R. (1995), 'Modele bankowosci inwestycyjnej-perspektywy rozwoju bankowosci inwestycyjnej w Polsce' (Models of investment banking and the perspectives for investment banking development in Poland), *Bank i Kredyt*, No. 6, 32–7.

Lipinski, S. (1994), 'Czy mozna ufac bankom?' (Can we trust the banks?), *Gazeta Bankowa*, No. 48, 3.

Luczka, T. (1996a), 'Problemy oprocentowania kredytu bankowego dla malego i sredniego przedsiebiorstwa prywatnego. Wybrane aspekty teoretyczne i prakyczne' (Price discrimination against SMEs. Theoretical and empirical discussion), *Bank i Kredyt*, No. 4, 4–11 (part I), No. 5, 87–95 (part II).

Luczka, T. (1996b), 'Surogaty kapitalu jako forma finansowania malego i sredniego przedsiebiorstwa prywatnego' (Alternative sources of external finance for SMEs), *Bank i Kredyt*, No. 11, 36–45.

Macmillan Committee (1931), *Report of the Committee on Finance and Industry*, Cmnd 3897, London: HMSO.

Maczynska, E. and M. Zawadzki (1996), 'Zadluzenie przedsiebiorstw-pomoc czy przeszkoda?' (External financing of enterprises – does it help?), *Bank i Kredyt*, No. 9, 19–27.

Mendelson, M. and J.W. Peake (1993), 'Equity markets in economies in transition', *Journal of Banking and Finance*, **17** (5), 913–31.

Mishkin, F.S. (1992), *The Economics of Money, Banking and Financial Markets*, 3rd edn, London: Harper Collins.

Monitoring Bankow 1992–1995 (1996), GUS, Department Finansow, Warszawa.

Pawlowicz, L. and P. Kulawczuk (1994), 'Udroznienie kanalow kredytowych' (Crediting SMEs), *Transformacja Gospodarki*, No. 49, Gdansk.

Pawlowska, A.E. (1997), 'Bank financing of small and medium size enterprises: an empirical investigation of credit rationing in Poland (1989–1995)', PhD dissertation, Birmingham University, Birmingham, UK.

Pohl, G., S. Djankov and R.E. Anderson (1996), 'Restructuring large industrial firms in Central and Eastern Europe. An empirical analysis', World Bank Technical Paper, No. 323, Washington, DC.

Polish Ministry of Privatization (1995), 'Information relating to the Universal Share Certificate', November.

'Powrot do lat piecdziesiatycyh ...' (Back in the 1950s ...) (1994), *Gazeta Bankowa*, No. 22, 20–21.

Radcliffe Committee (1969), *Report of the Committee on the Working of the Monetary System*, London: HMSO.

Rostowski, J. (1994), 'Inter-enterprise arrears in post-communist economies', *IMF Staff Paper*, No. WP/94/43.

Schaffer, M.E. (1995), 'Government subsidies to enterprises in Central and Eastern Europe: budgetary subsidies and tax arrears', *Center for Economic Performance Working Paper*, No. 671, September.

Stiglitz, J.E. and A. Weiss (1981), 'Credit rationing in markets with imperfect information', *American Economic Review*, **74**, 194–9.
Storey, D.J. (1994), *Understanding the Small Business*, London: Routledge.
Thorne, A. (1993), 'Eastern Europe's experience with banking reform: is there a role for banks in the transition?', *Journal of Banking and Finance*, **17** (5), 959–1001.
Wilson Committee (1979), *The Financing of Small Firms, Report of the Committee to Review the Functioning of the Financial Institutions* (1979), Cmnd 7503, London: HMSO.

APPENDIX 5A

Survey Design and Basic Characteristics of the Populations

In designing the questionnaire, we have drawn heavily on the experience of other studies examining the issue of financing the SMEs. At the time of preparing the questionnaire, there was no comparable research on the SME sector in Poland or other countries of Eastern Europe known to us.[1] The innovative and pioneering nature of our research proved to be disadvantageous. A number of errors and omissions have undoubtedly been made, despite modifications to our questionnaire made in the light of pilot studies. Yet, our investigation not only provides a valuable insight into financial relationships between the banking and SME sectors in Poland, but should also be recognized as a starting point and frame of reference for future studies.

The questionnaires were initially prepared in English, and only after extensive consultations were they translated into Polish. Pilot surveys were conducted in five firms and in one bank in mid-September 1994,[2] leading to the implementation of a number of amendments. The final versions contained about 65 questions grouped into six parts.[3]

Sampling and implementation

SME sector In our research we included firms fulfilling three main criteria: (i) they were registered companies, (ii) the number of employees at the time of the survey ranged between 20 and 500 people, and (iii) they were engaged primarily in manufacturing or construction. From the Business Foundation, an organization located in Warsaw providing a wide range of services for firms operating in Poland, we obtained a list of 500 firms which fulfilled these criteria. After the first selection process, in which we excluded non-profit institutions, government-affiliated establishments and all banking institutions, about 400 enterprises remained as potential respondents. We contacted by phone the managers of approximately 350 firms, of which 250 expressed their interest in participating in our research. In total, 82 questionnaires were returned (giving a response rate of 32.8 per cent). Responses were checked for completeness and elementary correctness, yielding generally satisfying results. Ultimately 60 questionnaires were sufficiently satisfactorily completed and representative (giving a response rate of 24.0 per cent) and these were used to form the population data base.

Banking sector Our plan was *not* to interview the highest number of banks possible, but to examine a sufficient number of types of banks divided on the basis of their size, location, ownership and so on, to enable us to conduct a comparative study among them in their approach to SMEs. Two groups of banks were excluded from the group of our future interviewers: cooperative banks (although this sector has a great deal of potential in becoming the leading force in the provision of banking services and external finance to the sector of SMEs) and two state-owned savings banks (namely, PKO SA and PKO BP).

In mid-October 1994 we referred to the Ministry of Finance, the Department of the Banking Sector and Financial Institutions, and the Polish Bank Association, with the request for support in conducting the interviews.[4] Between November 1994 and February 1995 we contacted first by phone/fax, then in person, 19 banks located around the country. Out of this number, only six banks were willing and/or able to comply with our request and completed the questionnaire.

The low number of respondent banks prevented us from making a cross-comparison of the treatment of SMEs among different types of banks. To overcome this problem, in addition to the questionnaire responses we used two sets of data: data describing the entire commercial banking sector published annually by the central bank and a complementary set of data constructed from financial information published in various issues of *Gazeta Bankowa* and covering 70 banks. Three groups of banks are distinguished: Group 1 includes four formerly specialized state-owned banks, Group 2 consists of nine commercialized banks hived off from the NBP in 1989 and the remaining private (domestic and foreign) banks constitute Group 3.

Basic characteristics of the population

SME sector In terms of *location*, the surveyed enterprises represented each region roughly in proportion to its contribution in the total number of firms nationwide. Almost one-third of respondent firms were located in Central Poland. Pomorze, Wielkopolska and Malopolska accounted for about 40 per cent. Enterprises from Slask contributed to just above 22 per cent. Two regions were underrepresented (Lubelszczyzna and Mazury, 10.5 per cent).

According to its *ownership*, the sample population is divided in two: 30 firms were state owned (including municipal firms) and 30 firms were privately owned (including cooperatives). Twelve firms had changed their ownership from public to private during the period under discussion.

The distribution of the sample population according to *the age of the business* is considerably skewed towards the more-established firms: 65 per cent of the survey population consists of enterprises of more than 25 years of age.

The distribution of responding firms in the *various sectors* of the economy diverges considerably from the distribution of enterprises nationwide, which

Table 5A.1 Representation of surveyed banks

Data on banks that responded to a questionnaire

	1990	1991	1992	1993	1994	1995	Average		Position in the banking sector*			
									Assets	Capital	Deposit	Credit
As percentage of banking sector												
Assets	12.3	14.7	16.3	15.1	13.2	16.7	14.7	Bank 1	6	6	8	4
Capital	40.8	23.8	17.1	18.1	19.2	7.3	21.0	Bank 2	14	12	12	12
Deposit	23.2	14.6	13.4	12.6	10.8	n.a.	14.9	Bank 3	5	15	12	13
Credit	21.2	19.3	19.5	17.7	17.7	18.7	19.0	Bank 4	8	7	7	7
As percentage of banking sector excluding banks of Group 1								Bank 5	19	19	21	25
Assets	32.0	43.0	43.1	35.9	37.3	39.1	38.4	Bank 6	38	39	n.a.	36
Capital	68.8	36.1	30.1	34.3	31.9	29.4	38.4					
Deposit	48.0	37.4	34.9	29.1	29.7	n.a.	35.8					
Credit	44.6	49.6	44.3	39.8	44.4	n.a.	44.5					

Data on banks published in *Gazeta Bankowa* (as a percentage of banking sector)

	1990	1991	1992	1993	1994	1995
Net assets (no. of banks)	n.a. (24)	91.7% (49)	87.3% (67)	86.4% (70)	78.3% (59)	86.4% (43)
Total loans (no. of banks)	89.9% (23)	85.9% (47)	90.1% (66)	90.0% (68)	79.5% (59)	81.4% (51)
Total deposits (no. of banks)	76.8% (21)	90.2% (47)	93.4% (65)	95.5% (69)	82.4% (59)	98.6% (52)
Total no. of banks	52	74	84	87	82	84

Note: * Ranking at end-1995 in the total population of 70 banks, including banks of Group 1.

follows from the approach adopted in our research. In our survey sample, heavy industry was overrepresented while light industry was underrepresented. The coverage of other sectors in the population is approximately in line with the national picture.

Before proceeding with the examination of the survey results in terms of the *distribution by employment*, it is necessary to mention that the requirements imposed on the firms participating in the survey were valid at the end of 1994. Hence there are enterprises in our population that at the end of 1994 fulfilled the employment criteria, but in the previous years their employment had exceeded the threshold of 500 people. In 1989 there were 11 firms with the number of employees exceeding 500 people, whereas in 1994 all the firms employed less than 500 workers. In general, the survey shows a bias towards medium-sized firms employing between 100 and 250 employees and away from those with very low or high employment. Moreover, the size of the firms measured in terms of the average number of employees in the six-year period has decreased by more than 50 per cent (an average sampled enterprise employed 470 people in 1989 and 221 in 1994).

Banking sector Out of the six interviewed banks, four were among the banks hived off from the NBP in 1989 (Group 2) and at the time of writing they were still operating in the form of joint-stock companies, fully owned by the State Treasury. Two remaining banks were established in 1990 and 1991 in the form of joint-stock companies, of which one had foreign participation (Group 3). In terms of location, two banks had their headquarters in Warsaw, two in Lodz, one in Cracow and one in Lublin.

Although the bank sample was small relative to the total number of banks, it does account for approximately 17.4 per cent of the total banking sector and almost 40 per cent of the state-owned banks from Group 1 are excluded (Table 5A.1). This is a consequence of the fact that four of them were on average ranked among the top ten banks, at 7.4th position, in the group of 70 commercial banks. Thus, even if we cannot statistically generalize from this sample to all banks, we can draw conclusions about an important segment of the loan market. Also, responses are usually expressed in percentage terms to eliminate problems associated with changes in sample size. Therefore, although with great prudence, one could treat the results of our analysis presented here as credible, but not free of possible exceptions.

NOTES

1. To be specific, there have been a number of empirical surveys conducted in Poland prior to the launching of our project (for a comprehensive list, see Kondratowicz and Maciejewski

1994, pp. 68–9); however, the vast majority of them covered a wide range of issues related to the private sector development (employment, production structure, capital utilization, export orientation, technology and finance). Thus, although these studies cast some light on the recent trends and tendencies in Poland, their relevance for those of us who were particularly interested in the bank–firm relationship, was rather insignificant. Only after the distribution of the questionnaires was completed, were a number of articles on private sector finance in Eastern Europe and Poland published.

2. We would like to thank Mr Bogusław Grabowski, at that time President of Petrobank Lodz, for his extensive assistance at this stage of our research at considerable cost of his time.
3. The questionnaire covered the following areas: (i) basic information; (ii) screening processes; (iii) borrowing activities; (iv) collateralization of loans; (v) monitoring; (vi) evaluation of banking/SME sector performance. A full version of the questionnaires is provided in Pawlowska (1997).
4. We would like to thank Mr Mieczyslaw Bojanczyk, at that time the vice-president of the Department of the Banking Sector and Financial Institutions, Ministry of Finance, for his kindness and invaluable help in recommending our research to the management of a number of interviewed banks. Also, we would like to express our gratitude to Professor Marek Balka, at the time of writing the Minister of Finance in the Polish government, for his interest, encouragement and for making it possible to conduct our research in two of the sampled banks.

6. Entry conditions, structure and performance in banking sectors in Central and Eastern Europe

Céline Gondat Larralde and Amine Tarazi*

1 INTRODUCTION

By way of introduction, we would like to summarize some recent or current trends experienced by Western banking systems. These new features, which underlie the themes developed in this chapter, must be seen as characteristic of the new organization of the whole financial industry.

The Growing Heterogeneity of Banking Structure

For more than two decades, the banking industry has been characterized by the growing heterogeneity of its structure: in fact, it is less and less confined to banks themselves, as more or less specialized firms have entered some segments of the banking market, each firm exercising skills and activities very different from each other's, and each entity adopting a very specific and rapidly evolving organizational configuration. This situation tends to enhance the distortions between the institutional definition of the banking system and the 'economic' definition of the banking industry.[1]

In such a context, the issue of the optimal organization of competition within the banking industry and between the banking industry and other financial industries has been revitalized. What kind of competition patterns are valid today in banking? This question may seem to be trivial at first sight; however, it may represent one of the most important challenges for the next decade. For instance, competitive distortions created by some privileges still granted to cooperative or mutual banks, to state-owned banks – especially in times of trouble, concerning the latter – or to other special financial institutions[2] have become recurrent banking events. So the optimal organization of

* We would like to thank Professors D. Lacoue-Labarthe and Andy W. Mullineux for their precious help and relevant remarks.

competition remains more than ever at the very heart of banking authorities' concerns, mainly because the banking industry is still granted some specificity in terms of regulation, if its situation is compared with other economic sectors. This fundamental feature derives from the banking firm's particular activity[3] which is at the root of its potential instability: any disruption, any interruption of its activity is regarded as extremely harmful to the community and justifies the existence of a specific regulation.

The Relative Instability of Banking Industry Performance

The progressive deregulation of financial and banking activities has considerably reduced the classical competition-orientated policy instituted by the Western banking authorities. Since the 1930s in the United States and in almost every domestic banking system since the Second World War, many banking rules were implemented that did not deal directly with safety and soundness issues, but instead aimed at restricting 'excessive' competition among banks themselves and between banks and other financial institutions.[4] Those restrictions were conventionally presented as counterparts of the banking system stability. By reducing actual and potential competition, the banking authorities succeeded in maintaining a higher profit distribution to incumbent firms. One consequence of this very strict banking regulatory framework has been the remarkable stability of domestic banking systems for almost three decades.

In the 1970s and in the 1980s, many studies emphasized the cost of entry regulation. The rise in competition stemming from deregulation and facilitated by progress in data-processing technology permitted considerable gains in terms of (allocative as well as production) efficiency, but some traditional 'fire walls' disappeared and as a consequence there has been a potential rise in several risks less easy to control. Banking authorities have endeavoured to offset this potential rise in instability by enforcing a more prudential (re)regulation-orientated policy towards banking risks. But this kind of control cannot be considered as neutral *vis-à-vis* competition and risk-taking behaviour: while it does not directly influence pricing mechanism, it still lays down conditions as for incumbency, exit, investment strategies and so on.

Until the end of the 1970s, with very few exceptions, banking authorities have usually succeeded in preventing banking crises, at least in limiting bank failures. This assertion is no longer valid, not since the US thrift débâcle that stands as a precursor of recent or current banking problems (see Brumbaugh 1993, and Kane 1985). The progressive financial deregulation permitted the conditions of trade-off between banking efficiency and stability to be renewed. This recent rise in instability – or more precisely the growing diversity of performance within the banking industry, or between domestic banking systems, mainly due to the fall in recurrent sources of profits – following a remarkably stable period has often been analysed as a symptom of 'excess capacity' in banking (see Llewellyn 1990), underlined by increasing competitive pressures, and it has often been compared with what happened in the US aircraft industry in the 1980s.[5]

These two tendencies – the growing heterogeneity and the relative instability of banking systems – are part of a wide movement of restructuring and reorganization of the financial industry. At the heart of the phenomenon, the role, the *raison d'être* of the banking firm and its integration into a more and more deregulated, competitive, globalized and market-orientated financial environment, but also the behaviour of public authorities and the efficacy of their actions as regulators, as supervisors, as shareholders of banking firms in some countries and as the entity in charge of monetary policy,[6] are triggering questions about banking regulation and its actual impact on the structure and performance of the banking industry.

Questioning Regulation Efficiency and Optimality

As banking activities are carried out increasingly within a market-orientated financial environment, some have called the application of the concept of efficiency to banking regulation itself and also for a reinforcement of 'market discipline',[7] rather than its replacement as the authorities had demanded in the past. In such a perspective, one should keep in mind that market exit then becomes the 'normal' sanction in the case of insolvency. So far, with only a few exceptions, it has been rather difficult for the authorities to apply this scheme in banking; failure in the banking industry is still granted a very particular status since some bank failures do not purely and simply prompt a competitor's exit without casting doubts over agents' confidence in the whole financial system.

Emphasizing regulatory conditions of admission to the banking industry today may, at first sight, seem somewhat extraordinary and outdated; this kind of analysis may seem much less relevant nowadays than it did twenty or thirty years ago, if you refer to the competitive and regulatory current framework in Western countries, where exogenous barriers to entry ensuing from regulation tend to decrease; besides, recent studies underline 'endogenous' economic barriers, those coming from the specificity of banking output process and banking assets.[8] As the protection from competitive forces that regulation provides tends to disappear, banking firms are today more inclined to make use of those endogenous or 'economic' barriers to impede or delay entry. However, this approach may be of interest because it may enable us to anticipate better any future changes in the structural and regulatory features of Eastern European banking systems.

Summing up the present theoretical and empirical work on the impact of entry regulatory conditions on competition and performance in the banking industry is not an easy and riskless task. Our inventory cannot be exhaustive and we hope it will at least be representative even though often allusive. After briefly reviewing the importance of (actual and potential) entry in competition theory (Section 2), we analyse the impact of regulatory entry restrictions on banking structure and performance in the light of empirical analyses developed from the 1960s to the 1990s (Section 3). Finally, we try to focus our attention on Central and Eastern Europe, searching for a potential link between their banking market structure and their performance (Section 4). Section 5 concludes.

2 ENTRY AND COMPETITION IN THE BANKING INDUSTRY: REVIEW OF THE THEORY

The Long Predominance of the Structuralist Approach

For several decades, the traditional model developed by industrial organization theory, based on the structure–conduct–performance paradigm (SCP or structuralist approach), which borrows some of it results from classic oligopoly theory (see, for instance, Stigler 1964), established a general framework to study competition by providing a general statement on the determinants of performance in an industry. It permitted effects due to some market structures on the state of competition to be explained, emphasizing the impact of entry conditions on concentration and, overall, the impact of concentration on prices and margins.[9] The structuralist argument is based on stylized facts underlined by Bain (1956) and others in the 1950s, in their inter-industrial empirical work: there would be a positive link between concentration and performance, particularly in industries characterized by strong barriers to entry.[10]

As has already been underlined in the late nineteenth century, potential as well as actual entry restricts the ability of firms present in an industry to maintain their monopoly position: the threat of entry by new competitors puts a constraint on the custom of established firms to conduct their operations in ways that adversely affect consumers, as an expectation of high profits entices new firms to enter the market. Incumbent firms then have two options: either they set an entry-forestalling price that makes it unprofitable for a new firm to enter, or they continue to charge the higher (monopoly) price. In the latter case, if entry is free, new entry may occur and the increased number of firms will eventually drive prices and profits down. In the former case, the mere anticipation of entry induces incumbents to lower their prices towards more competitive levels and thus entry does not necessarily have to occur to have an impact on market performance.

A benchmark in this respect has been established recently by Baumol et al. (1988) who applied the label 'perfectly contestable' to markets in which incumbent firms and potential entrants share the same technology and potential competitors can enter and exit without loss during the time taken by incumbents to change prices. The theory of contestable market – or the theory of 'ultra free entry' as Shepherd (1984) called it – is an extreme characterization of market performance that relies on the assumption that entry and exit are cost free. In such a context (absence of barriers to entry and exit[11]), oligopolistic firms granted with very important market shares – and in the extreme case, a monopoly firm – cannot develop any market power and their performances will be similar to those obtained in a perfectly competitive market. This theory suggests that in order to reduce market dominance, policy should be directed at entry (and exit) barriers, while the traditional approach recommended that policy should be directed to internal conditions such as antitrust actions.

The Relevance of Industrial Organization Models and Concepts in Banking

In view of recent changes in banking, are industrial organization models relevant in describing bank behaviour and the functioning of the banking industry? One should rather admit that the functioning of the banking industry cannot be described by a unique model, since market structures today differ from one banking product or one banking service to another. Some market segments may be characterized by a strong elasticity of demand while others may not. Oligopoly situations may exist in some banking segments while other segments may face a very competitive environment. Competition in every banking activity has not intensified in the same way and according the same pattern.

The limits of the traditional model of industrial organization

Although the traditional approach underpins our current understanding of bank behaviour, it does not provide a complete explanation of it. In the early 1960s, the banking industry in the United States was brought under the jurisdiction of antitrust law; then economists began to investigate the SCP relationship in US banking. Rejecting the traditional explanation – a non-competitive price behaviour in concentrated markets obtained by collusion – the Chicago–UCLA thesis, developed in the 1970s by Stigler (1968) and others, stipulates that market concentration reflects the differential efficiencies of incumbent firms (concentration is then considered as a consequence of high market shares obtained by efficient firms which earn economic or Ricardian rents (because of lower costs), not monopoly rents) and most of the important types of barriers to entry arise from restrictions on market conduct imposed by the authorities (see Scherer and Ross 1990). An important public policy question is at stake in this debate since the Chicago–UCLA thesis suggests that any antitrust action or any action impeding or delaying mergers is likely to be counterproductive from an efficient point of view. It seems that this approach has been welcomed favourably by the Western banking authorities for several years now.[12]

The structuralist approach is based on an oversimplified description of the banking firm which is usually considered as a single-product firm maximizing its non-risk-adjusted profit. The progressive cut in entry, or more generally mobility, barriers enhances the significance of 'economic' barriers to entry; nowadays, established firms are more often inclined to reinforce or to make better use of this tool to impede any potential competition: the 'cost structure' factor has become even more central today in strategic decisions of banking firms. Although it is essential in such a context to focus on the specific nature of the banking output process and banking asset characteristics (for example, the minimal efficient size of the banking firm, joint-cost economies and multiproduct analysis), structuralist studies trying to estimate the impact of regulatory barriers never take into account those endogenous barriers to entry and the potential interactions that might result.

Dietsch (1992) focuses on two limits of the SCP approach. First, he emphasizes the SCP limit that stems from the meaning granted to the notion of market power: firms' preferences may change as their market power increases or decreases, a factor which is certainly not taken into account in the SCP approach. As the Edwards–Heggestad–Mingo hypothesis stipulates,[13] the portfolio structure of a bank (whose market power has increased) may change but this result may not necessarily be reflected in its performance. Moreover, a firm increasing its market power may be more likely to incur a rise in operating costs (in particular staff expenses) as models of the managerial firm stipulate. Finally, introducing the notion of market power in banking analysis raises some serious questions: even in the case of collusion, the ability of banks to set prices (interest rates on loans and deposits) is limited by the presence of a very special agent in banking markets, the Central Bank, which is in possession of a wide range of regulatory/economic actions in order to influence prices charged by banks. As noted by Meltzer (1969), if a market power exists in the banking industry, this market power is the Central Bank's power to which banks' market power is tightly subordinate.

Second, borrowing some results from the classical oligopoly model, the SCP approach concludes that an industry characterized by economies of scale will be inefficient as it may lead to a situation of destructive competition; so it is necessary to regulate and control such an industry. This model lays the foundations of financial regulation, implemented until the beginning of the 1980s, which was specially orientated to restrict 'excessive' competition. The contestable market theory challenged this result at the beginning of the 1980s, asserting that this result cannot be relevant in the case of a multiproduct industry.

Contestability as a new reference to analyse competition within the banking industry?

The contestable market literature challenges the methodology and the conclusion of the traditional framework. The feature of markets which determines performance in this model is barriers to entry and exit, not the number of incumbent firms on a market. This model has been developed in order to describe markets (even monopoly markets) in which firms are unable to exploit their internal market power because there are no barriers to entry or to exit. It turns out to be a very useful model to understand and analyse competition in some segments of banking activities while it integrates some very interesting concepts pertinent in banking (for example, sunk costs,[14] cost subadditivity and multiproduct analysis); some of its results are compatible with those of recent oligopoly models. But its scope may be rather limited by its complexity; and the conditions under which a contestable configuration is efficient are very restrictive. In fact, the relative importance of sunk costs determines the nature of competition that prevails in the different segments of the financial industry. If there are no sunk cost investments to be incurred in order to enter one particular segment of the banking industry, the results and performance may be in accordance with those of perfect competition, even if firms have to incur important sunk costs, But the absence of sunk costs does not prohibit price warfare or collusion. The existence of sunk costs to be incurred in order to enter one particular segment of an industry prevents it from being 'contestable'.

Dietsch (1992) proposed a typology of sunk costs in banking based on their nature:

- there can be technological sunk investments that can only be used in banking, such as investments in some data-processing tools;
- there may be some institutional sunk costs if, for instance, there are no second-hand markets in which some banking equipment can be traded; and finally,
- sunk costs may be of a strategic kind, such as advertising outlays – although they represent only a tiny part of operating costs in banking – or more generally any expenditure linked to non-price competition strategies. Excess capacity in branch offices by banks (emphasizing the

proximity link between a bank and its customers) in order to maintain their pre-emptive right on their local markets should be considered as a frequent example of strategic sunk investments.

Dietsch underlined sunk costs in traditional loan activities focusing on the informational asymmetries between a borrower and a lender. In order that the bank loan contract can play its incentive role, the bank must incur investments that commit it for a long-term period. The bank will then obtain private information on borrowers that no other banks can easily get and use – this information has no value outside the bank – so these investments should be considered as sunk.[15] Some economists, such as Sharpe (1990), have gone further in this analysis asserting that banks incurring this kind of sunk investments may thus be able to 'capture' their customers.

3 ENTRY REGULATION AND BANKING INDUSTRY: REVIEW OF EMPIRICAL WORK

There are no empirical studies estimating directly the impact of one particular regulation on the performance realized by agents subject to such regulation. The studies analyse this issue indirectly: first, economists try to conjecture, more or less implicitly, the effects of regulation on the structure of the industry under regulation, and then they try to estimate the impact of structure on performance. Banking studies have not found a positive relationship between concentration and profitability as consistently as it has been found in the inter-industry studies.

Studying the Impact of the Conditions of Entry in Banking on Actual Entry

Observing entry rates and changes in banking regulation

To achieve its goal – maintaining a safe and sound banking system, avoiding any disruption in the payments system and preventing any contagion effect – banking regulation is aimed at both market structure (regulating the context in which banking activity is conducted) and banking behaviour (influencing directly banking conduct by constraining some individual decisions). This distinction is useful in the study of banking regulation although both regulations are linked. We shall focus on the first type of regulation, operating directly on market structure, that is to say, regulatory provisions and actions aiming at restricting entry or controlling the size of the firms (chartering laws, branching and bank holding company expansion restrictions) and which can be summarized as dealing with the issue of an optimal size and the risk that excessive concentration may cause, although other provisions may interact with them and bias or exacerbate their impact on actual banking structure.

Regulatory conditions limiting access to national and/or local banking markets A new entrant wishing to set up a business in the banking industry has to apply for a charter from national (and/or in some cases, for example in the United States, from regional) chartering agencies who used to rely heavily on the 'convenience and needs of the community' criterion to refuse or to delay entry. By observing entry rates through periods marked by changes in these kinds of entry legal restrictions, it seems that they have put a significant constraint on bank entry or branch office openings. But graphical analyses which consist only in paralleling several tendencies – or more precisely what is intuitively perceived as tendencies – rapidly reach their limits since no serious statistical analyses are conducted to confirm or to invalidate conclusions that have been reached.

The US has a dual banking system with entry regulation divided between the state and several federal authorities. State regulations are not uniform, some states being considerably more severe than others; there are also differences between the federal agencies.[16] At any moment, a bank has the right to switch charters in either direction. This key attribute of the dual system – this element is not a product of any original intent or design, according to Scott (1979) – has been considered sometimes as 'an opportunity to escape arbitrary supervision' and 'a vital check against the development of oppressive or capricious supervisory practices'. In general, competition among chartering agencies would seem to limit any single agency's power to restrict entry in the United States: if one agency restricted entry severely, banks seeking charters would go to another agency. Scott (ibid.) studied the impact of this competition between chartering agencies. He has observed significant bank conversion trends for 1950–74, but this situation has to be mitigated in terms of the percentage of assets in the whole banking system. However, his analysis emphasizes the dual banking system as a dynamic and interactive regulatory structure and as a potential strength in relaxing entry restrictions.

In Figure 6A1.1, Keeley (1985)[17] plotted entry rates for US commercial banks between 1921 and 1983. According to him, the evidence supports the notion that there was a significant decline in the rate of commercial bank entry during the period following the Banking Act of 1935 (which set up a federally administered 'needs' criterion for chartering federally insured banks) until 1962. In 1961, a much more liberal Comptroller of the Currency was appointed. It seems that his policy did have a significant effect on raising entry rates.[18] But looking at entry in banking only in terms of entry by new commercial banking organizations introduces a bias and probably understates entry because of the possibility of entry through branching, or because of increased competition by non-depository institutions. The deregulation trend in banking seems to have occurred in an environment in which entry restrictions have been substantially relaxed. The fundamental role played by innovations in data-processing technology in the 1960s and 1970s in eroding restrictions on entry and competition should also have been emphasized.

Until the mid-1960s, the French banking system was known for its low 'birth rate' and low 'mortality' as De Boissieu (1990) noted: its oligopolistic structure after the Second World War was quite remarkable. At the end of the 1960s, a major change appears in the current attitude of French banking authorities: the 'need' criterion has been replaced by a more prudential approach (capital requirements); authorities' fears of an excess supply of banking services seemed to have disappeared, or at least they have been mitigated. The impact of regulatory changes on evolution of branch openings is obvious (see Muldur 1993). Shortly after the first deregulation shock in 1966, a sharp rise in the number of branch office openings can be observed until 1975. This period is known in France as *la course aux guichets* (or the run for branch office openings). The implementation of a (flexible) control in 1982 and 1986 does not seem to have had a strong impact. At the end of 1986, total free branching was implemented for networks that were granted no tax privilege. However, the number of openings remained stable; so it seems that today, openings are more sensitive to economic and financial conditions than to changes in entry regulation.[19]

Selective monetary policy tools and prudential regulation These factors may also impede or delay entry. Prudential regulation, as it is applied to everyone, cannot be considered as a genuine barrier to entry. But some researchers have shown, for instance, that in the United States, the legal lending limit of 10 per cent of capital to any one borrower might force unit banks to raise significant capital before obtaining a charter (thus delaying entry), otherwise they could have had little flexibility in competing for business loans with other types of banks. One should also insist on some specific regulatory or tax entry conditions applied in case of mergers and acquisitions, specially when the acquirers are foreigners.

Testing the impact of entry restrictions on banking structure

In a classic study dealing with the effect of chartering on the rate of bank entry, Peltzman (1965)[20] concluded that chartering reduced the rate of entry by at least 50 per cent compared to what would have occurred without such restrictions; for a long time, this result has been widely accepted by economists and government officials. Peltzman's finding is based on a comparison of the rate of entry prior to the passage of the Banking Act of 1935 and the creation of the Federal Deposit Insurance Corporation (FDIC), which he characterizes as the 'free banking' era, to the 1936–62 period during which, he argues, federal–state competition for chartering insured banks was effectively eliminated (although we can raise doubts about this assertion). He tried to estimate what conduct would be adopted (entry) if chartering regulation did not exist and then he compared this result to what actually happened; the difference between both situations is supposed to represent a measure of the impact of this regulation.

Edwards and Edwards (1974) cast doubt upon this result although they agree with the final conclusion: the significance of the impact of entry regulation on actual entry. They rightly noted that Peltzman's (1965) work fails to take complete account of the indirect effects of regulation – restrictions on entry cause firms in the industry to earn higher profit rates so the profit rate used to predict (desired) entry in Peltzman's equation is higher during the period of entry restrictions than it would have been in their absence. They develop an alternative model using the expected profit rate as a guide for regulators' policy while Peltzman implicitly assumes that regulators refuse entry to applicants in each year by an amount equal to a constant proportion of the existing bank population in that year (a constant refusal rate policy).

Even if these studies may seem today to have been superseded and 'simplistic' – without mentioning the interactions that exist between the different kinds of regulation which are not taken into account as Jacobs (1965) had already noted – they have constituted one of the very few attempts to evaluate statistically the impact of one particular regulation on the banking structure.

Charter value, market power and changes in regulatory entry barriers
According to Keeley (1990), regulatory restrictions on entry and on competition in the 1950s and 1960s made bank charters valuable. One consequence of this situation is that with valuable charters as assets, banks had the incentive not to fail since the owners of the banks cannot sell the charter once the bank is declared insolvent: its potential loss created a regulatory bankruptcy cost from the point of view of the bank owners. Keeley examined the relationship between changes in regulatory entry barriers and the market power of US commercial banks in order to create an instrument for charter value, and then he estimated the relationship between market power and risk taking from 1970 to 1986.[21] As suggested by Lindenberg and Ross (1981), Keeley (1990) uses Tobin's q – the ratio of market value of the firm to replacement costs of its assets – as a measure of a bank's market power. The branching variables are dummy variables reflecting the liberalization during a previous period of branching, multibank holding company and interstate expansion laws in the state in which the bank is located. Liberalization of branching or multibank holding company expansion laws in the previous period is associ-

ated with a statistically significantly (at the 1 per cent level) lower market-to-book asset ratio. This result seems to suggest that both branching and multibank holding company expansion restrictions did provide banks a degree of protection from competition.

Estimating the Structure–Performance Relationship in Banking

There are two kinds of studies designed to provide evidence on how market structure influences the performance of banks: some studies estimate the relationship between measures of bank market structure and performance; others estimate the cost structure of the banking industry. In this survey, we have paid attention only to the first category, but some recent studies have tried to integrate some cost structure analyses into structure–performance estimations.

Searching for a possible positive statistical link between concentration and performance

A first approach is to estimate the behaviour and the performance of an industry whose structure has actually been modified, that is to say, to perform a comparative analysis (the situation before/after the change). This approach allows us to answer two questions. First, one is able to analyse the motivations governing entry: is the performance of banks located in a local market that is about to experience changes in its structure significantly different from the performance of similar banks located in a market whose structure will not change? Second, what is the actual impact of entry on the performance and behaviour of incumbent banks? Studies using this analytical framework reached contradictory conclusions: for instance, while Fraser and Rose (1972) found that entry significantly improves performance, especially in the portfolio selection of existing firms, Peltzman (1968) showed that entry rates reduce the returns of existing banks.

An alternative and much more common approach is to include in performance models explanatory variable(s) representing the regulatory conditions of entry: the simultaneous impact of barriers to entry and concentration as well as other factors can then be estimated. Shortly after the Philadelphia National Bank case in 1963, economists began to investigate the SCP relationship in US banking in a similar way to that done in inter-industrial studies which found a positive relationship between concentration and performance, although it is difficult to define what a banking market really is (for example, local market, industry specificity in terms of regulation, in terms of output processing). The US banking industry at this time perfectly lent itself to this kind of analysis: although it had more than 14 000 banking ‘entities’, it was highly concentrated on a local basis.

Many studies (see Appendix 6A2) implement this analytical framework and several surveys have been carried out since Benston's (1973) survey. They reach relatively contradictory conclusions. For instance, reviewing 39 studies between 1961 and 1977, Rhoades (1982) concludes that 30 of them found a positive link between concentration and performance (although he includes some studies in which only a minority of tested equations reached this conclusion), while Osborne and Wendell (1978) conclude that no real empirical evidence of a positive link is found.

Focusing on specification and estimation problems, Heggestad (1979) notes that all these studies share a common weakness: there is no rigorous theoretical model connecting concentration and equilibrium price (or any other measure of performance) and many of the banking studies make no attempt to develop a conceptual model. As a result, they often omit important variables and are subject to interpretation problems. However, basing his conclusions on the most rigorous studies (Gilbert (1984) eventually reaches the same conclusion), he considers that the level of concentration of market in which a bank is located is a significant positive determinant of performance. But the impact of other structural variables, such as those relating the impact of entry regulation to performance (studies which tried only to distinguish between different types of branching and bank holding company laws), is markedly less foreseeable. Therefore, these studies cannot support any general conclusions concerning the influence of state branching restrictions on measures of bank performance. Moreover, Gilbert notes that the issue of the potential impact of other types of regulation, such as ceilings on interest rates on time and savings deposits and usury ceilings on the relationships between concentration and performance, is never taken into account.

In order to explain this weak relationship between concentration and performance in banking, some economists noted that the linear form adopted by most studies might be unsatisfactory: there might exist some critical concentration level above which the relationship is no longer valid. Jackson (1992) re-estimated the equations used by Berger and Hannan (1989), dividing their sample into three subgroups according to concentration level, and found that the structure–price relationship was valid only for the weak concentration subgroup. Although Berger and Hannan (1992) argue the robustness of this result, they agree that the relation between price and concentration varies according to concentration levels and time periods.

Both Heggestad (1979) and Gilbert (1984) call attention to 'extra market structure', that is to say, any potential competition that might influence the behaviour and the performance of banks on a local market: for instance, Hannan (1979) finds that the number of relatively large banks that could establish branches in a market area, but have not yet done so, helps to explain the interest paid on savings deposits by commercial banks. Similarly,

Heggestad and Mingo (1977) report that the minimum service charge on standardized personal deposit accounts was about $1.5 per month lower in areas in which thrift institutions were also allowed to offer cheque account.

Discriminating between the two potential explanations of the structure–performance relationship

A new wave of empirical studies have tried to perceive which one of the two theoretical models[22] is the most appropriate one, as both reach contradictory conclusions in terms of regulation.

The first studies trying to distinguish between both hypotheses included another structural variable among the independent variables used to explain performance, accounting for each bank's market share. Once each bank's market share is properly accounted for, concentration of the market in which the bank is located adds nothing towards explaining bank profit rates. Market share is positively and significantly related to profitability, even after controlling for concentration. Smirlock (1985), using this methodology based on Weiss's (1974) work, suggests that any effect of concentration reported in previous studies is spurious and probably due to a correlation between profitability and the omitted market share variable, and he views his findings as supporting the efficient-structure hypothesis over the traditional hypothesis as a description of banking markets. However, this methodology supposes that market share reflects only efficiency or relatively large efficiency, not their market power: according to Smirlock (1985), only efficiency allows a large market share to be acquired and market power can only be obtained by collusion.

An obvious solution to Smirlock's problem is to include a measure (or even two) of bank efficiency directly into the model, using a stochastic cost frontier, as Berger (1995) proposed. By testing the relationship between performance and efficiency directly, the relationship between performance and concentration has a clear-cut interpretation. Although these recent studies do not reach clear conclusions, in a sense they permit a unification of both methods used to analyse how market structure influences the performance of banks since they integrate cost structure estimations of the banking industry in studies focusing on the relationship between measures of bank market structure and performance.

Moreover, while past studies focused almost exclusively on US local banks servicing individuals and small businesses, some of the recent studies have adopted a national framework as the reference market instead of a local market: they try to investigate the structure–performance relationship for European banking (for example, Molyneux and Thornton 1992 or Goldberg and Rai 1996). This issue is especially important today as the Second Banking Directives now allows European banks chartered in one country to open branches in other European countries. Although there is general agreement that the recent liberalization will result in cross-border mergers and alliances, it is still unclear whether the banking industry in Europe will eventually be dominated by a few supranational banks. The nature of the structure–performance relationship must be understood better in order that the European governments can determine whether to strengthen or weaken existing anti-trust laws.

4 AN EMPIRICAL ANALYSIS OF CENTRAL AND EASTERN EUROPEAN BANKING

The aim of this empirical analysis is to assess the effect of market structure on bank profitability in Central and Eastern Europe. The main goal is to check whether the standard results obtained in the case of the United States and Western Europe hold for banking firms established in Central and Eastern Europe. Of course, the results we obtain should be considered with extreme care since information on these banking systems is still poor and certainly not reliable enough to draw rigorous conclusions.

The data in this study are composed of balance sheet and income statement information for banks for the year 1994. Standardized accounting data were obtained from IBCA (International Bank Credit Analysis Ltd), a London-based credit agency. After sorting the data for statistical purposes a sample of 177 commercial banks, operating in 11 countries in Central and Eastern Europe (Bulgaria, Croatia, the Czech Republic, Estonia, Hungary, Latvia, Lithuania, Poland, Slovenia, Romania and the Slovak Republic) could be retained. The sample includes most of the major banks in each country in order to allow concentration analysis, but in some cases information could be collected for only ten or fewer banks.

List of Variables

Dependent variables

ROA: return on assets % (net income/assets)

ROE: return on equity % (net income/equity)

Independent variables

CONC: three-bank asset concentration ratio %

PARM: market share of a bank % (bank assets/total assets)

LTA: bank size variable (log of bank assets)

KOA: capital ratio % (equity/assets)

Di, $i = 1, \ldots, 11$: dummy variable for country i.

Presentation of the Sample

Table 6.1 shows descriptive statistics on performance measures and concentration for our complete sample and Table 6.2 gives detailed information for each country included in the sample. The three-bank asset concentration ratio (*CONC*) and average return (*ROA*) both reveal high differences among countries. Note that the measure of concentration for each country is sample specific and its reliability depends essentially on the inclusion of the largest banks in each banking system. From a casual inspection of our samples, the largest banks do not seem to be omitted in our study. However, because our definition includes commercial banks only, it may yield results that differ from those obtained by other studies.

Table 6.1 Structure and performance measures in the global sample

	Total assets (US$ thousands)	*CONC*	*ROA*	*ROE*	*KOA*
Mean	723 034.6	60.39680	1.347428	–99.61017	14.16369
Median	199 298.0	60.75000	1.027961	8.108108	11.52250
Maximum	11 175 903.0	89.10000	18.49377	211.7370	66.39004
Minimum	5 529 000.0	42.19000	–12.57297	–16110.00	–3.996815
Std deviation	1 392 760	13.84872	2.995077	1247.633	11.07610
Observations	169	169	169	169	169

Table 6.2 Structure and performance for each country in the sample

	Number of banks	Total assets Mean (US$ thousand)	*ROA* (%) Mean	*CONC* (%)
Bulgaria	18	536 684.70	1.26	60.75
Croatia	23	502 256.20	0.28	70.43
Czech Republic	16	1 776 398.00	0.26	78.08
Estonia	9	57 758.01	1.54	71.57
Hungary	28	632 230.90	1.34	42.19
Latvia	8	77 419.50	2.68	54.07
Lithuania	7	83 280.86	0.23	66.83
Poland	31	922 551.60	2.36	45.73
Romania	9	926 777.80	3.30	72.56
Slovenia	13	336 435.80	0.92	63.40
Slovak Republic	7	1 688 554.00	0.74	89.10

Method and Results

The method used in this chapter is essentially based on Smirlock (1985), Berger and Hannan (1989) and Molyneux and Forbes (1995). A cross-sectional profit equation which includes market share and concentration as well as bank size (log of total assets) and capital ratios is estimated using OLS procedure. Correction for heteroskedasticity was implemented using White's method. Variables *LTA* (log of total assets) and *KOA* (equity/total assets) are control variables defined to capture diversification effects and capital structure effects that may differ among banks. Dummy variables are also used in some of the equations to capture country-specific effects. Table 6.3 shows the results obtained for the global sample of 177 banks and Table 6.4 those obtained for two subsets of countries differentiated by the degree of concentration of their banking systems.

The results in Table 6.3 show that concentration is negatively related to profitability (equation with *ROA*), whereas studies in the case of the United States and Western Europe show the opposite effect (for example, Molyneux and Thornton 1992). Moreover, the positive link between market share and profitability, a standard result that holds in the case of the United States (Smirlock 1985), is not confirmed here. Since our measure of concentration is highly sample specific and therefore may be considered as arbitrary, we removed it from the regressions including dummy variables for each country. The lack of a link between market share and profitability is still confirmed in that case.

Since previous studies showed that the positive link between concentration and profit was stronger when the considered markets were less concentrated originally, the tests were carried out for two samples of countries depending on the level of concentration of their banking markets. The low concentration group includes banks operating in markets where the three-bank asset concentration ratio is lower than 60 per cent and the high concentration group includes banks operating in markets with a ratio higher than 60 per cent (Table 6.4).

The results in Table 6.4 show that concentration has a positive impact on profit only when the considered banking markets are originally weakly concentrated (*CONC* < 60 per cent) that is, when considering banks operating in Latvia, Hungary and Poland. For the remaining countries (*CONC* > 60 per cent), higher concentration does not affect profitability and therefore the results obtained above for the global sample are invalidated. Thus the results we obtain for Central and Eastern European countries appear similar to those obtained in the case of the United States and Western Europe.[23]

However, since our measure of concentration is less reliable in this case where even fewer observations are available, the more reliable test of the

*Table 6.3 Global sample (*ROA *and* ROE *as dependent variables without/ with country dummies)*

	ROA	*ROA*	*ROE*	*ROE*
C	1.650		−2104.757	
	(0.465)		(−1.117)	
CONC	−0.035[2]		−2.222	
	(−3.163)		(−1.057)	
PARM	0.018	−0.036	−10.524	8.169
	(0.652)	(−1.0236)	(−1.077)	(0.781)
LTA	0.061	0.379	155.651	0.558
	(0.231)	(1.449)	(1.129)	(0.014)
KOA	0.067[2]	0.088[2]	19.536	12.432
	(2.048)	(2.88)	(1.130)	(1.245)
D1		−4.793		−244.506
		(−1.43)		(−0.491)
D2		−5.358		−170.507
		(−1.53)		(−0.336)
D3		−2.741		−292.413
		(−0.782)		(−0.568)
D4		−3.175		−410.494
		(−1.155)		(−0.910)
D5		−6.08		−327.023
		(−1.827)		(−0.634)
D6		−4.402		−2504.452
		(−0.959)		(−1.078)
D7		−4.992		−237.976
		(−1.510)		(−0.476)
D8		−4.02		−199.948
		(−1.133)		(−0.423)
D9		−2.232		−231.203
		(−0.720)		(−0.546)
D10		−3.546		−188.17
		(−1.047)		(−0.369)
D11		−4.592		−206.845
		(−1.365)		(−0.411)
R^2	0.074	0.162	0.036	0.146
Observations	169	169	169	169

Notes:

1. Dummy variables are defined by decreasing concentration levels: *D1* (Slovak Republic), *D2* (Czech Republic), *D3* (Romania), *D4* (Estonia), *D5* (Croatia), *D6* (Lithuania), *D7* (Slovenia), *D8* (Bulgaria), *D9* (Latvia), *D10* (Poland), *D11* (Hungary).
2. Significantly different from zero at 5 per cent level (*t*-statistics in parentheses).

Table 6.4 *Low concentration (LC) and high concentration (HC) samples (ROA as dependent variable without/with country dummies*[1]*)*

	ROA LC	*ROA* LC	*ROA* HC	*ROA* HC
C	–22.582[2]		1.261	
	(–4.108)		(0.208)	
CONC	0.325[2]		–0.019	
	(3.58)		(–0.491)	
PARM	–0.166[2]	–0.187[2]	0.029	–0.001
	(–3.5)	(–2.995	(0.751)	(–0.018)
LTA	0.769[2]	0.847[2]	–0.018	0.170
	(3.302)	(3.342)	(–0.044)	(0.315)
KOA	0.067[2]	0.068[2]	0.073	0.102
	(2.126)	(2.051)	(1.519)	(1.954)
D1				–2.619
				(–0.372)
D2				–2.947
				(–0.406)
D3				–0.688
				(–0.096)
D4				–1.553
				(–0.277)
D5				–4.084
				(–0.589)
D6				–2.619
				(–0.35)
D7				–2.817
				(–0.408)
D8				–1.772
				(–0.249)
D9		–5.553[2]		
		(–1.993)		
D10		–8.757[2]		
		(–2.731)		
D11		–9.729[2]		
		(–3.036)		
R^2	0.282	0.285	0.051	0.127
Observations	67	67	102	102

Notes:

1. Dummy variables are defined by decreasing concentration levels: *D1* (Slovak Republic), *D2* (Czech Republic), *D3* (Romania), *D4* (Estonia), *D5* (Croatia), *D6* (Lithuania), *D7* (Slovenia), *D8* (Bulgaria), *D9* (Latvia), *D10* (Poland), *D11* (Hungary).
2. Significantly different from zero at 5 per cent level (*t*-statistics in parentheses). White heteroskedasticity-consistent standard errors and covariance.

effect of market structure on profits is the one that considers market shares instead.

As we can see from Table 6.4, market share does not affect profitability in all cases. A negative significant link can be observed for banks operating in markets (countries) with weak concentration whereas there is no significant link for the highly concentrated markets. Again, the regressions which include dummy variables instead of the concentration variable (*CONC*) confirm our results. This puzzling negative link between market share and profit obtained for weakly concentrated markets suggests that banks should have no incentives to gain market shares when they operate in markets which are not concentrated originally and which may be closer to perfect competition. However, this result could be biased for several reasons. For instance, the larger banks in the banking industry (which are generally state owned) might be less concerned about their profitability than the smaller banks.

Thus, on the whole, it appears that market shares do not explain differences in profitability and therefore the expected positive link which is obtained in US studies does not hold for Central and Eastern Europe. However, the expected effect of concentration on profits can be detected for weakly concentrated markets.

5 CONCLUDING REMARKS

The French and the American banking system experiences mentioned above may be relevant, not because of any lesson that can be learned from their recent changes – every banking system has its specificity and structural features that cannot be replicated elsewhere – but perhaps these experiences may help us to understand and better anticipate some potential effects of banking regulation concerning entry and exit (and more generally concerning competition) that have been implemented recently since the 1990s in Eastern European countries.

Banks have played a prominent role in the transition restructuring reforms: they have been one of the most efficient 'tools' of national authorities to influence firm adjustment indirectly through monetary policy, through banking regulation evolution and more generally through the new institutional and regulatory framework concerning the new relationship between a bank and a firm. In the context of transition, moral hazard has been reinforced because of the 'capture' of banks by some large firms and more generally by agents' resistance to strengthening competitive and financial constraints. The second banking reforms recently implemented in Eastern European countries aim at endowing the bank loan market with structures and mechanisms intended to encourage banks to carry out their usual functions. In order to create the conditions of a real competitive banking industry, new entry must be authorized and failure regulation must be implemented. One of the main challenges faced today by Eastern European countries as well as Western banking systems is the issue concerning the optimal size of their banking system. To what extent should entry regulation be implemented? Moreover, as long as insolvent banks are permitted to remain open and as long as frequent calls for help are made to central banks and banking authorities, the last phase of banking transition (when all financial intermediaries will be governed by competitive process and strong financial constraints) will be delayed. Future empirical work is needed to assess not only the structure–performance link more thoroughly but also to measure the sensitivity of bank cost and profitability to market conditions as well as the risk of failure of banking institutions.

NOTES

1. If you refer to the definition of an industry according to industrial organization, an industry is a group of firms producing a homogeneous good or service (or a basket of goods or/and services) demanded and sold on a unique market.
2. These are not subject to the same legal and financial constraints as, for instance, *la Poste* (Post Office/Girobank) or *les Caisses d'Epargne* (savings and loan associations/building societies) in France, or the 'non-bank' banks in the United States and in Western Europe.
3. Characterized by informational asymmetries, and consequently potential negative externalities.
4. Restrictions on entry – such as government control of chartering, geographic restrictions on branching or product-line restrictions – or restrictions on competition (as monetary authorities were controlling both the quantity of credit available through credit ceilings and the level of interest rates).
5. There would exist a cyclical Darwinian logic: while making markets more disputable, deregulation enhances competitive pressures; excess capacity that ensues and the fall in profitability should prompt less-efficient firms to exit the market, emphasizing the role of concentration to reach a new equilibrium.
6. We voluntarily stay outside the current debate for or against the institutional separation of banking and monetary functions.
7. Market discipline can be defined as any measure by which shareholders of a firm are induced to absorb a portion of losses undergone by this firm, but in return they are entitled to require a higher risk premium as soon as they perceive a rise in the firm's risk-taking behaviour.
8. For instance, sunk costs ensuing from special long-term relationships – as a way of reducing informational asymmetries – between a bank and its customers.
9. Scherer and Ross (1990) for a review of the SCP paradigm. The conduct or rivalry in a market is determined by market structure conditions. Higher seller concentration lowers the cost of collusion, then fosters tacit or explicit collusion on the part of incumbent firms which, as a consequence, may earn monopoly rents.
10. There is no theoretical consensus on how to define and how to measure a barrier to entry; there are several definitions, depending whether you adopt a normative – like Bain (1956) – rather than a comparative point of view – like Stigler (1968), or the theory of contestable market. A barrier to entry, or more generally a mobility barrier as defined by Caves and Porter (1977) should rather be considered as a cost of adjustment which an entrant must incur to penetrate into a market successfully. In fact, in the short run, any barrier will be

considered as a much more imposing set of obstacles by the entrant than it will be when viewed over the medium to long run and after the entrant has had a chance to develop a strategy to deal with its 'disadvantage': given time, money and imagination, many apparently imposing obstacles can be circumvented.

11. For a review of barriers to exit, see Caves and Porter (1976). Barriers to exit can affect entry in two ways: first, they affect the risk of an entry decision by adding to the cost that an entrant would have to bear if events subsequent to entry prevent it from leaving the market; second, barriers to exit may also influence the competitive incentives of incumbent firms: if these barriers are relevant and if entry occurs, you may expect established firms to act as if 'they have their back to the wall'.
12. A recent study by Jayaratne and Strahan (1997) confirmed that the performance of US commercial banks between 1975 and 1992 improved significantly after restrictions on bank expansion were lifted because better banks grew at the expense of their less-efficient rivals.
13. A firm increasing its market power may become more risk averse.
14. Sunk costs are closely associated with the entry and exit process. The sunk cost of an investment project may be defined as the difference between the *ex ante* opportunity of this project and the value that can be realized *ex post*, once the project has been carried out until the end. That is, sunk costs generate long-term earnings to a firm incurring them but they cannot be recovered if the firm has to exit the market.
15. In this sense, see Caves and Porter's (1976) concept of asset specificity.
16. Currently, a bank wishing to start business can either apply for a federal charter from the Comptroller of the Currency, or apply to the appropriate state banking agency for a state charter. However, to obtain federal deposit insurance, newly state-chartered banks must either receive approval directly from the Federal Deposit Insurance Corporation or become members of the Federal Reserve System (national banks are all members of the Federal Reserve System and all have federal deposit insurance).
17. Entry is defined as the number of bank openings regardless of whether they were new openings or reopenings (this feature is particularly important for the years 1931–35, as reopenings of suspended banks were especially high before FDIC insurance reduced the number of bank failures). Because entry rates might be somewhat overstated by the procedure adopted, Keeley (1985) excluded data for 1933 and 1934 from the analysis (so this has the effect of reducing the average entry rate between 1921 and 1935).
18. But there may be another interpretation of the data: entry restrictions seem to have gradually relaxed beginning perhaps as early as 1950, since the data would not be inconsistent with an upward trend starting then (as no statistical study is conducted here, one should be rather cautious with any conclusion on data trends).
19. This first deregulation shock consisted of several important steps: the complete liberalization of bank lending rates except for the usury rate while deposit rates were kept under control, the liberalization of bank branching which created competition for market shares and the traditional distinction between commercial and investment banking since the Second World War was kept in force but somewhat relaxed. But Mulder (1993) insists that this obvious stability conceals in fact an important phenomenon: the rise in branch office openings by foreign banks relative to domestic ones.
20. He estimated the following equation, with annual data from 1921 to 1962: $E_t = f(P_{t-1}, Z_t) - k.\ R_t$, where: E_t is the rate of formation of new banks in period t, P_{t-1} is the expected rate of return on invested capital in banking (adjusted for risk) in period $t-1$, Z_t is all variables (other than regulation and lagged expected profits) that determine entry in period t and R_t is a dummy variable which takes the value of 0 between 1921 and 1935 and the value 1 in the regulated period. The estimated value of k in this equation is 0.579, a value which is interpreted by Peltzman to mean that the rate of entry during the period of regulation was about half as large as it would have been, had there been no regulation.
21. A recent study by Demsetz et al. (1996), confirmed that high franchise value banks hold more capital and take on less portfolio risk leading to lower levels of overall risk, highlighting the importance of continued monitoring of franchise value in the banking industry.

22. The traditional hypothesis emphasizes non-competitive price behaviours in concentrated markets obtained by collusion while the efficient-structure hypothesis focuses on lower costs achieved through superior management or production processes or more efficient scale, permitting to increase size and market share, and as a result, leading to higher market concentration.
23. Moreover the data seem to fit the model better in this case compared to the regression carried out in previous studies with data for Western Europe or the United States.

REFERENCES

Aglietta, Michel (1993), 'Comportement bancaire et risque de système', *Revue d'Economie Financière*, Hors Série, l'industrie bancaire, 439–64.

Alhadeff, David A. (1962), 'A reconsideration of restrictions on bank entry', *Quarterly Journal of Economics*, **76** (2), May, 246–63.

Artus, Patrick and Jean-Paul Pollin (1989), 'Les effets de la réglementation et le comportement des banques', *Document de Travail n° 1989–26*, Caisse des Dépôts et Consignations, Service des Etudes Economiques et Financières.

Bain, Joe S. (1956), *Barriers to New Competition*, Cambridge, MA: Harvard University Press.

Baltensperger, Ernst and Jean Dermine (1990), 'European banking: prudential and regulatory issues', in Jean Dermine (ed.), *European Banking in the 1990s*, Oxford: Basil Blackwell.

Baumol, William J., John C. Panzar and Robert D. Willig (1988), *Contestable Markets and the Theory of Industry Structure*, rev. edn, New York: Harcourt Brace Jovanovich.

Benston, George J. (1973), 'The optimal banking structure: theory and evidence', *Journal of Banking Research*, **3**, Winter, 220–37.

Berger, Allen H. (1995), 'The profit–structure relationship in banking – tests of market power and efficient-structure hypotheses', *Journal of Money, Credit and Banking*, **27** (2), May, 404–31.

Berger, Allen H. and Timothy H. Hannan (1989), 'The price–concentration relationship in banking', *Review of Economics and Statistics*, May, 291–9.

Berger, Allen H. and Timothy H. Hannan (1992), 'The price–concentration relationship in banking: a reply', *Review of Economics and Statistics*, **74**, February, 376–9.

Berger, Allen H., David B. Humphrey and F.W. Smith (1993), 'Economies d'échelle, fusions, concentration et efficacité: l'expérience de la banque américaine', *Revue d'Economie Financière*, Hors Série, l'industrie bancaire, 123–54.

Brumbaugh, Dan Jr (1993), *The Collapse of Federally Insured Depositories: Savings and Loans as Precursor*, New York, London: Garland.

Caves, R. and M. Porter (1976), 'Barriers to exit', in R. Masson and P. Qualts (eds), *Essays in Industrial Organization in Honour of J.S. Bain*, Cambridge, MA: Ballinger.

Caves, R. and M. Porter (1977), 'From entry barriers to mobility barriers: conjectural decisions and contrived deterrence to new competition', *Quarterly Journal of Economics*, **97**, 247–521.

De Boissieu, Christian (ed.) (1990), *Banking in France*, London: Routledge.

Demsetz, Harold (1982), 'Barriers to entry', *American Economic Review*, **72**, 47–57.

Demsetz, Rebecca S., Marc R. Saidenberg and Philip E. Strahan (1996), 'Banks with something to lose: the disciplinary role of franchise value', *Economic Policy Review*, Federal Reserve Bank of New York, **2** (2), October, 1–14.

Dewatripont, Mathias and Jean Tirole (1993), *La réglementation prudentielle des banques*, Lausanne: Payot.

Dietsch, Michel (1991), 'La concurrence bancaire, vers de nouvelles règles du jeu', *Revue d'Economie Financière*, **19**, Winter, 43–56.

Dietsch, Michel (1992), 'Coûts et concurrence dans l'industrie bancaire', *Rapport*, Conseil National du Crédit et Direction des Etudes de l'Association Française des Banques, March.

Dietsch, Michel (1993a), 'Localisation et concurrence dans la banque', *Revue Economique*, 779–90.

Dietsch, Michel (1993b), 'Les surcapacités bancaires en France', *Revue d'Economie Financière*, Hors Série, l'industrie bancaire, 169–98.

Edwards, Linda and Franklin R. Edwards (1974), 'Measuring the effectiveness of regulation: the case of bank entry regulation', *Journal of Law and Economics*, **17** (2), October, 445–60.

Fraser, Donald and Peter S. Rose (1972), 'Bank entry and performance', *Journal of Finance*, **27**, March, 65–78.

Geoffron, Patrice (1993), 'Réglementation des industries bancaires: entre efficacité et stabilité du système financier', *Revue d'Economie Industrielle*, **66**, 4ème trimestre, 69–82.

Geoffron, Patrice (1994), 'Analyses structurelles des industries bancaires et nouvelles concurrence financière', *Revue d'Economie Financière*, **30**, Spring, 27–48.

Geroski, Paul, Richard J. Gilbert and Alexis Jacquemin (1990), *Barrier to Entry and Strategic Competition*, Chur: Harwood Academic Publishers.

Gilbert, R. Alton (1984), 'Bank market structure and competition', *Journal of Money, Credit and Banking*, **16** (4), November, 617–45.

Gilbert, Richard J. (1989), 'Mobility barriers and the value of incumbency', in Richard Schmalensee and Robert D. Willig (eds), *Handbook of Industrial Organization*, Amsterdam: North-Holland.

Goldberg, Lawrence and Anoop Rai (1996), 'The structure–performance relationship for European banking', *Journal of Banking and Finance*, **20**, 745–71.

Hannan, Timothy H. (1979b), 'Limit pricing and the banking industry', *Journal of Money, Credit and Banking*, November, 438–46.

Hannan, Timothy H. (1991a), 'Foundations of the SCP paradigm in banking', *Journal of Money, Credit and Banking*, **23** (1), February, 68–94.

Hannan, Timothy H. (1991b), 'Bank commercial loan markets and the role of market structure: evidence from surveys of commercial lending', *Journal of Banking and Finance*, March, 133–49.

Heggestad, Arnold A. (1979), 'Market structure, competition and performance in financial industries: a survey of banking studies', in Franklin R. Edwards (ed.), *Issues in Financial Regulation*, New York: McGraw-Hill.

Heggestad, Arnold A. and John J. Mingo (1977), 'The competitive condition of US banking markets and the impact of structure reform', *Journal of Finance*, **32**, June, 649–61.

Huveneers, Christian and Alfred Steinherr (1993), 'Economie industrielle des institutions bancaires', *Revue d'Economie Financière*, Hors Série, l'industrie bancaire, 13–46.

Jackson, William E. III (1992), 'The price–concentration relationship in banking: a comment', *Review of Economics and Statistics*, **74**, February, 373–6.

Jacobs, Donald P. (1965), 'The interaction effects of restrictions in branching and other regulations', *Journal of Finance*, **20**, May, 332–48.

Jayaratne, Jith and Philip E. Strahan (1997), 'Entry restrictions, industry evolution and dynamic efficiency: evidence from commercial banking', *Staff Report No. 22*, Federal Reserve Bank of New York, March.

Kane, Edward J. (1985), *The Gathering Crisis in Federal Deposit Insurance*, Cambridge, MA: MIT Press.

Kaufman, George G. (ed.) (1990), *Restructuring the American Financial System*, Boston: Kluwer.

Keeley, Michael C. (1985), 'The regulation of bank entry', *Federal Reserve Bank of San Francisco Review*, Summer, No. 3, 5–13.

Keeley, Michael C. (1990), 'Deposit insurance, risk and market power in banking', *American Economic Review*, **80** (5), 1183–200.

Lindenberg, Eric and Stephen Ross (1981), 'Tobin's *q* ratio and industrial organization', *Journal of Business*, **54**, January, 1–32.

Llewellyn, David T. (1990), 'Competition and structural change in the British financial system', in Edward P.M. Gardener (ed.), *The Future of Financial Systems and Services: Essays in Honour of Jack Revell*, New York, St. Martin's Press.

McCall, Alan and Manfred O. Peterson (1976), 'The impact of *de novo* commercial bank entry', Working Paper No. 76–77, FDIC Division of Research.

Meltzer, A.H. (1969), 'Controlling money', *Federal Reserve Bank of Saint Louis Review*, May.

Molyneux, Philip and William Forbes (1995), 'Market structure and performance in European banking', *Applied Economics*, **27**, 155–9.

Molyneux, Philip and John Thornton (1992), 'Determinants of European bank profitability', *Journal of Banking and Finance*, **16**, 1173–8.

Muldur, Ugur (1993), 'Les barrières à l'entrée dans le marché bancaire français', *Revue d'Economie Financière*, Hors Série, l'industrie bancaire, 75–122.

Neven, Damien J. (1990), 'Lessons from industrial organization to retail banking in Europe', in Jean Dermine (ed.), *European Banking in the 1990s*, Oxford: Basil Blackwell.

Osborne, D. and J. Wendell (1978), 'A criticism of the traditional analysis of banking competition', Research Paper No. 78–01, Federal Reserve Bank of Dallas.

Peltzman, Sam (1965), 'Entry into commercial banking', *Journal of Law and Economics*, **8**, October, 11–50.

Peltzman, Sam (1968), 'Bank stock prices and the effect of regulation of the banking structure', *Journal of Business*, **41** (4), October, 413–30.

Rhoades, Stephen A. (1982), 'Structure–performance studies in banking: an updated summary and evaluation', Staff Study No. 119, Board of Governors, Federal Reserve System.

Rochet, Jean-Charles (1991), 'Déréglementation et risque du système bancaire', *Revue d'Economie Financière*, **19**, Winter, 57–68.

Rochet, Jean-Charles (1992), 'Concurrence imparfaite et stratégie bancaire', *Revue Economique*, No. 2, 261–76.

Scherer, F.M. and D. Ross (1990), *Industrial Market Structure and Economic Performance*, Boston: Houghton Mifflin.

Scott, Kenneth (1979), 'The dual banking system: a model of competition in regulation', in Franklin R. Edwards (ed.), *Issues in Financial Regulation*, New York: McGraw-Hill.

Sharpe, Steven A. (1990), 'Asymmetric information, bank lending and implicit contract: a stylized model of customer relationships', *Journal of Finance*, **45** (4), September, 1069–87.

Shepherd, William G. (1984), 'Contestability vs. Competition', *American Economic Review*, **74** (4), 572–87.

Shepherd, William G. (1990), 'Mainstream industrial organization and "new" schools', *Revue Economique*, No. 3, 453–80.

Smirlock, Michael (1985), 'Evidence on the (non) relationship between concentration and profitability in banking', *Journal of Money, Credit and Banking*, **17** (1), February, 69–83.

Smirlock, Michael, Thomas Gilligan and William Marshall (1984), 'Tobin's *q* and the structure–performance relationship', *American Economic Review*, **74** (5), December, 1051–60.

Stigler, George (1964), 'A theory of oligopoly', *Journal of Political Economy*, **72**, February, 44–61.

Stigler, George (1968), *The Organization of Industry*, Homewood, IL: Richard D. Irwin.

Tirole, Jean (1988), *The Theory of Industrial Organization*, Cambridge, MA: MIT Press.

Weiss, Leonard W. (1974), 'The concentration–profits relationship and antitrust', in H. Goldschmid, H.M. Mann and J.F. Weston (eds), *Industrial Concentration: The New Learning*, Boston: Little, Brown & Company, pp. 184–233.

APPENDIX 6A1 OBSERVING ENTRY RATES AND CHANGES IN ENTRY REGULATIONS

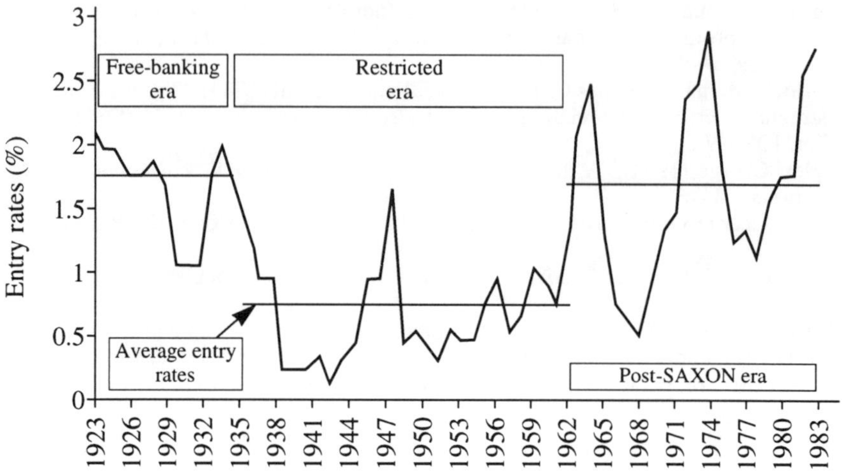

Source: Reprinted, by kind permission of the Federal Reserve Bank of San Francisco, from Michael C. Keely (1985), 'The regulation of bank entry', *Federal Reserve Bank of San Francisco Economic Review*, No. 3, Summer, 5–13.

Figure 6A1.1 Entry rates for US commercial banks, 1923–1984

APPENDIX 6A2 EQUATION GENERALLY TESTED IN STRUCTURE–PERFORMANCE MODELS

The estimated linear equations are generally of the form:

$$P = f(D, C, M, S, X)$$

where

- P is the price of a specific product (automobile loan rates, mortgage rates, business loan rates, saving rates …) or other dimension of performance (return on equity, return on assets, market value of bank stock relative to book value …),
- D is a set of variables to reflect market demand conditions,
- C is a set of variables to reflect differences in costs across firms and the market,

M is the degree of monopoly in the market as measured by the concentration ration,

S represents other market structures, such as proxies for entry restrictions (most studies use dummy variables for differences in US state branching restrictions), and

X is a set of control variables related to a specific product characteristics.

7. Financial reforms in Poland: an analysis with a computable general equilibrium model

Robert Lensink*

1 INTRODUCTION

Many studies describe the package of financial liberalizations in Poland (see, for example, Calvo and Coricelli 1992; Ebrill et al. 1994; and Lamacz 1995). However, there are virtually no formal assessments of these reforms, because of a lack of suitable models. This chapter tries to partly fill the gap by developing a general equilibrium model, which can be used to formally analyse financial reforms in Poland. The working of the model is explained by presenting the effects of an interest rate deregulation and changes in reserve requirements, which are among the most important financial liberalization measures in the Polish stabilization programme.

The chapter is organized as follows. Section 2 presents the model. Section 3 describes the simulation results and finally, Section 4 summarizes the chapter and outlines some issues for further research.

2 THE MODEL

The model contains a commercial banking sector, a central bank, a government sector, a consolidated private sector and an external sector.

* The author would like to thank participants of the conference on 'Economic Performance and Financial Sector Reform in Central and Eastern Europe,' held in Tallinn, 20–21 September 1996, for comments. This chapter is based partly on Gupta and Lensink (1996b). The research for this project was supported by the European Commission's PHARE/ACE programme 1994 under contract number 94–0685–R.

Commercial Banking Sector

The commercial banks are assumed to hold five assets: required reserves (*RR*), excess reserves (*ER*), loans to the private sector (L_p), loans to the government sector (L_g) and net foreign assets (NFA_b). Liabilities consist of domestic currency and foreign currency denominated deposits (*D* and *FCD*, respectively). Net wealth (NW_b) is given by

$$NW_b = RR_{-1} + ER_{-1} + L_{p,-1} + L_{g,-1} + eNFA_{b,-1} - D_{-1} - eFCD_{-1} + S_b \quad (7.1)$$

where e is the exchange rate and S_b are the commercial bank's savings. Net saving (bank profits) is modelled as:

$$S_b = i_g L_{g,-1} + (1 - d_p) i_p L_{p,-1} + i_f eNFA_{b,-1} - i_d D_{-1} - i_{fd} eFCD_{-1} \quad (7.2)$$

where i_g is the lending rate on loans to the government; i_p is the lending rate on loans to the private sector; i_d is the zloty deposit rate; i_{fd} is the deposit rate on foreign currency denominated assets; i_f is the foreign interest rate (exogenous) and d_p is the default rate (exogenous). It is assumed that neither the excess nor the required reserves earn any interest, which is in accordance with practice since neither type of reserves is remunerated in Poland (Ebrill et al. 1994, p. 32).

Commercial banks are assumed to determine L_p, L_g, *ER* and NFA_b by means of an approach originally set out by Rosensweig and Taylor (1990). They assume that commercial banks maximize expected utility from total assets, subject to a wealth constraint. Using a constant elasticity of substitution (CES) utility function, the following block of equations can be derived

$$teta_{b,1} = A_{b,1} \frac{1}{q_b} \quad (7.3)$$

$$teta_{b,2} = A_{b,2} \frac{\left[\frac{1 + i_p(1 - d_p) - d_p}{1 + i_{p,0}(1 - d_{p,0}) - d_{p,0}}\right]^{\sigma_b - 1}}{q_b} \quad (7.4)$$

$$teta_{b,3} = A_{b,3} \frac{\left(\frac{1 + i_f + \dot{e}^e}{1 + i_{f,0} + \dot{e}_0^e}\right)^{\sigma_b - 1}}{q_b} \quad (7.5)$$

$$teta_{b,4} = A_{b,4}\frac{\left(\frac{1+i_g}{1+i_{g,0}}\right)^{\sigma_b-1}}{q_b} \tag{7.6}$$

$$q_b = A_{b,1} + A_{b,2}\left(\frac{1+i_p(1-d_p)-d_p}{1+i_{p,0}(1-d_{p,0})-d_{p,0}}\right)^{\sigma_b-1} + A_{b,3}\left(\frac{1+i_f+\dot{e}^e}{1+i_{f,0}+\dot{e}_0^e}\right)^{\sigma_b-1} + A_{b,4}\left(\frac{1+i_g}{1+i_{g,0}}\right)^{\sigma_b-1} \tag{7.7}$$

$$ER = teta_{b,1}(NW_b + D + eFCD - RR) \tag{7.8}$$

$$L_p = teta_{b,2}(NW_b + D + eFCD - RR) \tag{7.9}$$

$$eNFA_b = teta_{b,3}(NW_b + D + eFCD - RR) \tag{7.10}$$

$$L_g = teta_{b,4}(NW_b + D + eFCD - RR) \tag{7.11}$$

where σ is an elasticity of substitution (all substitution elasticities are exogenous),[1] A is a distribution parameter; *teta* is the share of a particular asset in total available funds; the subscript b refers to commercial banks; the additional subscript 0 denotes the start value of the relevant variable and q_b is the mean return. The approach explained above enables the portfolio effects to be considered by 'guesstimating' one substitution elasticity, which is convenient, given the small amount of data available.[2]

Central Bank (NBP)

Net wealth of the central bank (NW_{cb}) is given by:

$$NW_{cb} = eFRES_{-1} + NGP_{-1} - RR_{-1} - ER_{-1} - CUR_{s,-1} + S_{cb} \tag{7.12}$$

where *NGP* is the stock of claims on the government; CUR_s is the stock (supply) of currency in circulation and *FRES* is foreign reserves denominated in foreign currency, and S_{cb} is saving by the central bank, assumed to be zero during the simulation period. The supply of money is the adjusting variable to clear the central bank's budget constraint:

$$CUR_s = eFRES + NGP - RR - ER - NW_{cb}. \tag{7.13}$$

The central bank controls the required reserve ratios. A fixed ratio between zloty and foreign currency deposits and required reserves is assumed (α_0 and α_1, respectively) since in Poland, from 1 February 1994, commercial banks are subject to a reserve requirement for both types of deposits (NBP, *Information Bulletin*, **6**, 1995, p. 7). Hence,

$$RR = \alpha_0 D + \alpha_1 eFCD. \tag{7.14}$$

In principle, commercial banks in Poland are free to set deposit and lending rates. However, in practice commercial banks set rates on the basis of NBP interest rates on refinancing credit or NBP rediscount interest rates, since they see the NBP rates as the official projection of inflation (Ebrill et al. 1994, p. 30). Therefore, I assume that i_d is set by the central bank and hence given for commercial banks. Moreover, i_{fd} is assumed to have a fixed relationship with i_d, and is thus indirectly also set by the NBP; hence

$$i_{fd} = \alpha_2 i_d. \tag{7.15}$$

With respect to the lending rate I assume, in line with the derivation of the portfolio balance model, that the rate is given for individual banks, but that for the sector as a whole i_p is determined by the condition that bank profits equal normal bank profits (*NPROF*, which is exogenously set and can be equal to zero), that is,

$$S_b = NPROF. \tag{7.16}$$

The endogenous determination of i_p implies, *ceteris paribus*, that an increase in the default rate, an increase in excess reserves, or an increase in the reserve requirements, automatically lead to an increase in the spread between i_p and i_d, which is in line with practice in Poland where costs of obtaining funds are starting to become important for the determination of interest rates. i_g is linked to i_p:

$$i_g = \alpha_3 i_p. \tag{7.17}$$

This specification allows us to assess the effects of governments borrowing against lower interest rates than the private sector, which is clearly a form of financial repression taking place in many former socialist economies.

The central bank is also assumed to set the exchange rate. The exchange rate in Poland is determined via a crawling peg system.[3] This implies that the monetary authorities preannounce the path of the exchange rate and that the exchange rate behaviour becomes predictable. In Poland, the change in the exchange rate is set (very often) below the projected inflation differences with the trading partners in order to reduce inflation. Therefore, I assume that the expected exchange rate equals the actual exchange rate and that the actual exchange rate is set by the monetary authorities via the following rule:

$$e = e^e = \alpha \frac{P_{ds,-1}}{P_{w,-1}} \tag{7.18}$$

where P_w is the world price (exogenous: small-country assumption) and P_{ds} is the price on domestically produced goods bought by the home country. The expected relative change in the exchange rate, used in the asset demand equations, is then determined as follows

$$\dot{e}^e = \left(\frac{e^e - e_{-1}}{e_{-1}} \right). \tag{7.19}$$

Government sector

Calvo and Kumar (1994) have pointed out that the governments in the former socialist economies rely mainly on borrowing from the commercial banks by issuing government securities and on direct finance from the central bank. In order to limit domestic direct borrowing from the central bank the Polish government also tries to fulfil its credit needs by foreign borrowing. Government borrowing from the private sector is still negligible, which is, therefore, not taken into account. The balance sheet constraint reads:

$$GDEBT = eFDEBT_{-1} + NGP_{-1} + L_{g,-1} + GDEF \tag{7.20}$$

where *GDEBT* is government debt, *FDEBT* is foreign debt and *GDEF* is the government deficit. Borrowing from abroad, in foreign prices ($\Delta FDEBT$), is exogenously given so that the evolution of foreign debt is modelled as:

$$FDEBT = FDEBT_{-1} + \Delta FDEBT. \tag{7.21}$$

Borrowing from commercial banks is determined by the supply of loans by commercial banks. The remaining government debt is financed by borrowing from the central bank, that is,

$$NGP = GDEBT - eFDEBT - L_g. \tag{7.22}$$

The government deficit is modelled as:

$$GDEF = Pg - T_d - T_{ind} + i_g L_{g,-1} + i_{fl} eFDEBT_{-1} + Ptr \tag{7.23}$$

where: T_d is direct taxes; T_{ind} is indirect taxes; g is real government consumption (exogenous); tr is real transfers (social security expenses and subsidies: exogenous) and i_{fl} is the foreign lending rate (exogenous) and P is a composite goods price (consumer price). Indirect and direct taxes are modelled as:

$$T_{ind} = \alpha_5 P_{dp} q \tag{7.24}$$

$$T_d = \alpha_6 \left[P_{va} q + i_{fd} eFCD_{-1} + i_d D_{-1} + i_f NFA_{p,-1} - (1-d) i_p L_{p,-1} \right] \tag{7.25}$$

where q is real aggregate supply, P_{dp} is a composite goods price (producer price); NFA_p is net foreign assets of the private sector; α_5 and α_6 are indirect and direct tax rates (exogenous) and P_{va} is a value-added price. Since the non-government sector, in line with statistics on the Polish economy, comprises the household sector and both state-owned and private enterprises, the model abstracts from government investments.

Private sector

The private sector is a consolidated sector consisting of households and firms. The private sector borrows from the commercial banking sector, holds currency (CUR_d) and holds claims on commercial banks in the form of domestic and foreign currency denominated deposits, net foreign assets (NFA_p) and a (nominal) stock of capital (Pk). Since equity markets are still relatively unimportant in Poland, it is assumed that the private sector does not issue equity to finance its expenditures. The balance sheet constraint, determining net wealth (NW_p), reads:

$$NW_p = Pk_{-1} + CUR_{d,-1} + D_{-1} + eFCD_{-1} + eNFA_{p,-1} - L_{p,-1} + S_p \tag{7.26}$$

where k is the real stock of capital. Saving of the private sector (S_p) is modelled as:

$$S_p = Y - Pc \tag{7.27}$$

where c = real consumption and Y = nominal disposable income, modelled as:

$$\begin{aligned} Y = {} & P_{va} q + i_{fd} eFCD_{-1} + i_f NFA_{p,-1} + i_d D_{p,-1} - (1-d_p) i_p L_{p,-1} \\ & + Ptr - T_d - \delta Pk_{-1} \end{aligned} \tag{7.28}$$

where δ is the depreciation rate and δPk_{-1} equals consumption of fixed capital. It is assumed that the private sector operates in a credit constrained world and therefore takes all the loans from the banking sector it can get. Hence a loan demand equation for the private sector is not specified. The production side of the economy is modelled as simply as possible. Assuming a Harrod–Domar production function and rewriting the equation in growth rates, aggregate supply is determined by

$$q = \left[1 + \eta_0\left(\frac{k - k_{-1}}{k_{-1}}\right)\right]q_{-1}. \tag{7.29}$$

Real private consumption is based on an econometric estimate, using quarterly data for the period December 1991 to August 1995. I assume that real private consumption depends on real disposable income, the different components of real net wealth, the increase in the supply of bank loans and the different interest rates used in the model. The inclusion of the real change in bank loans in the consumption function (and the investment function; see below) is meant to represent liquidity constraints for the private sector, which may be caused by the presence of incomplete credit markets in the former socialist economies. It allows the importance of credit availability on production in Poland to be taken into consideration, as emphasized by Calvo and Coricelli (1992). In order to avoid serial correlation, I estimated the consumption equation in first differences. Interest rates and the net wealth variable were skipped from the equation since all coefficients with respect to these variables appeared to be insignificant. The preferred regression result for the consumption equation is as follows (t-values are given in parentheses, after the coefficients):

$$\begin{aligned}(c - c_{-1}) = {} & 0.40(5.40)\left(\frac{Y}{P} - \frac{Y_{-1}}{P_{-1}}\right) \\ & + 0.27(1.99)\left[\left(\frac{L_p}{P} - \frac{L_{p,-1}}{P_{-1}}\right) - \left(\frac{L_{p-1}}{P_{-1}} - \frac{L_{p,-2}}{P_{-2}}\right)\right] \qquad (7.30) \\ & + 0.46(1.28)\left(\frac{CUR_d}{P} - \frac{CUR_{d,-1}}{P_{-1}}\right); \text{adj. } R^2 = 0.80.\end{aligned}$$

The equation for gross real investment (ir) is also based on an econometric estimate, using quarterly data for the same period as the equation for private consumption. The equation is based on an investment model in which a stock-adjustment process is assumed, and in which the desired real capital stock depends, in addition to real disposable income (which is included in line with a simple accelerator-type investment model), on the availability of external funds (the change in the real supply of loans). The equation used is as follows (t-values in parentheses)

$$ir = 0.31(2.20)\frac{Y}{P} + 0.68(2.35)\left(\frac{L_{p,-1}}{P_{-1}} - \frac{L_{p,-2}}{P_{-2}}\right) \tag{7.31}$$

$$-0.06(-1.09)k_{-1}; \text{adj. } R^2 = 0.58.$$

Having determined investments, the real stock of capital is:

$$k = (1-\delta)k_{-1} + ir. \tag{7.32}$$

Given the stock of capital and the stock of loans to the private sector, the demand for other assets is determined in the same way as the demand for assets by the commercial banking sector. The block of equations, determining financial asset demands are:

$$teta_{p,1} = A_{p,1}\frac{1}{q_p} \tag{7.33}$$

$$teta_{p,2} = A\frac{\left[\dfrac{1+i_d(1-\alpha_6)}{1+i_{d,0}(1-\alpha_{6,0})}\right]^{\sigma_p-1}}{q_p} \tag{7.34}$$

$$teta_{q,3} = A_{q,3}\frac{\left[\dfrac{1+i_{fd}(1-\alpha_6)+\dot{e}^e}{1+i_{fd,0}(1-\alpha_{6,0})+e_0^e}\right]^{\sigma_p-1}}{q_p} \tag{7.35}$$

$$teta_{p,4} = A_{p,4}\frac{\left[\dfrac{1+i_f(1-\alpha_6)+\dot{e}^e}{1+i_{f,0}(1-\alpha_{6,0})+\dot{e}_0^e}\right]^{\sigma_p-1}}{q_p} \tag{7.36}$$

$$q_p = A_{p,1} + A_{p,2}\left[\frac{1+i_d(1-\alpha_6)}{1+i_{d,0}(1-\alpha_{6,0})}\right]^{\sigma_p-1} + A_{p,3}\left[\frac{1+i_{fd}(1-\alpha_6)+\dot{e}^e}{1+i_{fd,0}(1-\alpha_{6,0})+\dot{e}_0^e}\right]^{\sigma_p-1}$$
$$+ A_{p,4}\left[\frac{1+i_f(1-\alpha_6)+\dot{e}^e}{1+i_{f,0}(1-\alpha_{6,0})+\dot{e}_0^e}\right]^{\sigma_p-1} \tag{7.37}$$

$$CUR_d = teta_{p,1}(NW_p - Pk + L_p) \tag{7.38}$$

$$D = teta_{p,2}(NW_p - Pk + L_p) \tag{7.39}$$

$$eFCD = teta_{p,3}(NW_p - Pk + L_p) \tag{7.40}$$

$$eNFA_p = teta_{p,4}(NW_p - Pk + L_p) \tag{7.41}$$

where the subscript p denotes 'private sector'. Rates of return on deposits, net of (direct) tax, are introduced to allow for the fact that the private sector considers after-tax returns in its portfolio allocation procedure.

External sector

The balance of payments in foreign currency reads:

$$\begin{aligned} \Delta FRES = {} & P_w \exp - P_w imp - i_{fl} FDEBT_{-1} + i_f(NFA_{b,-1} + NFA_{p,-1}) \\ & - \Delta NFA_p - \Delta NFA_b + \Delta FDEBT \end{aligned} \tag{7.42}$$

where *imp* is real imports and *exp* is real exports. The balance of payments determines the change in foreign reserves. The stock of foreign reserves is determined as follows:

$$FRES = \Delta FRES + FRES_{-1}. \tag{7.43}$$

The modelling of imports is based on the so-called Armington approach (Armington 1969), now commonly used in general equilibrium models. This means that imports and domestically produced goods are assumed to be imperfect substitutes and that domestic agents demand a composite good of imports and domestically produced goods, which are combined according to a CES aggregation function. This approach implies that import ratios adjust in response to a change in prices on domestically produced goods bought by the home country, relative to the home currency price of imports (P_m). The specifications I use are:

$$imp = ratio_m ddd \tag{7.44}$$

$$ddd = \left(\frac{1}{1 + ratio_m}\right)(c_p + ir + c_g) \tag{7.45}$$

$$ratio_m = \frac{imp}{ddd} = A_m\left(\frac{P_{ds}}{P_m}\right)^{\sigma_m} \tag{7.46}$$

where *ddd* is real domestic demand for domestic goods and $ratio_m$ is the ratio of imports with respect to domestic demand for domestic goods. Exports are derived similarly. It is assumed that producers produce a composite good of exports and goods supplied on the home market, which are again combined using a CES aggregation function. This implies:

$$exp = ratio_x dsd \tag{7.47}$$

$$dsd = \left(\frac{1}{1 + ratio_x}\right)q \tag{7.48}$$

$$ratio_x = A_x\left(\frac{P_x}{P_{ds}}\right)^{\sigma_x} \tag{7.49}$$

where *dsd* is real supply of domestically produced goods at the home market, $ratio_x$ is exports over domestic supply of goods and P_x is the export price.

Goods prices and equilibrium conditions

The model distinguishes seven goods prices. The equations for P_m, P, P_x, P_{dp} and P_{va} are given below (P_w is exogenous).

$$P_m = eP_w \tag{7.50}$$

$$P = \frac{P_{ds}ddd + P_m imp}{c + ir + g} \tag{7.51}$$

$$P_x = eP_w \tag{7.52}$$

$$P_{dp} = \frac{P_{ds}dsd + P_x \exp}{q} \tag{7.53}$$

$$P_{va} = P_{dp}(1 - \alpha_5). \tag{7.54}$$

One price (P_{ds}) is not explicitly modelled. This price is endogenously determined by the goods market equilibrium condition. Hence, it follows from the condition:

$$dsd = ddd. \tag{7.55}$$

Except for the money market, all other markets are cleared by either the demand or supply side of the market (quantity rationing). The money market equilibrium condition is automatically fulfilled by means of Walras's law. Finally, actual (and expected) inflation is determined by the relative change in consumer prices, that is,

$$\pi = \frac{P - P_{-1}}{P_{-1}}. \tag{7.56}$$

3 SIMULATION RESULTS

This section presents simulation results for a deregulation of the zloty deposit rate and a change in the reserve requirements on zloty deposits. I start with a base simulation in which all coefficients and variables have the values as given in Table 7A.1 in the appendix. Next, I perform the simulations with the model by introducing one financial liberalization measure. Results are presented as percentagewise differences from the baseline: they could be interpreted as 'multipliers'. A positive value implies that the financial liberalization measure leads to an increase in the variable under consideration.[4] Since I am interested mainly in the effects on real production, figures for this variable are presented. Moreover, for different time periods and in percentagewise differences from the base run, figures for the nominal supply of bank loans (L_p), real consumption (c), the real capital stock (k) and the price level (P) are given in a table.

Increase in the Zloty Deposit Rate

An interest rate deregulation is often an important instrument in the package of financial liberalization measures. It is assumed that an increase in the deposit rate stimulates investments, and hence production. This follows the ideas of McKinnon (1973) and Shaw (1973), that a rise in the deposit rate stimulates private sector savings by an increase in demand for deposits, and hence also, investment, since investment is assumed to be determined by available funds.[5] However, it should be noted that at first glance the total effect on investment is not clear since the increase in the deposit rate may, via an increase in demand, lead to an increase in the price level, which negatively affects real private investments.

I assumed that the central bank doubles the zloty deposit rate from the base simulation value of 3.3 per cent to 6.6 per cent during the whole simulation period. Figure 7.1 shows that real production is positively affected by the interest rate deregulation during the whole simulation period. However, it can

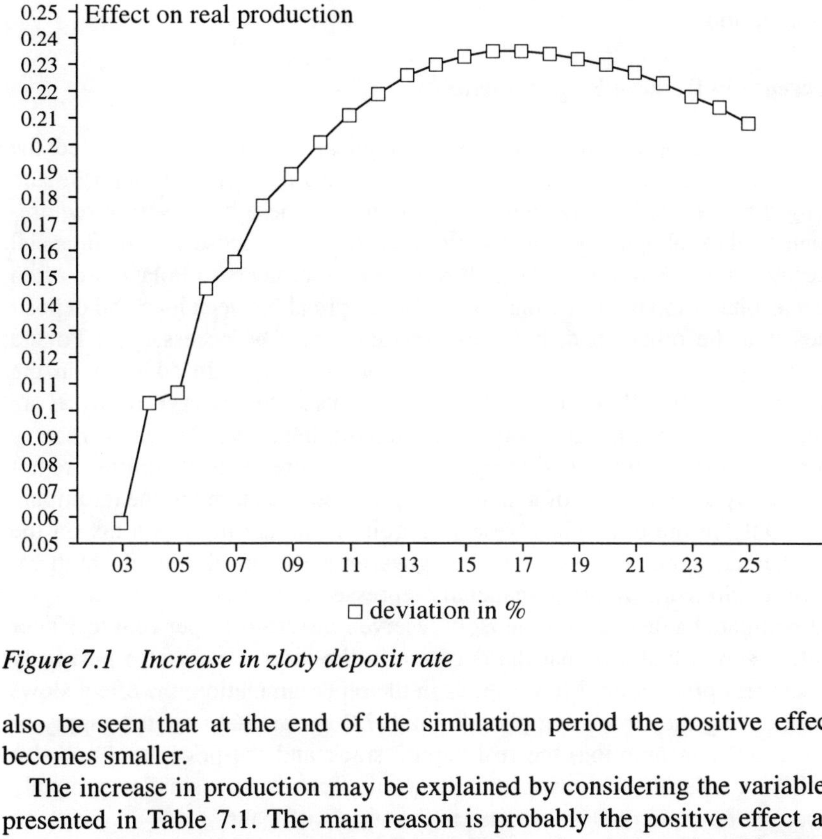

Figure 7.1 Increase in zloty deposit rate

also be seen that at the end of the simulation period the positive effect becomes smaller.

The increase in production may be explained by considering the variables presented in Table 7.1. The main reason is probably the positive effect an interest rate deregulation appears to have on the real capital stock. An interest rate deregulation positively affects the supply of bank loans, and hence it stimulates investments and the capital stock. However, it also appears that an interest rate deregulation leads to a rise in prices, which partly counteracts

Table 7.1 Simulation results: increase in zloty deposit rate (percentage differences from base run)

	5	15	25
L_p	2.1	5.3	15.8
c	0.8	0.9	1.2
k	0.4	0.8	0.7
P	2.7	13.0	25.6

the positive effect. This negative price effect becomes larger during the simulation period.

Decrease in Reserve Requirements

In many developing and transition economies, governments repressed the financial system by requiring high reserve ratios against bank deposits and using the receipts for government expenditures. These high reserve requirements lead to suboptimal financial intermediation and impose a tax on financial intermediation. Moreover, the high reserve requirements in Poland are often seen as one of the main reasons for the large spread between loan and deposit rates. On the other hand, high reserve ratios may be necessary in Poland because of the high default rates of the private sector. In addition, in the beginning of the 1990s the NBP has often used the reserve ratios as an instrument to limit the liquidity of banks, and hence has increased reserve ratios in order to limit inflation. High reserve requirements, therefore, are not necessarily an indication of a financially repressed economy in the traditional way. Only in the case where reserve requirements are used as a tax on the commercial banks to finance higher government expenditures, do high reserve requirements imply a financially repressed economy.

I simulated a decrease in the zloty reserve ratio from 15 per cent to 10 per cent. Figure 7.2 shows that the decrease in the reserve ratio also positively affects real production. Moreover, as in the other simulation, the effect slows down during the simulation period. Table 7.2 shows that now the supply of loans, real consumption, the real capital stock and the price level are also positively affected. However, the effect on prices is now smaller, probably because of a more modest increase in the supply of loans.

4 CONCLUSIONS

This chapter presents a simple general equilibrium model for assessing financial reforms in Poland. It appears that the financial liberalization measures considered are not the miracle cure their proponents often suggest. On the one hand, an increase in the zloty deposit rate and a decrease in the reserve ratio do stimulate the supply of bank loans and real production. However, on the other hand, the simulations suggest that financial liberalization may have an identifiable cost: both measures stimulate inflation. This result may be a somewhat depressing outcome for Polish policy makers, since the Polish financial liberalization programme is primarily geared towards reducing inflation.

The inflationary effect of both financial liberalization measures may be explained by the positive effect of an increase in the supply of bank loans on

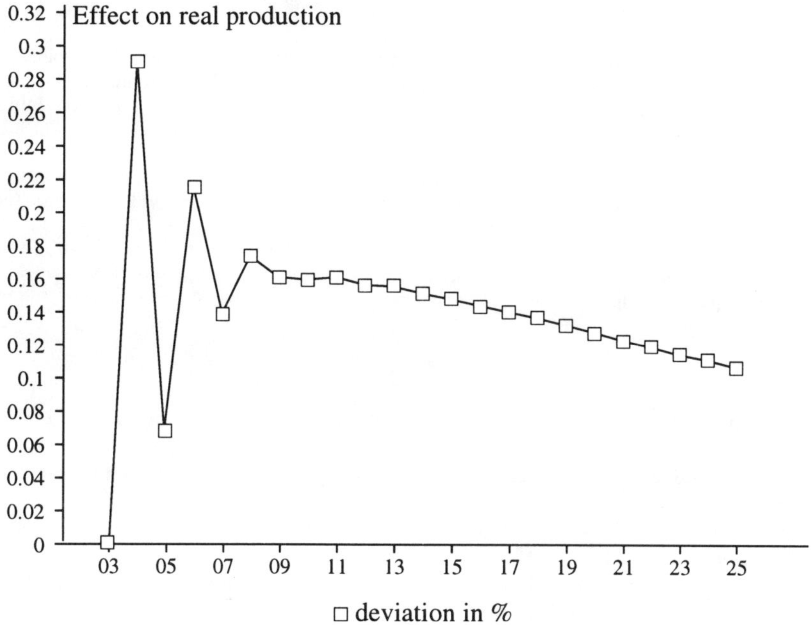

Figure 7.2 Decrease in zloty reserve ratio

Table 7.2 Simulation results: decrease in reserve ratio (percentage differences from base run)

	5	15	25
L_p	4.8	4.6	4.6
c	1.0	0.2	0.2
k	0.2	0.5	0.3
P	2.4	2.8	3.03

private consumption. This suggests that measures to liberalize the financial sector should be accompanied by some restrictions on consumer credits.

The results presented should be taken with caution. One of the principal shortcomings is that the main part of the model is not based on econometric estimates using Polish data. Hence, an obvious extension of the work presented in this chapter is to try to give a better econometric foundation for the coefficients used in the model. Given the short time period for which data are available, this would probably imply using monthly data.

NOTES

1. It refers to an elasticity of substitution between two inputs, holding the other input (and utility) constant. The elasticity of substitution is the same for each pair of inputs.
2. However, see Gupta and Lensink (1997) for a first attempt to estimate a standard multi-asset partial adjustment portfolio model (see Parkin 1970 and Brainard and Tobin 1968) for the commercial banking sector in Poland, using monthly data.
3. In May 1995, the NBP introduced a new system of setting the zloty rate. The system implies a partial flotation of the zloty within 7 per cent bands of a fixed daily rate (see, *PlanEcon Report*, 30 September 1995).
4. It should be noted that the shocks refer to *permanent* shocks, so that the series of differences from the base run do not give information on the stability properties of the model.
5. See Gupta and Lensink (1996a) for an extensive theoretical study on the effects of interest rate deregulations.

REFERENCES

Armington, P.S. (1969), 'A theory of demand for products distinguished by place of production', *IMF Staff Papers*, **16**, 159–78.

Brainard, W.C. and J. Tobin (1968), 'Pitfalls in financial model building', *American Economic Review*, **58**, 99–122.

Calvo, G.A. and F. Coricelli (1992), 'Stabilizing a previously centrally planned economy: Poland 1990', *Economic Policy*, April, 176–226.

Calvo, G.A. and M.S. Kumar (1994), 'Money demand, bank credit, and economic performance in former socialist economies', *IMF Staff Papers*, **41**, 314–49.

Central Statistical Office, *Biuletyn Statystyczny* (Statistical Bulletin), Various issues, Warsaw.

Ebrill, L.P., A. Chopra, C. Christofides, P. Mylonas, I. Otker and G. Schwartz (1994), *Poland: The Path to a Market Economy*, Occasional Paper 113, Washington, DC: IMF.

Gupta, K.L. and R. Lensink (1996a), *Financial Liberalization and Investment*, London: Routledge.

Gupta, K.L. and R. Lensink (1996b), 'Rozwoj Sektora Finansowego W Polsce: Podejscie Symulacyjne I Wstepna Specyfikacja Modelu', in A. Janc and T. Kowalski (eds), *Reformy Finansowe W Krajach Tworzacych Gospodarke Rynkowa*, Poznań: Akademia Ekonomiczna W Poznaniu, pp. 51–81.

Gupta, K.L. and R. Lensink (1997), 'Financial reforms and commercial bank behavior in Poland', in K.L. Gupta (ed.), *Experiences with Financial Liberalization*, Boston: Kluwer Academic Publishers, pp. 217–40.

International Monetary Fund (IMF), *International Financial Statistics*, Washington, DC, January.

Lamacz, T. (1995), 'Financial sector development and macroeconomic policy in Poland in 1990–3', in S. Griffith-Jones and Z. Drabek, *Financial Reform in Central and Eastern Europe*, London: Macmillan Press, pp. 151–76.

McKinnon, R. (1973), *Money and Capital in Economic Development*, Washington, DC: Brookings Institution.

Narodowy Bank Polski (NBP), *Information Bulletin*, various issues (November/December 1992 to June 1995).

Parkin, M. (1970), 'Discount house portfolio and debt selection', *Review of Economic Studies*, **37**, 469–97.
PlanEcon Report, various issues.
Rosensweig, J.A. and L. Taylor (1990), 'Devaluation, capital flows, crowding-out: a CGE model with portfolio choice for Thailand', in J.A. Rosensweig and L. Taylor (eds), *Socially Relevant Policy Analysis: Structuralist Computable General Equilibrium Models for the Developing World*, Cambridge, MA: MIT Press, pp. 302–31.
Shaw, E. (1973), *Financial Deepening in Economic Development*, New York: Oxford University Press.

APPENDIX 7A STARTING VALUES AND COEFFICIENTS

Table 7A.1 presents the parameters which are needed to simulate the model.

Table 7A.1 Data for the base year (August 1995: in million new zloty) and coefficients

Commercial banks	Government	Private sector	Interest rates	Other start values
D 54908.3	$eFDEBT$ 105853.2	c 30539.62	$i_{p,0}$ 0.059	
ER 1429.8	$GDEBT$ 147272.4	ir 7099.0	$i_{f,0}$ 0.014	Y 37568
$eFCD$ 21033.6	g 8069.28	d_p 0.2	i_f 0.014	P_{-1} 0.996
$eNFA_b$ 13051.7	tr 13546.7	Instruments	i_{fl} 0.024	Other coefficients
L_g 28716.8	External sector	α_0 0.15	$i_{g,0}$ 0.059	η_0 0.15
L_p 50353.2	imp 15397.18	α_1 0.01	$i_{d,0}$ 0.033	η_1 0.40
$L_{p,-1}$ 46327.0	exp 14292.20	α_2 0.182	$i_{fd,0}$ 0.006	η_2 0.27
RR 7341.8	$\Delta FDEBT$ 0.0	α_3 1	Elasticities	η_3 0.46
Nw_b 24951.4	Private sector	α_4 1	σ_b 1.4	η_4 −25956.4
Central bank	$eNFA_p$ 3046.6	α_5 0.22	σ_p 1.4	η_5 0.39
CUR 19879.7	Pk 111507.0	α_6 0.3	σ_m 1.0	η_6 0.19
NGP 12702.4	Nw_p 160022.0	$NPROF$ 2315	σ_x 1.0	η_7 0.13
$eFRES$ 13051.7	q 44602.85			δ 0.015
Nw_{cb} −2897.2				

Sources: Most data are obtained from various issues of the *Information Bulletin* of the Narowdy Bank Polski (henceforth, INBP). The description behind the variables refers to the line in this bulletin. The following issues of the INBP have been consulted: November–December 1992; October 1993; June 1994, June 1995 and December 1995. In addition, various issues of the *PlanEcon Report*, the statistical bulletin of the Central Statistical Office and, occasionally, IMF *Financial Statistics* have been used.

Notes:

D: zloty deposits of non-financial sector (INBP);

ER: from assets due from financial institutions the rules vault cash and NBP receivables plus NBP bills plus NBP bonds minus liabilities to NBP minus required reserves (RR) (INBP);

$eFCD$: foreign currency deposits of non-financial sector (INBP);

$eNFA_b$: assets due from abroad minus foreign liabilities (INBP);

L_g: assets due from general government plus Treasury Bills plus Treasury Bonds minus liabilities due to general government (INBP);

L_p: assets due from corporate sector plus assets due from personal sector;

RR: total required reserves held (INBP);

NW_b: calculated as $RR + ER + L_g + L_p + eNFA_b - D - FCD$;

$CUR = CUR_s = CUR_d$: the row coin in circulation (INBP);

NGP: the assets due from general government plus securities minus liabilities due from general government (INBP);

$eFRES$: approximated by central bank assets due from abroad minus central bank foreign liabilities (INBP);

NW_{cb}: $NGP + eFRES - ER - RR - CUR$;

eFDEBT: approximated by gross foreign debt of Poland (Table 11, INBP, various issues). The value is converted to zloty by using the free market average exchange rate (INBP);
GDEBT: calculated as $eFDEBT + NGP + L_g$;
g: calculated as $q - c - ir - exp + imp$;
tr: derived from Table 13, Central Statistical Office (January 1996);
exp; *imp*: figures are taken from *PlanEcon Report* (7 February 1996). They refer to hard-currency exports and imports on BOP basis;
$\Delta FDEBT$: exogenously set;
$eNFA_p$: approximated by the cross-border bank deposits of non-banks by residence of depositor (IMF, May 1996, Table 7xrd). These figures, as well as *exp* and *imp*, are converted to zloty by using the free market exchange rate (INBP);
Pk: capital stock data for Poland are not available. The base year value of the capital stock is assumed to be 2.5 times *q*. The capital stock data for the period before August 1995 (needed for the regressions, see below) are calculated as: $k_{-1} = k - ir$;
NW_p: calculated as $CUR + D + eFCD + eNFA_p + Pk - L_p$;
$q = c + ir + g + exp - imp$: calculated as $(c + ir + exp - imp)/(1 - gshare)$, where *gshare* is the share of collective consumption in GDP (as given by *PlanEcon Report*, 7 February 1996);
c: calculated by three times the average monthly per capita expenditures by households times the population (both given in *PlanEcon Report*, 7 February 1996);
ir: gross investment in fixed capital (*PlanEcon Report*, 7 February 1996);
d_p: based on the ratio between bank claims on businesses in bad financial standing and total corporate outstanding debt to the 15 principal banks (INBP);
α_0, α_1: based on INBP;
α_2, α_3: based on the base year ratio between i_{fd} and i_d and the ratio between i_g and i_p;
α_4: exogenously set;
α_5: based on the standard value added tax rate (Ebrill et al. 1994);
α_6: based on the average of the income tax rate for households (0.2) and firms (0.4) (Ebrill et. al. 1994);
NPROF: based on base-year savings of commercial banks;
$i_{p,0}$: approximated by the lowest risk principal zloty lending rate for commercial banks (INBP);
$i_{d,0}$: approximated by the average of 6 months' zloty deposit rates and demand zloty deposit rates (INBP);
$i_{f,0}$ and i_f: approximated by libor rate;
i_{fl}: exogenously set;
$i_{g,0}$: approximated by the series on yields on 13-week Treasury Bills;
i_{fd}: approximated by the average of 6 months' foreign currency deposit rates and demand foreign currency deposit rates (INBP).
Note that all interest rates are recalculated quarterly.
σ_b, σ_p: based on Rosensweig and Taylor (1990);
σ_m, σ_x: based on Rosensweig and Taylor (1990);
P: calculated by using equation (7.50), presented in the main text;
η: residual coefficients;
Y: calculated by using the equation for *Y*, presented in the main text;
δ: exogenously set.

Consumption, investment and production The coefficient in the production equation is exogenously set and based on model simulations. The coefficients for private consumption and investment are based on simple OLS regressions, using quarterly data for the period December 1991 until August 1995. In the estimates, nominal values are converted to real values by using the consumer price index (*Information Bulletin* of the NBP: INBP). August 1995 is normalized to one.

Base year asset shares and import/export shares In the base year, all prices and exchange rates are normalized to one. This implies that A_m and A_x can be derived from the initial values, and are calculated as: $imp/(c + ir + g - imp)$ and $exp/(c + ir + g - imp)$, respectively. The parameters A in the asset demand equations are derived from the initial year shares of the different assets. In the base year the interest rates are equal to the base-year interest rates, which implies that the As can be derived from the base-year asset shares.

PART II

Exchange Rate Regimes and Capital Flows

8. Fixed exchange rate regime in the stages of transition: lessons from the Czech case

Miroslav Hrnčíř

1 INTRODUCTION

At the start of the 1990s, the lively discussion on exchange rate regimes for transition economies and on the relevance of the arguments of standard theories could be only hypothetical. Since then, several years of reforms in the countries of Central and Eastern Europe have already provided empirical evidence on exchange rate developments in the conditions of transition. Accordingly, the discussion on the factors affecting the choice of exchange rate regime and on the merits of various adopted options can be developed in a comparative setting and on the basis of data and lessons already learned.

In 1990, the authorities of former Czechoslovakia pegged the Czechoslovak koruna (CSK) to a currency basket. The adopted policy of nominal exchange rate stability was targeted to anchor the stabilization process after sweeping price and foreign exchange liberalization in the beginning of January 1991. However, no binding commitment was made publicly to keep the introduced type of fixed exchange rate regime and the given exchange rate level unaffected, neither indefinitely nor for any preannounced period. The regime pegging the domestic currency to the basket within a rather narrow band of ±0.5 per cent in the Czech Republic was maintained unchanged (despite the dissolution of the former federal Czechoslovakia and of its common currency) up to the end of February 1996, that is for 62 consecutive months. Such a long-run exchange rate stability has indeed been exceptional in a transition economy and even in comparison with some OECD member countries. On 27 February 1996, keeping the central parity untouched, the applied band of the Czech koruna (CZK) was widened to ±7.5 per cent.

Although the move to an exchange rate arrangement allowing for more flexibility was in the air for some time, the markets were caught by surprise both by the extent of the band widening and the timing of its announcement, given the approaching parliamentary elections to be held at the end of May 1996.

Compared to the parallel experience in other countries, two features of the regime's shift and its aftermath distinguished the Czech case:

- unlike a number of other emerging market economies (EMEs), the Czech exchange rate arrangement did not switch to a crawling type of band to correct for inflation differential, although in the conditions of a transition economy the horizontal type of band with the same parity was adhered to;
- despite the widened margin, the CZK market exchange rate has also continued to fluctuate within a relatively narrow band in the follow-up period.

Figure 8.1 illustrates the exchange rate developments in the first half of 1996, that is in the period when the regime shift was implemented. After the band was substantially widened at the end of February, both the official rate (Czech National Bank, CNB, fixing) and market rate of the CZK maintained remarkable stability with respect to the central parity for some time, the deviations not exceeding two percentage points.

From mid-1996 until March 1997 the CZK fluctuated in the stronger part of the band and its rate of nominal appreciation with respect to the central parity exceeded 4 per cent in August–September 1996 and 5 per cent in February 1997, despite increasing deficits in trade and current accounts. The capital account's impact clearly dominated, supported by an increasingly restrictive stance of monetary policy since mid-1996. This trend reversed in late April 1997 with the shift of the CZK to a weaker part of the band.

In spring 1997 a further step was made in the move towards flexible exchange rate arrangements. As of 26 May, the Board of the Czech National Bank discontinued the pegging of the CZK to the basket and allowed for the shift to a floating option. Since then there has been neither an official nor an internal fluctuation band of the CZK and the exchange rate has been left to the market to determine its new level and development path. However, while 'not leaning against the wind' the Bank declared its readiness to intervene in the market to correct for the excessive volatility at whatever level of exchange rate it may be developing. This readiness to act has been demonstrated via stabilizing interventions which occasionally have been resorted to. It follows that a managed float option has been maintained in reality since May 1997.

The exit of the CZK from the pegged regime was effected under the pressure of currency turbulences and, in particular, under the risk of repeated speculative attacks. As in some other cases, the Czech currency became

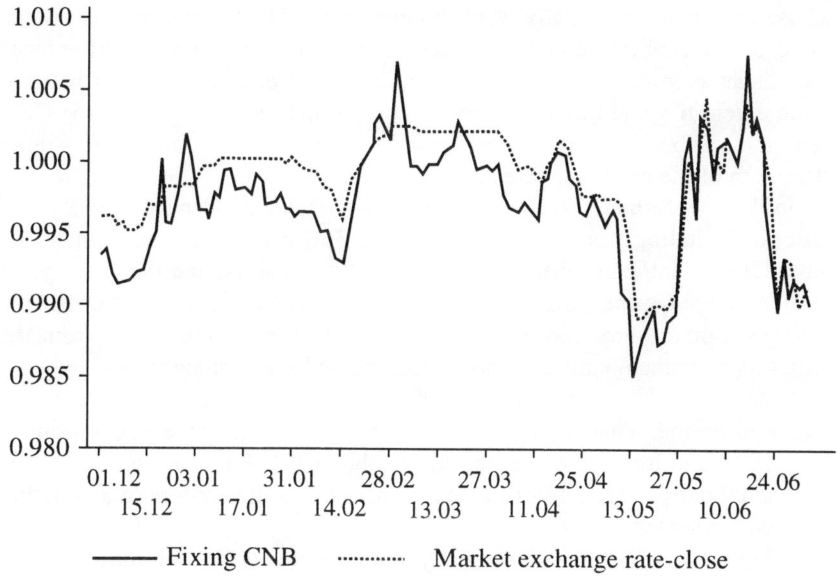

Note: CZK depreciation if > 1; CZK appreciation if < 1; CNB fixing = official rate.

Source: Czech National Bank.

Figure 8.1 *CZK official and market exchange rates (index with respect to the central parity pegged to the currency basket, December 1995 to June 1996)*

vulnerable especially because of the high current account deficit which had been developing since 1995. In 1996 it reached an unsustainable level of 7.6 per cent of GDP and it peaked in the first quarter of 1997. Bad news came from the unexpected slowdown in the macroeconomic performance and from the increasing gap in budgetary revenues. Moreover, the half-hearted package of policy measures to correct evolving imbalances, which was adopted by the government in April 1997, disappointed the expectations of investors.

Apart from macroeconomic imbalances and a non-credible policy package to cope with them, the sensitivity of the situation and its susceptibility to speculators' interests were further aggravated by deepening political instability. The very survival of the governing coalition became increasingly questioned in a country where political stability had been one of the assets in the previous period.

Macroeconomic and political weaknesses combined were increasingly perceived by investors and observers to resemble those in other EMEs elsewhere whose currencies eventually went through crisis. These were, among others, some of the ASEAN countries, Thailand in particular. Despite differences and distance from those countries the Czech currency turbulences were to some extent triggered by contagion effects. In the given conditions the CZK depreciated about 10 per cent compared to the previous central parity in an aftermath of the exchange rate regime shift.

Unlike the former Czechoslovakia, most EMEs of Central and Eastern Europe, including, for example, Slovenia, Bulgaria, Russia and almost all other CIS[1] countries resorted to a managed float (that is, to a flexible type of exchange rate regime), from the very beginning of the political and economic changes. Some others sooner or later found it necessary to depart from the initial fixed exchange rate, among others, Poland and Hungary.

Poland started its transition in 1990 with a fixed rate pre-committed to a specified period. That regime was replaced by an adjustable peg system in May 1991 and by a crawling peg in October 1991. Later on, the band was widened to ±7 per cent (May 1995) and, as a result, the system of a crawling band was imposed.

Hungarian authorities traditionally pursued the policy of mostly small irregular discrete realignments (devaluations) with respect to the basket. The aims of the policies, however, changed in the course of time. In some periods the devaluations just corrected for the inflation differential, that is, real exchange rate was maintained stable in principle, in others some real exchange rate appreciation was allowed to materialize. Starting from March 1995, the previous policies of occasional small adjustments were replaced by a preannounced crawling. Hungary joined Poland and a number of other EMEs, including Israel, Colombia, Chile and Mexico, in applying a crawling band system.

Contrary to the trends towards a more flexible arrangement, Estonia in 1992 and Lithuania in 1994 moved in the opposite direction, introducing a currency board system. This regime imposed a fixed exchange ratio on the 'pilot' currency (Deutschmarks and US dollars, respectively), which meant relinquishing the central bank's authority in devising and calibrating monetary policies.

With the benefit of hindsight, the following conclusions seem to follow from an evaluation of exchange rate arrangements in EMEs of Central and Eastern Europe:

- exchange rate regimes have developed in a wide variety of ways across individual transition economies, from currency board systems to various options of managed float;
- in the course of time the trend to more flexible exchange rate forms has clearly prevailed;

- although the available evidence on the comparative merits of applied exchange rate regime options in the conditions of transition is as yet only partial, the early peggers (countries like Poland, the Czech and Slovak Republics, Hungary and Estonia) seemed to fare relatively better in their stabilization efforts and macroeconomic recovery.[2]

Can we draw on the standard theory and on the experience of others in the world economy when explaining exchange rate developments in the specific conditions of transition? The discussion on the properties of alternative exchange rate regimes in economic theory already has a long tradition, and has been developing for decades. In the postwar period, especially, the theory on optimum currency areas[3] proved to be an inspiration and a point of departure for numerous applied studies.

Because of extensive attention and elaboration, a fairly high degree of consensus seems to exist on the comparative advantages and drawbacks of exchange rate regime options as well as on the factors which may affect their choice. Those factors are, in particular:

- dimensions of the economy, its real and financial properties and structure;
- type and frequency of shocks, whether real or monetary, endogenous or exogenous;
- macroeconomic conditions, policy objectives and priorities of the given country.

This consensus notwithstanding, the claimed correlations are not easy to validate in the real world. The experience shows

- a wide diversity of exchange rate regimes, for example, within relatively homogeneous groups of countries, that is, across countries which, according to standard criteria, could be expected to have similar exchange rate arrangements,[4] and
- the identification of relative merits of exchange rate regime options for those countries is far from evident.

Does this imply that the advantages and disadvantages of alternative exchange rate regimes are so inconclusive, as some authors seem to suggest?[5]

In our view the explanation should be looked for in a diversified and changing country- and/or period-specific conditions. The properties of exchange rate regimes have been derived on the basis of stylized market economy conditions or assuming the existence of such conditions. The concrete situation of a given country and/or period may, however, diverge more or less from that assumed. Accordingly, the more it deviates from the 'standard', the more the ratio of merits and flaws of adopted exchange rate options is likely to be affected.

The whole body of development economics emerged to reflect specific features, imperfections and rigidities of the local markets of EMEs. In that respect, the former centrally planned economies formed the group of countries which diverged most from the stylized setting of developed market economies, especially at the start of transition. While they shared some parallel constraints and goals with developing countries in macroeconomic dimensions, especially in the challenges of stabilization, liberalization and deregulation, beyond those they had to cope with the situation of almost entirely absent institutions of a market economy. In the course of transition, profound systemic and institutional changes had to materialize, accumulated into relatively short time spans of a few years. As a result, the environment for exchange rate and the requirements addressed to its role were changing relatively quickly in the follow-up transition stages. This is a specific, distinguishing feature of countries in transition compared to the conditions in other parts of the world economy. The issue is how intensively and in what ways those macroeconomic, institutional and systemic changes affected exchange rate arrangements in the countries of Central and Eastern Europe relative to the factors envisaged by the standard theory. Can we identify the diverging impact of individual transition stages for the choice of exchange rate regime, for its successive adjustments and for the role of an applied exchange rate?

The postwar developments in the world economy provide parallel experience from the situations when the conditions for the applied exchange rate regimes and for their pros and cons in the countries concerned substantially changed. The collapse of the adjustable peg system of Bretton Woods and its replacement by mostly floating rates of major currencies resulted from the changed conditions and policy priorities in the world economy in the early 1970s. Sweeping deregulation of financial markets in the 1980s, and later on the European monetary integration projects, are recent examples of the world- and European-wide shifts in the institutional setting which also affected the relative advantages and disadvantages of alternative exchange rate regimes, although because of different factors and in much more extended time horizons compared to transition economies.

The hypothesis is therefore advanced that in terms of transition economies the exchange rate arrangements and developments interacted with extensive institutional and systemic adjustments. Accordingly, to assess the rationale of a given exchange rate regime and its relative costs and benefits, not only the country-specific, but also the stage-specific conditions must be accounted for.

To discuss and to examine this type of causality in the concrete case of the Czech Republic, the chapter is structured as follows. Using the concept of financial openness as the organizing framework of the discussion, four development stages (model situations) are distinguished. The following sections examine the conditions, role and impact of the exchange rate regime at two crossroads of the Czech development. The first one was associated with the departure from the centrally planned economy framework and with the start of transition. The second one reflected the shift to a more mature stage of financial openness. The concluding part of the chapter derives policy-relevant lessons from the Czech experience with a fixed exchange rate regime. They confirm that the extensive changes and adjustments in underlying conditions in the course of transition co-determined the adoption and adjustment of exchange rate arrangements and their pros and cons.

2 STAGES OF TRANSITION AND EXCHANGE RATE REGIME

Reflecting the institutional and systemic trends and making use of the concept of financial openness[6] as an organizing criterion, a four-stage scheme is devised to study exchange rate developments in the transition economies:

1. *Stage A: financially closed economy* Exchange rates, although in 'nominal' existence, were in reality only exchange rate coefficients. They were derived from calculated data and isolated from the developments of domestic price ratios. Tightly regulated and, as a rule, diversified, they lacked the properties of an exchange rate proper and failed to reflect the market value of the given currency. As a consequence, the set of black and shadow exchange ratios developed, mostly widely diverging from the official rates.[7]

   Trade, capital and foreign exchange flows were subject to administrative control, both inward and outward. Domestic currency was non-convertible. This model situation reflected the pre-transition period of the former centrally planned economies.
2. *Stage B: rudimentary financial openness* Compared to the previous stage, the principal change in exchange rate sphere was the shift from exchange rate coefficients to an exchange rate proper. Because of the initiated price, trade and foreign exchange liberalization some degree of financial openness was achieved, albeit only partial.

   Liberalization steps being confined in principle to current account items only, capital flows were of limited importance and consisted mostly of long-term official capital. As a result, only current account fundamentals mattered for balance of payments and exchange rate developments.
3. *Stage C: advanced financial openness* The type and extent of currency convertibility was in principle already matching the standard of devel-

oped market economies. The shift was accomplished from 'internal' to external currency convertibility on current account items and the domestic currency complied with the requirements of Article VIII of the IMF.

The liberalization process was extended to capital account flows. Unlike the previous stage, private capital flows surged, supported by the upgrading of domestic financial markets and financial intermediation. As a result, the capital account's fundamentals mattered increasingly.

4. *Stage D: financially opened economy meeting the criteria of the European monetary integration projects* The entry into this stage implies that the transition process was successfully accomplished and the given country achieved the standard required to be eligible for membership in the projects of European monetary integration.

In the suggested four-stage scheme, the transition itself takes place in the two phases, B and C. The other two, stages A and D, respectively, reflect pre-transitional and post-transitional conditions. Although there are no clear-cut dividing lines in reality and the distinguishing features may overlap, passing from one stage to another reflected qualitative upgrading of financial openness of the given transition economy. This implied at the same time a parallel change in the exchange rate's environment and in the requirements addressed to the exchange rate's role.

Apart from the institutional and systemic changes, the macroeconomic situation of the transition economies also went through very divergent stages. As seen in Table 8.1 covering Central European Free Trade Area (CEFTA) countries, the deep and protracted 'transition' recession of the first years turned into the economic recovery and robust growth of the recent period.

In a parallel way, the disinflation process advanced from the initial price-level jump following liberalization package, to the challenge of how to cope with relatively moderate, but stubborn inflation levels (compare Table 8.2). The interaction between changes in the macroeconomic and institutional

Table 8.1 GDP growth rates in CEFTA countries

	1990	1991	1992	1993	1994	1995	1996
Czech Republic	–1.1	–14.2	–6.4	–0.9	2.6	6.4	3.9
Hungary	–3.5	–11.9	–3.0	–0.8	2.9	1.5	1.3
Poland	–11.6	–7.0	2.6	3.8	5.2	7.0	6.1
Slovak Republic	–2.5	–14.5	–6.5	–3.7	4.9	6.8	6.9
Slovenia	–4.7	–8.1	–5.4	1.3	5.3	4.0	3.1

Source: National statistics 1996.

Table 8.2 Consumer price inflation in CEFTA countries (change in % against preceding year)

	1990	1991	1992	1993	1994	1995	1996
Czech Republic	9.9	56.7	11.1	20.8	10.0	9.1	8.8
Hungary	28.9	35.0	23.0	22.5	18.8	28.2	23.6
Poland	585.8	70.3	43.0	35.3	32.2	27.8	19.9
Slovak Republic	10.6	61.2	10.0	23.2	13.4	9.9	5.8
Slovenia	549.7	117.7	201.3	32.3	19.8	12.6	9.7

Sources: National statistics.

setting therefore played a key role in the formation of individual transition stages.

Both from analytical and policy-making points of view the 'crossroads' of the identified follow-up stages are of particular importance. The Czech economy accomplished the turnaround from stage A to B in early 1991, implementing the package of sweeping liberalization and stabilization measures. To pass the crossroad between B and C became the challenging issue in the mid-1990s.

3 EXCHANGE RATE IN A RUDIMENTARY STAGE OF FINANCIAL OPENNESS

Fixed or Flexible Exchange Rate Regime for the Start of Transition?

The move from pre-transition stage A to stage B of our scheme implied the move from an exchange rate coefficient to a proper exchange rate. At that point, the choice of an exchange rate regime which would correspond to the conditions of the first phase of transition had to be made. On the one hand, the goals of the exchange rate were the same as elsewhere in the world economy: to support macroeconomic stability and, at the same time, to secure international competitiveness. While in principle complementary in the long run, the mentioned goals are as a rule competing in the short run. The specific conditions of the very start of transition, that is, the discontinuity of the previous centrally planned economy framework and the resulting uncertainties as to the evolving macroeconomic magnitudes, made the trade-off between those goals even more complicated.

As a consequence, the types of exchange rate policies suggested for adoption in the transition economies diverge widely according to the priority and weight attributed in each particular case to the competing objectives of competitiveness and macroeconomic stability. When reacting to the uncertainties in the assessment of the present situation in the country's competitiveness and in its future developments, the flexible option of exchange rate was put forward repeatedly. When, on the other hand, the priority was attached to the objective of restoring macroeconomic stability, the fixed exchange rate option was claimed to be the right choice.

Properties of transition seemed to provide powerful arguments for at least some degree of exchange rate flexibility:

1. The inherent features of transition were the discontinuity with the past and the uncertainty as to what a reasonably competitive exchange rate level could be.
2. The transition process itself, apart from exogenous shocks, implied turbulent developments because of the extensive liberalization, adjustment and restructuring in the domestic economy. In the given conditions, a persistent disparity in fundamentals compared to partner countries, in particular a higher level of inflation, seemed inevitable, at least for several years.
3. Apart from the disparities in fundamentals, the EMEs of Central and Eastern Europe mostly lacked the prerequisites for a sustainable fixed exchange rate regime. They missed in particular

    - a satisfactory level of international reserves and funds to defend a fixed exchange rate;
    - a workable infrastructure of factor markets, especially of financial markets; and
    - the reputation of monetary stability.

Reflecting on those conditions of transition, many observers argued for some form of exchange rate flexibility in the EMEs of Central and Eastern Europe:

- Willett claimed that the need to peg the exchange rates of the transition economies has often been exaggerated. Flexible types of exchange rate arrangements were obviously more consistent with the underlying conditions (Willett et al. 1992).
- H. Schmieding's conclusion was that a flexible exchange rate corresponds to the nature of transition (Schmieding 1991).
- Fry and Nuti, reacting to the persistent inflation differential, suggested a real exchange rate anchor instead of a nominal one as the proper concept for transition economies (Fry and Nuti 1992).

- Also, the lessons from the cases of currency overvaluation, experienced in particular in a number of Latin American countries in the 1970s and early 1980s, prompted the warnings against repeating such a mismanagement in the transition economies (Williamson 1991).

The floating rate was seen as a way to circumvent the unavoidable uncertainty about the competitive market-consistent exchange rate. The floating option should also allow for macroeconomic policies, including monetary, to be calibrated, without worrying about the competitive level of the exchange rate. It therefore looked attractive for EMEs as a way to avoid a potential foreign exchange constraint as well as the risk of either an undervalued or an overvalued rate. The fixed exchange rate option seemed hardly sustainable and credible. The lessons from elsewhere were unambiguous: if not credible, the costs of a fixed exchange rate regime were likely to become too high to be borne.

Nevertheless, the arguments in favour of the choice of fixed exchange rate regime were not less compelling:

1. A fixed exchange rate regime and nominal exchange rate stability should be a major instrument of macroeconomic stabilization in an economy which was rigidly regulated in the past and which was heading for sweeping liberalization. The exchange rate was expected to take over the role of a key nominal anchor.
2. By the same token, a fixed exchange rate could provide a benchmark for the extensive price ratios' adjustment initiated by price and foreign exchange liberalization. Potentially volatile exchange rate fluctuations, on the other hand, were likely to obscure price signals and distort expectations.[8]
3. A fixed exchange rate regime should have disciplining effects on economic agents, including government authorities and trade unions. After decades of arbitrary and non-transparent exchange rate ratios in the centrally planned economy framework, the disciplining impact of the fixed exchange rate 'norm' could contribute to the reorientation of behaviour patterns.
4. The traditional flaws of a floating rate, especially high volatility and the risk of substantial misalignment, were likely to be much greater than in consolidated market economies of a similar size. This was due to nonexistent or rather thin currency markets, underdeveloped institutions, missing foreign exchange markets and short-term arbitrage flows which, under certain conditions, could work towards stabilizing the exchange rate (Williamson 1991). The instability of a key price, the exchange rate, was feared to undermine the main aim of the pro-

gramme of currency convertibility: to 'import' rational price ratios and to discipline domestic agents.

The nominal anchor approach was advocated in particular in the IMF-sponsored stabilization programmes launched in former Yugoslavia in 1989, in Poland in 1990 and in former Czechoslovakia in 1991. The inflationary pressures were in transition economies inherited from the past as well as generated in the course of the transition itself. The parallel with the destabilized situation elsewhere in the world economy and, accordingly, with the IMF policy prescriptions already tested in the course of the 1970s and 1980s seemed, therefore, evident. A fixed exchange rate regime and a nominal exchange rate stability were in those IMF programmes targeted as major instruments of macroeconomic stabilization, anchoring both the current flows and expectations.[9]

The IMF resolution was the major causal factor behind the fixed exchange rate regime in the Polish and Czechoslovak cases. Slovenia and Bulgaria, on the other hand, opted for managed floating primarily because of the lack of foreign exchange reserves. In their 'starting' conditions the fixed exchange rate regime appeared unsustainable.

Estonia and Lithuania, the newly independent republics of the former USSR, resorted to a currency board solution. Because they were very small economies and lacked the institutions and experience in monetary management, the currency board was looked upon as a feasible way to radical disinflation. Inflation was reaching hundreds of per cent in the former and more than a thousand per cent in the latter country in the early 1990s.

The above examples suggest that eventually the country-specific priorities and constraints proved to have the final say in exchange rate regime choice at the start of transition. As could be expected, most transition economies adopted exchange rate arrangements 'in between' polar cases, that is, in between 'irrevocably' fixed and freely floating rates. To satisfy competing requirements of stability and competitiveness in the circumstances, the exchange rate policies as a rule resorted to compromise solutions. Those included adjustable peg, crawling peg and various forms of managed floating.[10] Polar regimes seemed unsuitable for transition economies except, possibly, for the short run. In that respect the revealed viability of the currency board experiment of Estonia and Lithuania provided an interesting experience.

The Fixed Exchange Rate Option in Former Czechoslovakia: Which Level in the Initial Period of Transition?

The official exchange rate of the CSK has been tied to a currency basket since the early 1980s. Accordingly, when the authorities of the former Czechoslovakia opted for a fixed exchange rate regime in 1990 pegging the CSK to a currency basket with a rather narrow band of ±0.5 per cent, the arrangement technically implied no change compared to the previous one. However, the peg could become operational and binding only after the departure from the rigid centrally planned economy framework.

Given this discontinuity, the monetary authorities were confronted with the selection of a proper 'entry' exchange rate level. The issue was twofold:

- what might be its equilibrium level in 1990, and
- how far to deviate initially from such a level to secure the exchange rate stability over, at least, a certain 'desirable' period, given the expected persistent disparity in fundamentals.

The standard definition of an equilibrium exchange rate says that this rate ensures the simultaneous attainment of internal and external balance (Williamson 1993). Although relatively clear-cut in theory, the concept of balance is much less straightforward when applied to real conditions. It refers to the identification of both external and internal equilibrium. The external equilibrium is considered to be in place when current account and sustainable capital flows are in balance. However, the identification of persistent capital flows is not unambiguous and their level may be subject to considerable changes in the course of time. By the same token, equilibrium rate being conceived as a medium-term concept, a cyclically average pressure of demand is to be assumed, not the actual one.

When the Czechoslovak authorities had to make the choice of exchange rate at the start of transition, the above-mentioned constraints in assessing what might be an equilibrium rate were even more severe. The very concept was alien to the former rigidly regulated centrally planned economy. Its discontinuity added new uncertainties. As a result, the assessment of macroeconomic variables and dimensions at the start of transition was exposed to a rather wide margin of error.[11] In those conditions, the lively discussion on the underlying equilibrium exchange rate which developed in the early 1990s was of intellectual interest, but it could hardly provide a policy-relevant benchmark.

Although the reliable assessment of the equilibrium rate was not available, the policy had to accommodate the arguments which called for an initial undervaluation of the exchange rate. Evidently the most compelling one was the decision to introduce an 'internal' currency convertibility and to implement a sweeping liberalization of foreign trade at the very start of transition. As a consequence, an undervalued exchange rate compared to that which could be conceived as an 'equilibrium' rate for the then existing situation was evidently necessary. The currency convertibility, however limited, would otherwise be hardly sustainable with a fixed exchange rate regime. The likely outcome would be the early necessity for another correction of the exchange rate and/or a retreat from the already established convertibility status.

Additional constraints made the requirement of entry undervaluation even more necessary:

- the level of foreign exchange reserves was too low to provide a desirable cushion for potential fluctuation in liberalized foreign exchange flows;
- the necessity to reorientate the bulk of the existing trade after the abrupt collapse of COMECON institutions and markets; and
- a persistent real exchange rate appreciation must have been expected in the conditions of a transforming economy.

There was, however, an obvious trade-off involved: larger undervaluation would on the one hand increase the chances of survival of the introduced exchange rate arrangements, but at the same time it would deepen inflationary cost–push pressures and mitigate the disciplining function of the applied exchange rate. Underestimated depreciation would result in unsustainable balance of payments deficits and/or protective measures, undermining the credibility and the very existence of currency convertibility.

The degree of uncertainty and the lack of consensus as to the proper entry level of the exchange rate were reflected in a rather wide dispersion of values suggested for the 'initial' exchange rate level in 1990. Those ranged from CSK 16 per US dollar, that is, from close to then existing 'commercial rate', up to CSK 35–38, that is, to the rates approaching non-legal parallel and 'shadow' market rates.

The controversial issue was not only the assessment of the equilibrium rate, but also how far to deviate from its value. The resolution of the authorities was to err rather in undervaluation than the other way round.

In accordance with that preference, the option finally implemented, CSK 28 per US dollar, was closer to then-existing parallel market rates, that is, closer to the upper ceiling of devaluation alternatives rather than to the medium value of the discussed corridor (compare Figure 8.2). The implied depreciation amounted to about 95 per cent, as follows from Table 8.3. This radical change in exchange rate level was not implemented all at once, but as a cumulative result of four follow-up realignments in the course of 1990.

This figure alone may provide a distorted and biased picture of the true extent of the implemented depreciation. The specific institutional conditions of the shift from the pre-transition period in 1990 must be accounted for.

- The exchange rate changes were made with respect to the level of the 'commercial rate', which was applied in the rigidly regulated frame-

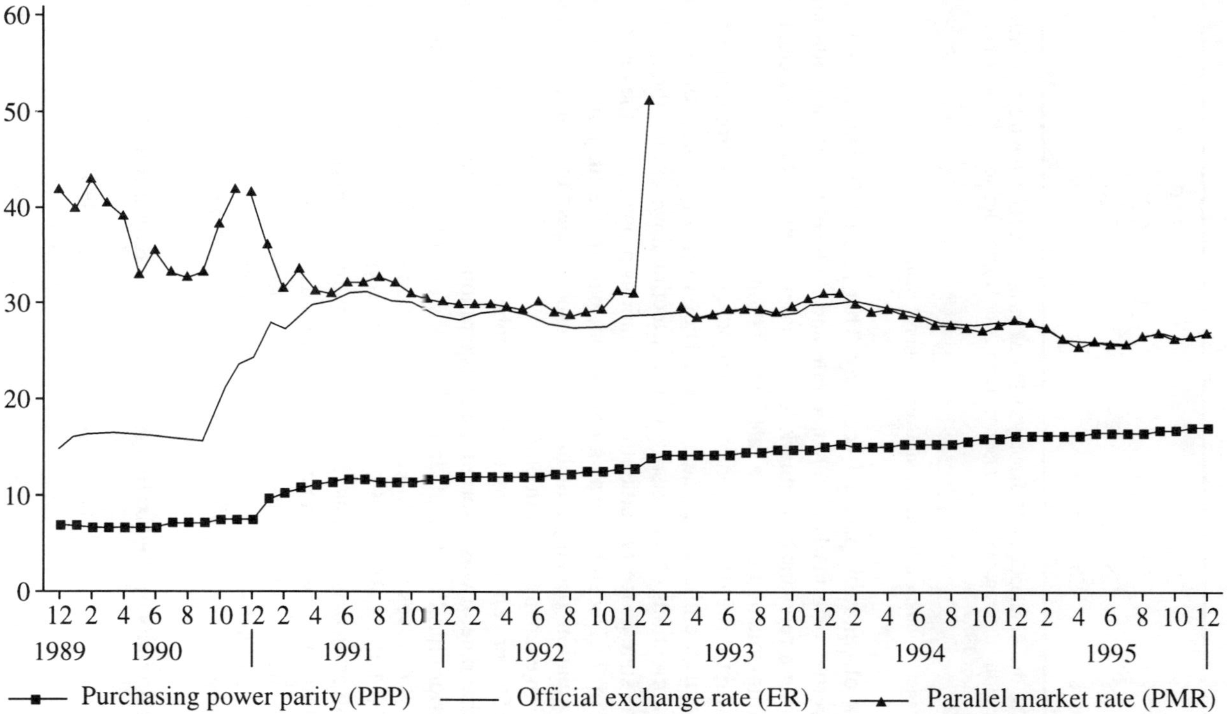

Sources: Financial Statistical Information, CNB; Monthly Statistics of the Czech Republic; Main Economic Indicators, OECD, Paris, August 1994.

Figure 8.2 Official exchange rate, purchasing power parity and parallel market rates of CZK (CZK per US$)

Table 8.3 Realignments of the Czechoslovak koruna in 1990

Date	Rate per US$*	Percentage change
2 January	CSK 14.62	2.10
8 January	CSK 17.00	16.30
15 October	CSK 24.00	55.20
28 December	CSK 28.00	15.90

Note: * The first devaluation of 2 January 1990 was made with respect to the 'commercial rate', that is, to the then applied exchange coefficient which amounted to CSK 14.31 per US dollar at the end of 1989.

Source: Financial Statistical Information, Czech National Bank.

work of centrally planned economy. That rate coefficient lacked the properties of a market exchange rate and its level therefore could not provide a relevant benchmark for the assessment of the real extent of the implemented exchange rate depreciation.

- The first three devaluations were introduced in an environment of as yet almost entirely regulated prices. They were, therefore, administrative corrections of the existing ratios, affecting flows among the entities of the state property, rather than devaluations proper. Only the last one, that of 28 December, was a component part of the liberalization and deregulation package, including domestic prices, foreign trade and foreign exchange liberalization.
- The 55 per cent realignment of 15 October 1990 was not programmed for that date. It was resorted to in desperation, under the pressure of the deteriorating liquidity of domestic banks and of the continued depletion of reserves due to capital flight and dramatically increasing imports in the latter half of 1990. These trends resulted from the spreading devaluation expectations, fuelled by the public discussion on the forthcoming massive currency devaluation as an integral part of the liberalization and stabilization policy package. Thus, the aggravating reserve constraint and the resulting 'unplanned' depreciation step in the second half of 1990 were to some extent self-inflicted.

Costs and Benefits of the Exchange Rate 'Entry' Realignments in 1990

Compared to expectations, the fall of economic activity in the early stage of transition was deeper and more protracted. At the same time, the price level also surged initially more than predicted. Although the phenomenon of specific 'transition' depression was quite common across transforming countries of Central and Eastern Europe and certainly not specific to the Czechoslovak economy (compare Tables 8.1 and 8.2 for evidence from relatively successful CEFTA countries), they seemed too high in the relatively stabilized macroeconomic situation of the former Czechoslovakia.[12]

In discussing the causal factors, the arguments have been put forward that the entry depreciation of the domestic currency and the restrictive stance of applied macroeconomic policies were overshot, thus repeating to some extent the Polish experience one year earlier. In that respect, measured by the difference between the effected depreciation and the actual black market rate, the extent of initial overshooting in the case of the Czechoslovak economy was substantially smaller. As reported by Rosati, the Polish zloty was depreciated to a level which was even lower than its black market rate (Rosati 1997). Nevertheless, the very fact that the nominal exchange rate of CZK could be maintained unchanged since January 1991 up to late May 1997 despite persistent real appreciation may be claimed as a sign of initial excessive undervaluation.

However, the assessment of the likely costs and benefits of entry devaluations must account for the specific conditions and goals of the initial transition period and discriminate between the short- and medium-run effects.

Given the discontinuities and uncertainty implied at the very start of transition, the risk of overshooting had to be offset against the risk of currency overvaluation, which could cause

- the retreat from the already established convertibility status;
- reimposition of protective measures; and/or
- repeated exchange rate corrections within a short time span.

The latter case, implying failure of the reform programme and the loss of its credibility, would certainly be more detrimental. The policy priority to avoid such a development, although running the risk of some overshooting (which the authorities demonstrated), must therefore be considered warranted, providing the extent of the overshooting did not exceed a tolerable corridor. Accordingly, the assessment, with the benefit of hindsight, should not be mixed with the stage of decision making.

The policy makers themselves were not unanimous with regard to the extent of the desirable devaluation; there was also disagreement between the members of the federal and the Czech governments of that period. Their diverging views were related to the alternative approaches suggested for the pace of liberalization in an external sphere, that is, for

- the advance of foreign trade and foreign exchange liberalization;
- the desirable level and time profile of remaining protection; and

- the timing of introduction of currency convertibility.

According to one approach the priority ought to be given to domestic liberalization while the regulations in the external sphere would be dismantled only later on, and step by step. The alternative approach, which was eventually implemented, argued for a sweeping liberalization on both domestic and external fronts simultaneously, together with the introduction of at least limited currency convertibility. Obviously, the advocated depreciation for the latter case was higher.

Even if due reservations as to the 'real' extent of the effected currency depreciation are made, the 'nominal' figures of Table 8.3 are too robust not to cause a substantial shock. It follows that the effected depreciation must have contributed to a higher than expected price level jump in the first months of 1991. Some 35–40 per cent of the surging price level in that period was estimated to be due to the depreciation of the currency. It may be argued, therefore, that the process of price adjustment materialized at a higher price level than, with the benefit of hindsight, would have been necessary. The favourable side of the developments was, however, that the initial inflation jump subsided in three months without further repercussions.

The implemented depreciation widened the already existing wedge between the current exchange rate and purchasing power parity rate (compare Figure 8.2). The scope for the hoped-for disciplinary impact of a fixed exchange rate was thus diminished or, possibly, its materialization was postponed. As a result, the environment for the performance of domestic enterprises became 'softer', especially with regard to exports and competition from imports.

The above drawbacks of depreciation overshooting were, however, mostly confined to the short run. As at least partial 'compensation', some benefits can be claimed to arise in the medium run:

- The initial undervaluation of exchange rate (widening of its wedge from the purchasing power parity, PPP, rate) formed an exchange rate 'cushion'. This cushion in the follow-up period contributed to the nominal exchange rate stability and to the positive inflation record of the Czech Republic compared to other EMEs of Central and Eastern Europe.[13] The nominal exchange rate could be maintained unchanged over a protracted period despite persistent real exchange rate appreciation and without any additional costs to defend it by specific policy measures.
- The extended time span allowed for equilibrating real exchange rate appreciation to materialize once the productivity and incomes started to grow again in the later stage of transition.

4. A FIXED EXCHANGE RATE REGIME WITH INCREASING FINANCIAL OPENNESS

The Nominal Exchange Rate

Extensive adjustment under way in the transition economies and persistent real exchange rate appreciations combined with exogenous shocks made a degree of exchange rate flexibility desirable in many countries and usually inevitable once financial markets were opened to international influences.

The distinguishing features of the Czech developments were not only the resolution of the authorities to stick to the fixed exchange rate regime in the later stage of reforms but also the capability to sustain stable nominal exchange rate for a much longer period than in most EMEs (see Table 8.4). This nominal exchange rate stability was achieved despite external shocks and continued real exchange rate appreciation even exceeding its rates in some other economies in transition.

After 62 months of a rigid fixed exchange rate confined to the band of only ±0.5 per cent, the CZK rate was freed to fluctuate in a wider band of ±7.5 per cent. This change implied that for the first time in the course of transition the

Table 8.4 Nominal exchange rates of CZK

	1991	1992	1993	1994	1995	1996
a. End of period – December						
CZK/US$	28.55	28.60	29.76	28.22	26.66	27.33
% over year earlier	18.02	0.18	4.06	–5.18	–5.53	2.50
CZK/DM	18.14	18.09	17.41	17.94	18.50	17.57
% over year earlier	12.11	–0.28	–3.78	3.03	3.17	–5.00
b. Year average						
CZK/US$	29.48	28.26	29.15	28.78	26.54	27.14
% over year earlier	64.17	–4.11	3.13	–1.26	–7.80	2.26
CZK/DM	17.79	18.13	17.64	17.74	18.52	18.05
% over year earlier	59.42	1.92	–2.70	0.56	4.40	–2.53

Note: + nominal depreciation; – nominal appreciation.

Source: Selected Indicators of Monetary Developments, Czech National Bank.

exchange rate level started to reflect the changes in its market assessment. It may therefore be of interest that until the spring of 1997 the CZK rate continued to fluctuate within narrower limits inside the band, short of stabilizing interventions of the central bank.

Since the very start of transition in 1990 to May 1997, the CZK (CSK until the split of the currency of former Czechoslovakia in early 1993) was pegged without interruption to a basket, but its composition was changed occasionally in the early stage of transition (see Table 8.5).

Table 8.5 Currency basket of the Czechoslovak and the Czech koruna

	US$	DM	ATS	UK£	FrF	Sw.Fr
1 June 1981	45.83	29.78	10.65	9.06	4.68	n
1 January 1989	32.88	40.93	12.32	n	4.82	9.05
28 December 1990	31.34	45.52	12.35	4.24	n	6.55
2 January 1992	49.07	36.15	8.07	n	2.92	3.79
3 May 1993	35.00	65.00	n	n	n	n

Source: Financial Statistical Information, Czech National Bank.

The amendments were motivated by 'technical' considerations. There was no deliberate intention to make the peg either harder or softer. The implemented changes were the product of the search for an optimum peg given the changed importance of individual major currencies in trade and payments flows. In the case of the last amendment introduced in May 1993, the number of basket currencies were reduced from five to just two, the Deutschmark and the US dollar. The intention was to make the basket more transparent and to save on transaction costs.

During the period 1991 to February 1996 nominal exchange rate developments of the CSK (and the CZK) reflected only the shifts in the cross-rates of the basket currencies. In situations of diverging trends of the Deutschmark and the US dollar, the basket arrangement contributed to a stabilization in the corresponding bilateral CZK's ratios.

The dominant share of the Deutschmark (65 per cent) in the basket since 1993 implied that the nominal exchange rate to some extent shadowed Deutschmark developments. Accordingly, the appreciating trend of the Deutschmark in 1994 and 1995 resulted in a corresponding minor appreciation of the nominal effective exchange rate of the CZK as well.[14]

On the other hand, the relative weakening of the Deutschmark *vis-à-vis* the US dollar, which developed in the first half of 1996 and in the course of 1997, worked in the reverse direction.[15]

After the widening of the band in February 1996, the impact of the cross-rates was combined with more extensive autonomous fluctuations of the CZK with respect to the central parity (that is, with respect to the basket). Figure 8.3 demonstrate those fluctuations (the index value) together with the developments of the bilateral CZK/US$ and CZK/DM rates.

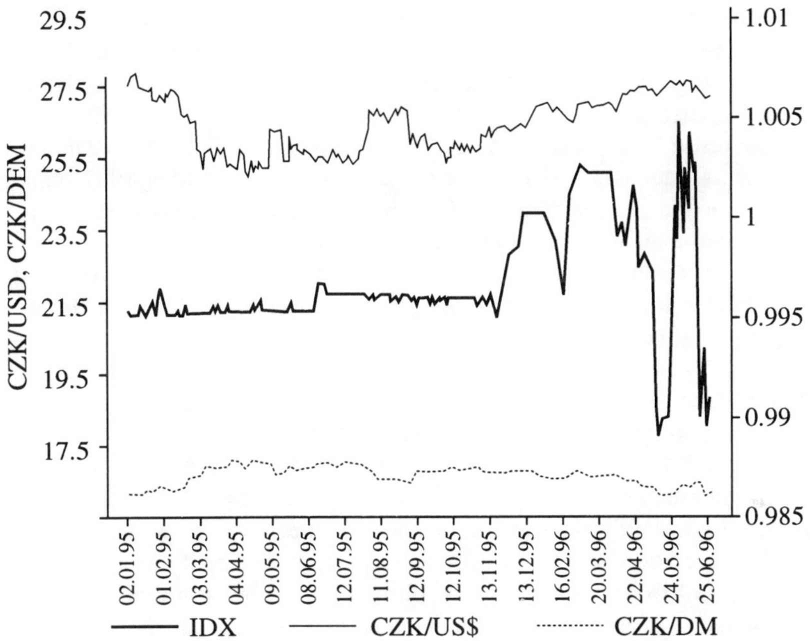

Note: IDX identifies the deviation of the CZK exchange rate from the central parity (central parity with respect to the basket = 1). Since the exit of CZK from the pegged rate in late May 1997, the index value has informative relevance only.

Source: Czech National Bank.

Figure 8.3 Exchange rates of CZK, 1995–1996

The Real Exchange Rate

The data on exchange rate developments in transition economies reveal a tendency to persistent real appreciation in the course of transition. The rates of real appreciation differed across individual countries, however. Those differences were due to the diverging developments in both components of the real rates, that is, in nominal exchange rates and in domestic price and costs levels *vis-à-vis* partner countries.

Three stages can be distinguished in the Czech developments since the start of transition:

- In 1990 the domestic CPI price level increased by only 9.9 per cent (see Table 8.2). The depreciation amounted cumulatively to about 50 per cent.
- During the period 1991–95, on the other hand, nominal exchange rate stability with respect to the basket was maintained despite much faster domestic price level increases relative to partner countries. A persistent real exchange rate appreciation developed.
- The resort to a wider band of ±7.5 per cent in late February 1996 and especially the shift to a floating regime at the end of May 1997 made more extensive fluctuations of nominal exchange rate possible. Thus, nominal exchange rate movements started to play a role in real exchange rate changes. While episodes of nominal depreciation partially corrected for the disparity, it nevertheless strengthened further during periods of nominal appreciation.

The real exchange rate appreciation of the CZK has been rather high in the examined period of transition, that is, since 1990 to mid 1997. In terms of both CPI and PPI it peaked in the first months of 1997. For the base January 1990, the cumulative real appreciation reached in February 1997 was, in terms of CPI and PPI, 41.8 per cent and 36.5 per cent, respectively. The nominal depreciation which has evolved since then, especially as a result of the induced exit from the pegged rate, diminished the level of real appreciation of the CZK. In June 1997 it amounted to 27.5 per cent and 22.1 per cent respectively, compared to January 1990 (see Table 8.6 and Figure 8.4). Although the gap between figures in terms of CPI and PPI has been widening, in principle their trends have continued to be parallel. Accordingly, in the Czech conditions it makes little difference whether we study the process of real appreciation in terms of CPI or PPI indices.

Compared internationally, the cumulative real exchange rate appreciation of the CZK was the largest among the countries of Central and Eastern Europe. Table 8.7 shows the figures based on trade-weighted indices for five CEFTA countries covering the period 1993–1997Q.2. The highest level of real appreciation in the case of the CZK developed in spite of a relatively favourable inflation record. The Czech economy was the first one among the EMEs of Central and Eastern Europe to reach and sustain one-digit CPI inflation (see Table 8.2 for CEFTA countries' inflation rates). However, while inflation was lower than in other transition countries, the nominal exchange rate remained stable for much longer.

Table 8.6 Real effective exchange rates of CZK

1. Change over year earlier (in %)

	1991	1992	1993	1994	1995	1996	1997[1]
a. End of period							
CPI based	27.38	9.06	14.65	8.18	6.53	8.12	–3.98
PPI based	36.12	8.13	10.01	4.17	6.00	4.99	–4.41
b. Year average							
CPI based	–8.71	8.28	16.65	7.31	7.89	7.55	4.35
PPI based	1.48	9.62	12.34	3.56	6.01	2.96	1.86

Notes: + real appreciation; – real depreciation.
1 June 1997 to June 1996 and first half 1997 to first half 1996.

2. Rate of change over base period (January 1990 = 100)

	Year average							
	1990	1991	1992	1993	1994	1995	1996	1997[1]
CPI based	94.01	85.82	92.93	108.40	116.32	125.50	139.50	127.47
PPI based	90.83	92.17	101.04	113.51	117.55	124.62	132.49	122.12

Notes: > 100 real appreciation; < 100 real depreciation.
1 June 1997.

Source: Selected Indicators of Monetary Development, Czech National Bank.

Real exchange rate developments, not nominal, co-determine a country's competitiveness and its current account balances. The conventional wisdom views real appreciation as a deterioration of international competitiveness with the resulting negative impact on growth and employment. Along those lines of reasoning, the data on the CZK's real exchange rate developments signalled an alarming loss of competitiveness and the risk of an increasingly overvalued currency. The constellation recalled developments in a number of countries with delayed adjustment which resulted in failures of the fixed exchange rate regime and in currency crises.[16]

The data on real exchange rate developments suggest that the 1990 'entry' depreciations of CZK were already eroded in the period 1993–94. However, this does not necessarily imply that the exchange rate has been increasingly overvalued since. There are two main reasons why it need not be so. One

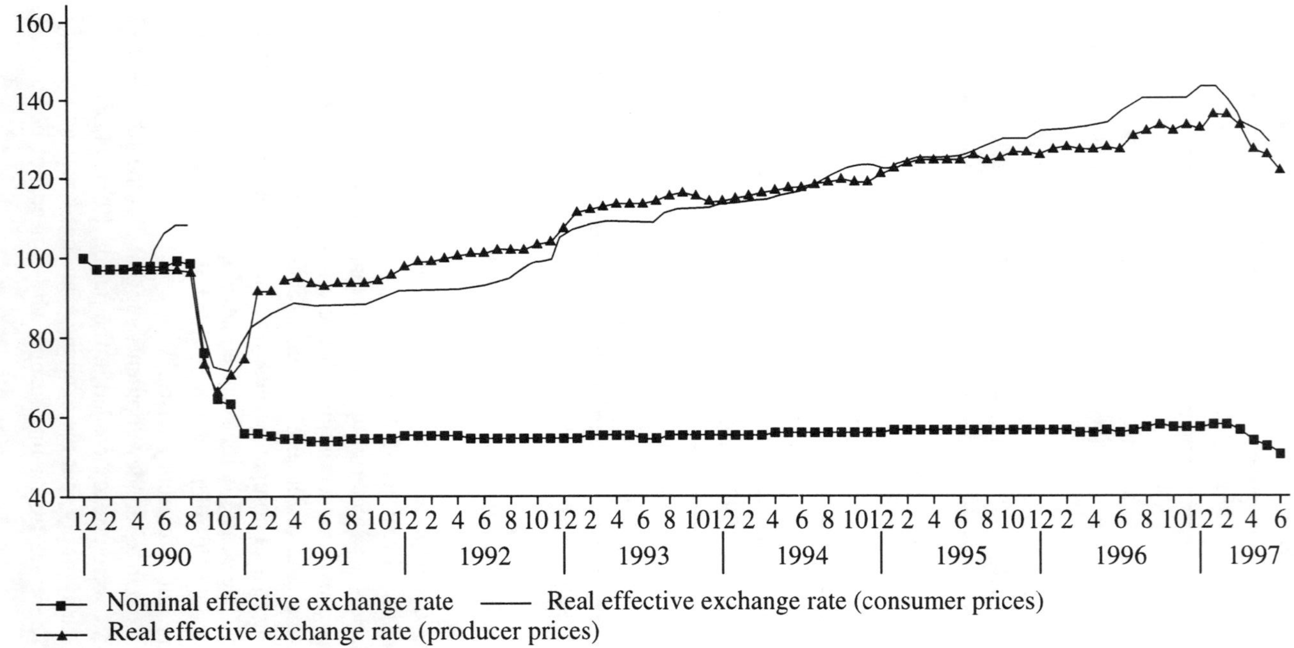

Note: > 100 real appreciation; < real depreciation.

Sources: Financial Statistical Information, Czech National Bank; Monthly Statistics of the Czech Republic, Czech Stastistical Office; OECD, Main Economic Indicators.

Figure 8.4 Effective exchange rates of CZK (0.65 DM + 0.35 US$ per CZK, January 1990 = 100)

Table 8.7 Real effective exchange rates of CEFTA countries' currencies

1. CPI based

	1993	1994	1995	1996	1997Q.1	1997Q.2
Czech Republic	122.3	130.4	136.4	147.4	158.8	150.2
Hungary	110.5	109.7	104.6	107.6	115.0	116.1
Poland	107.6	108.0	114.9	125.5	128.9	132.4
Slovak Republic	118.9	123.6	129.5	134.8	141.5	144.3
Slovenia	100.7	101.8	110.9	106.9	107.4	109.0
2. PPI based						
Czech Republic	117.9	122.0	125.4	132.6	142.0	133.8
Hungary	105.9	100.6	96.0	98.9	109.0	108.5
Poland	107.4	103.1	107.4	111.4	109.4	108.0
Slovak Republic	116.7	119.1	123.4	128.6	134.9	136.2
Slovenia	95.5	97.2	105.0	100.4	100.8	103.9

Note: Trade weighted indices *vis-à-vis* 21 industrial countries, 1992 = 100.

Source: BIS, Economic indicators for Eastern Europe, Basle.

reason is that the initial base period's level (January 1990) was most likely not an equilibrium rate. Another argument is that the equilibrium rate has changed over the transition years.

As discussed in Section 3, the exchange rate adjustments of 1990 were declared relative to the 'commercial rate' inherited from the centrally planned framework. This rate was a mere calculated coefficient, not the exchange rate proper. Accordingly, it was likely to diverge substantially from the market equilibrium level.

The other possibility is of particular interest. It suggests that a significant change in the equilibrium exchange rate level may have taken place in the course of transition. The PPP doctrine assumes an underlying tendency in the movements of the nominal exchange rate to offset changes in the ratio of national price levels. The real exchange rate as a currency-adjusted ratio of national price levels ought, therefore, to be constant in the long run. The observed deviations from the PPP benchmark reflect the temporary gains or losses in the country's external competitiveness.

A number of empirical studies concluded that in the conditions of standard market economies the PPP doctrine more or less holds in the long run. In the case of transition economies, there is in fact as yet no 'long run', and the validity of PPP as a benchmark can be questioned. Specifically, the large systemic and external shocks, abrupt shifts in productivity and in income levels taking place within a relatively short time span are not consistent with the assumptions of PPP theory relying on the stability of relative prices. There are grounds for expecting that those abrupt changes in real dimensions of the economy, discontinuities and shocks may have shifted the equilibrium real exchange rate in the course of transition.

It follows that, to assess the impact of real exchange rate appreciation and its consequences on the competitiveness of an economy in transition, the specific features of transition must be accounted for. In the concrete case of the Czech economy there were several arguments which warranted real appreciation: initial real undervaluation was particularly pronounced; prior to the opening up the prices of non-tradables were artificially low; and the productivity growth in the tradables sector significantly outpaced that in the non-tradables sector. However, the increasing current account deficits in the period 1996–1997Q.1 and some other indicators suggested that the degree of real appreciation might become excessive, eroding the cost competitiveness of exporting and import-competing industries.

5 CONCLUSION EXCHANGE RATE PEG IN AN ECONOMY IN TRANSITION: SUSTAINABLE AND DESIRABLE?

The experience of the EMEs of Central and Eastern Europe suggests that there has been a tendency to more flexible exchange rate regimes as transition advances. It refers also to the case of the Czech Republic. Although the koruna remained rigidly pegged to the basket for a relatively long period, the substantial widening of its fluctuations band in February 1996 and especially the move to a managed floating in late May 1997, implied the shift to a flexible type of regime. At the same time, the shift from pegged exchange rate regimes to various more flexible options turned out to be a more general phenomenon in EMEs worldwide, particularly in recent years. Are the pegged rates no longer either sustainable or desirable for the conditions of economies in transition or for EMEs in general?

There are considerable potential merits of pegged exchange rates for EMEs, the stabilization and disciplining impact of exchange rate anchor in particular. The nominal exchange rate stability may, however, become a controversial property once its level deviates substantially from the underlying fundamentals. A pegged exchange rate implies that its changes are, in principle, given up as an instrument of restoring a country's external balance and competitiveness. In those conditions the burden of adjustment rests with domestic variables, especially with wage rates, and the success depends on their flexibility.

Reflecting theoretical arguments and the experience of exchange rate pegs in EMEs, the role for exchange rate as a nominal anchor is conventionally attributed to two types of situations (compare Corden 1991):

- in conditions of high inflation rates when the country is ready to disinflate. In this case the role of exchange rate as a nominal anchor can only be temporary, in principle confined to a short period of radical disinflation;
- in countries with a positive price stability record and which have already earned credibility for their anti-inflationary policy stance. In their case there may be a prospect for a sustained nominal exchange rate anchor.

Given the character and magnitude of the adjustment required, Begg concluded for countries in transition: 'The original anchor is unlikely to survive intact as transition continues ... Where countries begin with an exchange rate peg, the issue may not be whether it should be abandoned but at what stage and with what it should be replaced' (Begg 1996, p. 57).

The Czech experience with the pegged exchange rate points to two different constellations which evolved in the course of transition and which affected its benefits and costs. In the first transition stage the fixed exchange rate of the CZK could be maintained without being tested and without the necessity for defending it. This was due to two specific features of the existing environment:

- the 'entry' undervaluation of the CZK made it possible for a persistent process of real appreciation to go on without undermining the competitiveness and balancing of external accounts;
- unlike sweeping liberalization in the trade sphere, only a rudimentary stage of financial openness was reached. Domestic financial markets and financial infrastructure were only in their infancy: according to the international standard the CZK remained non-convertible currency and capital flows were subject to extensive regulation. As a result, the domestic variables continued to be relatively isolated from external financial flows, and the implied interest rate differential had only a marginal impact on capital flows.

In these conditions, monetary policy could focus on the requirements of domestic stabilization and disinflation, without being constrained by its impact on capital flows or on current account balancing. It follows that the rudimentary stage of financial openness and transition-specific factors made a fixed exchange rate regime consistent with autonomous monetary policy. Monetary targeting, while addressing the requirements of disinflation, worked at the same time towards nominal exchange rate stability, that is, towards a slower flattening of the exchange rate 'cushion' created through initial undervaluation.

The institutional environment and the underlying conditions for the sustainability of a fixed exchange rate regime changed radically in the later stage of transition:

- the Czech Republic has reached a stage of an advanced financial openness in which domestic markets are open to strong influences from foreign financial markets;
- the continued real appreciation of the CZK's exchange rate has already eroded the previous undervaluation of the currency. This implies that, on the one hand, the peg and its disciplining impact could become increasingly binding for the cost and price developments in the open sectors of the economy. At the same time, however, the external competitiveness and current account developments became the function of real exchange rate changes;
- although open to external influences, some inherent properties of an economy in transition have as yet persisted, in particular: large inflation and interest rate differentials *vis-à-vis* basket currencies; the domestic financial markets and institutions are as yet not 'mature' and established; the banking sector is burdened with bad loans.

Given those features of transition, the advanced stage of financial openness of the Czech economy has proved to be increasingly inconsistent with the existing rigid fixed exchange rate regime. The room for monetary policy autonomy became severely constrained and, at the same time, the pressures arising from massive capital flows and from their volatility became an increasingly important destabilizing factor. The resulting policy response was a substantial widening of the fluctuation band in February 1996. This shift reduced the mentioned constraints and enhanced the desirable autonomy of monetary policy, providing more room for manoeuvre.

However useful such a regime change was, it was not a panacea. One consequence of the advanced stage of financial openness was that the exchange rate could not deviate for long from 'equilibrium' rates as assessed by financial market participants. The shift to a wider band alone could neither secure the maintenance of such an equilibrium rate, nor substitute for a proper policy mix to achieve it.

Like all transition economies, the Czech Republic has gone through a long period of real appreciation. An important question is whether this apprecia-

Table 8.8 Czech Republic: balance of payments, 1989–1992 (US$ million)

	1989	1990	1991	1992
Current account	508.9	–121.4	1708.2	–455.7
Trade balance	–148.3	–860.6	740.0	–2052.2
Service balance	561.5	121.6	910.6	1485.0
of which				
Travel balance	150.9	–69.5	436.0	659.3
Factor income balance	–58.8	–173.2	14.6	5.6
Transfer balance	95.7	184.8	57.6	105.0
Capital account	–188.1	504.8	–1331.0	1.9
Direct investment	170.6	132.6	513.1	982.9
Portfolio investment	n	n	n	–26.0
Other long term capital	–511.3	370.3	1142.2	319.7
Credits extended	–593.6	–192.0	153.2	105.1
Credits received	82.3	562.3	989.0	214.6
Net short term capital	152.9	1.9	–2986.3	–1274.7
Errors and omissions	221.5	–839.6	221.4	223.1
Change in reserves (increase –)	–542.6	889.0	–598.6	80.1

Source: Czech National Bank.

Table 8.9 Czech Republic: balance of payments, 1993–1997 (US$ million)

	1993	1994	1995	1996	1997
Current account	455.8	–786.8	–1369.1	–4292.2	–3155.8
Trade balance	–525.3	–1381.2	–3677.9	–5877.3	–4589.6
Service balance	1010.8	488.3	1842.0	1923.0	1731.9
of which					
Travel balance	1031.4	645.1	1242.4	1121.8	1267.3
Factor income balance	–117.5	–20.2	–105.6	–722.5	–650.2
Transfer balance	87.8	126.3	572.4	384.6	352.1
Capital account	–554.8	0.0	6.8	0.6	10.2
Direct investment	563.3	748.9	2525.6	1387.9	1275.2
Portfolio investment	1600.4	854.6	1362.0	725.5	1085.7
Other long term capital	861.1	1767.6	4338.3	2183.3	–1279.0
Credits extended	–2878.2	–2417.7	–2489.0	–2381.5	–4499.4
Credits received	3739.3	185.3	6827.3	4564.8	3220.4
Net short term capital	56.0	658.0	971.2	–926.8	–1686.6
Errors and omissions	103.5	–212.7	594.5	–833.1	297.0
Change in reserves (increase –)	–3029.3	–2371.6	–7458.1	828.0	1766.7

Source: Czech National Bank.

Table 8.10 Unit labour costs (real) in Czech industry (1989 = 100)

	ULC	*W/P*	*Y/L*
1990	100.6	100.3	99.7
1991	81.1	69.2	85.3
1992	90.3	75.3	83.4
1993	100.1	82.4	82.4
1994	104.6	90.6	86.6
1995	102.9	98.5	95.7
Annual changes (%)			
1991/90	–19.4	–31.0	–14.4
1992/91	11.3	8.8	–2.2
1993/92	10.9	9.4	–1.2
1994/93	4.5	10.0	5.1
1995/94	–1.6	8.7	10.5

Notes: The formula used for calculations of *ULC* was as follows:

$$ULC = (W/P)/(Y/L),$$

where
W = wages in industry
P = producer prices
Y = output in industry
L = employment in industry,
W/P = 'real product wage'
Y/L = labour productivity.

Enterprises with 100 employees and above.
1992–94: enterprises with 25 employees and above.

Source: Monthly Statistics of the Czech Republic, Czech Statistical Office.

Table 8.11 Profitability trends in the Czech manufacturing industry (1990 = 100)

	1991	1992	1993	1994	1995	1.–7. 1996
1. Producer prices	165.2	180.9	206.4	218.0	236.3	249.1
2. Average export values	157.0	158.4	162.1	168.4	176.1	184.3
3. Unit labour costs (nominal)	140.0	172.3	218.0	241.1	254.8	270.0
4. Domestic profitability (1)/(3)	118.0	105.0	94.7	90.4	92.7	92.3
5. Export profitability (2)/(3)	112.1	91.9	74.4	69.8	69.1	68.3

Notes: Unit labour costs (nominal) = (W) : (Y/L).
Enterprises with 100 employees and above.
1992–94: Enterprises with 25 employees and above.

Sources: Monthly Statistics of the Czech Republic; Hájek (1997).

Table 8.12 Net foreign assets (NFA), domestic credits (DC) and money supply (M2) developments

	ΔNFA	ΔDC	ΔM2	ΔNFA/ΔM2	ΔDC/ΔM2
1993/92	54.1	110.3	121.8	44.4	90.6
1994/93	105.1	103.6	150.0	70.1	69.1
1995/94	116.7	112.0	169.2	69.0	66.2
1996/95	–44.5	101.0	77.8	–57.2	129.8

Sources: Report on the Monetary Development in the Czech Republic; Czech National Bank.

Table 8.13 Drainage and injection of liquidity, 1990–1995 (annual averages, CZK billion)

Year	Liquidity injection (+)	Liquidity drainage (–)			Balance
		Open market operations	Minimum reserves requirements	Deposits with CNB	
1990	17.4	0.0	0.0	0.0	17.4
1991	21.1	0.0	21.8	0.0	–0.8
1992	15.1	11.8	25.3	0.0	–22.0
1993	6.5	26.4	40.0	0.0	–58.8
1994	7.1	70.4	47.2	0.8	–111.3
1995	7.3	89.4	64.3	20.6	–166.9
1996	13.4	138.4	94.6	–	–
Change in period					
1990	17.4	0.0	0.0	0.0	17.4
91/90	3.7	0.0	21.8	0.0	–18.2
92/91	–6.0	11.8	3.5	0.0	21.2
93/92	–8.6	13.6	14.7	0.0	–36.8
94/93	0.6	45.0	7.2	0.8	–52.5
95/94	0.2	19.0	17.1	19.8	–55.6
96/95	6.1	49.0	30.3	–	–

Sources: Czech National Bank; Selected Indicators of Monetary Development.

Table 8.14 *Scale of sterilization of foreign exchange inflow (monthly average, CZK billion)*

	A ΔNFA	B ΔMonetary base	A/B Sterilization ratio*	C ΔNDA
1993/92	64.3	43.2	1.49	–21.1
1994/93	96.3	67.0	1.44	–29.4
1995/94	181.8	162.3	1.12	–18.9
1996/95	–22.6	–9.2	(2.46)	13.4
1995/92	342.4	272.5	1.26	–69.4
1996/92	319.8	263.3	1.21	–56.0

Note:
* Ratio of the change in NFA to that in reserve money.
NFA is net foreign assets of the central bank (its net international reserves), NDA is its net domestic assets.

Source: Czech National Bank.

Table 8.15 *Foreign debt and foreign exchange reserves (in convertible currencies, US$ billion)*

	As of 1.1.93	Change in 93	94	95	As of 31.12.95	Change in 96	As of 31.12.96
Gross foreign debt	7.1	1.4	2.2	5.8	16.5	4.3	20.8
Short term	1.8	0.2	0.9	2.1	5.0	1.0	6.0
Long term	5.3	1.2	1.3	3.7	11.5	3.3	14.8
Foreign exchange reserves	3.5	2.8	2.6	8.5	17.4	–0.5	16.9
Official reserves (CNB)	0.8	3.1	2.3	7.8	14.0	–1.6	12.4
Commercial banks	2.7	–0.3	0.2	0.7	3.3	1.2	4.5

Source: Czech National Bank.

tion has already reached the dimensions where the Czech economy is losing competitiveness or whether the appreciation is primarily a reflection of 'equilibrium' real exchange rate changes caused by relative price and productivity developments. The long period of nominal stability and fixity of the Czech

Table 8.16 International comparison of price level and GDP per capita ratios, 1993 (Austria = 100)

	*P/P**	GDP per capita according to	
		Exchange rate	PPP rate
Czech Republic	30.1	13.3	44.1
Slovenia	57.9	27.9	48.2
Hungary	52.6	16.4	31.2
Slovak Republic	30.1	9.1	30.2
Poland	40.1	9.8	24.4
CEFTA	40.2	n	29.7
EU15	89.9	n	89.6
United States	84.0	107.0	127.0

Source: European Comparison Programme, Results 1993, Eurostat.

currency – achieved without really trying – led to the belief that real exchange rate changes could be consistent with the requirements of competitiveness. This belief was reinforced when the currency was allowed to float within a wide band in February 1996 and the exchange rate continued to fluctuate close to central parity and later moved to the strong part of the band.

However, for some time the path of the nominal exchange rate has primarily reflected the impact of capital flows motivated by lucrative interest rate differentials. At the same time the current account deficit has been increasing persistently, reaching the unsustainable ratio of 7.6 per cent of GDP in 1996. The positive productivity differential linked to the process of catching up was not high enough to correct for the inflation differential and, consequently, the Czech fundamentals became increasingly misaligned, given the existing pegged ratio. As a result, the CZK became vulnerable and sensitive to the changing perception of market participants. In May 1997, it became the target of speculative attacks with the resulting exit from the pegged regime and depreciation in the range of 10 per cent with respect to the previous central parity.

NOTES

1. CIS refers to Commonwealth of Independent States, the institutional framework linking the majority of republics of the former USSR.
2. This conclusion is broadly in line with the findings of some other studies which pointed to the relative advantages of fixed rates in fostering macroeconomic stabilization. Among the

studies covering EMEs of Central and Eastern Europe compare, for example, Fischer et al. 1997. Nevertheless, the implied causality could be subject to a discussion. The arguments may be formulated the other way round: because of more favourable inflation and stabilization records, the given countries could 'afford' to maintain fixed rates.

3. This theoretical body developed from the contributions by Mundell and McKinnon in the early 1960s (Mundell 1961, McKinnon 1963). For a more recent discussion, see Wihlborg and Willett 1991.
4. Austria and Switzerland, for example, are small open economies, closely integrated in real terms with the neighbouring Germany and subject to the impact of parallel external factors. Although the achieved degree of price stability and of macroeconomic performance used to be close to each other, their exchange rate regimes persistently remained completely different.
5. 'Which is better, a fixed exchange rate or a flexible one? No question in economics has been debated more fiercely or more inconclusively. The reason is that neither system is without its flaws, and nobody has been able to quantify the trade-off' (Krugman 1995, p. 17).
6. This concept reflects the conditions in which residents acquire assets and liabilities in foreign currencies and non-residents operate in the given country's financial markets. Accordingly, the degree of financial openness reflects the ease for both inward and outward transactions as well as for domestic transactions in foreign currencies.
7. In the case of former Czechoslovakia, the diversity of exchange rate ratios were as follows at the end of 1989, that is, just before the start of transition:

   - official exchange rate CSK 7.20 per US dollar;
   - so-called commercial rate CSK 14.30 per US dollar;
   - parallel market rates in the range of CSK 40–45 per US dollar.

   It should be noted, however, that both the extreme variables were of only marginal relevance. The official rate was maintained unchanged in the whole postwar period (since the currency reform of 1953) despite its growing overvaluation. Such a rigidity was possible only because of administrative regulation and was of no real importance. Parallel market rates, that is, CSK unofficial rates quoted by some foreign banks, were heavily biased as they reflected only a very narrow and specific market segment.
8. The argument followed Friedman's logic on extracting the information on relative prices in the conditions of volatile inflation. 'The broadcast about relative prices is, as it were, being jammed by the noise coming from the inflation broadcast' (Friedman 1976, p. 20).
9. However, the programmes for some other countries in transition which started later on, opted mostly for a managed floating arrangement.
10. Their differentiation into fixed and flexible options was not, however, unambiguous in the concrete cases. As put by Willett, when frequent adjustments are taking place, the case is one of managed flexibility. When the adjustment are only rare and occasional, the regime is a form of pegged rate (Willett 1992).
11. The extent of potential errors in assessing macroeconomic developments in the first transition year is demonstrated by the comparison of the predicted and actual magnitudes for 1991:

   - current account surplus of US$0.3 billion was achieved instead of an envisaged deficit of US$2.5 billion estimated by both government and IMF experts,
   - compared to the government's prediction of the 5–6 per cent drop in the GDP the actual fall was almost 15 per cent, that is, three times greater than expected.

   Obviously, the opposite deviations in the financial and real spheres were interrelated: the deeper fall in GDP was 'counterbalanced' by the more favourable current account result.
12. Sachs, for example, concluded: 'In Central Europe, Czechoslovakia stood out as the sole case of a country that began the reform period without extreme prior macroeconomic instability' (Sachs 1996, p. 147).

13. The BIS 1993 *Annual Report* claimed 'The Czech and Slovak Republics maintained remarkable macroeconomic stability last year ... To a large extent this stability must be ascribed to the fixed exchange rate policy, which contained inflationary pressures despite a relaxation of macroeconomic policies' (BIS 1993, pp. 39–40).
14. The effective exchange rate of the CZK appreciated in nominal terms by 1 per cent between January 1994 and December 1995, from 54.6 per cent in January 1994 to 55.7 per cent in December 1995, January 1990 = 100 per cent (see Hrnčíř 1995). Compared to the initial stage of transition, the December 1995 level implied some 0.5 per cent of nominal appreciation against January 1991.
15. In mid-1996, the CZK has depreciated by about 5 per cent against the US dollar but gained about 2 per cent against the Deutschmark since the beginning of the year.
16. Several countries in Latin America were hit by such failures, among them Chile, because of the overvalued fixed rate in early 1980s. Learning the lessons, competitive exchange rate and export-orientated development have become its policy priorities and Chile became a Latin American success story in the 1990s.

REFERENCES

Bank for International Settlements (BIS) (1993), *63rd Annual Report*, Basle, June.

Begg, D. (1996), 'Monetary policy in Central and Eastern Europe: lessons after half a decade of transition', IMF Working Paper No. 108, Washington, DC: IMF.

Corden, W.M. (1991), 'Exchange rate policy in developing countries', in de Melo and Sapir (eds), *Trade Theory and Economic Reform*, Oxford: Basic Blackwell.

Fischer, S., R. Sahay and C.A. Végh (1997), 'Stabilization and growth in transition economies: the early experience', in S. Zecchini (ed.), *Lessons from the Economic Transition*, Paris: OECD.

Friedman, M. (1976), 'Inflation and unemployment: the new dimension of politics', the 1976 A. Nobel Memorial Lecture, Stockholm, December.

Fry, M.J. and D.M. Nuti (1992), 'Monetary and exchange rate policies during Eastern Europe's Transition', *Oxford Review of Economic Policy*, Spring.

Hájek, M. (1997), 'Macroeconomic analysis of the Czech economy 1996', Working Paper CNB, No. 67, Prague.

Hrnčíř, M. (1995), 'Exchange rate regime in the stages of transition', Conference Paper, Prague.

Krugman, P. (1995), 'Monetary virtue leads two-peso tussle', *Financial Times*, 13 June, p. 17.

McKinnon, R. (1963), 'Optimum currency areas', *American Economic Review*, **53**, September.

Mundell, R.A. (1961), 'A theory of optimum currency areas', *American Economic Review*, **51**.

Rosati, D. (1997), 'Exchange rate policies in post-communist economies', in S. Zecchini (ed.), *Lessons from the Economic Transition*, Paris: OECD.

Sachs, J.D. (1996), 'Economic transition and the exchange rate regime', *The American Economic Review, Papers and Proceedings*, May, 147–52.

Schmieding, H. (1991), 'Lending stability to Europe's emerging market economies', Kiel Working Paper No. 481.

Wihlborg, C.G. and T.D.Willett (1991), 'Optimal currency areas revisited', in C.G. Wihlborg, M. Fratianni and T.D. Willett, *Financial Regulation and Monetary Arrangements after 1992*, Amsterdam: North-Holland.

Willett, T.D., F.Al-Marhubi and R. Dahel (1992), 'Currency policies for Eastern Europe and the Commonwealth countries', Conference Paper, July.

Williamson, J. (1991), 'Advice on the choice of an exchange rate policy', in E.M. Classen (ed.), *Exchange Rate Policies in Developing and Post-Socialist Countries*, International Center for Economic Growth, San Francisco: ICS Press.

Williamson, J. (1993), 'The management of capital inflows', International Finance Corporation, Conference Paper, December.

9. Macroeconomic policy and capital flows: evidence from transforming economies of Central and Eastern Europe

David G. Dickinson and Andy Mullineux

1 INTRODUCTION

This chapter considers some implications of macroeconomic policy for formerly centrally planned economies during their transition to 'market economies'. In particular, the relationship between (currency) convertibility, capital outflows (including capital flight) and inflows, and policy credibility is examined. These factors are mutually related, and their interaction is highlighted. The chapter considers these issues by focusing on the experiences of a number of the countries of Central and Eastern Europe (CEE), specifically Poland, the Czech Republic (up to January 1993 federated with Slovakia as the CSFR), Bulgaria and the three Baltic states.[1] In addition, Hungary appears in the empirical analysis as it has been a major recipient of foreign capital in the region. The concluding part of the chapter considers the recent issues with regard to capital flows and exchange rate policy which have been faced in Central and Eastern European countries and evaluates the lessons which can be learned from the experiences.

The globalization of financial capital markets has had major impacts on the developing economies. While the 1980s were a period when developing economies, particularly in Latin America, experienced the problems of capital outflows (flight) as a result of the debt crisis, the reverse trend has been observed in the 1990s. At the same time, the 'Tiger' economies of South East Asia have been experiencing major inflows of capital. However, both the Mexican crisis of 1994 and the South East Asian crisis (still developing) in October 1997 have demonstrated that financial liberalization and capital inflows are very much a two-edged sword.

In the early stages of their transition, Central and East European countries did not experience major capital inflows (capital flight was more of a problem). Indeed, it can be argued that their performance with regard to foreign direct investment (FDI) has been rather disappointing. For example, in 1991 the Asian newly industrialized economies (NIEs) had net FDI at US$19.1 billion, the Latin American economies experienced US$11.2 billion, while Central and East European economies benefited from $2.2 billion. By 1994, this had risen to $57.5 billion for Asian NIEs, to $25.9 billion in Latin America and edged up to $3 billion in CEE. The figures for portfolio investment are even more stark although, as we shall argue later, this is distorted by the lack of development and hence liquidity in financial markets in Central and East European economies.[2] These figures may partly reflect the importance of regional factors (very strong growth in the South East Asian region, proximity to the United States for Latin America) but the failure of the Central and East European economies to improve their performance in the early stages of their transition path suggests that the relative degree of stability of the economies is an important determinant. Indeed, more recent evidence over 1995 and 1996 supports this view in the sense that as the transition economies of CEE have stabilized, this has encouraged a much stronger FDI performance. This is the issue which we wish to investigate in this chapter. At the same time, development of financial markets, and particularly the stock market as privatization has proceeded, has encouraged inward portfolio investment.

This chapter synthesizes a number of distinct (but related) areas of analysis. The issue of convertibility in the case of transforming former socialist economies has been analysed in considerable detail (Williamson 1991; Greene and Isard 1991; Quirk and Evans 1995) and will be considered in the next section. Section 3 looks at the key variables which can explain international capital movements, particularly for economies such as the ones currently being considered. Of particular relevance is the work on capital outflows from developing, particularly Latin American, economies (Lessard and Williamson 1987). In addition, however, it is necessary to consider the level of capital inflows, particularly as economies become more stable and attract the attention of international investors. Indeed the success of economies in their stabilization plans is often also associated with increasing but more volatile capital flows which create a new set of issues which policy must attempt to tackle. Since risks and changes in them are cited as a major reason for capital flows, the issue of policy and its credibility also rests neatly within the analysis of capital flows. However, we need to be more specific about what factors lend a policy stance credibility, particularly for economies which are undergoing major structural adjustment. In Section 4, empirical analysis relating to the relationship between capital flows (specifically FDI) and macroeconomic (policy) uncertainty is presented. This will be informative since the macroeconomic and political experience of these countries differs quite considerably and it will be of interest to examine how the diverse performance of the economies has impacted upon the level of capital flows. Section 5 then reviews the policy implications of these experiences with a view to assessing reasons for the different performances of the economies examined, and Section 6 concludes with a summary of the major lessons which can be learned, about the interaction between policy and capital flows, and hence allows consideration of the decision to move full convertibility of the currency and the appropriate exchange rate regime to follow.

2 (FOREIGN EXCHANGE) CONVERTIBILITY AND THE EXCHANGE RATE REGIME

The issue of currency convertibility and choice of exchange rate regime has been recognized as a key one which needs to be faced by the transforming economies of CEE. Foreign exchange convertibility may be limited to current account transactions or extended through a spectrum of interim stages to full, current and capital account, convertibility. The terms internal and external convertibility are also used frequently.[3] In broad terms, current account (or internal) convertibility relates to individuals' rights to obtain foreign exchange at the prevailing market rate, in order to conduct normal international trade in goods in accordance with the IMF's Articles of Agreement. Capital account or external convertibility is the extension of access to foreign exchange for the conduct of cross-border trade in both financial and real assets by removal of all foreign exchange controls.

The basic argument for current account convertibility[4] is that it exposes domestic producers to the full rigour of international competition and allows the pricing of key inputs, particularly energy, to be consistent with world market conditions, thereby revealing comparative advantages and disadvantages, enhancing microeconomic efficiency. The adoption of current account convertibility, along with trade liberalization and the removal of distortionary price subsidies, was regarded as an important step in the process of promoting a market economy, and was adopted at the outset of their transitions by Poland (in January 1990) and the CSFR (in January 1991). Similar policy measures were taken (to varying degrees) by the other countries which form part of this study.[5] From the early stages of transition, the Central and East European economies which restricted convertibility have moved to liberalize their capital accounts such that most of them now have almost fully convertible currencies.

The integration of the financial sector into the international community, implied by a move to full convertibility of the currency, can have major benefits for the efficient allocation of capital, and allows full access of domestic enterprises to international sources of finance. The possibility of substantial capital outflows as a result of the high risks associated with domestic currency assets, while the credibility of the economic transformation programme is being established, means that it is not possible to establish this level of convertibility at an early stage in the transformation process. However, repatriation of profits is a necessary precondition for attracting FDI and the ability to repatriate investment capital is also desirable. For this reason EMEs (emerging market economies), which need to generate capital inflows to supplement low domestic savings pools, typically combine restricted (especially for the non-trading sector) internal and current account convertibility with capital account convertibility for foreign investors while maintaining restrictions on domestic capital outflows.

The choice of exchange rate regime is closely linked to the degree of currency convertibility. The policy adopted by the Central and East European economies has been variable in this regard. Some chose to peg the currency, others adopted a crawling peg while a smaller number opted for a flexible exchange rate regime.[6] Since, to achieve current account convertibility, it is necessary to unify the official and black-market exchange rates, currencies were generally undervalued since black-market rates typically contained risk premiums. However, from that time most have experienced real exchange rate appreciation as domestic inflation remained persistently high. Allied to this has been the problem of currency appreciation from inflows of capital as these are liberalized. Clearly, then, transition countries need to take into account the costs of freeing convertibility of their currency when there is likely to be resulting significant inflows of capital.[7] They also need to adopt an exchange rate regime which allows for the effects of domestic inflation on the real exchange rate in order to ensure that domestic industry can compete in world markets.

In this respect the credibility of policy is a key factor. There is a balance to be struck between the efficiency effects of a fully convertible currency and the risk of large-scale capital flows resulting from the high (and variable) risks associated with domestic financial assets. The choice of exchange rate regime is also clearly crucial – the effects of speculative capital flows on the ability of countries to maintain exchange rate pegs is well known both for developed and less-developed countries. Of particular relevance to the transforming economies of CEE are the recent trends in Latin America and South East Asia. These two regions have been the receptors of large-scale capital inflows during the 1990s. In the case of Latin America, particularly, this has been the response to improved macroeconomic conditions following the international debt problems of the 1980s. However, such inflows have resulted in a variety of potentially undesirable developments: nominal and real exchange rate appreciation, consumption booms, large trade deficits and, under fixed exchange rate regimes, increases in reserves with resulting monetary growth and inflation (for a detailed discussion, see Corbo and Hernandez 1996). Such developments have also been observed in economies which had appeared to be relatively successful (the Czech Republic in CEE and Thailand in South East Asia). The problems arise when attempts to maintain a fixed exchange rate are clearly at odds with the underlying fundamentals. In this case the policy is not credible and the domestic currency is at the mercy of currency speculators. In addition, as the Mexican crisis in late 1994 indicated, confidence in these economies is rather fragile and a sudden deterioration in overall macroeconomic conditions in one country triggering a currency crisis can generate major capital outflows in others (contagion effects). Such a situation has also been seen in CEE where the problems with the Czech Koruna has had effects on the Polish zloty.

To summarize then, the issue of currency convertibility and the choice of exchange rate regime are linked. A pegged exchange rate can assist in creating macroeconomic stability in the early stages of transition as long as the economic fundamentals are consistent with maintaining competitiveness at the chosen pegged rate. Countries which adopt rather liberal policies towards the capital account must take this issue very seriously, since currency crises happen very quickly and policy response cannot be quick enough to avoid the costs of such crises. Thus, until a country has developed a stable policy environment it should forsake the potential benefits of opening up the capital account, and even then, must ensure that the currency peg is sustainable and hence credible.

3 CAPITAL FLOWS AND THEIR CAUSES IN ECONOMIES IN TRANSITION

There are a number of different types of capital flow which need to be distinguished. Capital may flow into or out of an economy as a result of the desire of multinational corporations to invest directly in other countries (FDI). In addition, financial capital can flow both ways as a result of risk-spreading behaviour of the management of international portfolios. Alternatively, such capital flows may be of a short-term, speculative, nature. It is this latter category which often presents a policy dilemma in countries where there is a desire to both open the capital account and preserve exchange rate stability, although longer-term investment can also create problems of exchange rate appreciation.[8]

In modelling capital flows it is necessary to recognize that empirical success has been rather elusive (for example, see Calvo et al. 1993; Churhan et al. 1993). However, there is also a literature considering private sector investment in developing countries. For example, Greene and Villanueva (1991) have found that real GDP growth, level of per capita GDP, rate of public sector investment, real interest rates, domestic inflation, debt service ratio and the debt/GDP ratio are all important determinants of the rate of private sector investment in developing countries during the period 1975 to 1987. We start from the position that such macroeconomic variables are likely to be important in explaining FDI.[9] Recent analysis of irreversible investment has highlighted the importance of volatility in explaining the aggregate level of investment (see, for theoretical discussion, Dixit and Pindyck 1994, MacDonald and Siegel 1986, and, for empirical analysis, Pindyck and Solimano 1993, Aizenman and Marion 1993, and Episcopos 1995). The basic idea is that irreversibility increases the 'hurdle' rate which enterprises require before undertaking investment and that the size of the additional return required is related directly to the uncertainty which the investor faces. Hence, not only is investment a function of the state of the macroeconomy but also of its volatility. Of course, there is a whole literature devoted to general analysis of the causes of FDI (for example, see Dunning 1981) but the particular focus of the empirical analysis here is the reason for the rather disappointing performance of the Central and East European economies at the beginning of the transition process. Our contention is that macroeconomic uncertainty has a major impact and the particular emphasis of the next section of this chapter will be on modelling, and investigating the impact of, such volatility on FDI.

In the context of capital flows associated with investment in financial assets, we would suggest the portfolio model to be an appropriate analytical starting point. Hence, investors will wish to invest in assets which provide them with the highest overall level of return given the risks faced, which can be considered in two categories: risks due to underlying shocks which hit the economy, and risks which result from policy actions, perhaps in response to the turn of economic events. In simple terms, there will be a desire to diversify into the EMEs as long as the prospects for the economy are not too uncertain and any risk differential is adequately rewarded. Of course, portfolio capital outflows (if allowed) will respond in the same way. Once again, we would expect key macroeconomic variables to be good indicators of the risks which investors face and consequently should find the specification of the model explaining portfolio investment to be very similar to that for FDI (although the ability to extract oneself from financial assets means that the investment is reversible and consequently the way in which risks are modelled may be slightly different).

However, developing countries, and particularly formerly centrally planned economies which embarked on the transformation process with extremely basic 'two-tier'[10] bank-based financial systems, are unable to offer as wide a range of financial assets as more developed countries (see discussion in

Mullineux 1995). Hence, as a result of portfolio diversification and risk management, a potentially large capital outflow is to be anticipated. This may be reversed as the financial sector develops, privatization progresses, and secondary equity and government bond markets are established. Thus institutional structures will be important in determining the pressure for capital flows to take place. This is the most important reason why the level of investment in domestic financial assets has been so small for the Central and East European economies in the early stages of the transition process. Even in a country which was relatively successful in stabilizing its economy (Czech Republic) we have not seen international investors taking advantage of the high returns available until several years after the major reforms were initiated.[11]

The above discussion has highlighted that in order to explain capital inflows and outflows we must first identify the risks faced by investors in domestic assets. In the context of non-policy shocks, the transforming economies are subject to the vagaries of the world economic environment, and the reform programme itself creates a high level of uncertainty. The process of economic transformation is itself a major generator of uncertainty, from the effects of price and trade liberalization to the timing and distribution of bankruptcies and effects on the healthy parts of the economy. The collapse of the Council for Mutual Economic Assistance (CMEA) was also an important early shock to the economy. There is also a great amount of policy uncertainty which results from the transformation process and from the failure to create a stable political environment in which difficult policy decisions can be made (the Polish case is a prime example here, where political instability can be seen as a prime cause of capital flight at the start of the reform process).

In the context of fiscal policy, governments face large-scale government funding difficulties both from the lack of an effective and broad-based tax-collecting system and from the need to construct a social security system from scratch. In addition, monetary policy is also subject to stringent controls in order to stabilize the economy. There are potential problems arising from the conflict between monetary and fiscal policy which some countries were more successful than others in solving (the Czech Republic had been the most fiscally conservative prior to starting its transformation process and hence was the most successful in stabilizing the economy, while, at the other extreme, Bulgaria failed to deal with the issue at all and consequently suffered from persistent high inflation which has prevented its economy from properly starting the transition process until the second half of the 1990s). Hence the credibility of the reform package as a whole, and the macroeconomic stabilization programme in particular, is a key factor in assessing the risks inherent of investing in the transition economies.

For the EMEs, the problem of policy credibility is of a different order of magnitude to the studies of inflation control found in the conventional macroeconomic literature.[12] In these countries, the aim is to change the nature of resource allocation. Initiatives are required at both the micro and macro level. The success of the programme depends upon the ability to deliver the desired result at both levels. Hence the need for successful macro-stabilization to complement enterprise reform, for, without a stable aggregate environment, enterprises cannot be expected to make efficient resource allocation decisions.

Two issues which we can identify as important in the context of this study are the choice of exchange rate regime and the decision on the degree of currency convertibility. The adoption of a pegged exchange rate (and, in the extreme, of a currency board) has been a way of increasing the credibility of the commitment to control fiscal deficits and to maintain monetary stability (the relative experiences of the Czech Republic, Estonia and Bulgaria are instructive in this regard). It is also clearly important for capital flows in the sense that an increase in certainty about the future path of the exchange rate will remove the risk associated with exchange rate movements. In addition, the decision as to the degree of currency credibility can affect the credibility of policy in that the more open the regime adopted the clearer the commitment to the reform process. However, there can be a downside as well. Liberalizing the capital account too quickly can destabilize the financial sector and hence create more volatile macroeconomic conditions. This can not only eradicate the benefits of such a policy but actually push the economy backwards in the sense that uncertainty increases and creates less attractive conditions for investment both from domestic sources as well as from those outside the economy.

For policy to be successful it requires credibility. Capital flows respond to the relative risks of investing at home and abroad, and the degree of policy credibility is an important component of those risks. The degree of convertibility permitted will relate closely to the degree of credibility of the overall policy stance. The choice of exchange rate regime is dependent on the credibility of attempts to control fiscal deficits and maintenance of a fixed exchange rate is easier for countries which do not have large amounts of international debt. In the early stages of reforms, even without full convertibility, the problem of capital flight means that governments should strive to make their chosen policy as credible as possible.[13] Otherwise, the costs of the reform process in terms of an even harsher macroeconomic stabilization package involving, for example, high nominal and real interest rates to support the exchange rate, will be greater. As the reform process generates both stability and growth, then the chosen exchange rate regime must be consistent with the underlying economic fundamentals and the lack of domestic policy coordination will open up the currency to speculative attack. This has been the experience of the Czech Republic during 1996 and more recently of Thailand and other South East Asian countries in 1997. What this implies is that policy should be flexible as well as credible. It has already been pointed out that economies are subject to the vagaries of the economic environment and policy should be capable of being adapted to changed circumstances while retaining its credibility. This may entail, in practice, significant costs. One of the more significant costs for the economies of CEE will be the failure to attract FDI.

The next section collects these issues together by analysing the behaviour of capital flows and relating it to policy and the path of key macroeconomic variables during the early stages of the reform process. The study involves looking at the experience of a number of the EMEs of CEE to highlight the important interrelationships. The results of the next section are then used to motivate a discussion of the future policy options which are open to the reforming economies of CEE as they move on to the next stage of their reforms.

4 AN ANALYSIS OF CAPITAL FLOWS DURING THE STABILIZATION AND POST-STABILIZATION PHASES

This section considers the evidence on capital flows in a number of EMEs of CEE, in particular, Poland, the Czech Republic, the Slovak Republic, Latvia, Estonia and Hungary.[14] Reference is also made to the experience of Lithuania and Bulgaria. The emphasis of the work here is on identifying factors that relate to the effects of the policy and its credibility, so that the analysis can be related back to the previous discussion. We shall adopt a multi-country approach in order to highlight key differences between countries which are undergoing similar structural transformations. Note also that some of these countries have been reforming longer than others and comparison of economies at the same stage of the transition process, although at different times in the European and world economic cycle, can also yield insights. We concentrate on the early stages of the reform process when the effects of uncertainty are dominant. As has been discussed previously, we consider three particular elements of capital flows, net foreign direct investment, portfolio and other investment (both short and long term) and capital flight (as measured by the errors and omissions entry in balance of payments statistics (see Table 9.1). Most data are taken from IMF *International Financial Statistics* (it will be indicated where data is obtained from an alternative source).

Casual observation can provide some insights into what has been going on. In terms of net FDI, Hungary, the Czech Republic and latterly Poland have

Table 9.1 *Capital flows in selected Central and Eastern European transition economies, 1991.1–1995.2 (maximum time period; some countries' data are for shorter period; data is quarterly)*

	Other capital	Net FDI	Errors and Omissions
Czech Republic			
Mean	420.5	186.6	–20.2
Standard Deviation	523.4	146.9	364.7
Minimum/maximum	–437/1497	–14/552	–520/648
Poland			
Mean	–37.2	104.3	–28.6
Standard Deviation	1404	77.1	218.9
Minimum/maximum	–4427/2831	10/252	–435/450
Latvia			
Mean	25	33.3	–103.8
Standard Deviation	92.3	29.6	114.8
Minimum/maximum	–130/185	6/81	–346/27
Estonia			
Mean	–3.2	36.9	–2.4
Standard Deviation	26.4	19.8	36.4
Minimum/maximum	–51.6/38.8	13/85	–47.5/52.1
Hungary			
Mean	310.4	398.5	53.2
Standard Deviation	598.6	317.1	136.5
Minimum/maximum	–572/1277	159/1515	–122/358
Slovak Republic			
Mean	–58.7	29	59
Standard Deviation	313.3	62.2	122.8
Minimum/maximum	–425/351	–98/141	–138/291

dominated. Hungary has had a long history of encouraging FDI and consequently has a well-established reputation. The Czech Republic has experienced the most stable macroeconomic conditions. Poland is by far the largest country and hence has the most potential for foreign investors in terms of size of domestic market. For the other countries, we may observe that there is a rising trend but from a small base. With regard to other capital flows we may observe that Poland is significantly affected by its inherited debt and subsequent restructuring. The Czech Republic has been on a marked upward trend, resulting from its successful privatization and consequently relatively active stock market. Hungary is also experiencing greater flows, particularly in the recent past, for similar reasons. With regard to trends outside of the data period reported we may note that the region, as a whole, saw a significant increase in the level of FDI.

One feature of the data is its highly volatile nature. This is to be expected given that it is quarterly and the nature of the variables being analysed, but it makes modelling a difficult process. The volatility in the flows may well reflect the volatility of the economies, and the consequent uncertainty which is the motivating force behind the capital movements. This is something to which we wish to pay particular attention. The degree to which the flows are volatile is indicated in Table 9.1, where the summary statistics are reported for each of the category of flows which we are analysing. It may be noted that, not surprisingly, FDI is less volatile than the other components of capital flows.

We now turn to consider the formal estimation of a model of FDI. Earlier discussion has indicated various variables which we should include as explanatory variables. Thus we would expect the growth rate of the economy, the trade balance or the current account to be important real variables indicating the strength of the economy. At a policy level, monetary growth and inflation are likely to be important. Note that we regard these explanatory variables to be exogenous to the determination of capital flows since we are dealing with a panel data set with a relatively short time period (about ten quarters).

In addition, we are also interested in the effects of credibility or volatility of policy on the behaviour of capital flows. There are various ways of trying to measure the effect of credibility of policy on the behaviour of key economic variables (in our case capital flows). Agenor and Taylor (1991) consider the use of the Kalman filter, but we have too short a time period to consider using relatively sophisticated tools to measure the uncertainty which investors face. However we start from the basis of a GARCH(1,1) model. This constructs a measure of the time evolution of the variance of a variable as follows:

$$\sigma_t^2 = \omega + \alpha\varepsilon_{t-1}^2 + \beta\sigma_{t-1}^2 \qquad (9.1)$$

where α, β and ω are constants and σ is the forecast variance and ε is the residual from the equation which estimates the variable in question. This can be re-written as:

$$\sigma_t^2 = \frac{\omega}{1-\beta} + \alpha\sum_{j=1}^{\infty}\beta^{j-1}\varepsilon_{t-j}^2. \qquad (9.2)$$

Hence the GARCH model generates a measure of the variance of a variable which weights relatively recent observations more highly. As indicated, we do not believe it useful to use such a model for our analysis but we adopt the principles involved by constructing a measure which writes the variance of a variable as follows:

$$V(X_t) = \left[\sigma_x + \alpha \frac{\sum_{0}^{t} \beta^{t-j} (X - \overline{X})^2}{t-1} \right] \Bigg/ 2 \qquad (9.3)$$

where $V(X_t)$ is the measured volatility (uncertainty) of the variable X at time t, while σ_x is the sample variance for the data period available and β is the weight, while α is chosen so that the second term of the expression converges to the sample variance over the full data set. Thus the measured uncertainty converges to the sample variance over the complete data period. Writing the uncertainty measure in this way ensures that the path of uncertainty over the sample period is not too volatile (compared to, say, representing the uncertainty at a particular point in time as the variance of observations to that time). The base level of uncertainty is proportional to the sample variance – this implies some element of rational expectations in the sense that the economy comes into the period with a level of uncertainty which to some extent reflects the outcome over the whole period, but if actual realizations at the start of the period are at the extremes of the (assumed) sample distribution then the uncertainty measure will tend to decrease over tOdï – this is the effect we wish to capture for economies which have stabilized relatively successfully. We need to specify a value for β in order to make this definition operational, and we come to this later.

Also, we wish to consider the country-specific effects since a particular feature of our study is to suggest how policy and its credibility has an influence on capital flows. We model this by using a fixed-effect model, allowing our estimated constant term to vary across countries. In addition, we wish to take into account the importance of exchange rate policy and its credibility. We do this through examining the experience of countries which have used alternative exchange rate policies.

We now report the results of single-equation estimation for FDI. All estimations have used a heteroskedastic consistent estimation method. We pool our individual country data and estimate across all countries. The sample is quarterly over 1991.1 to 1995.4, although note that we have data over the whole sample for Poland, Hungary and the Czech Republic (for the Czech Republic pre-1993.1 we use data for the CSFR) while we were able to obtain data from 1993.2 for Estonia and Latvia. We were unable to obtain data for the other countries in our study.

First we shall discuss the outcome of calculating our measure of uncertainty. We tried different values of β but found that we did not get significantly different results. We therefore chose the simplest specification which was to set β to 1. The variables which were to represent uncertainty were: variance of inflation, variance of real growth, variance of monetary growth (both narrow and broad measures were tried). A brief review of the pattern identified from our adopted measure of uncertainty shows it to be consistent with the macro-stabilization of the economy with the success (or otherwise) of different countries clearly identified. If we take the most successful country, the Czech Republic, we observe a decline in inflation uncertainty and in the early part of the period in growth, with an increase later on as the economy starts to recover from the effects of the reform process. There is a large increase in monetary growth uncertainty half-way through the period as a direct result of the split of the CSFR. Broad money growth (and hence its variance) also reflects the effects of (unsterilized) capital inflows. For Poland we find a similar pattern for inflation uncertainty, although the magnitude is higher than in the Czech Republic, while growth shows greater volatility caused by the more prolonged recession followed by significant improvement later in the period. The large increase in variance of monetary growth is due to the stabilization measures which took hold during 1991. Hungary shows a similar inflation response as the other countries while its growth performance is indicative of a steady improvement in the real economy over the period once monetary growth behaviour is strongly influenced by stabilization measures early in the period. Similar patterns emerge for Latvia and Estonia, although later during the period to reflect that their reform process started after that of the other three economies. The patterns for monetary growth reflect that both countries adopted (modified) currency board systems and, in addition, Latvia also introduced full convertibility of its currency, impacting particularly on broad monetary growth.

The results of our estimation across the cross-section of countries, allowing for fixed effects across countries are shown in Table 9.2. The result of the estimation suggests that general uncertainty has been a significant factor in determining the relative success of Central and Eastern European economies in securing flows of FDI. A number of features are worth mentioning. First, GDP enters positively, as expected – the larger the economy the greater its attractiveness for FDI, although note also that during the period studied these economies were experiencing output falls so the positive effects of GDP growth only appear later in the period. Second, growth uncertainty (*VGROWTH*) appears with a negative sign. This may appear perverse but recall that the economies were going through stabilization. Those economies

Table 9.2 Equation for FDI as a function of macroeconomic variables and macroeconomic uncertainty

Variable	Coefficient	Standard error	*t*-statistic	Probability
C	492.3351	102.3264	4.811416	0.0000
GDP	0.217578	0.135022	1.611426	0.1126
M3GROWTH	0.951722	0.378174	2.516625	0.0147
VGROWTH	–5.204768	2.417902	–2.152597	0.0356
VINF	–0.556696	0.108230	–5.143613	0.0000
CR	–205.1566	58.61350	–3.500160	0.0009
PL	–189.4387	32.59037	–5.812719	0.0000
D1	1175.935	28.61190	41.09950	0.0000

R^2	0.850188	Mean dependent variable	183.8046
Adjusted R^2	0.831790	Standard deviation dependent variable	219.8913
Standard error of regression	90.18487	Sum squared residual	463598.7

with high *VGROWTH* were the first to stabilize and then start on a growth path, hence becoming the most attractive for FDI. The same reasoning applies to the positive sign for *M3GROWTH* – stabilization was often associated with large falls in M3 (during the stabilization phase we do not see much FDI) which then allowed for some positive monetary growth, encouraging confidence in the domestic economy and resulting increase in FDI flows. Of particular interest here are the negative effects of the uncertainty variables. We have already discussed the interpretation of the sign on *VGROWTH*. The variance of inflation appears with a negative sign – the larger this variance the higher the uncertainty about the economy and its prospects; certainly policy credibility will be damaged. The two country-specific effects, picked up by the dummy variables *CR* (Czech Republic) and *PL* (Poland) are also interesting. They show that these two countries are picking up a relatively small amount of FDI compared to Hungary (the major recipient). One interpretation of this is that the length of time a country has been open to FDI is important (Hungary has been doing so since the mid- to late-1980s). If this is the case we would expect to see the other countries in the region gradually improve their performance, particularly as they become more stable. In addition, we may note that the equation performs badly with respect to Estonia. The forecast FDI is declining while in fact FDI has been rising. One interpretation of this is that the success of the Estonian currency board has offset the effects of general macroeconomic uncertainty by creating a credible policy regime. If true, we would expect that Estonia should benefit in the post-sample period from a relative surge in FDI (as we shall discuss, this is indeed the case).

To summarize, our empirical results are supportive of the contention that uncertainty is a key factor in determining the amount of FDI which a country receives. If we interpret this at a regional level then we would expect that the amount of FDI coming into the Central and Eastern European region should increase as the constituent countries increase their stability.

5 MONETARY AND EXCHANGE RATE POLICY, CREDIBILITY AND CAPITAL FLOWS: THE RECENT PAST

In this section we turn to consider the implications of the empirical analysis which we have reported in the previous section. We have identified that volatility, in the way in which we have measured and analysed it, is important. In addition, we have considered how different countries have performed in attracting capital inflows and we have found that those economies which have the advantage of a history of openness to the rest of the world or where macroeconomic stability was sustained or where the size of the country makes it attractive, have done relatively well. The implication is that relatively small countries should open themselves to the outside world as much as possible but will have to wait some time before experiencing the benefits of this while at the same time ensuring macroeconomic stability. Now we shall briefly discuss the implications of this analysis for the recent history which Central and Eastern Europe has experienced.

The experience of the economies of CEE during 1996 and 1997 has demonstrated that whilst they have had mixed success with stabilization (or, at least, the speed with which it has been achieved) the future still holds the prospect of a fairly 'bumpy ride'. The flows of FDI have quite clearly grown during the period. In addition, as the financial markets have continued to develop there has also been a marked increase in the levels of portfolio investment (which had been negligible up to 1995). Table 9.3 reports the flows which have taken place. As would be expected, increasing size of average flows has also been accompanied by more volatility. This reflects not only that capital flows are volatile but that the economic environment in the Central and Eastern European economies has become more unstable. The Czech Republic experienced a currency crisis and as a result eventually had to devalue the currency in mid-1997. The underlying causes of this crisis were a rapidly deteriorating trade balance and a weak banking system. Of course, a trade deficit is not necessarily an indicator of weak economic

Table 9.3 Recent experience of capital flows for selected Central and Eastern European economies (US$ million)

Country		95.1	95.2	95.3	95.4	96.1	96.2	96.3	96.4
Hungary	FDI	228	238	332	3677	459	274	605	648
	PI	–139	1148	861	342	20	–35	–509	–345
Czech Republic	FDI	111	280	1580	560	299	137	517	435
	PI	30	344	321	675	–129	398	324	178
Lithuania	FDI	12.2	17.3	18.5	23.4	15.6	25.7	45.2	65.3
	PI	20.4	4.1	–4.1	–4.3	31	23.8	–9.1	–33
Estonia	FDI	45.5	38.9	80.5	34.1	25.6	–12.8	31.9	54.5
	PI	–0.5	5.3	–35.7	8.9	–14.9	70	–6.6	93
Latvia	FDI	16	49	81	83	70	56	35	116
	PI		–21	–17	1	–1	6		6

Note: PI = portfolio investment.

Source: IMF, *International Financial Statistics*.

performance but the real appreciation of the Czech koruna, which took place as a result of the nominal exchange rate peg in the face of a persistent positive wage inflation and a lack of growth in labour productivity, was always likely to bring about a situation where continuation of the parity was no longer feasible. Similarly the weakness of the banking system is not, of itself, necessarily a cause of currency crises, but once the speculators get to work the crisis will feed on a lack of confidence in domestic financial institutions, exacerbated by increases in the domestic rate of interest in an attempt to protect the currency. Such a situation characterizes the experience of the Czech Republic, and, indeed, has very recently hit the high growth economies of South East Asia.

Despite the more unstable environment, generally, we have seen that the relative success of the early stages of the transition has encouraged FDI. The performance right across the region has been increasingly impressive and does suggest that there is the potential for really significant flows in the future. In this case we would expect the effects of uncertainty to be reduced and for the more fundamental economic forces such as flexibility of the labour market, the level of real unit labour costs and the size of the potential market, to take over as key influences. In a similar way, at least until the very recent past (October 1997), we would expect the stock markets of these economies to continue to offer very attractive investment options and for major inflows of portfolio investment to continue. The fundamentals are basically favourable and while it may take time for confidence to be restored we would expect to see an improving position with regard to portfolio inflows.

However, for this to happen we would like to see an increasingly flexible policy response. It can be argued that the recent problems of the Czech economy are attributable, at least in part, to a commitment to an unsustainable exchange rate peg. Furthermore, the resulting crisis may well have harmed the economy more than if the exchange rate peg had been abandoned earlier. But, as we have also argued, an exchange rate peg has the benefit of making credible the commitment to achieve low rates of inflation. Thus there is the standard conundrum of flexibility against credibility. But this may be too stark a choice. Increasingly central banks are adopting the concept of policy rules. As long as these are transparent then markets will feel able to predict policy fairly accurately. The advantage of a fixed exchange rate policy is that it is predictable. But it also makes the policy inflexible. It would be better to develop a policy rule which allows for maintenance of a fixed exchange rate unless and until the economic fundamentals are inconsistent with the maintenance of the peg. Since market participants are able to judge this as well as policy makers then it would allow the markets to recognize when a currency peg would be abandoned and for the devaluation to take place as smoothly as possible. Adopting increasingly wider bands on the target exchange rate would be one way of achieving this at the policy level.[15] In other words, widening the bands in response to economic fundamentals would be part of the policy rule. Such a policy would have the advantage of building in a mechanism for adjusting policy once it became non-credible.

CONCLUSIONS

This chapter has examined the behaviour of capital flows during the early stages of the reform process of the EMEs of CEE, a time period which required stringent macroeconomic stabilization measures. These measures have generated uncertainty which, it has been argued, has been a significant hindrance to FDI. This uncertainty has been accompanied by a major devaluation of the exchange rate which has, for some countries, became a source of instability (Poland is a clear example) while others were able to operate a stable exchange rate successfully, either through a clear policy decision (Czech Republic) or through adopting a currency board system (Estonia). The speed at which macro-stabilization is achieved will depend very much on the initial conditions and, certainly in the case of the Czech Republic, these were conducive to the stabilization process. Estonia's initial success with the currency board has been noteworthy but, like the pegged exchange rate of the Czech Republic, the strictures of the currency board system have created problems. For example, currency inflows caused inflation to increase and required sterilization by the central bank and, indeed, in recent months the system has come under increasing strain in response to the general speculative pressure against currencies in the region. However, certainly a currency board is one way of building credibility in an anti-inflationary monetary policy and has appeared to have had a beneficial impact for Estonia during the period of our analysis.

The development of the financial sector can do much to encourage capital flows. Privatization has been seen as a way of encouraging direct investment as well as financial (stock) markets. Recently the Czech Republic has experienced the benefits of the relative speedy programme of privatization, and the length of time Hungary has been undergoing reform means that it is well ahead of the game. The repeated delays with the mass privatization process in Poland have clearly hindered the inflows of capital that should result, while the Baltic states have been developing their privatization strategies and are now benefiting from the process by attracting an increasing level of capital inflows. Until the 1996/97 crisis, Bulgaria had been very reluctant to privatize any enterprise except those which are in serious financial distress. It is not surprising that this has been costly to an economy which has not experienced much benefit from the reform process to this time and certainly has not experienced any consistent foreign investment.

The danger with becoming too attractive an investment is that capital flows inwards and creates pressure for the exchange rate to be revalued and a resulting loss of competitiveness. This was the experience of the Czech Republic. We have considered the potential policy responses to this development and the danger of continuing to operate an inflexible pegged exchange rate. Hence we suggest that policy rules which allow for a more flexible policy response should be introduced. Adopting wider bands in which the exchange rate is allowed to move, where the size of the bands is consistent with the underlying economic fundamentals is one possibility. Of course, one of the key fundamentals will be the degree of currency convertibility which is allowed. Adopting a fully convertible currency requires a sustainable stable macroeconomic environment. Hence most of the economies of the region have moved towards or have fully adopted full convertibility later in their reform process once stabilization had taken place. This should improve the efficiency of the financial system. However, capital inflows in the presence of a rather weak banking system which is poorly regulated creates an environment where bank failure is likely – particularly if there is an implicit or explicit deposit insurance scheme as a result of the moral hazard problem which is created. Thus the underlying economic fundamentals may mean that financial liberalization generates significant economic costs before the benefits are apparent. Such a situation has happened in Thailand recently.[16] So the issue of economic fundamentals relates not only to the macroeconomic but also to the microeconomic environment. Hence if the banking system is not in a satisfactory condition then, despite correct macroeconomic fundamentals, it will not be possible for full convertibility to exist alongside the maintenance of a pegged exchange rate.

To summarize, then, we have found that uncertainty about the economic environment and policy credibility are significant factors affecting capital inflows into the economies in transition in Central and Eastern Europe. In addition the experience of the different economies of the region point towards how policy choice of exchange rate regime can influence the credibility of policy, although this is as much dictated by the economic fundamentals as the ability of policy makers to win the confidence of economic agents. As these economies move towards greater stability, the issue of currency convertibility becomes more important, and in order to promote competitive pressures in the financial sector a move to full convertibility of the currency plays the same role as current account convertibility for the goods and services market. However, a move to capital account convertibility in haste will create instability which may feed on itself and lead to a loss of policy credibility. In addition, poor microeconomic conditions in the financial sector will exacerbate problems and highlight the inconsistency between the objectives of economic policy.[17] One route through this is for the policy makers to adopt a policy-making system which recognizes these potential inconsistencies and to make policy as transparent as possible by using rules which respond to the underlying economic fundamentals. Such a policy framework has the benefits of being both credible and flexible.

NOTES

1. These are the countries with representatives in our ACE research group.
2. See Turner (1995) for more details. Note that the Central and Eastern European countries chosen for comparison are Poland, the Czech Republic, Hungary, Bulgaria, Estonia, Latvia and Lithuania.
3. See Greene and Isard (1991) for a more detailed discussion of the slight differences between these terms.
4. See Asselian (1991), Bofinger (1991), Bomhoff (1992) and Polak (1991).
5. For example, Bulgaria adopted internal convertibility, Estonia full current account convertibility and Latvia and Lithuania introduced full convertibility of the currency.
6. Thus the CSFR (later, two countries, the Czech and Slovak Republics) chose to peg the exchange rate, while Poland moved to a crawling peg after its fixed rate regime failed. Estonia adopted a currency board as did Lithuania after experimenting with a floating currency, while Latvia has also moved to an exchange rate peg. Bulgaria has introduced a currency board after several years of a floating rate regime and very high inflation.
7. Such an outcome has been typical, resulting from the return of flight capital as well as the inflows of foreign capital attracted by the high returns associated with emerging market economies. In the next section, we consider, in detail, the factors which affect capital flows.
8. Note that Claessens et al. (1995), considering both developed and developing economies, have suggested that the distinction between short- and long-term capital flows is not

helpful, in the sense that their time-series properties are similar and hence it is no longer appropriate to consider short-term flows as more volatile (thus a policy problem) than long-term ones.

9. Note that our earlier analysis showed that this was effectively the only source of capital inflows in the early stages of the transition.
10. Prior to the introduction of 'the reforms', a 'monobanking' system prevailed, then, typically in the late 1980s, a two-tier system was created by separating central banking functions from commercial banking functions, which were to be performed by a number of 'commercial' banks. The latter were newly created state-owned institutions or existing state-owned, formerly 'specialized' banks, and were usually organized on a(n) (industrial) sectoral or regional basis (Corbett and Mayer 1991).
11. Note that our own work (Dickinson and Mullineux 1996) has found that there was a significant amount of capital flight during the early stages of the transition in Poland and the CSFR which is likely to be a response to the risks which were faced and the desire to move into more developed financial markets. It could also be the consequence of round-tripping as a result of the relatively favourable tax treatment of foreign investment (see Khan and Ul Haque (1985) for a full explanation of this behaviour).
12. The early literature on credibility has concentrated on inflation control (Backus and Driffil 1985; Barro and Gordon 1983). Some more recent studies have tackled the issue of policy credibility during a major reform process, for example, Baxter (1985), Rodrik (1989). Rodrik (1991) has also looked specifically at investment and policy credibility in developing countries. Van Wijnbergen (1985) has developed theoretical analysis of the credibility of trade policy reforms and capital flight.
13. The ability of capital controls to restrict capital flight is an open question (see Phylaktis 1988). Note also that currency substitution may be a major problem when internal convertibility is adopted (Rogers 1992).
14. A considerable amount of analysis has been conducted on the transition of these countries (for example, see Begg (1991) and Hrnčíř and Klacek (1991), on the Czech and Slovak Republics (CSFR as it was) and Berg and Sachs (1992) and Calvo and Coricelli (1992), on Poland).
15. Note that such an approach was used by the Czech Republic as a way of counteracting speculative pressure in 1996, but the return of a crisis and eventual devaluation in 1997 demonstrate that such a policy cannot be used as a method of defending an unsustainable exchange rate. When the fundamentals have been consistent the policy has been used by countries with more success (for example, for some members of the Exchange Rate Mechanism in the aftermath of the September 1992 crisis).
16. Note that the property bubble which burst in 1996 exacerbated this process.
17. It is important to ensure that a proper regulatory and supervisory agency is in place and that appropriate measures have been taken to deal with any bad debt problem.

REFERENCES

Agenor, P. and M.P. Taylor (1991), 'Testing for credibility effects', *IMF Staff Papers*, **39**, 545–71.

Aizenman, J. (1991), 'Exchange rate flexibility, volatility, and domestic and foreign direct investment', *International Monetary Fund Staff Papers*, **39**, 890–922.

Aizenman, J. and N. Marion (1993), 'Macroeconomic uncertainty and private investment', *Economics Letters*, **41**, 207–10.

Allesina, A. and G. Tabellini (1989), 'External debt, capital flight and political risk', *Journal of International Economics*, **27**, 199–220.

Asselian, J.C. (1991), 'Convertibility and economic transformation', *European Economy*, Special Issue, June, 215–41, Commission of the European Communities.

Backus, D. and J. Driffil (1985), 'Inflation and reputation', *American Economic Review*, **75**, 530–38.
Barro, R.J. and D.B. Gordon (1983), 'A positive theory of monetary policy in a natural rate model', *Journal of Political Economy,* **91**, 589–610.
Baxter, M. (1985), 'The role of expectations in stabilisation policy', *Journal of Monetary Economics*, **15**, 343–62.
Begg, D. (1991), 'Economic reform in the CSFR: should we believe in Santa Klaus?', *Economic Policy*, **13**, 244–86.
Begg, D. and R. Portes (1992), 'Enterprise debt and economic transformation: financial restructuring of the state sector in Central and Eastern Europe', CEPR Discussion Paper No. 695, London: Centre for Economic Policy Research.
Berg, A. and J. Sachs (1992), 'Structural adjustment and international trade in Eastern Europe: the case of Poland', *Economic Policy*, **14**, 118–73.
Bofinger, P. (1991), 'Options for the payments and exchange rate system in Eastern Europe', *European Economy*, Special Issue, June, 243–61, Commission of the European Communities.
Bomhoff, E.J. (1992), 'Monitory reform in Eastern Europe', *European Economic Review*, **36**, 454–8.
Business International/ Credinstalt (1992), '*East European Investment Survey*', October, Vienna.
Calvo, G. and F. Coricelli (1992), 'Stabilisation in Poland', *Economic Policy*, April, 176–226.
Calvo, G., L. Liederman and C. Reinhart (1993), 'Capital inflows and real exchange rate appreciation in Latin America: the role of external factors', *IMF Staff Papers*, **40**, March, 108–51.
Churhan, P., S. Claessens and N. Mauiwgi (1993), 'Equity and bond flows to Latin America and Asia: the role of external domestic factors', Mimeo, Washington, DC: World Bank.
Claessens, S., M. Dooley and A. Warner (1995), 'Portfolio flows: hot or cold?', *World Bank Economic Review*, **9**, 153–74.
Corbett, J. and C. Mayer (1991), 'Financial reform in Eastern Europe: progress with the wrong model', *Oxford Review of Economic Policy*, **7** (4), 57–75.
Corbo, V. and L. Hernandez (1996), 'Macroeconomic adjustment to capital flows: lessons from recent Latin American and East Asian experience', *World Bank Research Observer*, **11**, February, 61–85.
Cuddington, J.T. (1986), 'Capital flight: estimates, issues and explanations' , Princeton Studies in International Finance, No. 58, International Finance Section, Princeton University, Princeton, New Jersey.
Dickinson, D.G and A.W. Mullineux (1996), 'Currency convertibility, policy credibility and capital flight in Poland and the Czech and Slovak Federal Republic', in C. Ries and R. Sweeney (eds), *Capital Controls in Emerging Economies*, Boulder, CO: Westview Press, pp. 203–25.
Dixit, A. and R. Pindyck (1994), *Investment under Uncertainty*, Princeton, NJ: Princeton University Press.
Dunning, J.H. (1981), *International Production and Multinational Enterprises*, London: Allen & Unwin.
Eaton, J., M. Gersovitz and J.E. Stiglitz (1986), 'The pure theory of country risk', *European Economic Review*, **30**, 481–513.
Episcopos, A. (1995), 'Evidence on the relationship between uncertainty and irreversible investment', *Quarterly Review of Economics and Business*, **35**, 41–52.

Greene, J.E. and P. Isard (1991), 'Currency convertibility and the transformation of centrally planned economies', Occasional Paper 81, Research Department, Washington, DC: IMF.

Greene, J. and D. Villanueva (1991), 'Private investment in developing countries: an empirical analysis', *IMF Staff Papers*, **38**, 33–58.

Hrnčíř, M. and J. Klacek (1991), 'Stabilisation Policies and Currency Convertibility in Czechoslovakia', *European Economy*, Special Issue, June, 17–39.

Khan, M.S. and N. Ul Haque (1985), 'Foreign Borrowing and capital flight: a formal analysis', *IMF Staff Papers*, **32**, 606–28.

Lessard, D.R. and J. Williamson (1987), *Capital Flight and Third World Debt*, Washington, DC: Institute for International Economics.

MacDonald, R. and D. Siegel (1986), 'The value of waiting to invest', *Quarterly Journal of Economics*, **101**, 707–28.

Mathieson, D. and L. Rojas-Suarez (1993), 'Liberalisation of the capital account: experiences and issues', IMF Occasional Paper No. 103, Washington, DC: IMF.

Mullineux, A.W. (1992a), 'Hard budget constraints, credit crunches and central bank independence', *University of Wales Business and Economics Review*, No. 8, 35–8.

Mullineux, A.W. (1992b), 'Banks, privatization and restructuring in Poland', *University of Wales Business and Economics Review*.

Mullineux, A.W. (1992c), 'Privatization and financial structure in Eastern and Central European Countries', *National Westminster Bank Quarterly Review*, May, 12–25.

Mullineux, A.W. (1995), *Financial Reform in Central and Eastern Europe: Lesson from the West, Poland and Further East*, New York: Nova Science Publishers.

Polak, J.J. (1991), 'Convertibility: an indispensable element in the transition process in Eastern Europe', in J. Williamson (ed.), *Currency Convertibility in Eastern Europe*, Washington, DC: Institute for International Economics, pp. 125–43.

Phylaktis, K. (1988), 'Capital controls: the case of Argentina', *Journal of International Money and Finance*, **7**, 303–20.

Pindyck, R.S. and A. Solimano, (1993), 'Economic instability and aggregate investment', *NBER Macroeconomics Annual*, 259–317.

Quirk, P.J. and O. Evans (1995), 'Capital account convertibility', IMF Occasional Paper, No. 131, Washington DC: IMF.

Rodrick, D. (1989), 'Promises, promises: credible policy reform via signalling', *Economic Journal*, **99**, 756–72.

Rodrick, D. (1991), 'Policy uncertainty and private investment in developing countries', *Journal of Development Economics*, **42**, 229–42.

Rogers, J.H. (1992), 'Convertibility risk and dollarisation in Mexico: a vector autoregressive analysis', *Journal of International Money and Finance*', **11**, 188–207.

Rojas-Suarez, L. (1991), 'Risk and capital flight in developing countries', in *Determinants and Systemic Consequences of International Capital Flows*, Research Department, Washington, DC: IMF.

Turner, P. (1995), 'Capital flows in Latin America: a new phase', BIS Economic Papers, No. 44, May, Bank for International Settlements, Basle.

Van Wijnbergen, S. (1985), 'Trade reform, aggregate investment and capital flight', *Economics Letters*, **19**, 369–72.

Vegh, C. (1992), 'Stopping high inflation: an analytical overview', *IMF Staff Papers*, September.

Williamson, J. (1991), *The Economic Opening of Eastern Europe*, Policy Analyses in International Economics, Washington, DC: Institute for International Economics.

10. The magnitude and determinants of capital flight in Eastern Europe

Niels Hermes, Robert Lensink and Victor Murinde*

1 INTRODUCTION

The issue of capital flight has gained much attention in academic as well as policy circles since the early 1980s. Research interest initially focused on Latin American countries.[1] Capital flight from these countries appeared to be voluminous in absolute terms; the sheer volume of the flows posed a threat to national solvency and economic stability. In addition, the flight of these countries' scarce resources occurred at the same time that they were in desperate need for foreign exchange to amortize their outstanding debt to commercial banks in industrial countries. In the context of highly indebted countries coexisting with commercial banks ridden with bad loans, the capital flight problem indirectly also threatened the stability of the international financial system.

This chapter investigates the issue of capital flight in a sample of Eastern European countries. These countries are going through a process of political and economic transition, and uncertainty over future outcomes of this process has been relatively high. The success of the ongoing policy reforms is, among other things, dependent on the availability of foreign exchange. Thus, akin to the Latin American case, the existence of capital flight in transition economies is very likely to interfere with the implementation of the policy reforms, and may be detrimental for the future economic prospects of these countries. In this context, it is of interest to investigate whether capital flight has been an important phenomenon in transition countries. Moreover, it is important to contribute to knowledge on the determinants of capital flight in these countries in order to adjust policy reforms in such a way that capital flight is

* The research for this chapter was financially supported by the European Commission's PHARE/ACE Programme 1994 under contract number 94–0685–R. The authors thank the participants of the conference on Economic Performance and Financial Sector Reform in Central and Eastern Europe, 20–21 September 1996, Tallinn, Estonia, for useful comments on an earlier version of this chapter.

reduced or even reversed. Hence, the chapter focuses on studying the magnitude and determinants of capital flight for Hungary, Poland and Romania. These countries have been selected purely on the basis of data availability for the relevant variables in this study.

The remainder of this chapter is organized as follows. Section 2 analytically explores the problems surrounding the issue of the measurement of capital flight, and subsequently presents data on the magnitude of capital flight for Hungary, Poland and Romania. Section 3 presents the model, which is used to describe the determinants of capital flight. In Section 4, the model is applied to econometrically investigate the determinants of capital flight for the three countries in our sample. Section 5 provides a summary and some concluding remarks.

2 MEASURING CAPITAL FLIGHT: METHODS AND ESTIMATES

The measurement of capital flight is difficult, since there is no general agreement on what exactly is meant by the term. In most studies, the phenomenon of capital flight is somehow related to the existence of high uncertainty and risk with respect to returns on domestically held assets (Murinde et al. 1996). Residents take their money and run in order to avoid extremely high expected losses on their asset holdings. In this sense, capital flight should be distinguished from *normal* capital outflows. These latter outflows may be based on considerations of portfolio diversification of residents – for example, in terms of portfolio or direct investment and trade credit – and/or activities of domestic commercial banks aiming at acquiring or extending foreign deposit holdings (Deppler and Williamson 1987, p. 41). Yet, in practice it is extremely difficult to distinguish empirically between such normal and abnormal capital outflows.

Consequently, several capital flight measures are available in the literature. Not surprisingly, this leads to huge differences in capital flight estimates for different countries. In general, four capital flight measures can be distinguished in the existing literature (Claessens and Naudé 1993, pp. 2–9). First, some studies measure capital flight indirectly from the balance of payments by comparing the *sources* of capital inflows – that is, net increases in external debt and the net inflow of foreign investment – with the *uses* of these inflows – that is, the current account deficit and additions to foreign reserves. If the sources exceed the uses of capital inflows, the difference is termed as capital flight. This measure is the so-called *residual method*; it has been the most widely used measure in the available literature.[2] The residual method acknowledges the difficulties of separating abnormal from normal capital outflows and, therefore, measures all private capital outflows as being capital flight. Second, in some cases capital flight is measured by adding up net errors and omissions and non-bank private short-term capital outflows. This measure corresponds to the idea that capital flight goes unrecorded, due to the illegal nature of these capital movements. These unrecorded capital movements are believed to appear in net errors and omissions. Moreover, by concentrating on short-term flows, medium- and long-term outflows are excluded, which may be more *normal* in character (Gibson and Tsakalotos 1993, p. 146).[3] In view of the foregoing arguments, this measure is referred to as the *hot money method*. Third, capital flight has been measured by looking at trade misinvoicing. Proponents of this measure stress the fact that abnormal capital outflows of residents may be included in export underinvoicing and/or import overinvoicing, since both these malpractices provide channels to siphon domestically accumulated wealth outside the country.[4] Finally, some take the total stock of capital held outside the country by non-bank residents as a measure of capital flight; this is the so-called *asset method*.[5]

Since all measures have their drawbacks in calculating capital flight, the most straightforward and broad one has been applied here. Thus, the calculations of capital flight in this chapter have been based on the residual method, and in particular the specification proposed by the World Bank (1985), where capital flight is measured as the sum of the change in gross external debt, (net) foreign direct and portfolio investment inflows minus the current account deficit and the (net) changes of foreign reserves.

Moreover, there are good reasons for not using the hot money, trade misinvoicing, or asset methods of measuring capital flight. The hot money method does not take into account long-term capital outflows and it is unclear why capital flight should consist of short-term capital outflows only. Trade misinvoicing may also occur in the presence of trade taxes. Calculated trade misinvoicing may therefore be unrelated to the phenomenon of capital flight (Gibson and Tsakalotos 1993, p. 150). The asset method is too narrow in the sense that it may leave out potentially large parts of total capital flight.

Using the residual method is appropriate for yet another reason. This chapter investigates capital flight as a phenomenon that is important for Eastern European countries, since it may aggravate the foreign exchange constraints of these countries, and thus endanger the success of policy reforms. In this context, all capital outflows may be seen as having an adverse impact on future growth prospects of transition economies.

The magnitude of capital flight for Hungary, Poland and Romania is shown in Table 10.1. Data on capital flight have been retrieved from two different sources. For the 1982–91 period, data have been taken from the World Bank estimates (1993–94 version).[6] For the 1992–95 period, capital flight has been

Table 10.1 The magnitude of capital flight (CF) for Hungary, Poland and Romania, 1982–1995

	Hungary			Poland			Romania		
	CF stocks (US$million)	CF to GNP ratio	CF to export ratio	CF stocks (US$million)	CF to GNP ratio	CF to export ratio	CF stocks (US$million)	CF to GNP ratio	CF to export ratio
1980	n.a.	n.a.	n.a.	2 568	4.7	15.9	4 006	12.0	32.9
1981	n.a.	n.a.	n.a.	3 019	6.0	23.9	4 115	10.1	30.3
1982	468	2.1	4.8	6 442	10.3	47.8	4 651	9.8	37.2
1983	971	4.8	10.0	6 533	9.0	47.4	5 329	12.1	43.2
1984	1 288	6.6	13.1	6 236	8.5	45.0	5 542	14.7	40.7
1985	2 627	13.3	28.0	14 778	21.6	111.8	6 127	13.0	55.5
1986	3 533	15.5	34.7	15 864	22.3	112.3	6 846	13.3	64.8
1987	5 256	21.0	43.7	19 865	32.6	143.0	7 456	19.7	65.4
1988	6 784	24.7	55.8	24 820	37.7	159.3	8 513	21.1	68.6
1989	6 562	23.6	51.3	23 465	29.7	159.0	7 423	17.9	64.5
1990	6 724	21.3	58.9	27 118	48.8	145.9	5 342	13.9	81.5
1991	9 031	28.2	74.1	33 491	45.5	219.9	6 540	22.7	129.5
1992	9 901	27.8	79.4	31 791	38.4	196.0	6 244	25.0	123.0
1993	9 556	25.6	89.3	30 249	35.7	189.4	6 067	23.1	105.4
1994	10 301	25.8	94.4	20 966	23.3	107.3	7 367	24.6	99.2
1995	4 560	11.3	35.6	11 754	12.3	51.4	7 897	24.7	114.4

Note: n.a. = not available.

Sources: World Bank diskette (1993–94 version), and *PlanEcon Report*, various issues.

calculated from monthly data of the relevant variables – provided by various issues of *PlanEcon Report* – to get monthly flows of capital flight, which are then added up to get annual flows.

Table 10.1 presents the absolute stocks of capital flight for the 1982–95 period. The table shows that capital flight for the three Eastern European countries rose continuously until 1988. Poland experienced steeply rising stocks of capital flight of up to US$25 billion in 1988, whereas the levels for Hungary and Romania remained in the order of US$7 billion in that year. In 1989 capital flight for all three countries fell, but rose again in 1990 for Hungary and Poland, whereas for Romania the reduction continued until 1990. The Polish capital flight problem was rather extensive in the 1980s, and this is illustrated by the fact that Poland belonged to the top ten countries, which reported the highest average annual flows of flight capital for the 1981–91 period (Claessens and Naudé 1993, Figure 6). From 1992, however, this country experienced a dramatic fall of capital flight stocks, reducing to just over US$10 billion in 1995. Thus, the data suggest that the country experienced a massive reversal of capital flight in the early 1990s. For Hungary, capital flight fell steeply in 1995, diminishing from US$10 to 5 billion. Capital flight for Romania rose slowly after 1990 to some US$7 billion in 1995.

The burden of capital flight for a country is better illustrated when it is related to a macroeconomic variable proxying for the total wealth or economic weight of the country. Table 10.1 presents the ratio of the stock of capital flight to GNP for the three Eastern European countries. For Poland this ratio rose from 10 in 1982 to almost 50 in 1990 and then dropped to 12 in 1995. For Hungary the ratio rose to 27 in 1994; thereafter it fell to 11. Finally, for Romania the ratio rose to 21 between 1982 and 1988, dropping back to 12 in 1990, and then rising to 23 in 1995. The burden of capital flight of the three countries was not extremely high, at least when compared to other developing countries. In terms of the ratios of capital flight to GNP in 1991 – the only year for which data for all developing countries were available – the burden of capital flight was highest for countries in North Africa and the Middle East (and especially Egypt, Syria and Jordan) and Sub-Saharan Africa (with Sudan, Gabon, Nigeria and Uganda being the most extreme cases). The average ratios for the countries in both these regions amounted to almost 120 and 85, respectively. For Hungary, Poland and Romania, the ratios in that year were 29, 45 and 22, respectively. Yet, the burden of capital flight for these three countries was in the same range as that of the Latin American countries (31 on average), the region for which the capital flight problem has traditionally been studied most extensively.[7] Thus, the burden of capital flight in the three Eastern European countries is a non-trivial matter.

If capital flight is related to exports, more or less the same general trends emerge as those shown for the capital to GNP ratio. One important exception is that in 1995 the burden of capital flight measured using the ratio of capital flight to exports is clearly larger for Romania than it is for the other two countries. Whereas the ratios for Hungary and Poland were about 40, the ratio for Romania amounted to more than 100, which indicates that export performance of Romania was behind that of the other two countries, at least in the mid-1990s.

3 THE MODEL

In several studies of the determinants of capital flight, emphasis is laid on factors relating to aspects of uncertainty over future policy and their outcomes. Capital flight mostly occurs in times when such uncertainty is important. In line with this literature, this chapter argues that when economic agents in Eastern Europe perceive an increase in uncertainty associated with holding domestic assets during the introduction of the economic reform process, they tend to shift their wealth holdings abroad on a long-term or short-term speculative basis. However, the economic reform process designed to engender a transition to a market economy in Eastern Europe seems to offer a mixed scenario. Indeed, as the data in the previous section suggest, the three sample countries have recently experienced not only capital flight, but also its reversal (that is, capital inflows), a situation especially relevant to the Polish case. It is, therefore, useful to model capital flight in a broad framework of capital flows. The model derived below will be used to investigate the determinants of capital flight for the three Eastern European countries based on monthly data for the 1990–95 period.

Standard modelling of capital flows captures the behaviour of risk-averse investors who diversify their asset holdings in order to maximize the returns on their wealth. It emphasizes the role of differences in rates of returns between different domestic and foreign asset holdings, the amount of wealth to be divided over asset holdings and risk factors. Thus, the stock held of a particular asset is given by:[8]

$$A_t = \alpha(V_t, R_t, D_t) \qquad (10.1)$$

where A is the stock held of a particular asset in a diversified portfolio; V is wealth; R are the rates of return on assets held; D are different risk factors.

On the basis of equation (10.1), it is argued that capital flows, that is, ΔA, respond only to changes in the determinants, and should therefore be modelled in the form of a short-run adjustment process, which results from changes of the desired stock of A:

$$\Delta A_t = \beta(\Delta V_t, \Delta R_t, \Delta D_t) \tag{10.2}$$

where Δ denotes change of a variable, thus representing the short-run adjustment process that transforms stocks to flows. The adjustment process is completed in one period, that is, the equilibrium stock of A is acquired, so that capital flows become zero.

As Gibson and Tsakalotos (1993, p. 151) argue, adjustment of desired stocks of asset holdings may occur over a number of periods, due to structural rigidities, such as, for instance, capital controls. In that case, a stock adjustment model may be more appropriate. Equation (10.2) is transformed into:

$$\Delta A_t = \lambda(\Delta V_t, \Delta R_t, \Delta D_t, V_{t-1}, R_{t-1}, D_{t-1}, A_{t-1}). \tag{10.3}$$

Although equation (10.3) would be the ideal specification to be used for econometrically investigating capital flows in general, several problems arise. One relates to problems with respect to data on the initial stock of capital flight and data on wealth. A second problem may be the use of the concept of a long-run equilibrium of asset holdings in the present setting, in which determinants of capital flight are established based on short-term data. In the light of the fact that the magnitude of capital flight has been shown to fluctuate over time, in some cases yielding a reversal of capital inflows in the short span, it appears not to be consistent with the realities of Eastern European countries to specify a stock adjustment model in terms of a long-run equilibrium. Moreover, as was mentioned at the beginning of this section, it has been argued that capital flight occurs in an uncertain environment, rather than in an environment characterized by risks. If uncertainty – rather than risk – is at stake, past experience may not give useful information as to how to adjust the asset holdings towards an efficient long-run equilibrium level. Finally, adjustment to a long-run equilibrium level of asset holdings may not be an important aspect, if factors determining uncertainty and/or behaviour towards uncertainty are constantly changing. In such a situation, flow factors will be the most important variables determining observed fluctuations in capital flight (Gibson and Tsakalotos 1993, pp. 152–3).

Based on the above considerations, the following model is used to explain the short-term fluctuations of capital flight (ibid., p. 153):

$$\Delta KF = \varphi(\Delta R_{t-i}, \Delta U_{t-i}, \Delta KF_{t-1}) \tag{10.4}$$

where *KF* is capital flight; and *U* denotes factors influencing uncertainty. Both the rate of return and uncertainty variables may appear in the capital flight equation with a lag structure, which is implied by the subscript $t - i$.

Several variables may have an influence on uncertainty. In the present study the following variables have been selected.

1. *External government and government guaranteed long-term debt* High foreign borrowing by the government leads to high future repayment obligations. Residents may then expect that the government will pass on to them the costs of these repayments in the form of, for example, an *inflation tax*. An additional argument why capital inflows may stimulate capital flight is given by the fact that the government offers guarantees on repaying private external debt. In the presence of implicit or explicit public guarantees, high private foreign debt, which may increase the likelihood of default of private borrowers, increases the expected tax obligations of other borrowers due to the budget constraint of the government. This increases the incentive for other borrowers to place their own funds abroad, and it increases the likelihood of default on their own loans as well (Eaton 1987, p. 379). Mikkelsen (1991, p. 73) refers to this last phenomenon as capital flight arising as a form of contagion. The impact of high government debt on capital flight depends on the magnitude of the increase relative to some macroeconomic variable which may proxy for income, normally GNP or GDP. Yet, since this study uses monthly data and neither GNP nor GDP data were available on a monthly base, monthly exports have been used to scale government debt. This was the best available proxy variable for total production.
2. *Increase in aid flows* If aid and other concessional flows increase this may indicate the existence of serious macroeconomic and financial difficulties and hence may lead to capital flight. In contrast, however, one may also argue that increased aid flows may add to the productive capacity of the country, which may contribute to the reversal of capital flight. Thus, the sign of the relation between this variable and capital flight remains indeterminate. As with the debt variable, this variable should be scaled by exports, since it is the relative, not the absolute increase in aid flows which affects the direction of capital flows.
3. *Exchange rate changes: overvaluation of the domestic currency* One of the most important sources of uncertainty is the loss associated with holding an asset in the event that the currency in which the asset is denominated depreciates. In the literature, currency overvaluation is seen as an important determinant of capital flight. The relationship between exchange rates and capital flight may be explained as follows. An overvalued currency leads to an expected future depreciation. This leads to a

rise in the prices of foreign goods as compared to domestic goods and thus to a loss in real income. To avoid such welfare losses resulting from a depreciation, residents are stimulated to hold their assets abroad. The problem, however, is to find a satisfactory proxy for currency overvaluation. In fact, this comes down to determining the equilibrium exchange rate to which the actual exchange rate may be compared to determine the extent of over- (or under)valuation. For the Eastern European countries in this study, it remains difficult to determine the right period for which the assumption of equilibrium exchange rates might hold. Therefore, data for the real effective exchange rates as reported in the *PlanEcon Reports* have been used. This source uses the exchange rate of January 1990 as the equilibrium exchange rate.

4. *Government budget deficits* An increase in government budget deficits leads to higher future repayment obligations and hence may stimulate capital flight. Residents may be more uncertain about the returns to their asset holdings in the future, since the government might decide to finance its obligations by increasing taxes or by using the inflation tax. Increases in budget deficits should also be related to exports for reasons explained above.
5. *Export growth* Bleak prospects for export growth spell remarkable uncertainty, whereas high export growth may indicate a favourable domestic investment climate. Thus, positive export growth should stimulate capital flight reversal.

In addition to the variables discussed above, the real rate of return differential between foreign and domestic deposits (not incorporating factors of uncertainty), adjusted for the exchange rate changes, is hypothesized to be an important determinant of capital flight. As this differential rises, capital flight also rises, since holding assets in foreign accounts now becomes more profitable as compared to domestic holdings.

Summarizing the above discussion, the short-run dynamics of capital flight can be modelled as follows:

$$\Delta KF = Q(FINC, PUBD, GRANTS, BDEF, REXH, XG, \Delta KF_{t-1}) \quad (10.5)$$

where ΔKF is capital flight (flows) divided by exports; *FINC* is the real rate of return differential between deposits held in the United States and deposits held domestically, corrected for exchange rate changes (+); *PUBD* is government and government guaranteed debt divided by exports (+); *GRANTS* is total unrequited transfers divided by exports (+/–); *BDEF* is government budget deficit divided by exports (+); *REXH* is the real effective exchange rate (January 1990 = 100) (+); *XG* is the export growth rate (–); and ΔKF_{t-1} is the dependent variable one period lagged (+/–). The signs between brackets indicate whether the estimated coefficients are expected to be positive or negative, based on the above discussion.

To test this model monthly data have been used for the period January 1990 to December 1995. The following section presents the estimation and testing results.

4 EMPIRICAL RESULTS OF THE DYNAMICS OF CAPITAL FLIGHT

The estimation and testing procedure adopted the general-to-specific methodology (Murinde 1996). The model was estimated and tested in a country-specific spirit for each of the three transition economies. Two lags were initially allowed on each of the explanatory variables, and the lag structure of the model for each country was explored by retaining significant variables and/or variables with the expected partial derivative sign. The results are reported in Table 10.2 for Hungary, Poland and Romania.

The estimation and testing results for *Hungary* are not very promising. Only the real effective exchange rate and grants to exports ratio are significant and have the expected signs. Thus, in the case of Hungary capital flight is stimulated by increased overvaluation of the exchange rate, leading residents to believe that a depreciation will occur in the near future and accordingly prompt them to hold their wealth abroad. The negative relationship between grants and capital flight may indicate that the country has gained credibility in the eyes of its residents, based on the fact that the country has received foreign aid flows as part of the reform process. The government budget deficit to exports ratio (one period lagged) is significant but has the wrong sign, a result that is quite curious in the light of the model of Section 3.

The estimation and testing results for *Poland* show that government and government-guaranteed debt to exports and the grants to exports ratios are significant and have the expected signs. Thus, a high level of foreign debt of the government is seen as an indication of high future financial obligations, which may be shifted to wealth holders, for example by using the inflation tax or by increased taxes. The outcomes for the grants variable suggest that in the case of Poland, residents take an increase in aid flows as an indication of existing serious macroeconomic and financial difficulties, stimulating them to bring their wealth abroad. The export growth variable is also significant, but has the wrong sign. One explanation for this result could be that increased exports lead to increased holdings of working balances of exporting firms at foreign banks. In this case, however, the export growth variables determines fluctuations in *normal* capital flows, rather than capital flight (Mikkelsen 1991, p. 77).

Table 10.2 Regression results of the determinants of capital flight in Hungary, Poland and Romania

	Hungary	Poland	Romania
Constant	0.955	–1.239	–0.357
	(1.528)	(–2.576)	(–0.728)
$PUBD_t$		0.645	0.108
		(9.471)	(7.551)
$REXH_t$	0.084		
	(2.415)		
$GRANTS_t$	–0.534	0.485	
	(–3.599)	(1.990)	
XG_t		0.951	–0.969
		(9.389)	(–2.796)
$BDEF_t$			1.515
			(2.022)
$BDEF_{t-1}$	–0.804		
	(–2.062)		
KF_{t-1}	–0.227	–0.106	–0.160
	(–1.620)	(–1.046)	(–1.071)
Adjusted R^2	0.27	0.63	0.60
SE	0.639	0.761	0.654
Durbin's H	1.43	2.45	2.68
F-statistic	13.89	14.69	10.67

In the case of *Romania*, the outcomes show that the foreign debt variable, the export growth variable, and the government budget deficit variable are significant and have the expected sign. Thus, high foreign debt of the government leads Romanian residents to believe that the resulting high future repayment obligations of the government will be detrimental to the real value of their domestically held wealth through government actions such as monetary financing or increased tax rates. Moreover, positive export performance is seen as an indication of a favourable domestic investment climate, which tends to reduce the willingness of residents to bring their money outside the country. Finally, increased budget deficits of the government raises fears of wealth holders that the government may turn to monetary financing of its domestic debts, thus leading to increased capital flight.

The real rate of return differential variable (*FINC*) appears to be insignificant in all estimations. Possibly, this is related to the way this variable has been constructed. Instead of using the US deposit rate as the foreign rate of return, one could have used the LIBOR rate, the German deposit rate, or a composite of deposit rates of Western European countries.

5 CONCLUDING REMARKS

Overall, the empirical outcomes of this study show that capital flight is a country-specific phenomenon for this sample of transition economies. No single variable suggested here as being of influence on capital flight appears to be significant for all the three countries. However, the results shown in Table 10.1 indicate that uncertainty with respect to the reform process during the 1990–95 period has an impact on capital flight. In this sense, it should be noted that the reversal of capital flight, which has been reported in Section 2, especially in the cases of Hungary (1995) and Poland (1992–95) appears to have been the result of reduced uncertainty in these countries during these periods. This result might point in the direction of concluding that, at least to some extent, the reform efforts in these countries have been successful. Residents seem to have demonstrated increased faith in the policy reforms of their governments. However, more extensive research is needed to better explain the dynamics of capital flight and capital reversal in Eastern Europe during and after the transition.

NOTES

1. Nevertheless, Hermes and Lensink (1992) and Murinde et al. (1996) have shown that capital flight is also an important phenomenon for African countries.
2. See World Bank (1985) and Morgan Guaranty (1986) for alternative approaches to applying the residual method. According to Claessens and Naudé (1993, pp. 5–7), calculation of capital flight as proposed by Dooley (1986) is in fact also based on the residual approach.
3. Cuddington (1986) recommends this measure of capital flight.
4. Gulati (1987) recommends this measure of capital flight. In some papers, the residual method is applied in combination with trade misinvoicing. This means that in those cases, exports and imports – to calculate the current account balance – are corrected for trade misinvoicing to get a better calculation of the magnitude of capital flight (see, for example, Lessard and Williamson 1987; and Vos 1990).
5. For an elaborate description and application of the asset method, see Hermes and Lensink (1992).
6. The data are available on diskette from the World Bank.
7. All data, except for the Eastern European countries, have been taken from Claessens and Naudé (1993, pp. 18–19, Figures 6–8).
8. The model presented below follows closely Gibson and Tsakalotos (1993, pp. 150–53).

REFERENCES

Claessens, S. and D. Naudé (1993), 'Recent estimates of capital flight', Policy Research Working Papers, WPS 1186, Washington, DC: World Bank.

Cuddington, J.T. (1986), *Capital Flight: Estimates, Issues, and Explanations*, Princeton Studies in International Finance, No. 58, Princeton: Princeton University Press.

Deppler, M. and M. Williamson (1987), 'Capital flight: concepts, measurement, and issues,' in IMF, *Staff Studies for the World Bank Outlook*, Washington, DC: IMF, August, pp. 39–59.

Dooley, M. (1986), 'Country-specific risk premiums, capital flight, and net investment income payments in selected developing countries', Mimeo, Washington, DC: IMF.

Eaton, J. (1987), 'Public debt guarantees and private capital flight,' *World Bank Economic Review*, **1** (3), 377–95.

Gibson, H.D. and E. Tsakalotos (1993), 'Testing a flow model of capital flight in five European countries', *The Manchester School*, **61** (2), 144–66.

Gulati, S.K. (1987), 'A note on trade misinvoicing', in D.R. Lessard and J. Williamson (eds), *Capital Flight and Third World Debt*, Washington, DC: Institute for International Economics, pp. 68–79.

Hermes, N. and R. Lensink (1992), 'The magnitude and determinants of capital flight: the case for six Sub-Saharan African countries,' *De Economist*, **140** (4), 515–30.

International Monetary Fund (IMF), *International Financial Statistics*, Washington, DC: IMF, various issues.

International Monetary Fund (IMF), *Balance of Payments Yearbook*, Washington, DC: IMF, various issues.

Lessard, D.R. and J. Williamson (eds) (1987), *Capital Flight and Third World Debt*, Washington, DC: Institute for International Economics.

Mikkelsen, J.G. (1991), 'An econometric investigation of capital flight', *Applied Economics*, **23**, 73–85.

Morgan Guaranty (1986), 'LDC capital flight', *World Financial Markets*, **2**, 13–16.

Murinde, V. (1996), *Development Banking and Finance*, Aldershot: Avebury.

Murinde, V., N. Hermes, and R. Lensink (1966), 'Comparative aspects of the magnitude and determinants of capital flight in six Sub-Saharan African economics', *Savings and Development Quarterly Review*, **XX** (1), 61–78.

Vos, R. (1990), 'Private foreign asset accumulation: magnitude and determinants, the case of the Philippines', Subseries on Money, Finance and Development, Working Paper No. 33, The Hague: Institute of Social Studies.

World Bank (1985), *World Development Report*, Washington, DC: World Bank.

11. Sterilization of capital inflows in transition economies: an econometric investigation of the Czech and Polish cases

Eric Girardin and Jan Klacek*

1 INTRODUCTION

The wave of capital inflows in emerging market economies over the last few years, followed by the collapse of the Mexican peso and its destabilizing effects on other Latin American countries, has shown yet again the major role that sterilization, or the lack of it, can play in conditioning the implications of such inflows for the economies which 'benefit' from them.

Transitional economies in Central Europe have been hit by the same wave, which has occurred on top of a rising trend of foreign direct investment. It thus seems useful to provide some evidence on the degree of sterilization of capital inflows in transitional economies. This chapter will pay particular attention to the experience of the Czech Republic, and will implement tests comparing it with Poland.

The Czech case is of particular interest because it is distinct from other Central and Eastern European transition economies in at least two important aspects. First, the Czech Republic is the only country which maintained an unchanged fixed exchange rate over a long period of transition, from January 1991 until February 1996 when in response to massive inflows of capital the central bank widened the band around central parity. Second, the capital inflows to the country were both of the structural type associated with the privatization programme and restructuring process and of the cyclical type determined by the interest rate differential. These two types of capital flow seem to have occurred simultaneously. Therefore one can observe a growing intensity of capital flows across the period of four years.

* This chapter was prepared with the support of the PHARE/ACE Programme. The ACE Research Project 'The Design of Monetary Policy for the Central European Countries', within which the chapter originated, was coordinated by Professor Maxwell Fry. We thank him and other partners for helpful comments.

The chapter is organized as follows. In Section 2, we shall review the experience of the Czech Republic with reference to the size and composition of capital inflows, and their impact on money supply. In Section 3, we shall briefly give some hints on the theoretical framework which can highlight the various effects at work and recall the main results of previous work on the extent of sterilization in both industrial and developing economies. We shall then estimate monetary policy reaction functions for the Czech Republic and Poland over the 1992–95 period with monthly data, and then analyse the dynamics of capital inflows and monetary policy with vector error correction models. Section 4 concludes. Appendix 11A contains data sources and definitions.

2 INFLOW OF FOREIGN CAPITAL IN THE CZECH REPUBLIC AND ISSUES OF STERILIZATION POLICIES

The Czech Republic belongs to a group of economies in transition which have passed the stage of 'attracting foreign capital' and have entered the period of 'managing abundant capital inflows'. While at the beginning of 1993, after the split of Czechoslovakia, foreign exchange reserves were at a level of US$200 million, the massive accumulation which followed resulted in reserves reaching US$14 billion at the end of 1995 (see Figure 11.1). Starting from 1994 onwards,

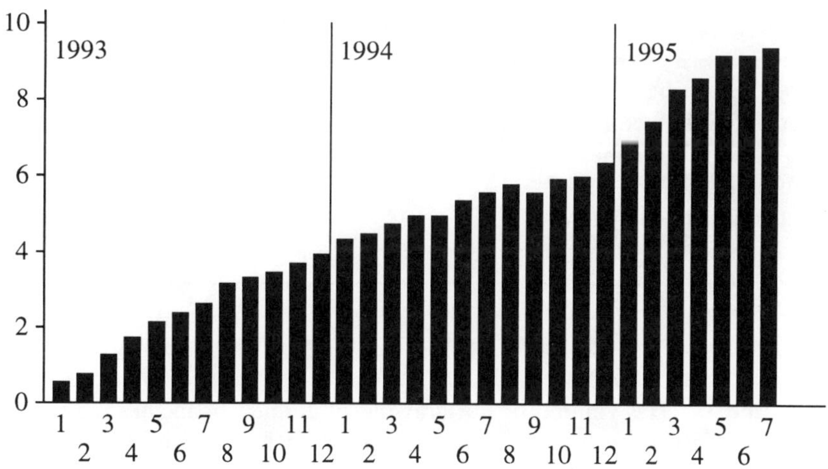

Source: Czech National Bank

Figure 11.1 Foreign exchange reserves

the build-up of foreign exchange reserves is attributable fully to a surplus in the capital account as the current account turned into a deficit. Since 1994 the Czech National Bank (CNB) has resorted to sterilization policies in order to contain inflationary pressures stemming from intensive capital inflows.

Structure of Capital Inflows

The factor of growing capital inflows can be seen on both the demand and supply sides. The growing demand for foreign capital was particularly connected to the need for long-term capital resources caused by the privatization process and the subsequent restructuring of the enterprise sphere. The relatively low level of the interest rate was especially motivated by the comparative advantage of the Czech economy (particularly lower wage production costs), the macroeconomic balance and, connected to this, the stability of the foreign exchange rate, the substantial potential for portfolio investment and expanding room for direct investment.

While during the first two years of transformation, capital inflows from official foreign sources dominated (from the IMF, European Union, World Bank and G24 governments), private capital in the foreign resources inflow became important during the transformation process (Table 11.1).

Table 11.1 Composition of gross foreign capital inflows, 1992–1995 (US$ billion)

	1992	1993	1994	1995
Official borrowing	0.6	0.25	0	0
Bonds of public sector, central bank	0	0.75	0.2	0.03
Direct foreign investment	1.1	0.6	0.9	2.6
Portfolio investment	0	0	0.9	1.6
Direct credits to companies	0.5	1.1	1.9	3.4
Total	2.2	3	3.9	7.7

Source: CNB.

In 1994, capital inflows were already dominated by *financial credits* drawn by enterprises. The volume of net drawing of foreign financial credits by enterprises during the first years of transformation was not substantial (approximately US$100–200 million per year) and was particularly related to the construction activities. These credits started to gain in importance from 1992, and since then their drawing has shown a strongly rising trend: in 1995, their gross drawing totalled US$3.4 billion.

From the monetary and economic points of view, the drawing of foreign credits by enterprises can be seen as:

- a cheaper source of long-term financing because of an insufficient supply of long-term resources on the domestic financial market,
- a replacement of foreign direct investment by joint ventures (this is also due to an effort to avoid higher domestic taxation of profits), and
- a source of additional demand for construction capacity and growth in this area.

Also, the structure of *portfolio investments* experienced noticeable changes in form. Unlike the previous period when the inflow of resources from portfolio investments was ensured only through issues of central bank bonds on international capital markets, at present, the capital inflow from this source is ensured by municipalities and private subjects. In 1995 and 1996, international institutions like the European Bank for Reconstruction and Development (EBRD), the Institute for International Finance (IIF) and the European Investment Bank for the first time issued bonds denominated in Czech koruna.

By the end of 1995, the value of Czech securities denominated in koruna owned by foreign investors amounted to US$2.7 billion. Of this amount, approximately 61 per cent was composed of shares, 23 per cent of state bonds, including those of the National Property Fund, and 16 per cent of enterprise bonds. By their nature, they belong to the short-term capital category. In 1995, the portfolio investment share of net capital inflows amounted to approximately 21 per cent.

Capital inflows underwent a major structural shift. Over the period 1992 to 1995, the structure of foreign capital inflow shifted from the official to the private sector, from direct investment to portfolio investment and direct credit and, more importantly, from medium- and long-term towards short-term capital inflows. (The sale of the Telecom company as part of its privatization in 1995 itself represents US$1.2 billion of foreign direct investment which inflated the total figure for FDI during this year.)

The culmination of capital inflows in 1995 coincides with the liberalization of most capital account transactions, the entry of the Czech Republic into the Organization for Economic Cooperation and Development (OECD) and the upgrading of the country rating by Moody's and Standard and Poor's.

Impact on the Money Stock

In a situation of massive capital inflows to a country, the stock of money tends to be determined by foreign investors and their decision making rather than by the central bank. While the capital account of the balance of payments of the Czech Republic was in surplus, representing 9.1, 6.6 and 16.9 per cent of GDP in 1993, 1994 and 1995, respectively, the incremental net foreign assets to broad money ratio reached 64 per cent in 1995 (see Tables 11.2, 11.3 and 11.4).

The CNB, which targets M2, was faced with a higher than targeted growth of the money stock. For example, in 1994, the CNB declared an interval of 14–17 per cent in the growth rate of M2 as consistent with the targeted rate of

Table 11.2 Broad money and net foreign assets (NFA) (CZK billion, end of period)

	1992	1993	1994	1995
(1) M2	598.6	720.4	870.4	1038
(2) NFA	35.5	89.6	168.2	275
Δ (2) as percentage of Δ (1)		44.4	52.4	63.8

Source: Czech National Bank, *Annual Report 1995* (1996).

Table 11.3 Capital account and GDP (US$ billion)

	1992	1993	1994	1995
(1) Capital account of balance of payments	0.002	2.6	2.4	7.7
(2) GDP	33.0	31.7	36.2	45.6
(1) as percentage of (2)	0	8.2	6.6	16.9

Source: Czech National Bank, *Selected Indicators of Monetary Developments in the Czech Republic* (1996).

Table 11.4 Rate of growth of M2 and inflation rate (percentages)

	1992	1993	1994	1–8/1995*
Broad money	23.0	20.2	20.8	19.6**
Consumer price index	11.1	20.8*	10.0	9.1

Notes:
* 8 percentage points of inflation rate in 1993 could be attributed to the introduction of VAT at the beginning of the year.
** Net of Telecom: 22.8 per cent, including Telecom.

Source: Czech National Bank, *Annual Report 1995* (1996).

inflation but the actual growth was 20.8 per cent and 19.6 per cent. This higher targeted growth rate of M2, fuelled to a large extent by the capital inflows, seems to correlate with the inflation rate which has not decreased in spite of either a balance or even a surplus in the government budget.

Because of a massive capital inflow the inflation rate could not be reduced further, and there was a rise of foreign credit both to the Czech banking sector as well as directly to the companies; these factors contributed to their financial vulnerability. The commercial banks could finance not just viable projects but also some rather risky endeavours. The companies and the public sector institutions such as municipalities who took credits from foreign banks or issued debt instruments on international capital markets, did not take into account exchange rate risk. Their experience up to that time had been of a fixed exchange rate regime.

Besides, open market operations aimed at reducing the liquidity of the banking sector. With the government's agreement, the CNB took over the proceeds from the privatization programme which had been deposited with the commercial banks. The CNB also increased minimum reserve requirements for commercial banks in order to limit domestic credits. The main instrument adopted was, however, open market operations conducted through CNB bills.

Sterilization Policies in the Czech Republic

Sterilization policies were started in 1994. Because of either a balanced budget or a budget surplus in the last two years, open market operations by the Central Bank had to rely on the bank's own issues of securities, the CNB bills, most of them with a three- or six-month maturity (see Figure 11.2). The issues of either the Treasury bills or the National Property Fund bills were insufficient to reduce liquidity of the banking sector. Therefore, emissions of the CNB bills through 1994 and 1995 had to increase threefold compared to 1993. The problem with the CNB bills is that the interest they bear is higher than the interest rate on foreign exchange reserves and the quasi-fiscal deficit which is implied represents the cost of this type of sterilization policy. Yet, the sterilization has not reduced the rise in the money stock. Therefore, the CNB decided to introduce an exchange rate risk by widening the fluctuation band from ±0.7 to ±7.5 per cent around parity, effective as of 1 March 1996. Subsequently the capital inflow has slowed down, but, the interest rate differential has again increased.

Theoretical Background and Previous Empirical Works

The standard open economy IS–LM model with capital flows, as formalized by Mundell and Fleming, is an appropriate framework to highlight in the simplest

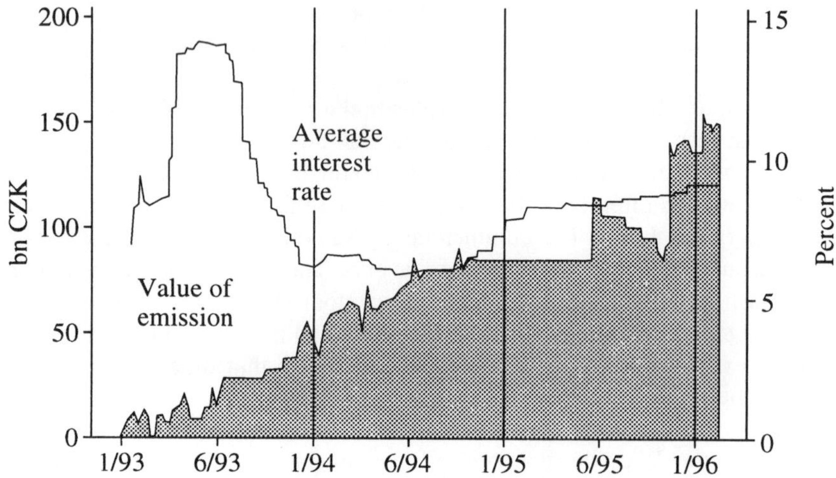

Figure 11.2 Emissions of CNB bills, 1993–1995

way the effects on a small open economy of capital inflows caused by a fall in the level of the foreign interest rate (see Frankel, 1994, and Calvo et al. 1993). Indeed, the improvement in the capital account of the balance of payments generated by such a fall leads to a downward shift of the external balance schedule (EE in Figure 11.3). Assuming imperfect capital mobility, that is, a positively sloped EE curve, the small open economy will have a lower interest rate, but it will remain higher than the foreign one. Two polar cases are of interest here. Under a regime of fixed exchange rates, reserve inflows translate into increases in the money supply leading to this fall in the domestic interest rate and stimulating aggregate demand. The LM curve thus shifts endogenously to the right and the economy moves southwestwards along the IS schedule and settles at point M. The other polar case is the one where the monetary authorities wish to target money supply. They then have to sterilize the reserve inflows by reducing domestic credit, keeping the LM curve at its initial position, and the economy remains at point E. However, this is an unstable situation. Indeed, the accumulation of reserve inflows through a capital account surplus should translate into an appreciation of the domestic currency and a trade balance deficit, leading the economy to point A. However, the authorities may be willing to keep the fixed exchange rate regime while targeting the money supply. The potential difficulty, which could even be faced by countries with a trade balance surplus, as shown by Calvo (1991), stems from the fact that the reduction in domestic credit is engineered through a direct or indirect increase in the stock of public debt. The service of this debt can become a burden for the government through a mounting budget deficit. The expected monetization or

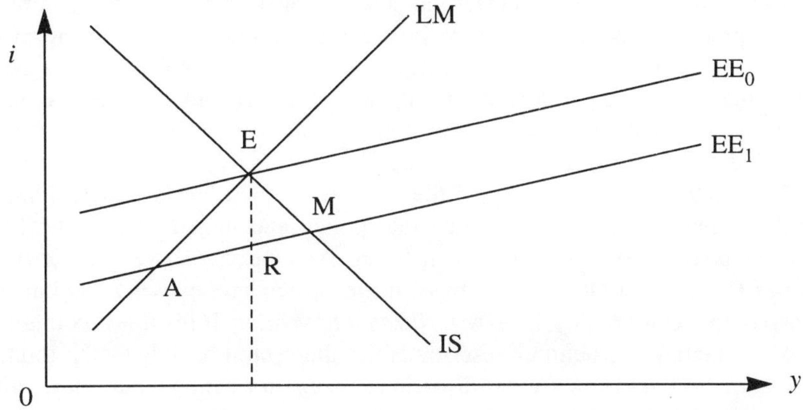

Figure 11.3 *Foreign interest movements, capital inflows and sterilization*

repudiation of the debt can spark capital outflows and ultimately a currency crisis (as happened in Mexico at the turn of 1994–95). This expected depreciation is associated with part of the interest differential between the country and the rest of the world.

At a practical level, governments faced with very large capital inflows have a variety of alternative policy instruments which they can deploy. The right mix for a particular country will depend on domestic country circumstances, on a perception of what proportion of the flows are likely to be permanent and on policy objectives (see Williamson 1994).

For a fully convertible currency, an initial level of intervention arises in the foreign exchange market. The purpose of intervention is to moderate trends towards the appreciation of the real exchange rate, since this rate has become one of the main instruments of export promotion. At this first level of intervention, two very different situations can be observed, depending on how central banks respond to increases in capital inflows. One response is not to intervene at this first level (not to accumulate reserves). In this case, capital flows would not bring about any changes in the international assets held by central banks and their entire increase would put pressure on the exchange market to reevaluate the currency. In this way, the international capital market is used for funding an increase in the current account deficit, which will lead to increased investment and/or consumption. The other situation occurs when the central bank intervenes at the first level by accumulating reserves. In this situation, a decision must be taken whether or not to sterilize the effects of the accumulation of reserves on the money supply. At this second level, intervention involves choosing between an active or a passive monetary policy (in terms of managing aggregate demand), which also determines its relationship with stabilization.

In the final instance, countries can always consider revising the nature of the capital account liberalization in order to regulate the composition of inflows. A third level of intervention then occurs. Some countries have chosen to open up the inflow of capital and to establish only those intervention mechanisms that will prevent the entry of short-term speculative capital which does not contribute to the investment process.

The possible combinations of the first and second levels of intervention yield different mixes of exchange rate policy and monetary policy which make it possible to distinguish two major intervention alternatives (see Griffith-Jones 1995). The first, favoured by countries which have chosen to maintain a passive monetary policy, is *non-sterilized intervention*. It involves accumulating substantial international reserves, since the central bank buys the foreign currency brought in by capital flows in exchange for national currency, without sterilizing the monetary effect of these operations. However, if adjustment by way of an increase in imports does not occur fast enough, this alternative can expand the monetary base beyond desirable limits. This usually results in inflationary pressures, causing appreciations in the real exchange rate and tendencies towards excesses and changes in the composition of expenditure.

The second alternative, adopted by countries which, together with defending the exchange rate, have chosen to pursue active monetary policies, is *sterilized intervention*. Like non-sterilized intervention, it involves accumulating reserves, but systematically approaches the second level of intervention by applying a sterilization of the monetary effects of these operations. The purpose is to isolate the money stock from fluctuations stemming from the mobility of foreign capital. This type of sterilization, if effective, prevents domestic real interest rates from falling. In economies that are making full use of their productive capacity, this has the advantage of helping to control aggregate spending and preventing further appreciation of the real exchange rate. However, with this option, if interest rate differentials persist, capital inflows continue to be stimulated, generating further needs for sterilization; at the same time, the intervention may be a source of quasi-fiscal deficits, since the central bank is placing commercial paper in the domestic market at higher interest rates than those it obtains on its international reserves. These quasi-fiscal losses may be partly offset by a subsequent capital gain derived from the appreciation of foreign exchange reserves.

It is for these two reasons that the alternative of sterilized intervention has been combined with other policy measures: (i) at the first level of intervention, to influence the exchange market; (ii) at the second level of intervention, to regulate aggregate demand through mechanisms other than the interest rate; (iii) at the third level of intervention, to modify the level and composition of capital flows, either directly, through restrictions and charges aimed particularly at short-term capital or indirectly, by generating exchange rate uncertainty.

It may be that, in some circumstances, sticking to fixed exchange rates does not imply that an independent monetary policy will be abandoned. Indeed, as shown by the experience of East Asian countries (Reisen 1993, quoted by Frankel 1994), such an autonomy can be kept in case the interest rate plays a minor role in the domestic economy for lack of liberalization, or of development, of domestic financial markets (Frankel 1994). In such circumstances, the various components of domestic aggregate demand, as well as the demand for money (as a possible result of financial repression, see Fry 1995), do not respond much to interest rate changes, making both the IS and LM curve in Figure 11.3 very steep, possibly even vertical. The fall in the foreign interest rate would then only lead to a downward movement of the economy along this IS/LM vertical curve, to point R, with a fall in the level of the domestic interest rate, but no effect on output.

This last possibility may be of interest when considering the effects of exogenous capital inflows on transitional economies of Central and Northern Europe. Indeed the interest elasticity of the components of aggregate demand and of money demand is ambiguous and its low level would give rise to similar effects. It then seems useful to try and measure the impact of capital flows in transitional economies of Central Europe in order to determine whether they have managed to sterilize the capital inflows of 1993–95.

3 COMPARATIVE TESTS ON STERILIZATION IN THE CZECH REPUBLIC AND POLAND

The existing empirical literature on the extent of sterilization in both developed and developing countries reaches well-defined results, which we shall briefly summarize in the first subsection. We shall then estimate monetary policy reaction functions using both the general to specific methodology and vector autoregressive models.

Empirical Evidence on the Degree of Sterilization

The extent of sterilization is usually measured by considering a monetary policy reaction function as follows:

$$\Delta D = \alpha + \beta Z + \mu \Delta NFA \tag{11.1}$$

$$\Delta(D/Y) = a + bZ + c\Delta(NFA/Y) \tag{11.2}$$

where ΔNFA is the change in net foreign assets, Y output, and Z a vector of other variables (such as inflation, output growth,and so on) which determine the response of monetary authorities (see Argy 1981). In the case when one considers only the balance sheet of the central bank, ΔD is the change in net domestic assets of this bank and ΔNFA the change in its net foreign assets. However, one can also use a broader approach and, in terms of the monetary survey, including net assets of the banking sector, consider that D is domestic credit and NFA the net foreign assets of the central bank and commercial banks combined. In both cases, μ is the sterilization coefficient.

Past evidence on the extent of sterilization for industrial countries, surveyed by Kreinin and Officer (1978), indicated a significant negative μ or c coefficient. More recent evidence also on industrial countries, is summarized by Fry (1995), with the common conclusion that such countries are able to sterilize capital flows substantially, or even completely.

In the case of developing countries, Fry's (1995) estimates imply rather low sterilization coefficients (–0.18 with a pooling of 27 countries over the 1960–88 period). This may be rationalized by the fact that some of these countries (such as Mexico, Turkey or Venezuela) responded to the growth in net foreign assets by expanding domestic credit rather than by restricting it, in order to stimulate investment and growth by financing imports of capital equipment and raw materials. By contrast, sterilization seems to be substantial in Pacific Basin countries such as Indonesia, Korea, Malaysia, the Philippines, Taiwan and Thailand. Overall they sterilized more than 40 per cent of increases in the net foreign assets of their banking systems (Fry 1995). Moreover, when one considers only the period starting in the late 1970s or early 1980s, the sterilization coefficient reaches at least 75 per cent in all Pacific Basin countries, except the Philippines.

Monetary Policy Reaction Functions and Sterilization

The data used in the tests that we implement cover the period January 1992 to November 1995 for Poland and December 1992 to December 1995 for the Czech Republic. The main source is PlanEcon's reports, except for the monetary survey data of the Czech Republic which come from a revised series by the Czech National Bank. We work with monthly data, given the short sample at our disposal. We consider the domestic credit of the banking system and its net foreign assets, as reported in the monetary survey. The tests implemented start with an unrestricted model from which a long-run solution is derived. We test for cointegration and when this test is positive, examine the associated error correction mechanism. In a second stage, we check the robustness of these results by using a vector auto-regressive model, and estimate a vector error correction model (VECM).

General auto-regressive distributed lag model

We shall examine an equation for the ratio of domestic credit to economic activity.

In the Czech case, the estimated equation is as follows:

$$\frac{DC}{Y} = \alpha + \sum_i \beta_i \left(\frac{DC}{Y}\right)_{t-i} + \sum_j \gamma_j \left(\frac{NFA}{Y}\right)_{t-j} + \sum_k \theta_k P_{t-k} + \sum_l \omega_l Q_{t-l} \quad (11.3)$$

where *DC* is domestic credit granted by the banking system, *Y* is retail sales in value, *NFA* is net foreign assets of the banking system, *P* is the retail price index and *Q* is industrial production at constant prices.

The impact of the net foreign assets ratio on domestic credit is very sizeable (Table 11.5) and positive with no lag while its negative contribution with a one-month lag mitigates this effect somewhat, but not enough to prevent the long-run impact from being very high (about 0.5). This long-run solution corresponds to a cointegrating relationship. In the error correction mechanism, where we add a seasonal dummy (for January), when account is taken of the coefficient of the error correction term the spillover from the net foreign assets ratio to the next month increase in the domestic credit ratio is 0.13.

In the Polish case, the estimated equation is as follows:

$$\frac{DC}{Y} = a + \sum_i b_i \left(\frac{DC}{Y}\right)_{t-1} + \sum_j c_j \left(\frac{NFA}{Y}\right)_{t-j} + \sum_k d_k \left(\frac{CGOV}{Y}\right)_{t-k} \quad (11.4)$$
$$+ \sum_l f_l P_{t-1} + \sum_m g_m i_{t-m}$$

The variables used have the same meaning as in the Czech case, except that *P* is the produced price index, *CGOV* is net credit to the government granted by the banking system, and *i* is the 0 to 1-month interest rate on inter-bank deposits.

The net foreign assets ratio clearly has a positive negative impact on the domestic credit ratio (Table 11.6). The long-run relationship corresponds to a cointegrating vector, but only at the 5 per cent level. The coefficient of the error correction term in the equation for the dynamics of domestic credit is sizeable and highly significant, confirming the evidence for cointegration and implying a quite rapid adjustment to the long-run level.

Table 11.5 General autoregressive distributed lag model: Czech Republic, 1992(12)–1995(12)

	Lag				
	0	1	2	F	Unit root t-test
$\left(\frac{DC}{Y}\right)$	−1	0.398 (4.21)		17.8 [0.00]**	6.36**
$\left(\frac{NFA}{Y}\right)$	0.620 (10.0)	−0.309 (−5.19)		61.3 [0.00]**	
P			−1.23 (−8.02)	64.4 [0.00]**	
Q		0.123 (3.27)		10.69 [0.00]**	
Cst	8.67 (8.44)			71.2 [0.00]**	

R^2 = 0.852; $F(5, 31)$ = 35.9 [0.00]; $\hat{\sigma}$= 0.02; DW = 1.57; RSS = 0.01 for 6 variables and 37 observations.
t-statistic in parentheses

Long-run solution

$$\left(\frac{DC}{Y}\right)^* = 14.4 + 0.517 \left(\frac{NFA}{Y}\right) - 2.06P + 0.204Q$$

(S.E.) (1.46)(0.08) (−0.35) (0.07)
Wald test χ^2 (2) = 51.6 [0.00]**

Error Correction Mechanism

$$\Delta\frac{DC}{Y} = \underset{(2.79)}{0.016} + \underset{(3.78)}{0.273}\,\Delta\frac{NFA}{Y} - \underset{(-4.23)}{0.318}\left[\left(\frac{DC}{Y}\right)_{-1} - \left(\frac{DC}{Y}\right)\right]_{-1} + \underset{(-4.89)}{0.095}DUQ1$$

R^2 = 0.843; $F(3, 32)$ = 57.3 [0.00]; $\hat{\sigma}$= 0.02; DW = 2.04; RSS = 0.013 for 4 variables and 36 observations.
Variance instability tests: 0.088; Joint instability test: 0.78; SC = −7.46; HQ = −7.58; FPE = 0.0005; AR 1–4: F(4, 28) = 0.121 [0.97]; $ARCH$ 4 $F(4, 24)$ = 0.43 [0.78];
Normality χ^2 (2) = 4.33 [0.00]**; $RESET$ F(1, 31) = 0.06 [0.81]

Table 11.6 *General unrestricted autoregressive model: Poland 1992(2)–1995(11) (dependent variable: DC/Y)*

	Lag				
	0	1	2	F	Unit root t-test
$\left(\frac{DC}{Y}\right)$	–1	0.541 (4.99)		24.9 [0.00]**	4.22*
$\left(\frac{NFA}{Y}\right)$	0.362 (9.81)	–0.242 (–5.08)		48.7 [0.00]**	
$\left(\frac{CGOV}{Y}\right)$	0.608 (13.9)	–0.296 (–3.33)		103.5 [0.00]**	
P	—	–0.108 (–2.83)		8.02 [0.00]**	
i	0.143 (1.99)			3.97 [0.05]	
Cste	0.914 (2.38)				

$R^2 = 0.979$; $F(7, 38) = 254.3$ [0.00]; $\sigma = 0.013$; $DW = 1.86$; $RSS = 0.0066$ for 8 variables and 46 observations.
Variance instability test: 0.098; Joint instability test: 1.74; $SC = -8.17$; $HQ = -8.37$; $FPE = 0.002$
AR 1–4: F(4, 34) = 1.31 [0.28]; *ARCH 4* $F(4, 30) = 0..26$ [0.89];
Normality χ^2 (2) = 0.027 [0.98]; *RESET* $F(1, 37) = 0.266$ [0.608]

Long-run solution

$$\left(\frac{DC}{Y}\right)^* = 19.9 + 0.261\left(\frac{NFA}{Y}\right) + 0.681\frac{CGOV}{Y} - 0.237P + 0.3i$$

(S.E.) (0.56) (0.06) (0.048) (0.04) (0.13)

Wald test χ^2 (4) = 277.0 [0.00]**

Error correction mechanism

$$\Delta\frac{DC}{Y} = -0.0009 + 0.357\Delta\left(\frac{NFA}{Y}\right) + 0.607\Delta\left(\frac{CGOV}{Y}\right) - 0.422\left[\left(\frac{DC}{Y}\right)_{-1} - \left(\frac{DC}{Y}\right)^*_{-1}\right]$$

(–0.36) (11.2) (16.5) (–4.19)

$R^2 = 0.976$; $F(3, 42) = 590.7$ [0.00]; $\hat{\sigma} = 0.013$; $DW = 1.87$; $RSS = 0.007$ for 4 variables and 46 observations.
Variance instability tests: 0.052; Joint instability test: 0.833; $SC = -8.37$; $HQ = -8.47$; $FPE = 0.0001$; *AR* 1–4: $F(4, 38) = 0.56$ [0.69]; *ARCH 4* $F(4, 34) = 0.21$ [0.93]; Normality χ^2 (4) = 0.18 [0.91] ; *RESET* $F(1, 41) = 0.35$ [0.55]

The Dynamics of Capital Inflows and Monetary Policy with a VECM

We now examine *VECMs*. We consider first the following system for the Czech Republic:

$$\text{System A}: \left(\frac{DC}{Y}, \frac{NFA}{Y}, Q, P\right). \tag{11.5}$$

We then examine another system for Poland:

$$\text{System B}: \left(\frac{DC}{Y}, \frac{NFA}{Y}, \frac{CGOV}{Y}, P\right). \tag{11.6}$$

The latter system is not estimated for the Czech Republic since credit to the government does not play a significant role in the latter country.

Czech Republic Case

In the unrestricted vector error correction model, estimated by full-information maximum likelihood, the variables in first differences had a non-significant contribution (and were thus omitted), except for the inflation equation (Table 11.7). The growth in industrial production and in the net foreign asset ratio depends on their own level in the previous month. We conclude that the net foreign asset ratio and industrial production are exogenous. Prices are only weakly exogenous. The domestic credit ratio and prices are not Granger caused by any of the other three variables, while domestic credit is the only non-weakly exogenous variable. The positive coefficient of $(NFA/Y)_{-1}$ in the equation for the dynamics of the domestic credit ratio implies that a high ratio of net foreign assets during a given month induces a rise in domestic credit the following month. This spillover of 0.17 is similar to that obtained earlier in single-equation error correction models.

The Polish case

In the vector error correction model for Poland (Table 11.8), the lag differenced variables are not significant and were left out. The coefficient of the lagged net foreign asset ratio in the equation for the dynamics of the domestic credit ratio is unambiguously negative, at about –0.4. This is strongly in contrast with the single-equation model, showing the necessity of taking into account interdependencies with a vector autoregressive model. Such a negative contribution is also to be strongly contrasted with the positive one uncovered for the Czech Republic.

Table 11.7 Unrestricted vector error correction model (FIML estimation): Czech Republic 1992(12)–1995(12)

	Variables							
	Cste	$\Delta\left(\frac{DC}{Y}\right)_{-1}$	$\Delta\left(\frac{NFA}{Y}\right)_{-1}$	$\left(\frac{DC}{Y}\right)_{-1}$	$\left(\frac{NFA}{Y}\right)_{-1}$	P_{-1}	Q_{-1}	Season *MTH*1
$\Delta\left(\frac{DC}{Y}\right)$	5.73 (5.41)			–0.411 (–4.21)	0.174 (4.66)	–0.809 (–5.16)	0.135 (3.79)	–0.157 (–8.55)
$\Delta\left(\frac{NFA}{Y}\right)$	–1.60 (–1.23)				–0.114 (–1.75)	0.403 (1.38)		–0.19 (–5.93)
ΔQ	2.90 (4.27)						–0.68 (–4.26)	–0.08 (–1.34)
ΔP	0.008 (4.93)	0.11 (3.02)	–0.046 (–1.89)					0.024 (4.21)

Table 11.8 *Unrestricted vector error correction model[a]: Poland 1992(2)–1995(11)*

	Explanatory variables				
Equation	$\left(\frac{DC}{Y}\right)_{-1}$	$\left(\frac{NFA}{Y}\right)_{-1}$	$\left(\frac{CGOV}{Y}\right)_{-1}$	P_{-1}	*Cste*
$\Delta\left(\frac{DC}{Y}\right)$	—	–0.428 (–3.92)	—	0.18 (2.82)	–2.5 (3.55)
$\Delta\left(\frac{NFA}{Y}\right)$	0.885 (4.62)	–0.770 (–5.39)	–0.558 (–4.73)	0.522 (5.40)	–5.50 (–5.47)
$\Delta\left(\frac{CGOV}{Y}\right)$	—	–0.392 (–3.47)	—	0.122 (1.87)	–2.06 (–2.82)

Note: [a] *FIML* estimation.

4 CONCLUSION

After Latin American countries, transitional economies in Central Europe have also been hit by a wave of capital inflows. The present chapter provides evidence on the degree of sterilization of such capital inflows in the Czech Republic and Poland.

Using first an unrestricted autoregressive general model, we estimate monetary policy reaction functions over the 1992–95 period with monthly data. The change in net foreign assets of the banking system have a positive impact on the dynamics of domestic credit in both countries.

Unrestricted vector error correction models show that mainly error correction variables matter for both countries. This shows that regressions of the change in domestic credit and of the change in net foreign assets, ignoring the error correction term, may lead to a misleading conclusion. There is now a very strong contrast between the two countries since the change in domestic credit reacts positively to the previous period level of net foreign assets in the Czech Republic, and negatively in Poland.

The results for the Czech Republic seem to correspond with the problem that the CNB had in targeting the money supply in the 1994–95 period. M2 is probably too wide a concept to target in the period when sterilization policies have to be adopted. Under these conditions (see Calvo et al. 1995) targets in

M0 or M1 plus some tentative evaluation of multiplier effects could be more adequate.

REFERENCES

Argy, V. (1981), *The Postwar International Money Crisis: An Analysis*, London: George Allen & Unwin.

Bernanke, B. (1986), 'Alternative explanations of the money–income correlation', *Carnegie-Rochester Conference series on Public Policy*, **25**, 49–100.

Calvo, G. (1991), 'The perils of sterilization', *IMF Staff Papers*, **38** (4), December, 921–6.

Calvo, G., L. Leiderman and C.M. Reinhart (1993), 'Capital inflows and real exchange rate appreciation in Latin America: the role of external factors', *IMF Staff Papers*, **40** (1), March, 108–50.

Calvo, G., R. Sahay and C. Vegh (1995), 'Capital flows in central Europe: evidence and policy options', IMF Working Paper.

Czech National Bank (1994), *Annual Report.*

Czech National Bank (1996), *Annual Report 1995.*

Czech National Bank (1993 to 1995), *Selected Indicators of Monetary Developments in the Czech Republic.*

Frankel, J.A. (1994), 'Sterilization of money inflows: difficult (Calvo) or easy (Reisen)?', International Monetary Fund, Working Paper, No. 94/159, December.

Fry, M.J. (1995), *Money, Interest, and Banking in Economic Development*, 2nd edn, Baltimore, MD: Johns Hopkins University Press.

Griffith-Jones, S. (1995), *Capital Flows to Latin America and Asia: Lessons for Central and Eastern Europe*, Sussex: Institute of Development Studies.

Hrnčíř, M. and J. Klacek (1991), 'Stabilization policies and currency convertibility in Czechoslovakia', *European Economy*, Special Issue.

Kouba, K. (1993), 'Systemic changes in the Czech economy', Paper for the Workshop on European Economic Interaction, Vienna, in Ch. T. Saunders (ed.), *Eastern Europe in Crises and the Way Out.*

Kreinin, M.E. and L.H. Officer (1978), 'The monetary approach to the balance of payments, a survey', *Princeton Studies in International Finance*, No. 43, Princeton University.

Narodny Bank Polsky (1992 to 1995), *Information Bulletin.*

Williamson, J. (1994), *The Management of Capital Inflows*, Washington, DC: Institute of International Economics.

APPENDIX 11A DATA SOURCES AND DEFINITIONS

Except when explicitly mentioned, data comes from PlanEcon.

Czech republic: data base: December 1992 to December 1995

DC = Domestic credit in Monetary Survey (current koruna, billions): commercial banks + central bank (*source*: Czech National Bank)

NFA = Net foreign assets in monetary survey (current koruna, billions): commercial banks + central bank (*source*: Czech National Bank)

P = Retail price index (Jan. 1990 = 100)

Y = Retail trade turnover (current koruna, billions)

Q = Industrial output (constant prices; 1990, monthly average = 100)

Poland: data base: January 1992 to November 1995

DC = idem = net domestic assets – balance of other items (new zlotys, billions)

NFA = idem = net foreign assets (excluding long-term debt) (new zlotys, billions)

P = Industrial price index (Jan. 1990 = 100)

CGOV = Net liabilities of the budget sector (new zlotys, billions)

i = Market interest rate (interest rate on 0 to 1 month inter-bank placements (*sources:* NBP, *Information Bulletin*, various issues for 1992–94 and IMF, *International Financial Statistics* for 1995)

Q = Industrial production index (1985, monthly average = 100)

PART III

Macroeconomic Effects of Financial Reforms and Panel Discussion

12. Simulation experiments of the macroeconomic effects of financial reforms in Poland and Estonia

Parminder Bahra, Christopher J. Green and Victor Murinde*

1 INTRODUCTION

The ongoing financial sector reforms in the transition economies of Eastern and Central Europe have involved difficult policy choices designed to steer the economy away from central planning to market-based pricing mechanisms and resource allocation. However, some macroeconomic problems have persisted; for example, widespread unemployment and high inflation have plagued most transition economies (see Ruggerone 1996). This is hardly surprising. At the genesis of the economic transition, there was no blueprint for these countries to follow.[1] Moreover, the central role of financial markets as well as the importance of ownership was not explicitly recognized, and for several years many transformation traps persisted (see Portes 1994; Doukas et al. 1998). In addition, recent attempts to focus on financial sector reform through bank restructuring have been continuously stalled by the bad debt problem facing commercial banks (see Murinde and Mullineux, Ch. 1 in this book). Nevertheless, some serious efforts are being undertaken by policy makers, politicians, foreign advisers and international organizations on devising optimal vehicles for facilitating the transition process.

In general, there are at least three main constraints to the designing and implementation of the reform packages (see Dewatripont and Roland 1995), namely, uncertainty of outcomes, complementarity and interactions between reforms, and political constraints. The first two constraints underscore the

* The authors acknowledge useful comments from participants at a conference on 'Financial Sector Reforms' held at Tallinn Technical University on 20–21 September 1996 where a preliminary version of this chapter was presented. The research for the paper was undertaken with support from the European Commission's PHARE/ACE Programme 1994 under contract number 94–0685–R. However, the interpretations and conclusions expressed in this chapter are entirely those of the authors and should not be attributed in any manner to the European Commission.

need to examine the effects of simultaneous financial sector reforms, especially since most of these reforms take place concurrently. In this context, it would be useful to have a framework within which financial sector reforms can be analysed in order to isolate the effects of different policy choices for transition economies. The idea is to be able to tease out the desired direction as well as the magnitude of change for policy instruments that represent the desired policy reform. Lack of this information set on the potency of policy instruments in transition economies impairs the provision of effective advice on policy design, implementation and sequencing.[2] Recent attempts to address these issues have involved the design of theoretical models to underpin the macroeconomic policy framework of transition economies (Green and Murinde 1998). While the theoretical models provide some reasonably reliable guidance on the desired direction of policy changes,[3] the magnitude of change may only be determined empirically.

It is therefore desirable to undertake some econometric estimation and testing of a theoretical model in order to shed further light on the expected direction and magnitude of policy effects. The main limitation of empirical work in this direction, for most transition economies, is the paucity of reliable macroeconomic data for estimating and testing economic relationships without unduly sacrificing degrees of freedom and asymptotic accuracy. Data are both sparse (characterized by low frequency) and of unreliable quality. In most instances, the longest available series is six years (1991–96) although a more reliable sample size is 1993–96; most of the data is annual. These data limitations seriously preclude the application of recent developments in econometrics, for example non-stationarity and cointegration testing as well as exploration of non-linearities, to the specification of an econometric model for a transitional economy.

In the meantime, while the quality of data is improving (with the OECD and IMF producing macroeconomic series and national income accounting data for most of the transition countries), it is imperative to explore alternative empirical methods of policy analysis. Generally, there are two promising avenues for empirically supporting the ongoing development of theoretical frameworks in which to analyse financial sector reform within the setting of large institutional change. The first avenue involves the use of panel data by innovatively pooling the sparse time series over the available cross-section of transition economies. However, this approach incorporates a loss of detail through generality; the approach may yield cross-country evidence but is unhelpful on country-specific policy exercises. Moreover, results obtained through this approach may require qualification, given the different histories and stages of development among transitional countries. The second avenue is to maintain a country-specific bias and innovatively use the available time series to calculate elasticities for the parameters of a theoretical model. The parameter estimates are then plagued in the model in order to carry out simulations and policy experiments on the potency of various policy instruments and reform packages.

This chapter is motivated to follow the second avenue. It proposes and implements a simulation experiments approach to shed light on the direction as well as the magnitude of policy effects on the macroeconomy during financial reforms undertaken in most transition economies. The approach utilizes a disaggregated variant of a macroeconomic model for a transition economy developed in Green and Murinde (1998) as a framework for conducting simulations and policy experiments. Poland and Estonia are taken as the testing ground for the model, being the two economies for which the theoretical model is most relevant.

The chapter makes a number of contributions to the literature on modelling the macroeconomic policy framework for policy reform, three of which are paramount. First, a complete model of a transition economy is specified to highlight the role of financial reform in overall macroeconomic performance; the structuralist issues on the supply side as well as the key aspects of the demand side are captured using structural (rather than reduced-form) equations. Second, the chapter circumvents the need to estimate and test a complete structural model, and the attendant problems with degrees of freedom and lack of asymptotic accuracy. Rather, we provide an estimate of the parameter value by taking ratios (comparable to comparative statics) to represent elasticities. Third, the chapter fills a gap in the literature that emphasizes the importance of the speed and sequencing of financial reforms in transition economies (see Hallagan 1997). A simulation approach which involves policy experiments is used to explore the forecasting of outcomes of financial sector reforms (up to the year 2005) within the setting of large institutional change.

In what follows, the remainder of this chapter is structured into four sections. Section 2 provides a background of the two transitional economies studied in this chapter; it discusses the salient macroeconomic aspects of the transition process in Estonia and Poland. These aspects are integrated into a disaggregated macroeconomic model in Section 3; the method used to calculate parameter values for use in conducting simulations and policy experiments is also explained. The results of the simulation experiments for Estonia and Poland are reported and discussed in Section 4. Section 5 summarizes and concludes.

2 SALIENT MACROECONOMIC ASPECTS OF THE TRANSITION PROCESS IN ESTONIA AND POLAND

Although the transition countries of Eastern and Central Europe share a broadly common central planning heritage, they have had different macroeconomic policy experiences during the transition process. It is therefore useful to highlight the salient macroeconomic aspects of the transition process in the two sample economies, Estonia and Poland, before we theoretically and empirically investigate their financial reform performance.

Estonia

The initial period of the transition process in Estonia was characterized by stagflation. By 1991, when Estonia gained its independence from the Soviet Union, the recession, which had started in 1990 when the country was part of the Soviet Union, was beginning to bite. In 1992, GDP fell by 23.3 per cent but recovered by 2.1 per cent in 1993. As part of the Soviet Union, prices were strictly controlled and hence official inflation remained low. However, price liberalization started in 1989 and by the end of 1992 virtually all prices were liberalized. This resulted in sharp increases in prices and inflation surged, reaching a peak of 1603 per cent (annual average) in 1992; by 1994 though, the annual average was 47.7 per cent. The coexistence of the recession and high inflation made the initial stages of financial reforms very difficult, as the domestic economy was severely weak.

In 1992, a new national currency was introduced at a rate of ten roubles to one Estonian kroon. The exchange rate was pegged to the Deutschmark at a rate of eight Estonian kroons to one Deutschmark; the government committed itself to keeping this rate until the year 2000. One further aspect of the currency reform was the introduction of a currency board system; the implication of this system in terms of current policy operations is that by law the central bank (Bank of Estonia) can only issue new money in proportion to its reserves. The idea was to reduce the possibility of political interference and the potential for government to print its way out of deficits.

Currency reform provided an appropriate platform for the initial stages of banking reform. Along with the new currency, a two-tier banking system was established with 42 domestic commercial banks. Generally though, the banks were small and undercapitalized; in 1993, these banks ran into operational problems and a banking crisis ensued. In response, the government raised the minimum capital requirements and imposed a greater degree of supervision. None the less, the problems persisted and the failure of the Social Bank in 1994 signalled increased supervision by the monetary authorities; troubled domestic banks were then asked not to issue dividends but rather retain them in order to strengthen their capital positions. Furthermore, interest rates were completely liberalized and because of the pegging of the currency to the Deutschmark, Estonian interest rates generally followed German rates.

On the supply side, especially in terms of the labour market conditions and the production process, wages in Estonia increased by an average of 3 per cent prior to the reforms; in 1990 when the reforms were introduced, workers realized real wage increases of more than 8 per cent. This was in part due to the introduction of a minimum wage and a wage-setting structure that was indexed to the rate of inflation. Subsequent reforms have introduced wage-setting structures that differentiate between the private, state and government sectors and these have led to increased disparity between the different groups, with the private sector enjoying the largest increases.

In terms of the external sector (the foreign balance schedule), Estonia has the most liberal trade regime in the Baltic region and is the only country which has refrained from imposing protectionist regimes as a member of the Baltic Free Trade Agreement, according to the EIU (1996a). By the beginning of 1992, licences on all imports, including currency, had been removed. Similarly, with the exception of antiques and works of art, all export tariffs were removed. Prior to independence, the trade sector was highly dependent upon the rest of the Soviet Union. In 1991, 94.7 per cent of exports went to the Soviet Union while 84.8 per cent of imports originated in the Soviet Union. Since then, Estonia has moved quickly to reorientate its trade towards the West. Finland now provides the greatest volume of imports (second-largest export market), while Russia is the largest export market. However, imports are outstripping exports and the trade deficit grew to EEK 5.5 billion. This was in part due to the country's dependency on energy imports from Russia and an overvalued exchange rate. Greater imports of machinery and mechanical imports may suggest, though, that the economy is moving out of recession. In addition, the 1991 Law on Foreign Investments removed any restrictions on foreign capital repatriation, although some business activities such as utilities and transport require licences and foreign investment has become significant, totalling $81 million in 1994. The sequence of policy reforms introduced in Estonia is presented in Table 12.1.

In general, the financial sector reforms in Estonia have achieved very important milestones, notwithstanding the problems in bank restructuring and the persistence of the informal sector. It is expected that bank performance will improve as the financial markets (especially the stock exchange) become fully functional (see Murinde and Mullineux, Ch. 1 in this book). The informal financial sector is still significant; Vensel and Wihlborg (1998) have found that out of 42 firms in the survey, the ratio of formal loans to total assets was 11.2 per cent in 1995 and 24.6 per cent in 1996, while the ratio of informal loans to total assets was 0.2 per cent in 1995 and 0.7 per cent in

Table 12.1 Chronological summary of the salient policy shifts and other aspects of the transition process in Estonia

1989	The phasing out of price controls begins; most (except in housing and natural energy monopolies) are removed by 1992
1989–1992	Forty-two domestic banks are established. Foreign investors are permitted to operate in Estonia. Interest rate liberalization.
August 1991	Estonia gains independence
June 1992	Independent national currency, the kroon (EEK), introduced. Initially pegged to the Deutschmark (DM) at 8 EEK/1 DM and is fully convertible
September 1992	Bankruptcy Law passed. By mid-1995, bankruptcy procedures are moved against 1000 firms
1992–1993	Banking crisis ensues. Government responds by increasing minimum capital requirements and more stringent supervision
March 1993	Privatization Act allows asset sales using vouchers and cash
June 1993	Securities Market Act is adopted
May 1994	Bank of Estonia advises commercial banks not to issue dividends but to strengthen their capital positions
September 1994	Computerized depository scheme opens. Shares in investment funds, enterprises and banks are traded over the counter
June 1995	The 'Europe Agreement' on trade is signed
July 1995	Estonian Securities Board has 18 investment funds registered
1996	Only 14 of the original 42 banks are now operational
May 1996	Tallinn Stock Exchange opens. Stock market capitalization by mid-1996 is approximately 11% of GDP
June 1997	The banking sector now consists of 13 commercial banks, two savings and loans cooperatives and one investment bank. Foreign ownership of banks is high at 40%, compared to the government stake of 7%
October 1997	Bank capital adequacy ratio raised from 8% to 10%
1998	Deposit insurance law guaranteeing 90% of private and company deposits up to a maximum of EEK 20 000 to be introduced

Sources: Compiled by the authors from various reports, especially EBRD (1996, 1997) and EIU (1996a).

1996. However, as the banking sector grows and financial markets become fully functional, the informal sector is expected to gradually diminish.

Poland

Following the breakaway from central planning, the Polish economy faced problems common among the other transitional economies. This included inefficient state-owned enterprises (SOEs), which were running up unserviceable levels of debt, a banking sector with many bad loans and portfolios that were concentrated both geographically and sectorally, an inconvertible currency, price distortions in the form of numerous subsidies in factor and product markets, an economy heading towards hyperinflation and in respect to the goal of a market-based economy, little if no experience of private property and the institutions necessary (for example, legal frameworks, financial markets, capital markets) for a modern market-orientated economy (see Bahra et al. 1997).

By 1989, the macroeconomic pressures had mounted. The government was running a budget deficit of about 7 per cent of GDP. Revenues were falling and the government sparked off strong inflationary pressures by financing the deficit through printing money. The new incoming Solidarity government prioritized the abatement of the impending hyperinflation and with advice from the IMF undertook a stabilization plan, the Balcerowicz stabilization plan. This was centred around two objectives; first, a fixed credible nominal exchange rate, and second, a tight tax-based incomes policy which became known as the *popiwek*. Imposed in 1990, the *popiwek* was a highly progressive income tax on wage increases and between 1990 and 1993 resulted in real wages declining on an average annual basis by 8.4 per cent. By 1994, though, real wages increased by 4.2 per cent and the incomes policy was replaced by a new law that resolved wage claims through negotiations involving labour, management and government. Additionally, the government imposed tight monetary policy, a credit squeeze and real positive interest rates (EBRD 1996; Rondinelli and Yurkiewicz 1996).

To address the immediate price distortion problems, the authorities introduced liberalization policies to run in tandem with stabilization policies. In 1990, most tariff and non-tariff barriers had been removed, with the effect that average tariffs had been reduced from 18.3 per cent in 1989 to 5.5 per cent in mid-1991. However, a subsequent deterioration in the trade balance led to the tariffs being reinstalled in late 1991 and average tariffs rose, to rise to 18.4 per cent in 1992. Between 1990 and 1991, most prices had been liberalized, the exceptions being domestic fuel, medicine, local authority housing and spirits. In January 1990, the zloty became convertible (although exchange restrictions on travel allowances and other invisible payments remained) and the 1991 Law on Companies with foreign participation allowed foreign investors to purchase foreign currency with zlotys for the transfer of profits and repatriation of capital as long as the initial investment was made with zlotys purchased at the official exchange rate. In October 1991, the currency regime changed to a preannounced crawling peg against a basket of currencies. January 1990 saw interest rate liberalization, with banks free to set deposit and borrowing rates.

The effects of these policies, in the light of the collapse of COMECON trading arrangements, was to dip the economy into its severest postwar recession. Between 1989 and 1991, GDP declined by 17.7 per cent but growth returned in 1992, increasing by 2.6 per cent as consumption increased. This trend continued, with growth increasing for the next two years. In 1995, growth increased by 7 per cent; figures for the next two years have been edged downwards, but by the end of 1997 the Polish economy seems to have returned to pre-reform levels of wealth. What is evident during this period is that growth was in no small part due to a dynamic private sector that has increased in size from 31 per cent of GDP in 1990 to 56 per cent in 1994. In terms of employment the private sector share of employment increased from 14 per cent in 1989 to 74.6 per cent in 1996. In contrast, the remaining state sector performed poorly, with sales declining over the 1991–94 period (EBRD 1996; EIU 1996b).

Generally, the stabilization plan is considered to have been successful in containing inflation from near hyperinflation levels in 1989. The stabilization plan also saw a turnaround of the budget deficit from 7 per cent of GDP in 1989 to a surplus of higher than 3.7 per cent post-1995. However, stabilization did have costs, as the people of Poland faced higher prices, incomes policies and higher unemployment; the government was under pressure to increase expenditure on social security. Furthermore, the tax base had changed considerably. Previously, the government was the sole controller of finances, funds were centralized and tax was taken from the turnover of SOEs. In the post-reform period, however, firms were being privatized, but a tax collection system based along the lines of a developed market economy was still in its infancy.

The freeing of prices meant that central government no longer had to supply subsidies, as firms were made to adjust to world markets. Similarly, the convertible exchange rate exposed domestic firms to world markets, thus providing incentives to produce more efficiently and encourage exports. In fact as the economy grew after 1994, investment and exports became the driving force of recovery as export growth increased from 1.2 per cent of GDP in 1992 to 18.9 per cent in 1996 and investment grew by 9 per cent in 1996 after a decline between 1989 and 1991 (EIU 1996b).

More recently, inflationary pressures are building up and the central bank and the finance ministry are at odds over the precise source of these pressures. The central bank (with a strong degree of independence and a commitment to low inflation) cites structural factors such as the increase in import protection as the cause for these pressures whereas the finance ministry suggests that the central bank has failed to sterilize strong foreign inflows through currency appreciation. After successful negotiations in 1994 with the Paris Club over rescheduling debt, repayments are set to increase towards the beginning of the 21st century. In April 1996, the government accepted a policy framework known as Policy 2000. It sets out specific targets such as single-digit inflation and is designed with a view to Poland becoming a full member of the European Union (EIU 1996b).

A chronological summary of the sequence of policy reforms introduced in Poland is presented in Table 12.2. In general, although the financial sector reforms in Poland have achieved very important milestones, three problems have persisted, namely, high inflation, bank restructuring and the persistence of the informal sector.[4] Like in Estonia, it is expected that bank performance will improve as the financial markets (especially the Stock Exchange) become fully functional and the informal sector will gradually diminish.

3 THE MODEL

The macroeconomic model used here is a disaggregated version of the reduced-form model in Green and Murinde (1998). The model comprises four main blocks, namely, the expenditures sector, the financial sector, the external sector, and the supply side.

The expenditure components of the income–expenditure identity for a transition economy are set out in identity (12.1), and fully explored in what follows. In equation (12.2), real consumption expenditure (C) is postulated to depend on real income (Y) net of real tax revenue (T); real wealth (V); and the relative price of domestic and foreign goods (Q^*E/Q). The ratio (Q^*E/Q) captures the foreign producer price (Q^*) converted into domestic currency by multiplication by the spot exchange rate (E), and the domestic component of the price level (Q); where E is a weighted average of the official exchange rate and the parallel market exchange rate. The nature of shortages in the goods market is such that Q is actually a weighted average of the domestic (producer) price level for goods produced in the official sector and the corresponding price level for goods produced in the parallel (informal) sector. The inclusion of Q^*E and Q in equation (12.2) reflects the fact that consumption includes both home and imported goods. Moreover, these two variables are used to tie down the basics of the dual economy; the parallel market in foreign exchange operates via Q^*E while the parallel market in goods operates via Q.

Table 12.2 Chronological summary of the salient policy shifts and other aspects of the transition process in Poland

1989	Banking reform begins through the Banking Law and the National Bank of Poland Law. The 'monobank', the National Bank of Poland (NBP), divests itself of its regional branches as a precursor to privatization; central bank activities begin
1989–91	Commercial banking operations and branches of nine regional departments of the NBP are transformed into independent commercial banks
January 1990	Polish zloty becomes convertible
February 1990	The Balcerowicz (stabilization) plan. Stabilizing and liberalizing the economy – share of GDP increases from 18% in 1989 to 56% in 1994
March 1990	Fixed exchange rate regime is introduced
April 1990	Banks are allowed to set deposit and interest rates freely
May 1990	Excess-wage tax is imposed on state enterprises
June 1990	Law on Monopolistic Practice passed along with the creation of the Anti-Monopoly Office (AMO)
July 1990	Beginning of privatization; multi-track approach involving liquidation, asset sales, leasing or 'commercialization'. Passing of Privatization Bill leads to first five sell-offs by the end of the year
September 1990	Most tariff and non-tariff barriers to trade are suspended and state's monopoly on foreign trade is ended
October 1990	Exchange rate regime changed to a preannounced crawling peg against a basket of currencies, with the rate of crawl at 1.8% per month
December 1990	Insurance Law establishes the criteria for the authorization of insurance companies, for example, minimum capital and solvency levels
1990–91	Most prices are liberalized (with the exception of domestic fuels and basic medicine)
January 1991	Collapse of COMECON trading agreements. Stabilization tips economy into recession, exacerbated by COMECON collapse. Shift from barter to intra-regional trade at market prices with settlements in hard currency
March 1991	Debt forgiveness agreed with official Paris Club creditors; two-stage agreement weights repayment heavier in the 21st century
May 1991	Deterioration in trade balance leads to reimposition of import tariffs
June 1991	Law on Public Trading of Securities and Trust Funds allows the establishment of open-end investment funds
September 1991	Warsaw Stock Exchange reopens. Legal criteria and framework outlined in the Act Establishing the Warsaw Stock Exchange

Table 12.2 (continued)

October 1991	Law on Public Trading in Securities and Trust Funds confers supervisory activities to the Securities Commission. Number of listed companies rise from nine in 1991 to 44 in 1994 with market capitalization rising from 0.2% to 3.5% of GDP for the same period
1991–1992	Many new private banks are licensed in light of the Banking Law
August 1993	Polish zloty devalued 7.4% against basket of currencies, returning to original 1.8% crawl
1993–1994	Privatization of two of the nine state-owned commercial banks
June 1994	Foreign Exchange Law is passed, allowing full current account convertibility
October 1994	Excess-wage tax suspended
December 1994	European Association (EA) agreement as prelude to membership of European Union
February 1995	Crawling peg monthly rate reduced to 1.2%
February 1995	Law on Banking Deposit Guarantee Fund comes into force. This provides a scheme of deposit insurance for all commercial banks
March 1995	New exchange rate regime allows zloty to fluctuate within ±7% around the central rate
May 1995	Securities Commission authorizes the establishment of three new investment funds
July 1995	Poland becomes member of World Trade Organization
August 1995	Currency reform in light of anti-inflationary policies. New zloty takes off four zeros from existing currency
September 1995	Mass privatization. Within the framework of a layer of investment funds to manage assets, 15 funds were chosen and given allocations from a first tranche of 415 state firms
October 1995	Ratio of total domestic credit to GDP is 35%, of which only half of the domestic credit is to the private sector
December 1995	Warsaw Stock Exchange has 53 listed companies with a total market capitalization of US$4.3 (approximately 3.8% of GDP). Over-the-counter service expected to open in 1996
March 1996	Further funds for recapitalization of the second of the state banks and the state agricultural bank
June 1996	By mid-1996, four of the nine state banks had been privatized; the consolidation of remaining state banks is considered following poor subscription to the privatization of two regional commercial banks
June 1997	Four of the nine commercial banks have been privatized; there is a significant level of foreign ownership

Sources: Compiled by the authors from various reports especially EBRD (1996, 1997) and EIU (1966).

In equation (12.3), it is argued that real tax revenues depend on the level of real income and real imports, as well as the tax parameters for income (*TY*) and imports (*TZ*), respectively.[5] These taxes are relevant to almost all transition economies as part of the transition process to a market economy. As Ruggerone (1996) observes, tax issues seem to have been side-stepped in some recent theoretical work, notwithstanding the special role of the tax system in the early stages of the transition process.

In identity (12.4), real wealth of the private sector (*V*) consists of the productive component of private capital stock (*K*), money (*M*/*P*) and loans (*L*/*P*) in real terms (where *M* and *L* are deflated by the retail price index, *P*). The retail price index is a weighted average of domestic and foreign producer prices, as specified in equation (12.5). The productive component of the capital stock is but a component of the total capital stock (*K*). The real productive capital stock changes over time in incremental fashion such that it comprises additions of real gross investment expenditure (*I*) to the capital stock in the previous period depreciated at the rate δ, as given in equation (12.6).

We postulate that real gross investment expenditure has both domestic and foreign components and is a function of real income and the official real interest rate, given by the difference between the regulated official nominal rate (*R*) and expected inflation ($\hat{Q}^e$). Borish et al. (1996) point out that during bank and enterprise restructuring in the transition economies, many enterprises turn to state-owned banks for credit to allow them to defer restructuring. Indeed, as earlier shown for Estonia and Poland, the financing of small- and medium-sized enterprises (SMEs) creates huge demands on a constrained state banking sector, and ultimately SMEs may have to resort to the informal financial sector. In this context, we recognize that in most transition economies, business firms tend to rely on informal market loans to finance their short-term working capital, so we include the real curb-market interest rate ($NR - \hat{Q}^e$) as an argument. In addition, since investment goods include imports, we postulate that real gross investment expenditure is influenced by the relative prices of domestic and imported goods (Q^*E/Q). We include overseas aid (K_0) as an additional variable in the investment function to hypothesize a direct positive relationship between overseas aid inflows and direct investment which overseas companies bring during the transition period, as shown in equation (12.7).[6]

Real government expenditure is exogenous, as specified in identity (12.8). In equation (12.9), we postulate that the level of real exports (*X*) is a function of relative prices for domestic and imported goods. The official and informal markets in goods and foreign currency, characterized in the transition economies, are reflected in these prices. The import function is defined to be consistent with the consumption and investment functions, each of which include an import component. In addition, a significant part of the government revenues in many transition economies is generated from import taxes. So, we include a tax on imports as another argument in the import function in equation (12.10).

The financial sector is modelled jointly with the budgetary process. This approach is consistent with the argument by Sachs (1996) that financial stabilization involves the end of the pre-reform monetary overhang, high repressed and open inflation, and large fiscal deficits. Specifically, we characterize the money supply process in transition economies by specifying the government budget constraint facing these economies, as in identity (12.11). The identity implies that fiscal and monetary policy instruments cannot be used independently. During the process of transition, the government may be forced into undertaking huge expenditures; for example during the recent process of reunification of Germany, former Western Germany had to foot the expenses of facilitating economic reform. At the same time, the sources of tax revenues for the government remain severely limited until the transition is completed. Thus the transition process is characterized by budget deficits, as government spending exceeds tax revenue. Stocks of assets cannot be constant as the deficit needs to be financed by printing money ($\Delta M/P$), by borrowing from commercial banks ($\Delta L/P$) or by drawing upon foreign reserves ($\Delta F/P$).[7]

We postulate the demand for real money balances (M^d/P) to be a function of real income, real wealth, and the real rates of return to money and loans. To capture the relative influence of these variables, we incorporate the relevant returns to money and loans by thinking of various economic agents as holding the following asset substitutes: (i) real (rather than nominal) assets are substitutes for money, amidst high inflation; thus, expected inflation ($\hat{Q}^e$) is a proxy for the opportunity cost of holding money; (ii) loans for working capital in the informal credit markets earn NR; in real terms, $[NR - (Q^e)]$; (iii) bonds or loans to government that earn R, which is the regulated official rate; in real terms, $(R - \hat{Q}^e)$. Thus, in specifying the demand for real balances in equation (12.13) we impose restrictions on the coefficients l_2 and l_3 such that $l_2 < l_3 < 0$. These restrictions on the two interest rate elasticities, to be discussed below, reflect the role of official and informal finance.

As earlier noted in the country experiences for Estonia and Poland (Section 2), we assume financial dualism as characterized by the coexistence of official and informal (curb) markets in loans (credit). While the official sector comprises the new financial institutions and markets that are being established as part of financial reforms, the informal counterpart comprises the lending and borrowing transactions of economic agents outside the official sector.[8] The nature of the dual financial markets has important implications for the financial reforms addressed in our model, especially with respect to interest rate policy. Unlike its official counterpart, the informal financial sector is not subject to interest rate ceilings and reserve requirements. In terms of a single period, the curb-market interest rate is assumed to have higher elasticity than the official interest rate; for example, the effect of a rise in the official real interest rate on the demand for real money balances is smaller than the effect of a rise in the curb-market rate. At the beginning of financial reforms, the experience of transition economies suggests some kind of financial repression in which the official interest rate is pegged, and credit rationing takes place; hence unsatisfied demand for credit in the official sector spills over to the informal sector. The curb-market interest rate is determined by the forces of demand and supply in the informal financial market, thus the rate rises with an increase in unsatisfied official-sector demand for credit. As the process of financial reform picks up, the official and curb-market interest rates are inversely related; as the official rate rises, more funds are deposited in official financial institutions for intermediation purposes, and as more demand for credit is met in the official sector, the curb-market rate falls due to diminishing spillage of unsatisfied demand to the informal sector. Successful financial restructuring is consistent with the expansion of the official financial sector to take over the activities hitherto carried out in the informal financial institutions and markets; the official and curb-market interest rates ultimately converge, and the former becomes a free market rate.

Ruggerone (1996) observes that what seems to have been neglected so far in recent macroeconomic modelling for transition economies is the interaction of inflationary finance and real variables during policy reforms. We attempt to address this issue by developing a specification in which inflation is underpinned by the supply side. Specifically, we build up the aggregate supply function from a production function and a simple but plausible set of labour market relationships. In equation (12.14), we postulate that for transition economies, production (*Yp*) in the short run is a function of labour inputs (*LB*), the availability of curb-market loans for working capital needs (*WK*), and imported materials input (*N*). As earlier explained, we incorporate the fact that transition economies are characterized by the existence of a part of the capital stock which is unproductive; this renders the capital stock fixed in the short run. We also incorporate in our specification a central feature of the labour market in transition economies. We note that a fundamental feature of the centrally planned economies was full employment, with state enterprises hoarding unproductive labour (Svejnar 1996). We argue that the current composition of labour in transition economies is such that part of the labour force, which was previously employed in government-owned corporations, has the wrong skills and has to be retrained to be able to work productively for private sector companies in a market economy. At the wage bargaining time, the supply of employable (productive) labour (L^s) is a function of the real wage package $(W - \hat{Q}^e)$ as specified in equation (12.15).

On the demand side, the marginal physical products of labour, informal-market finance, and imported materials at wage bargaining time are derived and equated by producers to their expectations of: the expected real product wage $(W^e / \hat{Q}^e)$, the expected real price of curb-market finance $(NR^e - \hat{Q}^e)$ and the expected real price of imported materials $(Q^* E^e / \hat{Q}^e)$, respectively, as specified in equation (12.16).

In modelling the external sector, it is assumed that at this initial stage of the transition process, some kind of fixed exchange rate regime is in operation, although the process of financial liberalization has been set in motion, including trade liberalization (see Hillman and Ursprung 1996). Exogenous capital inflows take the form of concessionary finance from donor agencies such as the European Commission, the IMF and the World Bank; these inflows also attract direct foreign investment. Hence, the basic flow of funds identity we adopt here for the foreign sector states that a change in foreign reserves equals the difference between export earnings and import payments, plus exogenous aid inflows and any possible net capital inflows in the form of investment from overseas companies (K_0),[9] as given in equation (12.17). Thus the coexistence of the formal and informal markets in goods and foreign currency is incorporated in the equations for imports and exports.[10]

The equation listing of the model is given below.

Equation Listing of the Model

The expenditure sector

$$\ln Y = \ln(C + I + G + X - Z) \quad \text{Identity} \tag{12.1}$$

$$\ln C = c_1 \ln Y - c_2 \ln T + c_3 \ln V + c_4 \ln Q^* E - c_5 \ln Q + \mu_1 \tag{12.2}$$

$$\ln T = t_1 \ln Y + t_2 \ln Z + \mu_2 \tag{12.3}$$

$$\ln V \cong \ln[K + (M + L)] - \beta \ln P \quad \text{Identity} \tag{12.4}$$

$$\ln P = \alpha \ln Q + (1 - \alpha) \ln Q^* E \quad \text{Identity} \tag{12.5}$$

$$\ln K = \ln[I + (1 - \delta)K_{t-1}] \quad \text{Identity} \tag{12.6}$$

$$\ln I = i_1 Y - i_2(NR - \hat{Q}^e) - i_3(R - \hat{Q}^e) + i_4 Q^* E + i_5 Q + \mu_3 \tag{12.7}$$

$$\ln G = \ln G^0 \quad \text{Identity} \tag{12.8}$$

$$\ln X = x_1 \ln Q^* E - x_2 \ln Q + \mu_4 \tag{12.9}$$

$$\ln Z = z_1 \ln Y - z_2 \ln TZ + z_3 \ln Q^* E + z_4 \ln Q + z_5 \ln V - z_6 (R - \hat{Q}^e) - z_7 (NR - \hat{Q}^e) + \mu_5. \tag{12.10}$$

The monetary sector

$$\ln(G - T) = \ln(\Delta M / P + \Delta L / P + \Delta F / P) \quad \text{Identity} \tag{12.11}$$

$$\ln M = b_1 \ln G - b_2 \ln Y - b_3 \ln Z - b_4 \ln Q^* E + b_5 \ln Q - b_6 \ln L - b_7 \ln F + b_8 \ln(M_{-1} + L_{-1} + F_{-1}) + \mu_6 \tag{12.12}$$

$$NR = d_1 Y - d_2 R + d_3 Q^* E + d_4 Q - d_5 M + d_6 L + d_7 \hat{Q}^e + d_8 K_{t-1} + \mu_7. \tag{12.13}$$

The supply side

$$\ln Y = \phi_1 \ln BL + \phi_2 \ln N + \phi_3 \ln WK + \mu_8 \tag{12.14}$$

$$\ln BL^s = \varphi \ln(W / P^e) + \mu_9 \tag{12.15}$$

$$\ln BL^d = \lambda_1 \ln(W^e / Q^e) + \lambda_2 \ln(Q^{*e} E^e / Q^e) + \lambda_3 (NR - Q^e) + \mu_{10}. \tag{12.16}$$

The external sector

$$\ln F = e_1 \ln Q^* E - e_2 \ln Y - e_3 \ln Q - e_4 \ln M - e_5 \ln L + e_6 R + e_7 NR - e_8 \ln K_{-1} - e_9 \ln \hat{Q}^e + e_{10} \ln K_0 + \mu_{11}. \tag{12.17}$$

The variables are defined as follows: Y = real income; C = real consumption; I = real investment; G = real government spending; X = real exports; Z = real imports; T = real tax revenue; V = real wealth; Q^* = foreign prices; E = exchange rate; Q = domestic producer prices; K = nominal capital stock; M = nominal money; L = nominal loans; P = retail price index; NR = curb-market loan rate; R = official interest rate; TZ = import tax rate; F = foreign reserves; EQQ = inflation rate; BL^s = labour supply; BL^d = labour demand; W = wage rate; and K_0 = exogenous capital inflows, including foreign aid. The term ln denotes natural logarithm; and the superscript e on a variable denotes expectations.

The policy instruments in the model consist of budgetary and financial instruments. The budgetary instruments are real government spending, income tax rate and import tax rate; the financial policy instruments are the official interest rate, loans from commercial banks, the exchange rate and foreign aid.

However, the model also has some important limitations. It is distinctively short run in the sense that it allows us to look at only one-period effects of policy changes. Clearly, we would not expect most policy effects to carry over to the long run. However, they do illustrate the practical difficulties of managing an economy in the short run with structural rigidities such as informal markets in goods, foreign currency and credit. Precisely, the disaggregation of the model makes it difficult to explore meaningfully the dynamic analysis of financial reforms. In addition, the model does not deal with some of the concerns of financial sector reforms in transition economies, for example the issue of equitable distribution of incomes.

4 SIMULATIONS AND POLICY EXPERIMENTS

Standard counterfactual dynamic simulations, in deterministic as well as stochastic spirit, are usually performed on the basis of coefficients obtained by estimating the equations of a model using standard econometric techniques. In this chapter, given that we do not have enough observations to estimate the model for Estonia and Poland, we innovatively use the limited available time series to calculate elasticities for the model parameters. The description of data and variables used in calculating the coefficients (elasticities) in the simulation model for Estonia and Poland is detailed in Table 12A.1 in the appendix. The calculation of the coefficients is carried out by an approximation of the 'comparative statics' empirical ratios as illustrated in Table 12A.1. The values of the calculated coefficients obtained are reported in Table 12.3. To check on the reliability of these parameter values, restricted versions of some equations were estimated on actual data, where possible, without violating the degrees of freedom. It was found that the empirical estimated coefficients are not significantly different from the calculated values reported in Table 12.3.

The parameter values were inserted into the model and the Gauss–Seidel method was used to solve the model. Given a simultaneous linear model of the form $Ax = b$, where A is a matrix of coefficients, x is the set of endogenous variables, and b is a vector of numbers (which may include functions of endogenous variables); the method involves solving the model directly by

Table 12.3 Calculated parameter values for use in simulation experiments for Estonia and Poland

Coefficient	Poland	Estonia
α	−0.06607	0.540416
b_1	−0.2449	−2.51E−05
b_2	0.092047	0.052581
b_3	−1.43559	4.76E−04
b_4	1.78835	−8.31E−03
b_5	1.01132	1.27E−03
b_6	0.017569	−0.01861
b_7	0.127483	0.081863
b_8	0.083644	−4.36E−03
β	6.39299	4.95921
c_1	−6.65E−03	−0.23945
c_2	−0.09388	5.20409
c_3	0.349405	−22.2425
c_4	0.363996	−4.14163
c_5	−1.53E−03	−2.75E−03
d_1	8.83E−07	−27.4635
d_2	0.021183	10.2
d_3	−4.87E−03	30.27196
d_4	−2.60E−03	−32.3421
d_5	8.03E−05	−29.2353
d_6	−0.21203	−38.0259
d_7	0.14499	−32.8948
d_8	−3.07E−04	−30.9493
δ	11.68051	7.97813
e_1	−7.1723	−0.04683
e_2	−2.23181	1.28E−04
e_3	24.3809	−2.99367
e_4	66.9532	7.60674
e_5	−54.5453	−4.81298
e_6	2.14E−03	−6.09E−05
e_7	−8.52E−03	3.84E−04
e_8	2.73426	0.071777
e_9	−33.4031	1.09717
e_{10}	−9.16185	−0.78431
i_1	−0.07745	5.24112
i_2	0.013381	0.051604
i_3	−12.6787	−9.8651

Table 12.3 (continued)

Coefficient	Poland	Estonia
i_4	0.816558	-3.89422
i_5	-0.01304	-0.0436
λ_1	0.050149	-0.61929
λ_2	0.057296	0.133746
λ_3	-6.55E-04	-1.06E-03
ω_1	-0.22102	-0.58995
t_1	-0.20644	-0.33084
t_2	0.53708	0.660793
x_1	1.04104	-0.17055
x_2	-0.17748	1.04958
ϕ_1	-0.45753	0.526273
ϕ_2	0.414872	-0.87393
ϕ_3	-0.56829	0.803912
ϕ_4	0.082956	0.55273
ϕ_5	0.956428	0.04397
z_1	0.129135	8.57E-04
z_2	0.724692	0.508904
z_3	-0.20458	0.017035
z_4	-0.01072	-4.83E-04
z_5	-0.4221	0.423013
z_6	0.011312	4.47E-04
z_7	-4.12105	-10.669

Note: The first column gives the theoretical coefficients as specified in the equation listing of the model; the second and third column report the empirical counterparts of the coefficients for Poland and Estonia, respectively.

inverting A and multiplying b by it, that is, $x = A^{-1}b$. Specifically, a base simulation run was conducted for all the endogenous variables of the main model equations in a dynamic counterfactual spirit, that is, for the historical period 1993–96. Given the short horizon of the base run (four years only), the use of standard criteria for evaluating the performance and tracking ability of the model was not emphasized.[11]

On the basis of the base simulation run, some counterfactual experiments were undertaken in order to highlight the effects of financial reforms in Estonia and Poland. The interpretation of financial sector reform used here was to consider the removal of rigidities in the formation of the single most important price in the banking sector and the budding financial markets, namely, the liberalization of interest rates. The simulation experiment for each country therefore consisted of assuming a step change of a 1 per cent rise in the official interest rate (100 basis points).

The results of the policy shocks are reported in Table 12.4 for Estonia. It is shown that a rise in the official interest rate leads to a fall in real consumption expenditures; the forecasts indicate that consumption is increasingly reduced towards the year 2005. It is expected that private sector economic agents tend to reduce consumption following an interest rate liberalization; in addition, economic agents reduce consumption because of the expected increase in the cost of credit. Investment expenditure also contracts, initially slowly during the historical period (1993–96) and thereafter at a faster pace during the forecast horizon to the year 2005. This result is consistent with the structural model in the sense that an increase in the official interest rate directly increases the cost of capital as well as the expected return on investment. The effects of credit rationing and the presence of an informal financial sector in Estonia, highlighted in the survey studies by Vensel and Wihlborg (1998), do not seem to constrain the potency of financial reform policy. Exports fall throughout the historical period as well as during the *ex-ante* forecasting horizon. The fall in imports is much more pronounced than the fall in exports. It would appear that interest rate costs reduce the volume of imported intermediate inputs, which form a predominant proportion of total imports during the transition process. As expected, money supply falls following a rise in the official interest rate; this is consistent with the evidence on the fall in consumption. Foreign reserves are shown to increase throughout the historical and the forecasting periods; this result is consistent with the fall in money and the fact that imports decline faster than exports, as shown above. Inflation increases modestly during the historical period, but the general trend during the forecasting period shows a trend of declining inflation rates. This result is consistent with the argument that an increase in interest rates tends to reduce the curb-market interest rates and thus leads to lower prices on the supply side.

For Poland, the results of the policy shocks are reported in Table 12.5. The results suggest that a rise in the official interest rate increases consumption but at a declining trend; income increases throughout the historical and forecasting periods. This result suggests that the curb-market interest rate effects are predominant; a rise in the official interest rate induces a fall in the curb-market rate (which approximates the market-free rate) and thus leads to an increase in credit and consumption. However, imports decline and foreign reserves increase throughout the historical and forecasting periods. Inflation falls during the historical period, and the general trend during the forecasting period shows a trend of declining inflation rates. This result is consistent with

Table 12.4 Simulation results and ex-ante *forecasts for a 1 per cent rise in the official interest rate in Estonia*

Change in	1993	1994	1995	1996	1997	1998	1999	2000	2001	2002	2003	2004	2005
C(R)	–0.9059	–0.9586	–0.98424	–1.00741	–1.02635	–1.04237	–1.05625	–1.06849	–1.07944	–1.08935	–1.0984	–1.10672	–1.11443
I(R)	–1.16909	–1.30137	–1.77854	–2.16555	–2.55256	–2.93957	–3.32659	–3.7156	–4.10061	–4.48731	–4.87364	–5.25998	–5.64653
X(R)	–1.08273	–1.16528	–1.22284	–1.26796	–1.30508	–1.33662	–1.36403	–1.38827	–1.40999	–1.42968	–1.44768	–1.46426	–1.47962
Z(R)	2.040936	–16.5442	–26.9518	–38.8916	–51.0856	–63.2856	–75.4918	–87.7042	–99.9229	–117.076	–129.539	–142.015	–154.504
M(R)	–1.98555	–1.88668	–1.97416	–1.98372	–2.01365	–2.03349	–2.05371	–2.07152	–2.08812	–2.10334	–2.11763	–2.13105	–2.14355
F(R)	3.591679	4.813257	8.264201	11.14279	14.0171	16.88969	19.76153	22.63334	25.50517	28.37511	31.24258	34.11056	36.98046
P(R)	0.08213	0.14349	0.16924	0.171011	0.16486	0.15526	0.14318	0.12964	0.11524	0.10032	0.08508	0.06965	0.05408

Note: The multiplier effects are given for C(R) = consumption; I(R) = investment; X(R) = exports; Z(R) = imports; M(R) = money supply; F(R) = foreign reserves; P(R) = inflation rate.

Table 12.5 Simulation results and ex-ante *forecasts for a 1 per cent rise in the official interest rate in Poland*

Change in	1993	1994	1995	1996	1997	1998	1999	2000	2001	2002	2003	2004	2005
C(R)	11.42367	11.27706	11.22546	11.11321	11.02252	10.93202	10.84088	10.74836	10.65368	10.55607	10.45463	10.34834	10.23599
I(R)	−12.6784	−12.6784	−12.6784	−12.6784	−12.6784	−12.6784	−12.6784	−12.6784	−12.6784	−12.6784	−12.6784	−12.6784	−12.6784
Z(R)	−0.8594	−0.8594	−0.8593	−0.8593	−0.8594	−0.8985	−0.8594	−0.8593	−0.8985	−0.8594	−0.8594	−0.8594	−0.8594
M(R)	9.43767	9.33838	9.22037	9.19986	9.17129	9.14338	9.1194	9.09818	9.07911	9.06167	9.04553	9.03042	9.01616
N(R)	2.124	2.148	2.149	2.148	2.051	2.148	2.051	2.149	2.149	2.051	2.051	2.149	2.149
F(R)	−7.13201	−5.65163	−1.70118	2.38408	7.56632	13.48872	20.13213	26.88689	34.13161	41.64778	49.38742	57.31466	65.39845
Y(R)	3.67888	4.51765	5.7975	6.0758	6.34475	6.59295	6.82067	7.03306	7.23217	7.42023	7.59874	7.76899	7.93201
P(R)	−0.30087	−0.2589	−0.3312	−0.26985	−0.25089	−0.23125	−0.21131	−0.1913	−0.17138	−0.15165	−0.13217	−0.11299	−0.09412

Note: The multiplier effects are given for C(R) = consumption; I(R) = investment; Z(R) = imports; M(R) = money supply; N(R) = curb-market interest rate; F(R) = foreign reserves; Y(R) = real growth rate; P(R) = inflation rate.

the argument that an increase in interest rates tends to reduce the curb-market interest rates and thus leads to lower prices on the supply side under cost-plus pricing rules and an imperfectly competitive market structure as in Poland.

It is useful to note that the financial reform effects for Estonia and Poland exhibit some important commonalties and differences. In general, Poland exhibits stronger curb-market interest rate effects which permeate the macroeconomy, while the effects tend to be rather concealed in Estonia. First, consumption increases in Poland but decreases in Estonia; however, in both economies there is a declining trend in consumption over the entire historical and forecasting period. Second, the results suggest that investment optimism in Estonia is curtailed by an increase in the official interest rate; in Poland, investment falls in the first period, but thereafter the simulations show no activity, indicating that investment is hardly responsive to interest rate changes. Third, import expenditures contract in both Poland and Estonia; as theoretically postulated in equation (12.3), interest rate effects on imports operate predominantly through imported intermediate imports. Following interest rate liberalization, a reduction in real credit volume and imported intermediate inputs leads to a general decline in expenditures on imports. In Poland, the curb-market effects are stronger; thus money increases as the curb-market interest rate falls. Fourth, the behaviour of foreign reserves is more straightforward in Estonia than it is in Poland. Estonia reflects clear-cut expansionary effects in foreign reserves, achieved through a decline in the money supply as well as a fall in imports. In addition, interest rate liberalization effects are expansionary in Poland; this is consistent with the increase in money and consumption, and signifies the predominant effects of the curb-market interest rate effects. The effects on Estonia are blurred, suggesting that a rise in the official interest rate is exactly offset by the fall in the curb-market interest rate. Finally, an increase in the official interest rate yields disinflationary results in Poland, suggesting further that curb-market effects are predominant. This is the reverse of the effects in Estonia where the inflation rate increases initially but declines thereafter.

5 CONCLUSION

In the light of the brief review of the experience with financial sector reforms in Estonia and Poland, it should be noted that although these two transition economies have a broadly common heritage there are some differences in the way financial reform has been implemented. However, in both countries there is need for further reforms in bank and enterprise restructuring.

By using a disaggregated variant of a macroeconomic model for a transition economy developed in Green and Murinde (1998) as a framework for conducting simulations and policy experiments, this chapter has proposed and implemented a procedure for studying the effects of standard financial reforms for Estonia and Poland. The results obtained from dynamic counterfactual simulations and forecasts up to the year 2005 suggest that the financial reform effects for Estonia and Poland exhibit some important commonalties and differences. It is found in general that Poland exhibits stronger curb-market interest rate effects which permeate the macroeconomy, while in the case of Estonia the effects are less obvious.

Future research should take advantage of increasing data availability in order to generate robust coefficient estimates for conducting simulations and policy experiments on the effects of financial and fiscal reforms that are not covered in this chapter. For example, it would be useful to study the effects of a money-financed increase in government spending in transition economies.

NOTES

1. The literature indicates that, over time, governments of transition economies have taken different paths and choices in their move towards becoming fully-fledged market economies (Doukas et al. 1998).
2. This argument is consistent with the observation made by Dewatripont and Roland (1995) that the design of reform packages under uncertainty remains on top of the policy agenda in the transition economies in Eastern and Central Europe; see also Rybczynski (1991).
3. Theoretical policy predictions may give indeterminate signs in the sense that the effect of a policy change may be positive or negative; sometimes only under special restrictions is it possible to have a clear result (positive or negative definite).
4. The last two problems are common to those in Estonia. In particular, as emphasized by Kaufman and Kaliberda (1996), the role of the informal financial sector in Poland should not be underestimated.
5. These are marginal tax rates; TY = the marginal rate of income tax in the private sector, and TZ = the marginal tax rate on imports.
6. Equation (12.7) underscores two issues. First, given that the influence of the curb-market interest rate is assumed to be more operative via the investment function than the consumption function, we use the investment function to capture the curb-market effect; the consumption function may be relevant but at a great cost of being more cumbersome. Second, in the context of financially repressed transition economies, the official rate of interest is ineffective because of credit restrictions. An interest rate reform (a rise in R) enables the banks to garner private savings and make funds available for investment; hence while credit restrictions exist, the reform affects investment positively, and thus the official interest rate is positively signed, in contrast to the negatively signed curb rate.
7. The specification of the government budget constraint in identity (12.11) ignores the interest on government and foreign debt. This is because, as characterized in most transition economies, under financial repression the interest rate is artificially pegged low and does not change in the short run.
8. Montiel et al. (1993, pp. 10–11) classify transactions in the informal credit markets into four categories: occasional lending category which involves lending by individuals and institutions with a surplus of funds; regular moneylending activities which involve lending by specialist individuals or institutions who use their own funds or borrow funds from banks in the official sector for onlending to borrowers in the informal sector; economic agents who tie credit to transactions in markets where primary activities lie (for example,

loans by landlords to their tenants, credit by a supplier to a purchaser); and group finance involving various forms of cooperative efforts to generate loanable funds for individual credit needs. Almost all the four categories apply to Estonia and Poland.

9. We do not specify the accumulation of foreign reserves to be sensitive to the interest rate; hence we omit the interest rate variable in (12.28). Rather, we argue that during the transition process, an increase in exogenous aid inflows seems to signal an improvement in credibility in economic reform, and foreign companies therefore gain more confidence and increase their investment flows into the reforming economy; thus K_0 is defined to encompass overseas aid inflows and (consistent with our specification of the investment function in equation (12.7)) the related inward investment from foreign companies .
10. The reduced-form version of this model yields aggregate demand, aggregate supply and balance of payments equilibrium equations that fully incorporate the economic structure of transition economies; these three equations can then be estimated directly if data are available (see Green and Murinde 1998).
11. These include the root–mean–square simulation error, root–mean–square percentage error, the mean simulation error, the mean percentage error, and the Thiel's inequality coefficient.

REFERENCES

Bahra, P., C.J. Green and V. Murinde (1997), 'Coping with financial sector reforms in transition economies: what have we learned?' in T. Kowalski (ed.), *Financial Reform in Emerging Market Economies: Quantitative and Institutional Issues*, Poznań: Poznań University Press, pp. 11–39.

Borish, M.S., M.F. Long and M. Noel (1996), 'Lessons from bank and enterprise restructuring in the transition economies of Europe and Central Asia', *World Economy*, **19** (1), 39–62.

Dewatripont, M. and G. Roland (1995), 'The design of reform packages under uncertainty', *American Economic Review*, **85** (5), 1207–23.

Doukas, J., V. Murinde and C. Wihlborg (1998), 'Main issues in financial sector reform and privatisation in transition economies: introduction and overview', in J. Doukas, V. Murinde and C. Wihlborg (eds), *Financial Sector Reform and Privatisation in Transition Economies*, Amsterdam: Elsevier Science Publishers BV, pp. 1–18.

Economist Intelligence Unit (EIU) (1996a), *Economist Intelligence Unit Country Report for Estonia, 1995–96*, London: EIU.

Economist Intelligence Unit (EIU) (1996b), *Economist Intelligence Unit Country Report for Poland, 1995–96*, London: EIU.

European Bank for Reconstruction and Development (EBRD) (1996), *Transition Report 1996*, London: EBRD.

European Bank for Reconstruction and Development (EBRD) (1997), *Transition Report 1997*, London: EBRD.

Green, C.J. and V. Murinde (1998), 'Flow-of-funds and the macroeconomic policy framework for financial restructuring in transition economies', in J. Doukas, V. Murinde and C. Wihlborg (eds), *Financial Sector Reform and Privatisation in Transition Economies*, Amsterdam: Elsevier Science Publishers BV, pp. 241–79.

Hallagan, W. (1997), 'Speed and sequencing of market reforms: The case of banking in Latvia', *Contemporary Economic Policy*, **15**, 2, pp. 24–34.

Hillman, A.L. and H.W. Ursprung (1996), 'The political economy of trade liberalisation in the transition', *European Economic Review*, **40** (5), 783–94.

Kaufmann, D. and A. Kaliberda (1996), 'Integrating the unofficial economy into the dynamics of post-socialist economies: a framework of analysis and evidence', in B. Kaminski (ed.), *Economic Transition in Russia and the New States of Eurasia*, Armonk, New York: M.E. Sharpe, Inc.

Montiel, P.J., P. Agénor and N.U. Haque (1993), *Informal Financial Markets in Developing Countries*, Oxford: Blackwell.

Portes, R. (1994), 'Transformation traps', *Economic Journal*, **104**, September, 1178–89.

Roberts, B.M. and Z. Zolkiewski (1996), 'Modelling income distribution in countries in transition: a computable general equilibrium analysis for Poland', *Economic Modelling*, **13** (1), 67–90.

Rondinelli, D.A. and J. Yurkiewicz (1996), 'Privatisation and economic restructuring in Poland: an assessment of transition policies', *American Journal of Economics and Sociology*, **55** (2), 145–60.

Ruggerone, L. (1996), 'Unemployment and inflationary finance dynamics at the early stages of transition', *Economic Journal*, **106** (435), 483–94.

Rybczynski, T.M. (1991), 'The sequencing of reform', *Oxford Review of Economic Policy*, **7** (4), 26–34.

Sachs, J.D. (1996), 'The transition at mid-decade', *American Economic Review*, **86** (2), 128–33.

Svejnar, J. (1996), 'Enterprises and workers in the transition: econometric evidence', *American Economic Review*, **86** (2), 123–7.

Vensel, V. and C. Wihlborg (1998), 'Financial constraints on entrepreneurship in Estonia', in J. Doukas, V. Murinde and C. Wihlborg (eds), *Financial Sector Reform and Privatisation in Transition Economies*, Amsterdam: Elsevier Science Publishers BV, pp. 35–67.

APPENDIX 12A

Table 12A.1 Variables used in calculating the coefficients (elasticities) in the simulation model for Estonia and Poland

Variable name	Source	Availability	Notes
Y – real GDP (total income)	OECD – Historical datastream	1992–1995	Real and nominal values same as IFS
X- exports	OECD – Historical datastream	1992–1995	Seasonally adjusted; same as IFS
C – consumption	OECD datastream	1991–1995	Real values for same period
Z – imports	OECD – Historical datastream	1992–1995	Real and nominal values; same as IFS
Q – GDP deflator	IFS	1991–1995	
K – capital stock	OECD	1991–1995	Generated using TSP
CR – curb rate	IFS (for nominal loan rate, NR1)	1992–1995	Curb rate (= NR1 plus 10.2)
BL – labour	Datastream	1991–1995	Total employment
N – capital imports	EIU – hard copy	1993–1995	*N* in US$ converted to kroons
WK – working capital needs	IFS (lines 32c and 32d in IFS)	1991–1995	Bank lending to private and government enterprises.
W – wages	OECD datastream	1991–1995	Average figures
F – external reserves	IFS	1991–1995	Also OECD
E – exchange rate	Datastream	1992–1995	Same as IFS
G – real government expenditure	Datastream	1991–1995	Nominal data also available
RPI – consumer price index	Datastream	1991–1995	Also OECD
I – real gross investment	EBRD	1991–1995	Also OECD
K_0 – aid and capital flows (line 78bed)	IFS (and World Development Report)	1992–1995	Converted to kroons
T – total tax revenues	GFS; EIU	1991–1995	Real values for same period.
TY – income tax rate	GFS; EIU	1991–1995	Also OECD
L – real loans	IFS	1991–1995	Loans to central government
R – official interest rate	IFS	1992–1995	OECD
M – reserve money	IFS	1991–1995	Real data available
Q^* – foreign prices	IFS	1989–1995	US CPI

Calculation of parameter values for use in the simulations

$$c_1 = \ln Y - \ln C; c_2 = \ln T - \ln C; c_3 = \ln V - \ln C; c_4 = \ln Q * E - \ln C; c_5 = \ln Q - \ln C$$

$$t_1 = \ln Y - \ln T; t_2 = \ln Z - \ln T$$

$$\beta = \ln P - \ln V$$

$$\alpha = \ln Q - \ln P; \text{ alternatively } \alpha = (\ln P - \ln Q * E) + 1$$

$$\delta = \ln K_{t-1} - [\ln(k_t - I)] + 1$$

$$i_1 = \ln Y - \ln I; i_2 = \ln(NR - \hat{Q}^e) - \ln I; i_3 = \ln(R - \hat{Q}^e) - \ln I; i_4 = \ln Q * E - \ln I; i_5 = \ln Q - \ln I$$

$$x_1 = \ln Q * E - \ln X; x_2 = \ln Q - \ln X$$

$$z_1 = \ln Y - \ln Z; z_2 = TZ - \ln Z; z_3 = \ln Q * E - \ln Z; z_4 = \ln Q - \ln Z;$$

$$b_1 = \ln G - \ln M; b_2 = \ln Y - \ln M; b_3 = \ln Z - \ln M; b_4 = \ln Q * E - \ln M; b_5 = \ln Q - \ln M; b_6 = \ln L - \ln M; b_7 = \ln F - \ln M; b_8 = \ln(M_{-1} + L_{-1} + F_{-1}) - \ln M d_1 = \ln Y - NR; d_2 = R - NR; d_3 = \ln Q * E - NR; d_4 = \ln Q - NR; d_5 = \ln M - NR; d_6 = \ln L - NR; d_7 = \ln \hat{Q}^e - NR; d_8 = \ln K_{t-1} - NR$$

$$\phi_1 = \ln BL - \ln Y; \phi_2 = \ln N - \ln Y; \phi_3 = \ln WK - \ln Y$$

$$\varphi = \ln W / P^e - \ln BL$$

$$\lambda_1 = \ln(W^e / Q^e) - \ln BL^d; \lambda_2 = \ln(Q^{*e} E^e / Q^e) - \ln BL^d; \lambda_3 = (NR - Q^e) - \ln BL^d$$

$$e_1 = \ln Q * E - \ln F; e_2 = \ln Y - \ln F; e_3 = \ln Q - \ln F; e_4 = \ln M - \ln F; e_5 = \ln L - \ln F; e_6 = R - \ln F; e_7 = NR - \ln F; e_8 = \ln K_{-1} - \ln F; e_9 = \ln \hat{Q}^e - \ln F; e_{10} = \ln K_0 - \ln F$$

The variables are defined as follows: Y = real income; C = real consumption; I = real investment; G = real government spending; X = real exports; Z = real imports; T = real tax revenue; V = real wealth; Q^* = foreign prices; E = exchange rate; Q = domestic producer prices; K = nominal capital stock; M = nominal money; L = nominal loans; P = retail price index; NR = curb market loan rate; R = official interest rate; TZ = import tax rate; F = foreign reserves; EQQ = inflation rate; BL^s = labour supply; BL^d = labour demand; W = wage rate; and K_0 = exogenous capital inflows, including foreign aid. The term ln denotes natural logarithm; and the superscript e on a variable denotes expectations.

13. The continuing debate

The panel discussion was chaired by Dwight Jaffee and summarized by Victor Murinde and Andy Mullineux.[1] The panelists were Marek Belka, Miroslav Hrnčíř, Andy Mullinuex, Alfred Vanags, Vello Vensel and Clas Wihlborg.[2] Jaffee allowed each panelist ten minutes speaking time, which could be used up in a single statement or in part, with time reserved for later rejoinders or observations. The opening statements raised a number of issues.

The primary focus of the discussion was on financial and monetary issues in the transition economies of Central and Eastern Europe. The issues included capital inflows and their impact on monetary policy; approaches to bank regulation and small and medium-sized business enterprise financing; and financial sector development. Emphasis was on policy and institutional aspects of recent experiences as well as current problems.

The opening statements by Hrnčíř, Belka and Vanags all covered the 'capital inflows problem'. Hrnčíř outlined the problem within the Czech context (1995/96), noting that it was associated with the post-stabilization phase of the transition; emphasizing the problems it was causing for monetary and exchange rate policy. In particular, upward pressure was being exerted on the pegged exchange rate, requiring lower interest rates despite the fact that inflation remained significantly above EU rates, or sterilization, which was problematic in the absence of a well-developed government bond market.

Belka also outlined the Polish approach to privatization and enterprise restructuring and explained its links with the resolution of the bank's bad debt problem. The importance of strategic investors was highlighted, but the problem of finding suitable long-term shareholders was emphasized. In order to prevent over-reliance on capital inflows and to stimulate long-term saving, Belka advocated increased (funded) private pension provision, perhaps based on the Chilean model.[3] It was also noted that greater privatization of pension provision would enhance the role of institutional investors, with positive implications for corporate governance. Mullineux also advocated private funded pensions as a means of developing capital markets and emphasized the link with the privatization programme, which would increase the supply of shares for pension funds to invest in. The development of investment and pension funds would 'deepen' the capital markets by providing demand for stocks and shares and enhancing liquidity. The development of institutional investors, such as pension and insurance funds, would also reduce reliance on banks as monitors of firms in the corporate governance mechanism in line with developments elsewhere, particularly in the US and the UK.

Vanags expressed the view that the 'capital inflows' problem was over-emphasized. It was by no means clear that such inflows would augment the money supply, since they might, for example, generate an offsetting demand for imports. Further, even if the inflows did lead to an increase in the money supply, the result need not be inflationary. In the case of foreign direct investment, for example, income streams would be increased, leading to an offsetting rise in the demand for money. Portfolio investment would also lead to a rise in the demand for money. Vanags further observed that normal money transmission channels (through interest rate effects) were likely to be weak in transition economies. Hence transition economies should welcome foreign direct and portfolio investment.[4] Vanags also expressed doubt about the usefulness of monetary targeting in transition economies. Mullineux supported this view, noting that rapid financial innovation, which is essentially what transition economies are experiencing, severely distorts the relationship between monetary aggregates and target variables, as demonstrated in the UK in the 1980s.

Relating to the enterprise restructuring debate, Mullineux emphasized the importance of a thriving small and medium-sized enterprise (SME) sector for the privatization of an economy and for creating jobs to absorb workers laid off by restructuring state-owned enterprises (SOEs). He also noted that credit rationing was normal (due to asymmetric information), but was likely to be more acute in transition economies given that bankers are inexperienced and there is a high level of uncertainty about economic prospects. Further, there is a dearth of assets suitable to serve as collateral prior to the resolution of the restitution claims. Unsurprisingly, the banks have tended to demand high levels of collateral and to operate with wide margins; in part due to lack of competition, but also in an attempt to cover 'risks' in a highly uncertain environment. Loan guarantees are commonly provided in 'western' economies and some countries also provide (explicitly or implicitly) subsidized medium to long-term, fixed and variable rate, finance to SMEs (for example, in Germany via KfW, the reconstruction bank). Any subsidies provided could be phased out as banks begin to enter the market, perhaps initially via co-financing arrangements with development banks such as KfW. An important function of a state-backed small business bank would be to gather information and share it with co-financing banks. Jaffee supported the advocacy of loan guarantees, and possibly also refinancing arrangements, to stimulate SME lending and noted that the paper he had presented at the conference had recommended a guarantee and refinancing scheme to help stimulate the provision of home loans (mortgages); an extremely important, but hitherto neglected, element of the transition. In the US, refinancing is overseen by government agencies (for example, Fannie Mae) and similar agencies might usefully be established in transition economies, where they could help develop a secondary mortgage market.

Vensel emphasized the need to develop a legal framework to support the restructuring of the enterprise and financial sectors.[5] He emphasized the scarcity of trustworthy information,[6] noting that improvements in national and corporate accounting were urgently needed. The system of national accounts (SNA), which had been introduced earlier in most transition economies, was not fully functional. Moreover, the share of officially unreported transactions in the grey and black markets was quite remarkable; for example, the survey by Eurostat in the Baltic states during 1996 found that the share of unreported transactions was 14 per cent in Latvian firms, 12 per cent in Estonian firms and 7 per cent in Lithuanian firms. Vensel argued that, given the paucity of information, there was a need for a substantial amount of comparative survey work of the sort undertaken by his team and reported in this book. He also reviewed financial sector (banking and stock market) development in Estonia, noting that greater attention needed to be paid to economic efficiency[7] and to potential trade-offs between efficiency, and stability. Vensel noted that early stage developments had focused much more on banks seeking a role in savings mobilization and lending than on their governance/monitoring roles and on providing an efficient payments system. He argued that attention now needed to turn to stock market development, which would be facilitated by the greater 'information efficiency',[8] and would broaden the scope of corporate governance.[9] In the discussion it was observed that while institutional and regulatory preparations needed to be made, the stock market's development would naturally follow progress with the privatization programme (which produced stocks to trade) and that the privatization of pensions and the development of the insurance market, by creating institutional investors, would provide a stable (domestic) demand for stocks, and thus reduce reliance on capital inflows.

The most heated debate revolved around the need for bank regulation and supervision, and the appropriate approach to depositor protection in particular.

Mullineux put the case for explicit deposit insurance (with risk-related premiums) based on the existence of information asymmetry and the need to protect depositors for social reasons and to avoid panics developing into damaging systemic crises in the highly uncertain transition environment. Vanags supported the social case for depositor protection, arguing that it was the *de facto* norm in developed countries (whether via an explicit deposit insurance scheme or an implicit, 'lender-of-last-resort'/'bailout'-based, one). He could see no reason for a harsher regime in transition economies given that there were fewer alternative repositories for savings, especially in the early stages of the transition. 'Saver beware' was simply not an appropriate response at a time when savings mobilization was important and full confidence in the banking system had yet to be established. It was also noted that a substantial loss of life savings early in a transition would have damaging macroeconomic consequences due to the consequent reduction in consumption.[10]

The case against explicit deposit insurance was put by Wihlborg (keenly supported from the floor by Kimball Dietrich), who also expressed strong reservations about government interventions to support SMEs, especially via a government-backed SME bank.[11] Wihlborg broadly argued that asymmetric information may well result in market failure, but that regulations simply add to the distortions and exacerbate the moral hazard and adverse selection problems arising out of information asymmetry. Further, regulation inhibits financial sector development, since flexibility is needed to provide incentives for the production of the information necessary to alleviate the information problem and to encourage rapid financial innovation. Additionally, learning from mistakes allows a more rapid ascent of the learning curve. Wihlborg also questioned the susceptibility of transition economies to system crisis given their diverse array of banks.[12] He further argued that this lack of depositor protection might lead to 'narrow banking', with 100 per cent reserve banking for demand deposit (current account) balances. Some doubts were expressed about the likelihood of narrow banking being adopted given that 'fractional reserve' banking was the prevailing model elsewhere in the world and, increasingly, free capital flows would force convergence on the norm. Additionally, it was noted that the banks should lend, rather than invest deposits in safe assets such as Treasury Bills, in order to facilitate economic development, and that bank lending was likely to remain the overwhelming dominant source of enterprise finances until capital markets had become much more developed. Further, even in the most financially developed economies, such as the US and the UK, bank lending remained the dominant source of enterprise finance.

The argument drew a number of comments from the audience and the prevailing view seemed to be that depositor protection was desirable both on social grounds and to prevent damaging system banking crises. In addition it would encourage savings mobilization. The regulatory system therefore needed to be designed to deal with the moral hazard by taxing risk taking; using risk-related capital adequacy requirements and perhaps also risk-related deposit insurance premiums, as for example in the US. It was pointed out that the Estonian example, where banks were allowed to fail early in the transition, was a double-edged sword. The monetary authorities got away with it because the depositors thought they were fully protected and thus did not panic. Now that they know better, are they more likely to somehow (in the presence of information asymmetry) discipline the banks themselves, or to panic and simply withdraw deposits next time their savings are threatened?[13] Mullineux also pointed out that the reason for preferring explicit deposit insurance (rather than relying on implicit lender-of-last-resort cover) is that explicit insurance is more certain, and thus more reassuring to depositors, and that its costs fall on the banks (and thus, in a well-functioning banks market, ultimately on the depositors, that is, the beneficiaries of the insurance), rather than on taxpayers in general. Vanags pointed out that, notwithstanding moral hazard and adverse selection issues, bank failures in the West usually involved bailouts and he did not see why a harsher regime was optimal in the transition economies.

In all, the panel discussion was but a reflection of the ongoing debate among academics as well as practitioners on the salient issues relating to bank restructuring, privatization and corporate governance in transition economies. We hope this book has added to the momentum for exploring these issues further.

NOTES

1. Victor Murinde and Andy Mullineux would like to thank Dwight Jaffee, Alfred Vanags, Vello Vensel and Clas Wihlborg for their input and comments.
2. The affiliations of the panelists are given in the 'Notes on contributors' section in the prelims of this book.
3. Belka went on to become the Finance Minister of Poland for a short period, during which time he helped develop the introduction of a scheme under which revenue from privatization is to be used to help ease the transition to greater private pension provision in Poland.
4. It was not clear that Vanags was so sanguine about short-term flows, which seem to have been the root of the capital outflow problem in Mexico (1994/95) and Thailand (1997).
5. Vensel observed that although the legal framework in these countries has progressed rapidly, the capacity of the legal system to implement and enforce a complex legal structure is still weak. He cited the interview study carried out on Estonian firms which clearly indicated that most firms were not satisfied with the current legislation and enforcement mechanism.
6. Especially macroeconomic data for model building and forecasting exercises.
7. In the sense of resource allocation and the efficient performance of financial institutions and markets, engendered by the degree of competition in the market.
8. In the sense that new information is rapidly internalized in decision making.
9. This is an important observation given that the quality of accounting data directly influences initial public offerings (IPOs).
10. The Permanent Income Hypothesis, for example, postulates that the loss of earnings from savings and the erosion of wealth would lead to reduced consumption.
11. Wihlborg emphasized that the case against external regulation is that the imposed regulatory structure may not adjust to changing conditions in the economy. Moreover, external regulation is often orientated towards non-economic objectives, at a time when transition economies are aiming at increasing their growth rates.
12. He observed that since most transition economies have a large number of banks of varying quality, the risk that a run on one bank may cause systemic failure need not be substantial.
13. Albania and Bulgaria have, of course, subsequently provided historical footnotes.

Index